D1473185

WE BEGIN ANEW

One of the greatest difficulties of strategy writing is that there is almost never the time, money, and ability to return to a beloved product and update the original material. With World of Warcraft, we've been given the opportunity to do just that: to update, improve, and expand on the original guide with no time or expense spared. It seemed like a rare luxury to spend over half a year in preparation for the release of the first World of Warcraft strategy guide. Yet, that is modest compared to the time placed on this guide. Players and writers who have been involved with World of Warcraft from Beta 1 forward have come together for this incredible task. And in case you can't tell, we're excited. This is an amazing chance to take a guide that we loved and bring it to life once again.

If you are wondering what has changed, the list is a bit daunting. Almost all text is entirely new; strategies have been broken apart and rebuilt from the ground up. We have new tables, data, and updated maps to handle the changes from the last year and a half of updates. Newer screenshots with greater character variety were taken while logging in thousands of hours between characters on all manner of servers. Searching for Rare or Epic items? We have them all in here. Planning equipment sets, trying out different PvP builds, looking for ways to excel in dungeons, raids, and in the battlegrounds? We have been too, and the results are in here.

Everything that could possibly fit between two covers is ready. New players: you are still going to receive the comfortable introduction to World of Warcraft that was present in the first guide (we'll take you through the early hours of play and explain everything to help you on your way). Experienced players fear not; there an amazing amount for you here as well. We've taken all of the resources from all over Azeroth and the real world and brought them into one place. Tired of keeping the Net up in the background or on another system to look up item drops in your favorite instances? Do you want to squeeze those last few percentage points of critical strike out of your character without losing precious Stamina or Attack Power? We found the best ways to do it. We'll help you level your second, third, and fourth characters to 60 in style. We'll get you to Exalted in all the battlegrounds. And, we promise that it's going to be fun this time too.

Glad to have you back.

GLOSSARY

This Glossary gives you a good idea what the common terms mean in World of Warcraft. Gaming slang, internal statistics, and other such ideas are explained in enough detail to get complete novices and gaming veterans speaking the same language.

Add	A creature that adds into an existing fight against you. As a verb, it is the act of having a creature add into a fight "That Ogre is going to add."
AFK	Away From Keyboard. This means that the person won't be available for a short time. There is also a specific /afk command to let others who message you know that you are AFK.
Aggro	Most often this is used to note that a creature is attacking you or your group "We've got aggro!" The term denotes the aggressive interests of a monster/npc. If a person says, "Go aggro that monster" if means to intentionally get the enemy to attack you.
Aggro Radius	This is the distance from which an enemy decides to attack a character. This radius is influenced by the level difference between the monster and the character (with relatively tougher monsters aggroing from farther away). This distance is also influenced by the type of creature involved, as a number of predators have a larger aggro radius to begin with.
Agility	Agility is an attribute in World of Warcraft. This attribute determines a character's ability to Dodge attacks, score Critical Hits (that deal at least twice the damage), and deal more damage in general with their attacks (though this is only true with certain classes).
AKA	Shorthand for Also Known As
Alt	A secondary character. This usually refers to a character that you put less time into or a character that is lower in level compared to your primary (Main) character.
Area of Effect	These are spells, abilities, and items that influence multiple targets over a given area. Sometimes these are based on a circle around a specific target person (the caster or an enemy off in the distance). These can also be based off of a selected area (these are called ground targeted AoEs).
Armor	This reflects the amount of protective armor your character is wearing. This statistic increases as you continue to find better equipment with higher levels. Your character's current armor is the primary factor in determining physical damage mitigation.
Artificial Intelligence	Or AI. NPCs of various sorts have a certain level of intelligence that determines their activities in and outside of battle.
Attack Power	This is a statistic that influences the physical Damage Per Second of your character. Having a higher melee Attack Power greatly helps in dealing more damage, especially with heavier weapons. Having a higher ranged Attack Power increases overall ranged damage.
Attack Skill	Each character has an Attack Skill with at least several weapon types. Your maximum Attack Skill is equal to five times your current level. Training with a weapon by attacking increases your Attack Skill towards this cap. During battle, Attack Skill (relative to your enemy's Defense) influences the chance to strike successfully and score Critical Hits.
Attribute	A major statistic for a character. Each attribute reflects on a major side of a character's capabilities (Strength for melee damage and blocking with shields, Agility for Dodging, Critical Hits, and some classes' Attack Power, Stamina for Hit Points, Intellect for Mana, and Spirit for recovery of Hit Points/Mana over time)
Auction House	Frequently shortened to AH. These areas allow characters to post many items for sale. The transactions have a modest fee, yet they allow your character to make sales and purchases without meeting other characters directly and investing major time in buying/selling.
Avatar	The visual representation of your character in World of Warcraft

Battleground	An instanced area for PvP conflict. Sign up today in the major cities or at specific instance portals. WSG is Warsong Gulch, AB is Arathi Basin, AV is Alterac Valley.
BBL	Be Back Later
Bind	To Bind to a certain inn with your Hearthstone (so that you can teleport there in the future). This can also be used to define when an item Binds to your character on pickup (BoP) or on first equip (BoE).
Bind on Equip	This means that a specific item will Bind to your character the first time it is equipped. After that point, it cannot be traded or put onto the Auction House. Before that time, normal trade is completely allowable.
Bind on Pickup	These items immediately Bind to a character when looted or crafted, and they can never be sold or traded for any reason. Most often, these items are of Rare quality (or higher) and are found from powerful enemies.
Boat/Zeppelin	Boats and Zeppelins are used for travel between the continents.
Boots	Not just an armor piece! This is also used to signify a power-up object in the Battlegrounds (Warsong Gulch) that increases run speed ("If you can make it to our base, the boots are up!").
BRB	Be Right Back
BRT	Be Right There
Buff	Using spells to increase the potential of your allies. This refers to both the act "Please buff me, good Priest" and to the actual spell effect "With this buff I have 4,240 Hit Points, woot!"
Bug	An in-game problem that causes something unexpected to happen. This may require Customer Service Representative/GM intervention (you will need to submit a ticket if the bug is dramatic).
Camp	To control a given area in the hopes of either getting all the monster spawns for yourself/your group, or for the purpose of stopping PvP enemies from having safety there. You can camp an area, a graveyard, the corpse of a fallen enemy, and so forth. This often involves multiple people to be done most effectively (the group fans out and watches for anything that will try to disrupt their activities).
Carebear	Somewhat derogatory name for a person who avoids PvP, plays on non-PvP servers, and so forth.
Cast	To use a spell. This may occur instantly with some spells (instant-cast spells have almost no delay of any sort) or require up to several seconds of time invested in the casting process during which interruptions may occur if the caster is struck.
Caster	A person who is capable of casting spells. Often used to refer to Mages, Warlocks, Priests, and Druids who stay in Caster Form. It is implied in the name that the person is a softer target who needs either protection or fast elimination, depending on their affiliations. "Kill their casters first, they are supporting the flag carrier!!!"
Chain Casting	Going from one spell directly into the next. "That Shaman Chain Casts Lesser Healing Wave every time she gets in trouble."
Cheese	A method of winning that isn't exploitive but appears to be unfair in one way or another. This may be quite inaccurate in some cases. This is a synonym for abuse.
Class	A set of abilities and statistics for your character that is chosen during creation. This greatly influences how you will play your character.
Combat Pet	Warlocks and Hunters have pets that can fight beside them and greatly affect the outcome of combat.
Con	Short for consider. This was used in many older MOGs to tell how powerful a creature was. In World of Warcraft, this is done with both a numeric level comparison and by the the background color of the mob's frame.
Corpse Camping	To stay near a slain enemy in world PvP in an attempt to prevent them from resurrecting at their body without being killed again. This is not griefing by definition. It is also not friendly and is considered a fair act of aggression against the party being camped.
Crash to Desktop	When the game kicks you back onto the desktop. In-game, people will likely refer to this as a DC (a disconnect).
Creep	Term for neutral creatures.
Crit	Short term for a Critical Hit (a blow that deals roughly twice normal damage).
Critters	Creatures out in the wild that have no combat capabilities (small snakes, rabbits, etc.). Killing these is absolutely necessary.
Crowd Control	Using spells or abilities to disable enemy targets for a substantial period. Sap, Polymorph, and Fear are major examples of POWERFUL Crowd Control (CC) that not only limits the enemies' options to act, but almost removes them entirely from combat. Lesser/limited Crowd Control may inhibit movement but still allow enemies a moderate amount of control; Frost Nova, roots, and Hamstring are good examples of limited control.
Customer Service Representative	The in-game staff that exist to help players with major problems. Often called GMs by the players.
Damage Mitigation	The Armor statistic is compared to a table of estimated Armor values for a given level. The result is your character's Damage Mitigation (found by highlighting the Armor stat on your character page). This value roughly explains the amount of damage absorbed by your armor when your character is struck by a creature of similar level. Abilities and Spells can influence both Armor and Damage Mitigation.
Damage Per Second	Base damage from a spell, weapon, or ability is only part of the story. Damage Per Second (DPS) is a way to figure out how effective, per unit time, a given action is. The higher the DPS, the more damage an activity can produce. This is often most important for attrition PvP or PvE situations. In short-term PvP, burst damage is more important than specific DPS.
Debuff	A debuff is any spell that goes on an enemy target and stays there for a period of time. Some deal damage; some reduce stats.
Defense	This stat determines how often your character is struck physically and how often such blows are Critical Hits. This stat has a cap of five times the character's level and increases toward that cap when your character is attacked.
Direct Damage	Spells, Abilities, or Items that deal damage immediately and directly to a target.
Dispel	To remove a Debuff from an ally or to remove a positive effect from a foe.
DMG	Shorthand for Damage.
DnD	Do Not Disturb
DOT	Shorthand for Damage Over Time. DOT abilities/spells are often very efficient but require slower tactics for the attrition to run its course. Warlocks are especially known for their cruel DOTs.
Duping	Creating multiple items from a single source. This is only possible through rare exploits (if at all during this stage of the game), and WILL lead to major penalties or banning of accounts.
Emote	An action (often with voice or animation) that is made by your character. Emotes are very useful for roleplaying and are covered in this guide.
Experience	Experience/XP measures your progress toward another level.
Exploit	Activities that are against the Terms of Use for World of Warcraft and capitalize on bugs to give players an unfair advantage over others.
Farm	To repeatedly kill a given target or type of target, often for desired drops of trade items or equipment
Flag	An object (target) in the Battlegrounds; these are right-clicked to pick up or activate. Also used to denote PvP activity, as in "That warrior is flagged for PvP! Get 'em!"
Flagged	To be PvP enabled. On PvE, Standard RP servers, and in the starter Zones, using /pvp is required before fighting against the other faction is possible. Once /pvp is used, you are Flagged.
Flight	Both factions use bats/gryphons/etc. to fly characters between cities and towns. People may refer to this as being "on the bird."
Free for All	This is a loot rule that allows any character to loot any body. Often reserved for VERY close friends and trusted allies.
Gank	Primarily a PvP server term and function. This is when characters of much higher level go after younger targets that have no hope of surviving or even escaping, or when people are unprepared due to combat with a mob. A person who does this activity is a "ganker."
GG	Short for "Good Game!" Spoken to buddies after the end of many battleground matches, even when on the losing side.
GJ	Short for "Good Job!" to signal approval or appreciation.
Gimp	To Gimp means to take a course of action with Talents or equipment that makes your character ineffective. Being a Gimp is to be such a character. An example would be a full Intellect gear Warrior with a side dose of +Healing improvements.
GM	In-game Blizzard representatives that try to correct for bugs or deal with harassment issues.
Graveyard	A place where characters return after death. The spirits can run back to their bodies for life to begin anew, or they can Resurrect at the Spirit Healer nearby (this damages their equipment and causes a status debuff for a short time).
Graveyard Camping	Staying in areas where enemies are spawned in the Battlegrounds or use the Spirit Healer in the normal world. This is considered to be in very poor taste by many players and may (in some servers) be defined as griefing.
Grief	Making an active effort to harass another player that goes beyond the rules of the game. Graveyard Camping another player, Kill Stealing, and other malicious acts are included in this.
Grind	To specifically gain experience by attacking monsters (as opposed to questing for experience). Often repetitive and mindless.
Group Loot	A standard set of loot rules for groups in instances. Group Loot does a Round Robin system for standard items, letting each person loot a fair number of bodies. Then, when items of a chosen threshold drop, window appears that allows people roll Need, Greed, or Pass on the item.
Group/Party	A team of up to five characters that are invited (/inv) to complete common goals. This is great for questing and almost mandatory for doing instance dungeons at their appropriate level.
GUI	Graphical User Interface

Guild	Groups of players get together and form guilds. Initially, this takes nine signatures from unguilded characters on unique accounts. This starts off by getting a charter from one of the three major cities in your faction.
Hate List	Monsters keep an internal list of the character they WANT to kill the most. This is the Hate List. Damage done, healing, and other activities against the monster's interests determine who stays high on the Hate List.
Heal Over Time	In shorthand, used as HOT. A healing spell that helps another character in doses instead of in one instant chunk.
Hearthstone	An item given to all characters that allows you to Bind at Inns for instant teleportation (once per hour). The process of leaving an area using the Hearthstone is "Hearthing."
Hit Points	The stat to measure how tough your character is (how much damage they take before dying). Stamina bonuses, levels, and buffs affect Hit Points.
Honor	Points gained from kills against enemies of similar (or higher) level and from Battleground victories.
Hybrid	A class that fills several niches or rests in-between them. Shamans, Paladins, and Druids are very good examples of Hybrid classes because they can switch between some tanking, healing, and damage dealing roles.
IC	In-character (often used to let people know that you are speaking as your character, in a roleplaying sense).
IMO	In My Opinion (or IMHO for In My Humble Opinion)
Incoming	Or INC, used to let people know that enemies are on their way.
Instance	An area that is privately loaded for individual characters or groups (e.g. instance dungeons, battlegrounds)
IRC	Used to denote the use of outside communication channels (like voice chat or instant messaging programs).
Intellect	Stat that determines the amount of Mana your character has, the speed at which Defense and Weapon Skills are learned, and improves the spell Critical Chance.
j/k	Common internet term to signal that someone is "just kidding" and that they should not be taken seriously.
Kill on Sight	Often used as a PvP term for someone that receives no mercy at all. "That guy used /spit on my boyfriend, he is KOS now!"
Kill Steal	To Tap enemies that another player is setting up to fight. This prevents that player from being able to get experience for the monster. This can be griefing if done repeatedly, and it's very poor etiquette in any event.
Kite	To Kill in Time, also summons the image of stretching enemies behind you like a person flying a kite. This is a technique of killing enemies slowly by using DOTs and ranged attacks to wound them while evading/running away from the foes.
Lag	Delays caused by poor Internet latency. Lag jumping is when your computer corrects for this and jumps things around onscreen to get people into their proper positions.
Leech	To be in a group or raid and contribute nothing "They just sat there and leeched Reputation in Alterac Valley for two hours."
Leet Speak	Also known as 1337 speak. The use of numbers for replacing certain letters and generally idiosyncratic grammar to denote allegiance to the younger geek culture.
Level	A measure of your character's power and progression in Azeroth. This ranges from 1-60 before the game's first expansion arrives. In the future, this will extend from 1-70, and who knows what the future will hold!
Leveling	Gaining levels, and through them abilities and power for your characters. This is done by completing quests, killing monsters, exploring the world, and so forth.
Line of Sight	The direct line between one entity and their target. Many abilities require a direct Line of Sight, and when LOS is broken the spells/abilities will fail to go off.
Link	To post an item in a channel so that others may see its statistics. Holding down Shift while clicking on an item will do this for whispers and guild chat, but not for private chat channels.
LOL	Laugh Out Loud; common Internet usage for anything amusing. ROFL (rolling on the floor laughing) is also used.
LOM/OOM	Low on Mana and Out of Mana; these are statements made by casters to let the group know that fun time is almost over.
Looking For Group	Or LFG–used to let people know that you are trying to find a group to accomplish a task. Groups with open slots may yell LFM, or "Looking for more."
Loot	Loot itself is the treasure that is taken from monsters after they fall; To Loot means to actually bend over and right-click on bodies to take said items.
Lowbie	A person of low level for a given activity. This can mean someone in the first few levels of a PvP bracket, even if that person is level 50-52!
Mailbox	Many Inns or Bank areas have Mailboxes. Auction items and money are delivered here. Money can also be sent to other characters, as can items and letters! The fee for this is trivial, even at low levels.
Main	Your current primary character as opposed to your alts.
Master Looter	A loot setting that only allows the group leader to handle treasure and its dispensation. This is time inefficient and is often used in DKP-type systems or when dealing with extremely valuable loot.
Med	To rest, eat/drink, and restore any fallen buffs while preparing for future fighting. This is often called by the group leader or a primary healer.
Melee	Direct physical combat at close range.
Mistell	Or MT. Done when you message the wrong person with a /tell or when you post to the wrong chat channel. Example: "Yeah, my guild sucks and I'm thinking of leaving them" said in guild chat. Response "YIKES, MT. I was talking about another guild!"
Mob	Short for Mobile. An old gaming term that persists. All of the world's monsters are Mobs.
MOG	Massive Online Game
Mount	A creature that your character can ride. At level 40, every character has the ability to learn to ride a mount and, for a fee, purchase one.
Need Before Greed	The honor system of loot in instance dungeons. This means that you do not try to roll NEED on items that your character doesn't actually want to equip. If you are going to equip something, you need it. If you want it to sell, or send it to one of your alts or friends, it's greed.
Nerf	When the game is patched and certain actions/abilities are reduced in effectiveness. "They finally stopped Nerfing Mortal Strike!"
Ninja	To loot an item that was up for discussion or to roll need on items that are quite clearly not ones that you need. This is akin to an act of stealing from a group. Don't do it if you want to have friends, good guilds, good groups. It is NOT worth the money.
NM	Nevermind. Sometimes used as NVM.
Noob/Newbie	An insult. This is often said when someone does something completely foolish that gets them or their group/team in trouble. "The Paladin bubbled while carrying the flag, NOOB!!!" It can also be used in a self-deprecating manner: "Even though I've been through Wailing Caverns 3 times, I still feel like a noob there."
NPC	Non-Player Character. The various people of Azeroth who give quests, offer services, and exist to support the backstory of World of Warcraft are all NPCs.
Offtank	Also known as Secondary Tanks. These are tough characters that back up the primary Tank by worrying about single targets that peel onto casters. When not needed for this role, Offtanks often attempt to deal high damage.
OMW	On My Way
OOC	Out Of Character. Sometimes signified on roleplaying servers with the use of parentheses, as in "The horn has sounded! I must leave this place! (gotta log guys)"
Own/Pwn	1337 speak for a major victory over someone or something.
PC	Player Character
Ping	To create a glowing yellow circle on the local map through right-clicking on an area; this indicates direct position of a target (especially useful in the Battlegrounds). This is also a specific Hunter ability that is used to uncover Stealthed targets.
Point Blank AoE	An area of effect ability that centers around the caster. Shortened to PBAoE.
Port	To Port or Portal is to immediately travel to a certain location. Mages do this by Porting to set locations, any player can use their Hearthstones to Port to an Inn that they have bound to, and Warlocks can Summon people to themselves.
Pot	Potions are often shortened to Pot in-game. Pot use is common in PvE and PvP for restoring Hit Points or Mana. Other important Potions include Free Action, Swiftness, and many stat-enhancing choices as well.
Powerlevel	To assist a lower-level character by helping them quest/grind at a much faster pace. Often more effective with slightly higher-level characters that stay out of group.
Proc	An item effect that goes off under certain conditions (on hit, when struck, etc.). These often occur somewhat randomly and are somewhat powerful when they do occur. Short for "P.rogrammed R.andom O.C.currence".
Profession	Trades for crafting and gathering. A character can only learn two normal Professions, as opposed to secondary skills.
PST	Please Send Tell, used with ads for items or requests for services. This lets people know that you want to be privately messaged with any offers.
Puller	The person designated to pull enemies back to a group (a task that is essential for safe play in tougher instance dungeons). Hunters are ideal pullers, but any class can take this role if they are skilled and cautious.
PvE	Player vs. Environment. Quests, dungeon delving, and monster grinding are considered to be PvE content.
PvP	Player vs. Player. Battlegrounds, world conflicts, and duels are examples of PvP content.
QFT	Quoted For Truth. Used to indicate an assenting opinion.
Queue	The waiting list for the Battlegrounds and log-in server.

Raid	Groups above five characters can form when a leader selects the Convert To Raid button. Although experience is reduced dramatically and quests are no longer completable (with several exceptions), the firepower (or camaraderie potential) of a large force can be quite beneficial, and necessary in late-game raid dungeons and battlegrounds.
Random	Used to figure out who gets certain items that many characters want. For instance, if there are several Miners in a group, they may /random for a Mithril Vein that they come across.
Rank	Gaining high Honor in a given week increases your Standing compared to other players of the same faction. Working hard allows you to increase in PvP Rank, allowing considerable rewards in your capital city.
Reputation	Different NPC groups can be courted in various ways. With increased Reputation you gain access to items, recipes, and resources. Or, if you go to war against a given faction, you can lose such opportunities and slaughter the masses of their people for fun and profit.
Res Sickness	When brought back to life by a Spirit Healer, there is a period of decreased combat effectiveness. This debuff cannot be cured by characters.
Resistance	Ability to negate or mitigate damage and effects from various magical or non-physical attacks. There are Resistances for Arcane, Fire, Nature, Frost, and Shadow.
Rested Bonus	Characters gain double the normal experience for kills while they are in a Rested state. This accrues while you are logged out or in an Inn/City. Note that Inn/City resting gives your character FOUR times the amount of Rested Bonus, so it REALLY helps to log off at such a location at the end of a day.
ROFL/ROFLMAO	Common internet term used as response to something very entertaining: "Roll on the Floor Laughing/Roll on the Floor Laughing my [butt] Off."
Resurrection/Rez	Being brought back to life. This is done by returning to a corpse, speaking to a Spirit Healer, or by having healing characters cast various types of Resurrection Spells.
Roleplaying	Staying in-character to promote a greater sense of depth to the world.
Root	To lock an enemy in place for a short time. They can fight, but they cannot move.
Run Speed	How fast your character moves across terrain. There are several ways to increase this, including potions or specific class Abilities.
Snare	To slow an enemy's movement. Hamstring, Wing Clip, Frost Spells of many types, and other such abilities Snare opponents. They can still move and fight, but it is much easier to Kite them during this time.
Spawn	Defeated enemies and gathered resources return to the world after a time. This event is called a Spawn (or a Pop).
Specialization	Often refers to Talent selections. This denotes a focus on playing your character in a specific way. Gear, Talents, and playstyle all come together to maximize a given Spec. Can refer to trade skills.
Spirit	Attribute that controls the rate of Hit Point/Mana regeneration for your character.
Stacking	Abilities that work in harmony instead of replacing each other are said to Stack. Snares often do NOT Stack. DOTs of almost all types absolutely DO Stack.

Stamina	Attribute that determines your character's Hit Point total.
Standing	A ladder for Honor gained in a week. You compete against your own faction for high Standing. Achieving extremely high Rank is impossible without consistently high Standing and a huge investment of time.
Stat	A Statistic that reflects on your gear, levels, Attributes, and current state. Your stats provide a general idea for your character's combat performance.
Stealth	An Ability that allows a character limited invisibility at the cost of movement speed, available to only Rogues and Druids (as well as some mobs). Stealth is broken when the character takes specific actions or takes damage of any type.
Strength	Attribute that determines melee damage and potential for damage mitigation from shield blocking.
Stun	Any ability/effect that COMPLETELY halts an enemy. They cannot move or escape this effect until it wear off. No combat is possible for them at this time.
Talents	Talent Points are used to invest in one of three Talent Trees. Each character class has three major fields of Talents to choose from, and you can absolutely mix and match from two or even three Talent Trees. Talent Points are given from levels 10-60, adding up to 51 total TPs.
Tank	A tough character designed to grab enemy aggro and hold it while mitigating as much of the damage as possible. Warriors are often the best tanks, but Paladins and Druids are useful here as well. In lower levels, Shamans and both Hunter or Warlock Pets can also be reliable tanks.
Tap	The first point of damage against any target Taps it for you/your group. This designates the monster as yours, turning its status bar grey to all others. Only you can get experience or loot from your Tapped target.
Taunt	An ability that pushes your character much higher or to the top of a creature's Hate List. Great for Tanking!
Tell/Whisper	A private message, sent directly to a person by typing /tell or /whisper and their name. You can also click on a character's name on the screen and send a /tell from there.
Threat	The amount of influence on the Hate List that a given activity causes. High Threat is GREAT if you want aggro. High Threat is horrible if you are squishy.
Toon	Another term for your character in-game.
Train	A term used to denote the process of gaining new abilities (which can be done every even level), as in "I'll go train in Ironforge." It can also be used to denote the act of pulling enemies through another person/group and getting those people engaged in combat. The second definition can be taken as griefing if done repeatedly to people of the same faction.
Twink	A character (usually low-level) that possesses gear/enchantments greatly above their abilities/means.
Uber	Common slang usage means that a person/monster/item is extremely powerful if it is uber.
WTB/WTS	Want to Buy/Want to Sell
Zerg	To gather in a large group and rush forward. This is often a foolish or risky tactic in the battlegrounds because it leaves points undefended/unwatched. Supporting Allies is good; blind rushing is bad.
Zone	Common term for a region of Azeroth. Wetlands, Hillsbrad, Barrens, Durotar are all Zones.

CREATING A CHARACTER

Choosing a name, race, and class for your character may seem like a simple start, but it's all about investment. You can pick the first class that comes to mind in any race and click on the button to give you a default name. Or, you can sit down and consider with full attention to detail what you want from a character, what each class provides, and which race fits you the best, then think about a name that reflects all of that. Though this is a very personal decision, there are still a few tips that might help along the way.

CLASS

Your intended class is the best thing to decide first. After all, you don't want to fall in love with a race and suddenly find that they don't have the class you were hoping to play. If you don't have a class in mind already, stop and think about yourself. Do you want to get up close and personal? Is ranged combat more your style? Is magic a way of life for characters in the games you love, and, if so, do you like to support/heal or go on the offensive with it?

If you don't have answers to those questions yet, perhaps because you are new to fantasy games, go deeper into your analysis. Do you lead well? Prefer to sit quietly and act suddenly, on your own? Is supporting others very important to you, or are you disinclined to be constantly involved with other people's needs and problems? There are no wrong answers here. It's better to be honest about what you want and seek the class that suits you.

The table below may help here. Though personality issues are extremely subjective, there is a tendency that you will notice in people that are happiest in a given class.

The Classes in a Nutshell

Class	Major Aspects of Play	Personality Leaning
Druid	Flexibility, Healing	People Who Crave Change
Hunter	Survival, Interception, Pulling	Those Who Hold Back From Direct Conflict
Mage	Crowd Control, Range, Fast Life/Fast Death	The Fearless
Paladin	Cannot Be Killed Easily, The Healer Who Won't Die	People Who Hate Losing
Priest	Massive Healing and Group Support	Supporters
Rogue	Sudden Damage, Many Stuns, High Preparation	Aggressive Players
Shaman	Specialization Can Lead to Strong Melee, Ranged Damage, or Healing, Many Paths to Succeed	All Types
Warlock	Tougher Than They Look, Major Utility Options, Gods of Attrition Warfare	Those Who Love to Win
Warrior	Grab Immense Aggro, Hamper Enemies, Requires Both Skill and Gear to Show Their Ultimate Beauty	Leaders

The people who end up being happiest in their classes almost always feel that way because the personality of the class matches their own. There are many folks who play a class for the "wrong" reasons and end up never quite clicking with it. This is because they chose the class based on stats instead of soul. Class X may be the flavor of the month, but nerfs/buffs come and go. Try everything, analyze what feels right, and run with that.

RACE

Though Racial Traits are discussed later and certainly have an influence in gameplay, it is still STRONGLY recommended that you choose a race based on feel. If you grow to love your character, you are going to spend hundreds of hours watching them fight, grow, and succeed. Don't pick a character that doesn't look or feel right to you; look at all of the races, try male and female versions of each, and see what clicks. Let no one influence your decision in this. Pick what you like. Love it, enjoy it, and mock anyone who doesn't understand. In World of Warcraft, all possible character/race combinations are fully viable for the endgame. Anyone can solo to level 60. Anyone can group up to 60. End of story.

NAME

You might be amazed to realize how much goes into a name and how much people assume about you based of this. Generic fantasy names are near-on impossible to remember, movie characters are almost despised, and comic names might not get you into all the best groups. Consider the following:

NAMING TIPS

The World of Warcraft Name Generator gives you random names to consider. You can click on this as many times as you like and keep what you want. At the minimum, this avoids many of the issues with offensive names.

Other fantasy name generators are found online as well. Search for these and see if there is anything you like.

Simple names are often much better than complex names. If people have trouble typing your name, they won't remember it either. This is bad! You want people to remember who you are and to enjoy typing in your direction (well, if you like grouping and roleplaying).

Strongly consider avoiding popular names from fiction. Almost no one is going to treat you well if your name is a variant on common characters. Drisst Entruri Pickkardd is not your friend. Seriously, there are already 50 Hunters on your server alone with the name xxLegolaxx. Nobody can remember which is which. Nobody wants them around. If you want to go for it, good luck! Enjoy. But, don't say we didn't warn you.

Real world names are right out too. Jaylow the Priest might be able to team with Bennnifer the Druid, but things just won't work out in the long run.

It also needs to be said that names of major religious figures may be taken as major insults by some of the playing community. Be considerate and try not to make major political/social statements with your World of Warcraft time. People are in-game to get away for a while and enjoy the beauty of Azeroth. Be kind to the folks out there; most of them are pretty good people and would be happy to be your friend. By the same token, racial slurs are right out, and, yes, GMs will change names without warning. If you see someone using a name that is offensive in these ways, have no guilt in reporting them to a GM. Odds are, you aren't the only person offended by such language.

You don't need to have the most creative or incredible name to get by. Just choose something that you like. Something that sounds good to you. Simple, concise, clear, and easy to type.

Etiquette in the World of Warcraft

Online games have their own systems of social rules; there are certainly more interactions in a game like World of Warcraft than with offline roleplaying games, where people are seldom able to compete or cooperate while playing. WoW creates an environment where both positive and negative interactions between players are intended to occur, but even the negative ones are set within certain guidelines. Behaviors that fall outside of normal etiquette can be considered rude or inappropriate or even as griefing. To make friends and have a smooth experience in game, it pays to learn the rules up front.

WHILE HUNTING

The environment is primarily cooperative in the open field (at least within your own faction), where players are aligned against the monsters that stalk Azeroth. Whether soloing or grouping to accomplish this, there are ways to keep from stepping on other peoples' toes. Beyond that, it's good to know when someone else is doing something that is genuinely disrespectful so that you can advise them (at first), avoid them if they continue, and ignore them if no change occurs.

You Took My Mobs!!!

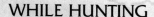

Mob ownership is often a point of contention during PvE hunting. Soloists and groups run into situations where other characters will come through and kill some of the same targets in the area where they were already hunting. The first point here is to use a cool head; everyone has a right to go after monsters. Even when a higher level person is attacking a beast, they may be after trade items that are useful, doing a backlog of old quests, or just farming something for their allies.

Instead of reacting with a negative attitude, see what can be done for both sides from the beginning. If you are on a kill quest, offer to bring the other person/people into your group—everyone benefits from this. By the same logic, if you are on a collection quest and someone else is going after the same targets for different reasons, it is STILL faster to group together and hunt. Take the time to ask them first before immediately moving to invite them; players often respond more favorably and happily to a verbal request for a party than if you ambush them with an invitation box.

For whatever reason, an alliance may not be an option. This happens often enough. No problem; you can state what you are doing and see if the other players are willing to give you the space to continue with what you were already doing. If they can't outright help, at least they can give you enough mobs to maintain the same kill rate and excitement. Fair enough for everyone concerned.

By asking people nicely and making your needs clear, you have every chance to get more of what you want if the other people are nice. Also, acting politely is less likely to trigger their obnoxious side (the side that might get them to intentionally stay longer and be even more obtrusive).

How to Handle Hunting Conflicts
Try to Work Together With Newcomers for Mutual Benefit
Agree to Leave Each Other Enough Targets and Space
Find a Better Hunting Spot If Nothing Can Be Arranged
Avoid Aggressive Players and Report Any Griefing to a GM AFTER You Are Certain That It Is Intentional

Most groups and conflicts are settled by the first two options. However, there are times when another group doesn't want to join with yours and is not willing to share anything in the region. That doesn't make them griefers—it's still within their rights to kill as much as they can within the area (that is your right as well). If the other group refuses to have a comfortable attitude, you may try another camp of the same creature (this DOES NOT mean that you are backing down or acting like a coward); there are often several camps of important monsters in a given region. Rather, it shows that you are sensible enough to have a good time and keep from wasting your night, experience points, and energy fighting for meager kills on a single quest. You can always come back later. Your fun, experience, and treasure are more important than making sure someone else ISN'T getting those things.

Okay, so is there any griefing at all that occurs in regard to mob ownership? Well, yes. Even with the tapping system in place, there are ways for people to make life difficult for many other classes. Someone with a real chip on their shoulders can use fast abilities to tap a monster just before your anticipated pull. This negates the experience and treasure you receive from the kill, so it's a bad situation. If someone does this once, ignore it entirely (it was most likely an accident). However, a person who follows your party around and does this multiple times is absolutely trying to get in your way. Ask the person what they are doing, then report anything foul in their response to a GM. If they ignore you and keep doing it, find a new place to hunt and ditch the offenders. Even at this stage, they may simply be too young, inexperienced, or otherwise hindered to know what they are doing.

It is still useful to know how to combat the people who try to tap "your" monsters. Note that your DOTs and debuffs aren't useful for tapping. You need to deal damage to a target, and deal it quickly. Find your fastest ranged ability and use that for grabbing monsters. If you are a melee class, see what works the best out of your existing options. For a Rogue, a fast thrown weapon or missile attack may be ideal. With Warriors, a Charge and immediate Hamstring. Obviously, Hunters and magic classes have the edge in doing this, but any skilled player who knows their class can learn to tap quickly and get the monsters they want.

One very useful thing to be aware of is the ability of certain classes to immediately lose aggro. Rogues and Hunters especially are able to grab creatures and then get them onto you (whether they are members of your faction makes no difference in this). What happens is that these characters gather the aggro, move over to you, then use deaggro abilities, such as Vanish or Feign Death. This puts the aggro onto you even if you haven't touched the monsters. Yikes! Most often this happens by accident when someone gets too many mobs at once on them and needs to escape; you are now the closest target for monster aggression and in the wrong place at the wrong time. However, a few nastier players of the community make an art form of doing this on purpose—and they are not usually subtle about it. If you see a suspicious/aggressive person gathering mobs into a tight group and then making a direct line toward you, prepare yourself for escape or an attack of your own against the monsters. Report those of your faction who do this consistently for griefing.

TREASURE DISTRIBUTION

When hunting in a group, especially when that group is composed of strangers, it is very wise to establish loot rules ahead of time. The dominant form of drop rules is to makes a pledge of Need Before Greed. This means that any character in the group who needs an item is placed in priority above someone who would just sell the item to a vendor or give it to an alternate character/guildie. This keeps parties together in a better atmosphere of cooperation. By agreeing on this BEFORE any powerful items drop, people save minutes of wasted hunting time trying to figure out who gets what.

Even with good loot systems in place, the game cannot police each player and make sure they don't roll for items in an honorable way. Indeed, Group Loot and Need Before Greed can't see into a character's inventory and determine whether they are actually going to equip an item. Thus, honor and trust play a huge part of proper treasure distribution.

Though individual definitions vary, the standard idea is that Need means that you are going to equip and use an item as soon as you possibly can, either the moment you get it or as soon as you reach the proper level. This item is an actual upgrade for your character, has an important place for you, etc. Greed is frequently used for items that aren't needed or for Enchanters who pretty much want everything that drops for their trade. Passing is done for items that aren't needed at all or for cases where guild groups are supporting their Enchanters (e.g., Need if you really need an item, Greed for Enchanters, and Pass for other people).

It's good to know what the loot systems do and do not do. This is useful for seeing why some things are very bad form. With Master Looter, a group leader is going to distribute things in the first place, so you don't have to worry about anything (just do what you are told, /random if asked to, etc.). More often, though, groups stick with Group Loot or Need Before Greed. In any event, you frequently have the option to roll on items that you don't need. Technically, a Warrior can equip plate, mail, leather, and cloth armor pieces. There might even be some leather with greater +Str and +Stam bonuses than your current equipment, so you might feel that you need it. Hold on before you click that Need button, and think!

If there are Rogues in the group, they are likely to have some serious need for such gear. It is very important to realize that the Need button carries certain subjectivity. If an item isn't ideal/perfect/godly for you, wait and see if other people are rolling Need on it. Ask people "This is actually an upgrade for me, if no one else Needs, can I roll?" They can always say no. This way, you are working with your group and avoiding the cries of "Ninja" or "I really needed that item."

The muddiest waters come when several people can use an item AND it is an upgrade, but one class may need the upgrade far more than others. Consider a party with a Mage who uses swords, a Warrior (also specializing in blades), and a Rogue who likes having a sword as well. Who NEEDS the epic sword that those lovely elite trolls just dropped? Do all of them? Yes and no, of course.

The Warrior would use it a great deal. The Rogue would too. For the Mage, it would be an improvement, but that player wouldn't be using it nearly as often. In these cases, it's better if the Mage backs off, but it isn't required either. So, the "right" thing to do for the Mage is to let the primary melee characters roll for it while looking for lesser swords. The "right" thing for the Warrior and Rogue is to accept the Mage's request to roll if he does push forward. Either side has the ability to walk away looking respectable, even if they don't come away with a rare item!

You can gain a great deal of respect from other people just by stating that although something would be nice for you to have, you would like someone else to receive the item. This is particularly true if you have had good luck and previously gotten some good drops during the run. By the same token, if someone else receives an item that you both rolled for, be a good sport and congratulate them on their good fortune. Everyone gets a little disappointed when they don't get what they really wanted, but behaving in a mature fashion increases the entire party's enjoyment of the game—and increases the chance that you can get a good party for the next run.

If someone in your group consistently tries to get every item that falls, talk to them about it first. Point out that they are pushing other people out of the way equipment wise and that it isn't fair. If they don't listen well, don't group with them again. If they are outright rude or unresponsive, boot them immediately and get another person for the group. The last thing you want is to reach the end of a long dungeon, defeat the boss, and have the best items of the night plundered by some jerk who came in with the very intention of stealing people's hard-earned gear.

FAST DROP GUIDELINES

- Set Drop Rules Before Leaving Town
- Don't Spend Large Amounts of Time Determining Treasure Distribution (More Fighting=More Treasure Anyway!)
- If a Player Acts Poorly, You Don't Have to Group With Them Again, But Making a Scene Hurts the Rest of the Group
- If People Continue to Be Greedy Even After It's Pointed Out, Cut Your Losses And Get Rid of Them

WHAT DO YOU DO ABOUT NINJA LOOTERS?

Put them on your Ignore List and don't group with them again. These players aren't likely to be considerate of your group's needs in the future, and it certainly brings down everyone's mood when the best items of a long instance go up in smoke. Move on, keep finding your favorite allies, and don't worry about it. Instances are repeatable, and there are more evenings, more encounters, and plenty more treasure for you. As for the Ninja Looter, imagine how things are going to go when nobody wants to group with them later for end-game content a couple months in the future. Having a bad reputation isn't much fun, and a few good items aren't worth the trouble.

Some people try to call out Ninja Looters on the boards. "This guy rolled need on everything, or formed a group and made himself Master Looter before we fought the bosses, etc." This usually isn't worth the effort. Go ahead if you feel that this person was so foul that others outside your circle of friends need to know, but the more sensible path is to inform friends/guild members and leave it at that. You can't stop everyone on the server from dealing with the bad folks, so it's often a more stable course to take care of your own.

Dealing With Incompetent Players

Not everyone has the same level of skill in World of Warcraft. Indeed, there is a huge gradient between the most adept and experienced players and those who are new to MOGs, WoW, and cooperative play in general. As with many suggestions, the best default should be to allow for some mistakes and be patient with others. Yet, there are still times when a player is performing so badly that something must be done about it.

When someone in your group (most likely a person in a pickup group) is performing poorly and getting others killed, have the group leader take the first step. The group leader should stop for a short rest (area allowing) and explain how the party should be performing. If the new player is pulling extra monsters onto a party, advise them on who to [/assist] and where to stand. When they outright pull monsters that aren't desired, tell them that they aren't responsible for pulling and that a different player is already handling that.

Unless the player is outright rude in their response to your party's suggestions, keep them around at least for the quest/expedition that you invited them to join. Good etiquette dictates that the group should stay together until the task is done, even if the weakest link in the party does not improve. Cutting a player for performing poorly is rude. That said, no one is obliged to take unskilled players out for every quest and every raid. If you aren't interested in helping that player improve their skills, don't group with them in the future. That is absolutely your choice. And, it's probably a wise decision.

Spam Invitations

It is best to look for groups with the tools available (general chat, Meeting Stones, looking for group world chat channel, asking in guild if people want to run X instance/quest, etc.). Walking around an area inviting everyone you see into a group is not polite. Ask first and you will find that it is much easier to collect a better grade of players!

The same is true for duels. Practicing with your character in 1-on-1 PvP is exciting, and many other players are happy to join you in duels, especially near towns when they are not engaged with quests, other parties, etc. However, spamming a person with duel invites is quite obnoxious and will land you on an Ignore List some of the time. The best duels take time to set up, with fun talk, mutual bows, and a brief discussion for any rules that are desired. Duels do not simulate true PvP anyway, and out-of-the-blue ones aren't worth the breach in manners.

Asking for Help

As long as you don't demand help from anyone, it is perfectly polite to ask for assistance when going after difficult fights, quests, and such. This can be done on the general chat channel, from guildies, or from people in the area. If you see people fighting their way toward a quest mob that you need to fight, there is nothing wrong with asking to join them. When you can't get close enough for [/say] to work, whisper to one of the members in the group. People rarely mind grabbing an extra person for a few kills.

A side issue of practicing good manners is when your party is standing close to an important quest NPC, getting ready for the fight. Because some of these monsters are hard to find (because of wandering, spawn problems, etc.), it is polite to either yell or send a message over general to let people know that that enemy is not long for this world. By doing this, you give others the chance to ask for an invite if they are close.

Requesting Buffs from Strangers

When soloing, you find that certain buffs make a huge difference to your performance. A Warrior out by his lonesome is greatly improved by a Priest's Stamina Buff (Holy Word: Fortitude). Getting conjured food and water from Mages is another boost to soloers, because it is effectively free to both parties. However, no one is obliged to help a character with abilities that cost time and Mana to cast. The best way to get what you want here is to approach characters that are out in the field and ask politely for the buffs or spells that you desire.

Don't be afraid to help the person in question polish off a few monsters; because of the tap system you receive 0 experience and they get their kills substantially faster. Be aware, this reduces the experience a player receives. That is usually a good way to help out while waiting for a response (ask first, either way, "May I have some food, my Mage brother? I can help you kill monsters for a time or give you some coin for your trouble!"). Also, if you have buffs that are useful, throw those on the stranger while they make up their mind (it won't hurt your request, certainly).

If a Mage conjures a large quantity of food/water for you, throw a modest tip in there even if the Mage doesn't ask for it; that person is going to have a short bit of downtime for what they gave you, and a tip makes them feel better about being generous. Besides, the cost of buying vendor food and water is so much higher that you save entire gold pieces at the moderate levels just by getting Mage assistance; encourage them!

From the buffer's perspective, it is nice to receive tips. However, a kind "thank you" is what you should expect and require for future assistance. When people don't thank you for your time and effort, it's not worth helping them time and time again. On the other side, if you do not demand a tip, don't expect one from every character you help (many may be too poor to make things sweet for you). Thus, if you aren't going to feel right about helping someone unless money is exchanged, TELL the other players up front. Selling your services is perfectly acceptable. Pretending to donate them and getting upset when people don't realize your expectations is a bit unfair.

All that said, people are strange. You can give offense to some people for things that don't hurt them in the least. They might be roleplaying or just misunderstand the system, but, whatever the case, don't always expect thanks for stepping in. If people don't ask for help directly, you assume a certain risk by charging forward. Shrug it off either way and do what you feel is right. In general, healing the people in trouble is least likely to upset folks, killing tapped monsters would be next, and snagging an untapped add is the most risky.

Perhaps the situation is entirely hopeless. When a dozen monsters get trained onto a small group, it is unlikely that they will evacuate safely. Don't jump in when the battle is hopeless (just get out of the way and hope for your own survival). Adding to a failing battle makes things even more chaotic and could even cause a fleeing group to stop and try to hold their ground.

TRAINS

Running through a region often causes a number of monsters to collect in your path, following behind. Even if you are high enough level to survive this, there are sometimes grave consequences to these trains (so called because it looks a tad like a train, with you as the engine and the monsters as cars following behind). When these monsters break off from the chase, they have a chance to aggro on various players during the trip home; this varies depending on the monsters and area, but it always has the potential for chaos. This can cause many deaths and problems to lower-level players in an area.

If you are running around with a train behind you, avoid other players by as wide a margin as possible. And, if your way is blocked by a group (at dungeon entrances or other such bottlenecks), be willing to move off to the side and wait until your train heads home before advancing. It's FAR better to die than to cause another group to wipeout. Besides, the characters you just protected may have a rezzer, offer you a group for future protection, etc. If you get them killed, they are not so likely to keep you on their friends list!

JUMPING IN

It is fairly common to see other players in trouble. A bad pull or just a poor turn of luck can place another character or entire group in a situation they cannot win. There is no hard and fast rule for what you are supposed to do at that point. If you believe your character would turn the tide of battle, feel free to jump in. When you KNOW the other group needs help, take a fresh target and pull that away (you get the experience and treasure, but they have one fewer problem to deal with). However, if you think the other group might be fine and are uncertain, jump onto a tapped mob; there is almost no way to give offense by doing that because the other party still gets their loot and experience.

If you are a Rezzer or your group has such a character that is willing, send one of the people in the doomed group a whisper and ask if they want a Rez (not everyone does if the map is small enough and the Graveyard is somewhat close by). It's worth a short moment to Resurrect the group if that is what they want. The good will is nice to have, and your group may need a Rez one day too. You never know who will be around when that time comes.

STAYING IN A GROUP

Groups may form for a single quest, an hour of play, or even a single battle. Proper manners here vary, but the basic key is to be honest about how long you intend to stay with a group and stick to your word. If you join someone for a quest, say that you are able to stay around for "X" amount of time and that is your limit. Work to get the quest done, then stay to make sure that it is done for everyone before leaving. In the event that you must leave unexpectedly, apologize, give at least some of the reason, and offer to make things up to people later.

When the task has been completed, make your intentions known then as well. If you like the party, ask them if they would like to continue grouping and see which quests you have in common. If you don't want to group any longer, thank them for the help and wish them luck (especially if the party wasn't very good; they'll need it). In any event, resist the urge to wander off and go back to your own business without saying anything to the group or suddenly separating from them after criticizing or demeaning them. Being polite and practicing good manners makes grouping more enjoyable for everyone.

By the same token, don't assume that everyone who leaves suddenly is being a jerk and ditching the group. Phone calls, family, lightning, penguin outbreaks, and other problems simply occur. If you group with someone a couple times and they consistently ditch after finishing their part of the quest, don't group with them in the future (at least, if that type of thing upsets you).

GRABBING RESOURCES

Resources that spawn at static points (e.g., Metal and Herbs) are available to everyone, and it is another case where first come, first served is the rule. Yet, there are a few ways to keep from doing unfair things while collecting. Because many resource points have monsters nearby, groups and solo characters must fight to clear the area first, unless they are high enough level to simply sneak past and grab what they want. Regardless, if you see a person clearing the area near a resource point, do not rush past and steal that point. Whisper to the person or group and ask if they are going after the resource node; if they say "yes", move on and look for another (you should get to the next point first since that person is still going after the last one).

If you badly need points for your skills, you may ask a person for a chance to access the resource point without taking anything. With Mining and Herbalism, the point is given for using the resource node, not for taking what is inside it. Thus, a whack on a vein of ore or a moment looking through the herb patch gives you everything you need without costing another person anything (either their point or the materials). There is no harm in asking for a chance to do this, and most harvesters won't have a problem letting you try, especially after they find that you are good to your word.

Note that some gatherers are from the other faction (thus you can't talk to them). When that is the case, go ahead and get the point without worrying about things. Competing with the other faction is a good thing! The neutral route is to get your point and leave the node for others, even if they are jerks; if they were clearing a point, let them have it. You've got your point either way. But, if you want to detract from the competing faction, go for it. Be ready for a /slap or /spit though (on a PvP realm, never gather from a node without killing the enemy first)!

In groups, there may be several resource collectors of the same type (two Skinners, two Miners, etc.). As the group is moving into the area, discuss how you plan to tradeoff resources. For mines, it may be that everyone gets a hit for points, then the metal is split evenly. For Skinning it may be that just one person skins each monster, for time reasons, and the Skinners trade who is on duty.

BACK IN TOWN

Even in the somewhat relaxed state of standing in town, hawking wares and seeking various trainers, there are proper ways to conduct yourself.

WHERE IS EVERYTHING?

Some of the NPCs in cities can be hard to find. A system is in place that allows players to ask the guards of major cities where to find various NPCs. Right-click on the guards to bring up a list of the NPCs and locations they are aware of, then choose the person you seek (a red flag on the mini-map appears to help guide you there).

Sometimes, people in the General Chat Channel ask where different NPCs and stores are located. Try to provide an answer for difficult questions. If the players are asking for answers to simple questions that they have access to, direct them to the source they should be using ("The Quest description tells you where those monsters are" or "Ask a city guard in Stormwind; they will put a marker on your map").

If you are the one who has questions, ask in General and see if people are willing and able to help. There is nothing wrong with asking every now and then if you don't receive assistance and are still having trouble. This is an area where "Please," "Thank You," and general courtesy go a LONG way. The more polite you are the more often future questions are answered. Also, players tend to provide more information when they feel connected to the person asking the question. "Does anyone know if the Mo'Grosh Crystal is a shared drop? :)" will get more attention than "Is Mo'Grosh Crystal shared?"

The best tendency is to try and find things you need on your own at first, because many items, stores, NPCs, and quest targets are quite accessible. Asking where to go and what to do the moment you receive a quest frustrates other players on chat, and they won't be as likely to help after several rounds of queries. Instead, wait until the tools available to you are exhausted. Look around, reread quests or pertinent text, ask your guild or group, then go into General Chat. Also, feel free to whisper a personal "Thanks!" to anyone who helps you. Showing that you are genuinely appreciative of their help is a suitable payment for the time they spent typing an answer.

ON THE BATTLEFIELDS OF PVP

Many of the rules that govern play in PvE change when dealing with players of the opposite faction. This is a desired aspect of the game for many people, and it is best to choose a server that fits your view of etiquette from the beginning if you are worried about certain aspects of competitive play. PvP is one of the rare times when the server is what dictates etiquette more than common sense, disposition, or morality.

When to Attack

Going after enemies of the opposite faction is a matter of duty on the PvP servers, to a fair extent. Disrupting another player of your faction when they are fighting a monster would be griefing; doing the same thing to an opposing faction's player is acceptable (perhaps even desired depending on how bitter the rivalry is on the server currently).

Indeed, attacking other players in a PvP environment is anticipated and encouraged. Any civility that you want to put into such combat (waiting until enemies are fully healed, outside of combat, have seen you, etc.) is above and beyond what others expect from you. Much like in real life, indulging your enemies in this way is a risk that won't always be returned. Let roleplay-ing and your sense of enjoyment dictate these responses instead of standard etiquette. If you want to be a dirty, rotten, backstabbing fiend that leaps onto hapless foes at the worst of times…go ahead and do it!

Is it possible to grief members of the opposition? Yes, there could be griefing, but this would only be an issue if there was a bug that was exploited against members of one faction. Things that would normally be considered griefing are often allowable otherwise. Training monsters into enemies is not griefing; it's a viable strategy. Again, you may not choose to do it, but your enemies have every right and ability to do it against your party. Be prepared.

Ganking

Ganking is the process of going after helpless characters or characters of MUCH lower level. If ganking doesn't do anything for you and it makes other people's lives difficult, is it wrong? No. Some people on both sides of the war see ganking as a practice of griefers. However, this is not an act of griefing because it is a game dynamic that is mutually agreed upon by the parties involved (the targeted players chose to come to a server where non-instanced PvP is a reality). Thus, they knew the risks and consented to the attack simply by joining the server.

That said in defense of gankers, it still is not an act that earns you respect from the majority of players unless you accomplish your attacks in novel and exciting ways. Using stealth or invisibility to get into contested areas where relatively low-level enemies are questing and going after solo targets is fairly simple. Charging in with raiding parties, fighting out in the open, going after larger groups, etc. is the way to have more fun and truly challenge yourself.

Play as you wish. Those who want to avoid this style of gaming are absolutely free to join the servers where Faction-based combat is restricted to instances and opt-in combat (e.g., defending city NPCs that are being attacked or flag-ging for PvP).

Corpse Camping

When an enemy dies, their corpse becomes a respawn point (when their spirit returns). Only in dire circumstances do PvPers take Durability penalties for their deaths, so it is probable that the person who died will return to their corpse. Corpse Camping is the act of patrolling the region where an enemy has died while waiting for the person to return (the followup is to attack the recently Rezzed character and kill them a second time).

Again, this is not griefing. However, it is both obstructive to the other person's enjoyment (since they can't even get enough health to have a good fight with you) and it holds your group in place instead of getting you more experience, money, combat, etc. The camped person is free to log off and return at a later point when you are gone, and it's impossible to know if that is the case. So, it is often better to get your kills, move on, and know that the victim could be after you at any time (enjoy the rush).

As far as etiquette goes, people are FAR happier on both sides when corpse camping is minimal. Very few players enjoy being camped this way, and most classes simply don't have the ability to get away safely when five or six people are boxing them into a small area. The flipside of this is what happens when a ganker/corpse camper goes down. Suddenly, tons of people are ready to camp the offending party, and the hunter quickly becomes the hunted.

BATTLEGROUND DOs AND DON'Ts

The PvP Battlegrounds have rules of conduct all to themselves. Some things are entirely fair there that would be mean in other parts of the game, yet other aspects are surprisingly cordial. Note, these are moral issues. Killing players is one of the key means of acquiring Honor, so many people feel the need to kill any and all, no matter the circumstances.

GRAVEYARDS

Graveyard camping in the battlegrounds is the most complex issue to bring out. In Warsong Gulch and Arathi Basin, this action is highly reprehensible. Many players on both sides turn nasty toward you if you stay in the area where the other faction is brought back to life. Don't attack these people until they have left the safety of the Graveyard. Not only is this a nice thing to do; it keeps people coming back for more even after their side has suffered a defeat. When people camp, it causes the other side to feel more than just defeated; they feel broken and humiliated. Then they don't come back. No more easy wins for you—often no more BGs at all for a few hours. Ouch!

Yet, in Alterac Valley, camping is a standard part of fighting strategy. This is because Graveyards are an active part of Alterac Valley warfare (they can be captured). Thus, the game encourages you to go after these sites directly.

EMOTING

The use of [/spit] is extremely unpleasant. Though realistic for roleplayers and an allowed action by Blizzard, many players find spitting to be rude/insulting. Reserve this for enemies who are vile. Graveyard campers perhaps?

The flipside of emotes is that they can be used to show respect or friendship, toward allies and enemies alike. Try [/salute] to let people know that they are respected even if you are trying to kill them. Or, [/love] and [/hug] work well for friendship. A good [/dance] is another way to let people know that things aren't always about fighting. If one side of a battleground is vastly outnumbered, the other side may choose to play around while accomplishing their goals as a way of saying, "we're going to try to win this quickly, but we won't fight you directly unless you attack us." Giving the understaffed side the initiative in this way is very good form.

EXITING BATTLEGROUNDS

Leaving a Battleground can be a point of contention as well. Because the game allows you to queue for multiple Battlegrounds, it's not a rare occurrence for a Battleground to pop up while you are already fighting in another. If your team is in trouble or

the fight is close, please don't leave unless you have a very good reason without telling your team first. Even if others take your place, the disruption might be enough to tip the other side toward victory. If you do have to leave, let people know and apologize, then leave the raid or [/afk] before logging out so a replacement can enter as soon as possible.

WHEN NOT TO ATTACK

In the Battlegrounds, don't attack enemies if they stop fighting entirely. When outnumbered or just outgunned, some people give up and pull back (this doesn't happen often, but it's worth knowing about). In these cases, the enemies want the match over as soon as possible so they can try to get more people into the next Battleground. Just win the match and don't attack them unless they attack you.

This also comes into play when other players are zoning into a Battleground that is already in progress. If you see someone standing absolutely still, despite combat going on around them, it's likely that they aren't being deceptive. They are probably just away from their keyboards or waiting for the area to load (especially if you see them doing this in their spawn-in points).

To be safe, go ahead and use crowd control or a snare on such targets, to make sure they can't quickly follow and attack you, but don't kill the poor people.

Eleven Things Worth Knowing

There are certain aspects of MOG play that are almost universal. Appropriately, these are present in World of Warcraft and should be explained for people who are new to the game, genre, or even to Blizzard games from the past.

PATIENCE IS THE KEY TO GLORY

It is invariably true that patience leads to greatness in many tasks. Most role-playing games have a huge element of this, and MOGs are even more representative of the idea. It's impossible for players to sit down and see everything there is to World of Warcraft in one day (or week, or month, or...). Thus, no matter how hard you try there is no way to rush through the game world and get to the "end." In fact, though there is an end-game portion of content where players are capped in level, there is never going to be a heavy hand on your shoulder saying "The game is over now, you win."

Regardless of anyone else's view of how fast someone should play, level, and enjoy the game, there is no specific time to reach a quest or an area. Take a week hunting for Kodo Leather in Mulgore, or try exploring all of Kalimdor at level 20 if you are truly brave. Nothing that you enjoy in World of Warcraft is wasted time. The world is here for you to enjoy! Take it easy and play as you wish. Indeed, the levels are more exciting, the gameplay refreshing, and every group a bit better when you remember that fun is more important than getting the next skill, level, Wombat of Slaying, etc.

LEARN WHAT YOU CAN HANDLE

It's exciting to push your character to the very limits of survivability. This is good to try on a limited basis for several reasons. First off, it provides a nice rush (even if you eventually lose and have to do a short corpse run). Beyond that, this type of testing brings you closer to your characters; understanding how to get every last bit of power out of a class makes every difference when it comes to complex challenges such as Player Vs. Player combat and dungeon Instances.

Though you naturally cover the limits of your character over time, simply by playing the game and dealing with the troublesome situations that arise from large pulls, trains from other groups, and ambushes out in the wild, testing still has its place. The issue here is that intentionally testing your class makes the process more analytic; you can prepare new strategies, test them out, and really see the effects. It's MUCH harder to keep a keen eye out when you are surprised.

Try finding situations that push your character to the limit to see what things your race/class/style combo are best for countering. Try going against single targets of high level in solo encounters; engage entire groups of equal or slightly lower-level monsters; grab wide aggro from a huge range of enemies and try to flee successfully. These tests reveal a great deal about the strengths of a player and that person's chosen character.

FIND A CLASS THAT SUITS YOUR MENTALITY

A character's class defines what they are capable of doing in so many ways. Though every class is quite impressive in World of Warcraft, even in solo encounters, there are styles of fighting that are more effective for certain classes. For Instances, Warriors handle groups of enemies FAR better than most alternatives (they have high health, impressive armor, and a Rage bar that is easier to fill when there are more targets aggroing). Casters, on the other hand, have more options for crowd control or healing, but must be quite careful of burst damage from enemies; success for casters involves damage at range, frustrating enemy advances, and using mana efficiently.

Class Style Quicklist	
Class Name	**Dominant Traits**
Warrior	Very High Survivability; Gather Aggro; Damage Mitigation; Versatile Melee
Paladin	Adequate Damage; Backup Healing; Resurrection; Strong Armor; Survival Abilities; Great Vs. Undead; Alliance-Only Class
Rogue	High and Sustained Damage; Many Stuns; Stealth; Low Armor; Light Hit Points, Lockpicking
Hunter	Powerful, Consistent Pets; Wonderful Sustained Damage; Traps, Tracking of Beasts and Sentient Enemies, Moderate Armor
Druid	Shapeshifting; Style Flexibility; Can Act as Substitute Tank, Rogue, or Healer; Damage at All Ranges; Great Roots; Backup Healing
Shaman	Totems for AoE Status Effects; Superb Group Support; Ranged Magic; Substantial Melee Damage; Moderate Armor; Resurrection; Horde-Only Class
Priest	Powerful, Fast, and Efficient Healing; Stamina Buff; Protective Shield Buff; Close-Range Fear on a Quick Timer; Anti-Undead Powers; Impressive Damage With Some Builds; Fragile Hit Points and Armor
Warlock	Multiple DOTs; Fear (LOTS of Fear); Extensive Pet Summoning; Many Channeling Spells; Blurred Line Between Hit Points and Mana (Can Use One to Gain the Other); Complex Class
Mage	High Ranged Damage; Snare Enemies With Cold or Root Them Briefly; Create Free Food/Water for Self and Others; Create Mana Gems for Personal Use; Many Instant Damage Options; In-Combat Crowd Control; Very Fragile Hit Points and Armor

Don't be afraid to message players of specific classes and ask them about their experiences. Use the WoW community site forums for the same purpose and see how actual players feel about their play experience. This avoids the path of reaching level 20-30 before realizing that a class is good but still not your style. Of course, it's good to try everything yourself in the long run, but that is a different issue.

CHOOSE A RACE THAT LOOKS AND FEELS RIGHT

Though class selection is dictated by logic, race is a decision based on aesthetics. Certainly, there are starting advantages to some race/class combinations (Tauren Warriors have higher starting damage per second and health, Gnomes have more mana to throw around than other races, etc.). Weigh the racial advantages against your aesthetic needs.

The choice of a character's race can be a great time to go with your heart. That character will charge about the screen for months to come, so pick a race that looks and feels right to you! This yields a starting location that suits your playstyle, since all of the starting areas are geared to the races that inhabit them. Also, it conveys an immediate sense of closeness between you and your character; the more you enjoy your character, the better each level seems.

VOICE EMOTES

Another fun thing to try is various voice emotes for the sex/race combination of your character. Create a character and try the [/flirt] and [/silly] commands five or six times each. If the humor of the combination works for you, the style of that race's quests are likely going to synch as well. Don't forget to sample the [/dance] of your choice as well, and know that there are male/female differences even within the races.

Don't let stats or racial traits decide race unless that is truly important to you! If you are interested in playing any combination, no matter how odd at first, go for it and have no regrets. In WoW, player skill and a good reputation gets you into high-quality groups far more often than race, class, etc.

INVEST IN FRIENDS AND SKILLED ALLIES

And speaking of good groups, there are a few tips to help with finding them. While you are playing, even at low level, try to see which people are active in General Chat in a helpful way. Make note of polite, informed players and how they are dealing with each other. Out in the field, see who is eager to buff ungrouped characters, jump in to help other characters when a pull goes poorly, etc. Don't be afraid to spend time getting to know the other players; the ones who stay involved with their characters into the higher levels may be your companions for months to come. And, the sooner you become friends with the more friendly and skilled players, the sooner pickup groups will be a thing of the past.

Ironically, to get away from pickup groups, people have to rush into many of them. The best times to do this are for kill quests, elite quests, and other activities where having more people around aids the process EVEN when they are strangers. Try to keep track of all the people you enjoy grouping with. Had a good time with Player A?—ask if you can put that person on your Friends list. They will most likely do the same for you. Continue this and there will be a cluster of a dozen or more people from other guilds that you know and like in no time (leading to faster groups with more familiarity, less down time, and more fun).

On the whole, the best players to choose for your list are the people who click with your personality and style of play. Even when some players are unskilled and make mistakes, they may be wonderful choices in the long run. You cannot train someone to be an exciting friend; skill in MOGs, on the other hand, is easily acquired over time by someone willing to learn. The vast majority of players who start off poorly but have the will to practice and learn end up being quite good by the time they reach high levels.

TRY EVERYTHING AT LEAST ONCE

There are many classes, races, and areas to explore. Even if one thing grabs you from the start, you become a better player by understanding where everyone else has been. Look into both factions even if you are sold on one of them. Playing a dedicated Alliance character, it is quite an eye opener to see the Barrens as a soldier of the Horde. Learning how the other side works together, quests, and levels aids in countering those tactics with your original character. Also, there is a chance that somewhere you haven't been will completely capture your heart. A player that immediately chooses to play as an orc may fall in love with Mulgore or even pine away for the beauty of Elwynn Forest.

For those with enough patience, try starting characters in each of the six initial regions to see if there is something special in one of them. Spending a couple hours on this your first day may pay off with a character you didn't even know you wanted to play.

In the same vein, be sure to experience world PvP, Battlegrounds, roleplaying, raids, and other such content several times, even if they don't seem to call to you. Some "carebear" players find that world PvP isn't their style at all, but Battlegrounds on a PvE or RP server are great for them. Or, you might discover that roleplaying is wonderful once you've met a few buddies and understand your character a tad better. Try it all!

IDENTIFY GOALS AND SUITABLE TARGETS

There are many goals for a player to seek in a given session. Sure, it is possible to play without more than an urge to beat monsters and have a good time (a goal unto itself, honestly). If that is all that you are looking for, recognize that and take a leisurely pace; fight the monsters you enjoy fighting even if there aren't any quests for that area. With a casual pace, it is entirely possible to group with a huge level range of friends and just do whatever you want!

When you have a more specific goal, do what you can to identify the best targets for accomplishing that. Indeed, someone looking for the best experience on a given evening should queue the most quests for an area, find a group that is willing to stay together for at least a few hours, and then plow through those quests with military efficiency. Or, when quests are dry for multiple areas, gather a high-kill rate party and grind elite mobs in an Instance (not entirely ideal for experience, but a fine way to work with others and increase your chance for higher-quality gear). By choosing the right group, activity, and monster type, you gain more money and experience without investing more time or energy.

Perhaps you want money instead. Taking professions to harvest resources is great for this. Mining, Herbalism, and Skinning are great ways to farm for cash. Sell the materials on the Auction House and watch the gold pieces roll into the mailbox. This will net your character far more money than grinding against even the best monsters for your class.

Another good money-farming technique is to hit instances that are far beneath you in level. Solo these and sell the green and blue items that drop (obviously only the Bind on Equip pieces can be sold, but instances drop far more of these). On many servers, items that are between 16-19 and 26-29 can be sold at painful buyout prices in the Auction House. This is because second-generation characters with heavy funding are buying such gear for use in the Battlegrounds.

The global point is to do what you like without worrying about experience per hour (unless experience per hour is your goal, of course). People love to

explore, roleplay, dance around Ironforge with stray Gnomes, etc. Experiment, find your favorite activities, then indulge.

THE RIGHT PLACE AT THE RIGHT TIME

While leveling, there are certainly better places to get the job done at any given point. Because questing is such a major aspect of WoW, it is quite useful to know where the most quests are throughout the game. One of the keys to progressing smoothly comes in traveling back and forth between equivalent regions; when quests are depleted in one area, try another for a time then return to see if new things are available.

In Alliance lands, a person may be hunting in Loch Modan from levels 12-14, then suddenly find a few of the remaining quests to be a bit challenging (or they will simply wish for something new). For a change of pace and some easy experience, move down into Westfall and do all of the quests there for the early levels. By the time Westfall becomes old news for your budding adventurer, Loch Modan's "tougher" quests should be just right. Or, there is always a trip out to Darkshore for yet another batch of level-appropriate quests. Horde characters often bounce between The Barrens and Silverpine Forest for the exact same reasons.

To find out about quests areas and new regions, read this guide, talk to people around your level, and see what other people are doing. Another trick is to do a search for people around your level. Try a [/who] for characters within a level or so and look at their location. You might find that some people are in places that you didn't expect.

USE ALL RESOURCES

In game, using your resources means that it is important to keep in touch with other players via the chat channels and the guild you choose. Be confident in yourself and try to find answers through exploring and testing, but don't be hesitant to ask others for help when things become muddled or frustrating. Buy quality items from other players as well, and be fast to sell the good things you find but can't use (this will make more coin than vendoring the items, and it substantially helps others at the same time).

Outside WoW, there are web sites, strategy guides, guild pages, and forums waiting for you. Each of these offers a different aspect of assistance for mastering World of Warcraft. Guild pages offer social interaction, networking, and a feeling of playing a game outside the game. Open forums have tons of information on quest problems, upcoming game changes, and developments in the world. Obviously, strategy guides have a good place because they can go into the game with you; kept beside your computer, they offer fast information, data charts, etc. Also, guides can be taken around for perusal when a computer won't be available (commute by train, long trips, and such).

If you want to know everything there is to know about WoW, play long, play hard, and use ALL of these sources. No single one of them is going to replace the others. Even with this guide and a few major websites about general WoW data, you may find great joy on the forum for your specific server. This is covered more in the Community Site section.

TAKE BREAKS

Eating, sleeping, work, friends, and all of the other needs demand their own time, but there are also breaks in game that can be useful to you. For one, it is nice to have a few characters to play unless you are madly driven to reach the level cap in the least possible time. Having a few characters gives a player the breathing room to play according to a given mood instead of being forced into the same style each evening. It is nice to have a tank for slugging things out, a caster for ranged spellwork, a crafting and farming character for making money and finding special gear, and whatever else calls to you.

By switching around the characters you play, the game stays more vibrant and has fewer demands on you. Instead, you get to go with your mood each time you play. The only serious downside of having multiple characters is that friends on the same server may out-level you. That is one of the many perks of having a guild; there is often a cluster of people in every region, so you won't be left out by leveling at a different pace than the "average" player. For that matter, it is pretty darn hard to find an average player when it comes to leveling, since there is a huge range in terms of speed and style of play.

Try keeping a character on both the Alliance and Horde sides on some servers. This is especially worthwhile on servers with heavier roleplaying groups because you can play off of more people and come up with better organization for cross-faction events. Very fun! This provides for breaks from the grind even while staying in game.

USING THE COMMUNITY

Being on online game, World of Warcraft has a number of components in the online community that are very useful for players. The community site, at www.worldofwarcraft.com, has an extensive forum for all users of the game. It also has news updates, contests, basic game info, support information, patch notes, account management, and a wealth of others treats.

TOOLS ON THE LEFT SIDE OF THE SITE

Account Management is the most essential function of the community site. This is shown at the very front of the page (on the left side, where many of the major navigation points are found), and it allows users to control their payment type, cancel accounts, and so forth. Password use, paid characters transfers, and parental controls are all based from here as well. If you have played WoW for a few weeks and it is something that you will play for a while, consider changing your billing information.

Using the Workshop gives everyone the ability to see PvP rankings, calculate talent templates for any character combination, look forward to events and raid resets in the game, and view major armor types.

The Media page is a repository for movies, music, screenshots, wallpapers, and the Blizzard Store. The Gadgetzan Times is also based there. WoW is not just an in-game community, check it out and get involved.

The Forums are a frequent stop for many players of all skill levels. There are always new people asking questions, veterans answering and debating the future of classes, and a full range of odd folks in-between. Though sometimes the Forums are a bit too much to take in all at once, they are often a very early source for knowledge about added areas, upcoming changes, and strategies for difficult encounters. Any major changes to classes show up here first, and much debate ensues. There are also server forums. If you are new and want to get the feel for a server, this is often a good first stop.

The Community pages have comics, contests, important links to events and community elements, and fan artwork. Guild Relations also have links here (to general discussions and the specific Guild Relations forum).

Use the Support pages if you are having trouble with billing, game access, and other major issues that prevent the game from working.

QUICK LINKS (THE RIGHT SIDE)

Look on the right side of the main community page for Quick Links of various sorts. These are sometimes in flux, as new content is added or being focused on during patch times and such.

Learn about new items or areas of the game, recruit buddies to play with you in World of Warcraft using the Recruit a Friend program, or set the PvP Rankings to your favorite server to see who is staying on top of the battlefield.

Don't forget to click on the In Development link to check on future elements of the game. Patches are always in the works, and these unleash entirely new challenges on the players.

Understanding Equipment, Enemies, and Levels

Levels of NPCs, monsters, and equipment means a great deal to new and veteran players alike. Just because there are items of stunning power out there doesn't imply that you should be wielding them from the beginning. Indeed, the theory behind World of Warcraft is that you must build your character's skills and abilities to the point where they are able to wield the items of greatest power. The same is true for which enemies you are able to fight with any degree of safety; the bitter and hard-fought skirmishes your friends have against Defias Pillagers in Westfall will seem like a fond memory in a few weeks when you begin engaging the Trolls of Stranglethorn Vale! And these are but minor foes in retrospect once your character steps into the flames of Stratholme in an attempt to stop the Scourge and Scarlet Crusaders that war there.

SHADES OF QUALITY: THE EQUIPMENT SYSTEM

For almost all forms of equipment, there are ways to quickly judge their approximate power and usefulness to you. The minimum level of an item reveals when you can use it, and the color of said item provides a rough sense of how powerful that piece is at that level.

The table below lists the different equipment tiers.

Equipment Color Scheme
Poor (Grey)
Common (White)
Uncommon (Green)
Rare (Blue)
Epic (Purple)
Legendary (Orange)

Items of Poor quality show up in an ugly grey color and are inferior to everything else; there are only useful when nothing else is available. This happens most often when you reach levels where new slots of equipment can be used (shoulderpads are the most common example beyond level one).

Common items are the standard ones for early trade/crafting or for crummy vendor equipment. Their color is a lifeless white. You won't use these items long at all, and only at the lowest levels is there much of a chance to intentionally equip such gear and care about it as an upgrade.

Uncommon items are frequently called "Greens" due to their color. Quite a large number of these pieces Bind on Equip and provide attribute bonuses to your character. This is the rank-and-file's base equipment. You can find green items from monsters all over the world, and the loot tables are very large. Sell or trade the pieces that you find and don't need while collecting the proper gear for your character from the Auction House.

Rare items start to get quite interesting. These appear in a wonderful shade of blue and offer bonuses that are substantially above what an Uncommon item would give at the same level. Some of these are Bind on Equip and can be found anywhere in the world (with a low drop rate), but a huge number are discovered in dungeons, where they are a Bind on Pickup drop from specific enemies. Thus, Rare items require more dangerous fighting to get, but they offer higher rewards and more specific character customization. Sell Bind on Equip blue items on the Auction House at a premium!

Everything from Epic gear onward is very difficult to get. These items require a massive investment in crafting, reputation quests that are repeatable and slow to complete, weeks of Battleground combat, or the farming of raid-level Instances. These items of the higher tiers are way above the power level of green and blue items. Anything that is purple, red, or orange is impressive! Some of these are only found once on an entire server.

NPCS, ALLIES, AND ENEMIES

Much like items, people and monsters you encounter in World of Warcraft are color coded. For both enemies and allies, there are color distinctions that are important to understand.

Other characters of your faction and NPCs will be either Blue or Green in appearance when you highlight their avatar. A bar appears that lists that person's name, class/job, and level. The color of that bar declares whether that person is flagged for PvP. A blue bar means that the target is not currently set for /PvP in that area. A green bar means that the person is a viable /PvP target for enemies from the opposing faction. NPCs are always viable targets.

Enemies and Beasts are different colors. Creatures out in the wilderness may be Yellow if they are passive. These neutral creatures do not attack anything on sight, regardless of proximity. You are free to walk up next to a Deer, Zhevra, or any other neutral creatures without fear of reprisal. If you attack these creatures, however, they will aggro on you and engage in battle just like any proper foe.

Aggroing Neutral Creatures

Even area-of-effect debuffs from your party can cause neutral creatures to aggro. To avoid this, use fire control and hold back on AoE activities when there are neutral creatures in the way.

Also note that many neutral creatures are shy and retreat from the area if there is a battle taking place. This prevents some problems with accidental aggro.

More aggressive creatures, such as various predators, undead beings, demons, members of the opposing faction that are PvP flagged and attacking, etc., appear with a Red bar when they are highlighted. Red stands for an aggressive creature; these foes aggro on you simply for stepping within a certain distance. That distance is determined by the difference between your level and the hostile creature's level.

Aggro Distance

Aggro distance, as stated, is computed by determining the difference in level between you and the enemy. Being lower level than the creature increases the distance at which it chooses to attack. Thus, very low-level characters for a given region have predators and enemies alike racing across fair distances for a chance at some fresh meat.

On the flipside, characters who are much higher level than the hostile monsters in an area won't aggro them without walking right next to them.

Finally, some enemies have a higher aggro range than others. Wolves, Coyotes, certain casters, and various additional foes aggro at a greater distance than your level difference dictates. It doesn't take long to learn which enemies do this for an area; you are then free to use greater caution when trying to avoid attacks from such targets.

Enemies from the other faction are a bit more complex, color wise. If you are on a PvE or RP server, the game doesn't assume that they are all red targets. If you aren't flagged for PvP yourself, the other team shows up as blue if they are also unflagged or as yellow if they are. When you flag and engage such targets, the coloring turns to red.

The Reputation System allows for more variety in certain NPCs. Regions with complex NPCs are given a faction of their own. Goblin towns, rogue elements of the Alliance and Horde, and fully independent groups feature this. If you improve relations with these groups, their mood changes to a Friendly one with your character. However, attacking NPCs of these factions turns them against your character.

NPCs just beneath Neutral are Unfriendly. Though they won't attack you outright, they don't offer to speak with your character, sell, or give quests to you.

Beneath Unfriendly is the Hostile Ranking; this turns previously passive NPCs into aggressive ones. Unless steps are taken to raise your faction with them dramatically, expect to be fighting these enemies for the rest of your days.

Be alert about attacking enemies from various factions. Fighting against the Bruisers in Booty Bay or the Timbermaw Furbolgs might seem like fun, but these actions hurt your reputation with certain factions by quite a margin. This can greatly hinder your interests in achieving quest goals, finding crafting recipes, or just reaching a safe haven. The general rule of thumb is that you should make as many friends as you can out in the world of Azeroth. You are likely to need them!

Reputation Quicklist	
Condition	**Effect**
Exalted	Final Tier; Rewards Are Very Specific to the Faction Involved
Revered	Rewards Are Specific to Faction Involved
Honored	10% Discount on Items Purchased from Vendors
Friendly	Standard Reputation Level for Friends of Your Faction
Neutral	Standard Reputation Level for Factions That Aren't On Your Side (Goblins, Many Gnomes)
Unfriendly	Cannot Buy, Sell, or Interact Extensively, But This Faction Won't Attack You
Hostile	NPCs From This Faction Will Attack You on Sight
Hated	All Members of This Faction Are Enemies

WHAT ARE THOSE SPECIAL PICTURES BY CERTAIN MOBS?

Elite monsters have special icons that surround their pictures in the interface. Elite monsters have a Gold Dragon border around their portraits; these creatures have much higher health compared with normal mob of that level (they also have more powerful attacks and abilities in many cases). Be wary of these mobs, but know that they drop better treasure and are worth more experience, so hunting them in groups can be lucrative.

Often, the strategies for fighting Elite mobs are different from those used against normal creatures. The general changes are that long-term abilities are even more powerful when fighting Elites (DOTs, debuffs, and short-term buffs are wonderful in these fights). Instead of using the philosophy of "Bring it down quickly to stay alive," the characters are pushed more toward "Bring it down safely and with maximal control of the situation." Use snares to keep these monsters from rushing off to heal or get allies. Healing is more important than ever when facing Elites, as your tanks won't always have enough health to survive against even a single Elite foe without assistance.

Now and then you also see creatures with Grey Dragon borders around their names. These are specific creatures instead of a racial type. Each monster of this type has a name ("Murgos Pugnose" instead of a generic Defias). The power level of named monsters varies tremendously. Some of these are rare but aren't especially powerful. Others may have new attacks, abilities not normally given to their race, and deal far more damage than one might expect. This is all a matter of experience and cannot be predicted simply by looking at the creature. So, rare spawns are noted by their grey borders and may or may not be Elite. They are often referred to as Treasure Mobs, as they have specific loot.

NOT EVERYONE COMES ALONE

There are several ways for enemies to get help from other creatures in the region. First, some creatures try to bring allies from the moment they are pulled. Humanoid mobs are the most notable for this, but there are beasts that do this as well. This makes camps of enemies harder to fight because even ranged attacks may bring several foes.

Another method that some humanoids and beasts have (especially with foes like Raptors) is to call for help. These calls can even bring creatures that are from different races; for example, an NPC Druid may respond to the call of a wounded Raptor. There is little to be done about these calls for help because they occur instantly. The best thing to do is pull such foes back to areas where their calls won't grab anything that you aren't already interested in fighting. The range on calls for help will vary by both creature and location (the distance is farther outdoors).

There is a third way for certain enemies to seek aid. When badly wounded, a number of wise foes run away (some of them at very high speed). If the monsters bump into any allies along the way, they will return with friends. Using snare or stun abilities can help quite a bit to prevent this problem. For classes without such tools, try to save damage for the end of the fight (by saving mana, instant abilities, etc.) so that the creatures can be struck down when they try to run.

The Basics of Group Dynamics

Grouping is such a central aspect of MOG play that it is discussed several times in this guide (each time with increased detail). Here in the Introduction, our examination of groups focuses primarily on the basic mechanics and reasons for getting into groups. Later on, we explain more about performing in high-level groups and in a wider variety of situations.

WHAT IS A GROUP

Groups are formed when characters decide to work together. By sharing the duties in combat, far more monsters can be brought to defeat, and safety is dramatically improved. Normal groups can be as large as five characters.

To start a group, one character targets another person and types [/invite] or they can invite a person from far away by using the character's full name [/invite Serene]. Using character portraits is another way to interact with people nearby (right-click on the person's portrait and choose invite from the list of options that appears). You can even right-click on a person's name on the text bar at the bottom of the screen when they enter areas/come online/speak/etc. and invite them from there or [/whisper] to them.

People who are invited into a group have a query box that appears on their screen; it asks whether they wish to join the inviter's group. If they decline, the inviter is informed by both a sound and a text message. If they join, the new character's portrait is added in the upper-left side of the screen. You are able to see their health and mana (or Energy/Rage). Even that character's pets are shown under their portrait.

So, a group, at its core, is a joining of characters who are going to attempt their challenges together. With two to five people, groups can attempt all of the quests or hunting activities that are normally available to characters. The quicklist below explains some of the changes when doing tasks in a group.

Changes Between Soloing and Grouping

- Groups Share Their Experience From Kills
- Looted Money is Divided Evenly Between Participating Group Members
- Bodies Are Lootable for Items Based on a System Decided by the Group Leader (Master Looter, Round Robin, Group Loot, Need Before Greed, or Free-for-All)
- Quests Can Be Shared Between Members (So Long as the Prerequisites Are Completed by All Members)
- Enables the Group Chat Channel (used by typing [/p "Text"])
- Character Information Is Displayed for All Group Members

Ultimately, groups are able to accomplish more things than a solo player, especially in the later stages of the game. The quantity or type of loot you receive improves dramatically when going through Instance dungeons, Raid areas, and other group-related content. The Battlegrounds are also far more viable when working and communicating well with your raid and within your group.

LOOT SYSTEMS REVISITED

Group loot systems are very important to most players. Unless you only play with friends and guildmates, it is important to find a fair system that distributes loot in a way that keeps everyone content.

Which system is the best to use? As you have probably guessed, it depends on the group, its leader, and the needs of the current mission.

Loot Systems		
Name	Best For	Description
Master Looter	Careful Distribution	Group Leader Distributes All Valuable Items
Round Robin	Not Ideal	Valuable Items Are Looted as if They Are Normal Treasure
Group Loot	Simplicity w/ Some Protection	Allows Everyone to Roll on Powerful Items
Need Before Greed	Raising the Fairness of Drops	Only Allows Characters Who Can Use an Item to Get It
Free-for-All	Pure Speed and Ease of Use	Everyone Can Loot Any Corpse

WHAT IS A RAIDING PARTY

Raiding parties are basically groups of groups. For difficult Instances, large-scale Player vs. Player attacks, or actual raid areas, these large groups are welcome (or even needed).

To form a raid, wait until a group is started normally, then open the raid tab (this is the final tab from the character screen). Press "O" to bring these pages up and select the raid tab from the bottom. There is a button on the page that appears to "Convert to Raid."

The next stage of a raiding party is to gather several fully-independent groups. This isn't a situation where everyone just clumps together and it doesn't matter which person is in which group. Indeed, leadership and organization are either the beauty or bane of raid work. Without organization, it is extremely hard to succeed when there are so many people together in a tight area.

Thus, groups should have an experienced leader at their head. The raid leader/organizer should often be the person with the most experience and skill in commanding for the given task. That means a talented PvPer should be at the head of a raiding party against another faction. A person who has done Blackrock Spire 30 times should lead two groups into the Raid.

Raiding parties are discussed at much greater length later in the guide, primarily in the Advanced Player vs. Environment chapter. Raids aren't needed or often done by characters at the lower or even mid-tier levels, so knowing what they are is more than enough for now.

WHEN TO GROUP

Groups offer many things to both casual and hardcore players. But, that doesn't mean they are perfect for everything. It's good to know what you want before seeking a group; this makes it much easier to achieve your goals.

Groups are able to complete quests at a faster pace for Kill Quests, Escorts, and Exploration/Delivery Quests. However, groups are far slower when dealing with Collection Quests (especially if ground spawns are involved). If pure speed is an issue, it's wise to solo while collecting items, and group when attacking monsters, escorting, or exploring high-level areas.

When it comes to farming coin, the situation is quite complex. Solo characters get a fair bit of money if they go after the right targets (farming lower Instance dungeons for Bind on Equip blues, harvesting metal and herbs, etc.). If money is your goal, try these activities by yourself or with a partner. Avoid large groups for cash!

Duos

Many duos work quite well, but certain combinations are even better for specific tasks. Remember that everyone has weaknesses; if you choose a duo that accounts for these weaknesses, it makes life much easier. For example, Warriors hold aggro, making the fighting safer for low armor classes (Rogues, Mages, Priests).

Even beyond the class pairings, try to find someone who is willing to play to the duos strengths and minimize weaknesses. If a Priest and Mage group, it is obvious that tanking isn't a strongpoint of the pair. Instead, those two would succeed quickly by using their high DPS and lean heavily on burst damage to keep enemies from engaging for long periods.

Fun is a fine goal, and groups are easily the best target for having a good time. Making friends with good players and nice people makes the game better no matter what you enjoy. Even for quests when groups aren't needed, having buddies around keeps there from being any tedium to slaying entire bands of roving wolves and bears.

Good Reasons to Group

- Trying to Complete Red, Elite, or Dungeon Quests
- Dealing With Kill/Explore/Escort Quests
- Taking on Instances in Full Groups
- Forming Raids for High-End Content
- Safety in PvP-Intense Areas (e.g., Hillsbrad)
- To Play With Friends!

WHEN NOT TO GROUP

Okay, so you see the reasons to group and the times when it is desired/needed. Here is the other side of grouping; there are goals that make grouping a bad idea.

Gaining experience in a group can be slow at certain stages of the game. Unlike a number of MOGs, World of Warcraft is dedicated to making it easy to level even when you play as a solo character. Indeed, leveling during solo play is fast if you keep your skills, gear, and items up to par. Take a great deal of food/water/bandages out with you and slash down the beasts of the open field. This pulls in experience at a very impressive clip, dwarfing just about any group that can't get into motion quickly. Find VERY target-rich areas, and stay focused the entire time.

During the low levels, quests are worth an even higher percentage of total experience gained. If you are trying to fly through the levels, jump into groups for the group-friendly quests (as listed above) but solo all of the collection quests. Grinding solo kills on the way to and from quests is also a major way to improve experience efficiency. These are efficient kills because you gain health and mana on the move, so your character is getting to fight without the same level of downtime.

It's not useful to group when the players you meet are unfriendly, uncooperative, or just don't match your style of play. If a group isn't enjoyable, it's not worth your time. Gold, experience, and levels mean so much more when you're having a good time, and players who enjoy the game have better characters. Even with a stat-specific view of things, happier players end up with more potent characters (these people play more because they are having a good time, and more hours equals more experience, treasure, and power).

WHAT COMPRISES A "GOOD" GROUP

This is certainly a subject for debate, but good groups are the ones that fulfill your goals without making game time stressful or obnoxious. You, as a player, get to decide what a good group is for your needs. If you want pure experience and money, simply look for the groups that are intense, dedicated to a high kill count, fast questing, and disciplined Instance running. If fun is your target, find players who relax a bit more, joke around, talk more, and explore.

There are so many players on each server that there are always people who share your interests and goals. Don't try to push other players into your mold; it takes less time and is better for everyone if you seek like-minded players from the beginning. Let the PvPers fight, let the roleplayers get into their roles, etc.

WHAT ARE QUESTS?

The World of Warcraft has a Quest system in place that not only helps you learn the history of the land but also gives experience points and treasure beyond those gained from any fighting. Experience earned from these quests does not count against your Rest State and automatically adjusts the experience needed until your State changes; this makes for very fast leveling when a player understands how to mix hard fighting with consistent questing.

There are many different types of quests players can take part in. This is designed to make leveling fun and interesting; the system also helps to guide players from one area to the next at appropriate times, making it easier to know where it's "safe" to continue adventuring.

TYPES OF QUESTS

There are many types of quests that are offered in World of Warcraft, from simple Kill Quests to the more involved Storyline Quests. They are designed to allow players to decide on the amount of time investment they want to make.

KILL QUESTS

Kill Quests ask you to go out and either kill a number of creatures or a named NPC. These types of quests are often best to do in a group if time is an issue. While the experience of the kills is spread out among the group, everyone gets credit for the kills. Often when killing an NPC for a quest you are required to bring back proof of the kill. These quests allow all the group members to loot the item off of the corpse and do not have to be repeated in order for all members to get the item. The few exceptions ask that you complete the quest alone.

Collection Quests

Collection Quests require that you go out and get a specific number of items either from a location or from creatures. These can be done in groups to accomplish the quest safely; note that only one of the item at a time is lootable from any creature. Unlike the Kill Quests requiring you to bring back a head or item, these are not shared quest items.

Collection Quests are often quite slow when done with other people. Even having competition in the same area for kills or ground spawns of the necessary type can be challenging. It is best to take care of Collection Quests when you are in the mood to solo and are playing during quieter server times. For example, if you log on during prime time, try to run instances or do Kill Quests, Battlegrounds, and those types of activities. Early in the day or late at night, Collection Quests become FAR more efficient.

Delivery Quests

These quests require that you deliver an item from one place to another. The risk isn't in facing any particular creature or killing anything on your way (generally speaking). The risk comes from traveling through hostile territory and making it through alive. As an additional challenge, some of these quests are timed. Packages must be delivered within that time in order to be successful.

Delivery Quests often have very poor rewards and are not enticing in the short run. Yet, it is useful to pick up such quests when you can and wait until you are in the right neighborhood before completing them. "Oh, I'm in Westfall tonight, I better drop off this letter." Keep such quests items in your bank to save bag space, and try to remember to take the goodies out before jumping on a flight.

The main reason to bother with Delivery Quests is that many lead into chains. Longer quest chain start in mundane ways at times, and the rewards at the end of the quests are sometimes quite nice.

Escort Quests

Escort Quests ask you to keep an NPC safe as you travel through dangerous territory. These are often difficult to solo, and an entire group can benefit from completing it together. Often you must defeat creatures that attempt to kill the person/creature you are escorting and keep the escort safe until they reach a designated location.

Stay close to the quest NPC at all times. Should you stray too far from the NPC, the quest fails and everything must be started again. When that happens, look in your quest log, abandon the quest, and talk to the escort NPC again when they respawn.

Quest Modifiers

Not all quests play by the same rules. Some quests are race/class specific, and others are only given by certain factions. These quest modifiers are explained below.

Faction Quests

Faction quests involve gaining faction with an NPC or group of NPCs in order to complete the quest. This can involve killing opposing NPCs or by doing some task that they would like done. Because the Reputation System can rise and fall based on your actions toward certain factions, these quests are often repeatable. Thus, you have a means of staying in good graces with a faction even if there are occasional problems (Sorry I killed your Auntie, but here is a Troll Necklace!).

Note that repeatable quests are designated with blue symbols over an NPC's head instead of the normal gold symbols.

Class Quests

Class Quests are specific to one class. These quests grant new abilities or special items to the character that completes them. These can be done in a group or solo depending on your own abilities, but the group gains little unless they are of the same class. Find other characters entering the Class Quest or try to help others doing their own quests in return for assistance on yours.

Class Quests are most often found from class trainers or with NPCs who are near your class trainers. At landmark levels (10, 20, 30, etc.) you are most likely to gain something of this sort; they are not found randomly or at unimportant levels.

Quest Chains

Quest chains are part of a larger and evolving storyline. As players accomplish each part of the quest chain the line gets more difficult. The last quest is often a final encounter against a boss monster. Many of the major quests in Instances start off in a mild way, with a quest out in the world. Look into quest chains for greater rewards.

Elite Quests

Elite Quests pit you against NPCs that are indicated as being elite. These NPCs have more health than others of their level and are much tougher to kill. These are generally group-friendly quests and may take you and your group into Instances. Elite Quests often take the most time to complete.

DUNGEON QUESTS

Quests that are specifically noted as Dungeon Quests are going to take your group into an Instanced Dungeon. These are major locations that many other players are likely to know. If you haven't been to such a place before, ask others to group with you and give you the full tour. Let people know ahead of time that you are new to the Instance so that they know to explain more complex aspects of the quest. Also try asking group members if there are sharable quests for the Instance that you don't have yet!

FINDING AND COMPLETING QUESTS

It's easy to find quests in many areas. Quest givers that have quests available in your level range have yellow exclamation points above their heads. NPCs that have a silver exclamation point above their head have a quest waiting for you in a couple of levels.

Once a quest giver has given you all the quests they can, no more exclamation marks hover over their head.

After right-clicking on a quest-giving NPC, a quest log appears to tell you what the quest is all about and what kind of reward you shall receive. Players have the option of either accepting the quest or turning down the request. Don't worry if you turn down a quest. It is possible to return to the NPC to get it once more. Just be careful about turning one down that may be a part of a series, because you might miss out of something fun later on.

Quests are stored in your log file on your hotbar and can be brought up by using the default 'L' hotkey. Twenty quests can be stored in your log at any time (any further quests are ignored until some of the current ones are completed or abandoned).

Your log file automatically organizes your quests for you and puts them into categories based on where the quest was received (or, in special cases, the log lists if the quest is a class or crafting quest). It also is color coded to indicate how difficult a quest is for you.

Clustering Quests

To save a lot of running time, cluster your quests by doing several in one area at a time rather than running around from place to place. For that matter, complete several quests in a specific section of a map before returning to town (this is very efficient and leads to faster leveling).

Grey indicates that the quest is easy and only gives a fraction of normal experience for having completed it at a lower level. Generally this is as little as 1/10th of the entire possible experience. Don't let fun or important quests fall to grey before they are turned in, and consider abandoning quests that are grey.

Green indicates that a quest is easy with a minimal amount of danger. The first level at which a quest becomes green does not reduce its reward. Afterward, you will receive slightly reduced rewards for quests that are completed after becoming green, but the ease of completing such tasks mostly negates this penalty.

Yellow indicates that a quest is within equal range of your level and has significant risk even with with proper preparedness. These can be accomplished either alone or with a minimal group. At this range experience is right on target for your level.

Orange indicates that the quest is difficult and will most likely need a group. Yet, with potions at the ready and a solid background in your class, most orange quests are doable.

Red indicates Danger! Danger! Danger! With a group you can certainly pull it off, but it's likely a good idea not to solo a red quest unless you already know it (by completing it with another character). Death may be the only thing you get out of going up against a quest that difficult so soon. Give it a level or two and watch to see when it changes to orange or yellow to make it more attainable.

Quest Colors

Color	Difficulty	Result
Grey	Trivial	Substantial Reduction of Quest Experience
Green	Easy	Almost Full Experience
Yellow	Standard	Full Quest Experience
Orange	May Require Group	High Quest Experience (Items of Higher Level)
Red	Requires Group	Very High Experience (Items of Considerable Power for Current Level)

It is as easy to find the end of a quest as it is the start of one. Ending quest NPCs have a yellow question mark over their heads. In addition, these NPCs appear on your mini-map, so guiding your character back to them is very easy. When returning to town, look for the golden dots that indicate a tracking target for the mini-map; quest NPCs show up when their quests are completed, and highlighting these dots will list the name of the NPC.

When finishing a quest, you are given a reward beyond experience. Rewards are often in the form of cash and/or a choice of objects. Even if you are unable to use an item, it is possible to sell it to a vendor. Quest items are soulbound and cannot be traded between players; sell unusable items to a vendor and enjoy the extra cash. Or, if you are an Enchanter, disenchant the item and use the ingredients to improve existing equipment.

Read through your combat log after completing quests. Notice that many major quests provide a healthy boost to your reputation with one faction or another. This is a great way to get various groups to like your character.

QUEST SHARING

An exciting feature of WoW is the ability to share quests. If your character is the only person in a forming group with a certain quest, it is easy to "give" the quest to everyone else in the party. In effect, you become the quest giver for the others, though they return to the normal NPC for their completion rewards.

You cannot share quests if there are prerequisites that the rest of the group members haven't accomplished (or if the quest is class/race related and they aren't of said class/race). You also cannot give them a quest that requires that a specific item given by the NPC (like a special Moonvial or package). A message lets you know if your quest has been successfully accepted or if the other person doesn't meet the requirements or has a full quest log.

You cannot receive quests again if you have already completed them. If your quest log is full, you have to abandon one of your quests and the other person will have to share it again.

To share a quest, open the quest log and click on the quest that you want to share. The option is there to abandon or share the quest; choose "Share" and your entire party is queried with that quest (if they accept it, you are good to go). When looking at the screen, it even says how many characters in your current group are also engaged in quests that you have. If a quest has a [3] to the left of it, three other people in your group have that quest as well.

ABANDONING QUESTS

At any time, you are free to abandon a quest. This clears the quest out of your log (making room for other quests). The original NPC that gave you the quest resets, thus enabling you to start the quest again at a later point. You can abandon quests for the quest log space, for convenience (if you know you won't do the quest again), or to make a second attempt at a quest you have failed. Timed Quests and Escort Quests are the most likely to fail; these should be abandoned and tried a second time.

DEATH AND REBIRTH

The lives of adventurers would be short indeed if death were a permanent fixture in MOGs. Either that, or people would spend FAR more time inside inns, hoping that various abominations wouldn't burst through the door. To make the game world a bit more fun, and a lot more survivable, Blizzard has implemented a system without vicious death penalties. This section explains the various types of death that your character could face and how to respond to these problems.

WAYS TO DIE

Characters that are slain drop to the ground and are taken out of your control. It is impossible to move, cast spells, emote, speak normally, or do anything of importance to yourself or your group. Private and guild messages are allowed, so you can message nearby folks to let them know if you need a Rez.

Your character enters this state when his or her health drops to zero. Falling from too high a distance, being struck by physical or mystic forces too many times, or drowning can do this. There is no starvation in WoW, nor are their status effects that directly cause death (though poisons and damage over time abilities can and will kill you whether you are still in combat or not). Keep your health high and life goes on.

When a character is slain by monsters, there is a 10% hit to the durability of all currently-equipped items. This can be a fairly painful slap to your money when it comes to repairing the pieces (especially at high levels). If you are planning to intentionally get your character killed off (for fun, roleplaying, etc.), consider taking off especially pricey gear ahead of time. Those who use Spirit Healers to Rez normally lose 25% of their durability to ALL carried items, not just equipped ones. Very painful indeed.

DEATHS IN INSTANCES

Instances won't allow characters to return to their corpses; this would make it too easy to regroup and continue fighting in difficult Instances. Though Resurrection spells and Soulstones work in the same manner inside and outside Instances, trying to Release and Return to your body fails. Instead, your character automatically revives when they enter the Instance.

The penalty here is simply that parties aren't able to survive losing a character during an Instance run without using either Resurrection or a Warlock Ritual of Summoning (once the person has revived normally). Of course, if the enemies of the Instance haven't respawned yet, the newly spawned character can run back to the group on their own without needing to clear anything.

DEATH ON THE BATTLEFIELD

Player versus Player deaths are the most trivial of all in terms of system penalties. Everyone is there is to fight honorably and die trying, so the game mechanics are extremely lenient on the characters. No durability hits are taken from PvP deaths. In fact, characters that are slain inside the Battlegrounds are brought back to life after a short delay; a nearby Spirit Healer does the work for them and returns the fallen fighters to full health and mana. Pets are even restored as well! Thus, hit release when your character falls in battle during the Battlegrounds and wait for the fun to start again.

THE PATH TO BETTER HEALTH

There are several ways to respond after your character dies. Each method of revival has different consequences, so it is wise to learn all three methods before stepping onto the field of battle.

RETURNING TO YOUR BODY (RELEASE AND RETURN)

The most common method of revival comes from Releasing and Returning to your corpse. Click on the Release button that appears once your character falls; this teleports you to the nearest Graveyard for your faction. As a spirit, you can see the world around you, but other characters and monsters are hidden from view. Only other spirits of your faction and the nearby Spirit Healer are visible.

A pointer on the mini-map appears to lead you toward your body; there is also a small gravestone to mark your corpse. Follow the pointer and don't worry about random monsters. Take a direct path and only avoid a fast route if the land prevents a direct run; as a spirit, you can even walk on water. Once you get near your body, the line between life and death blurs (this causes monsters to become visible to your spirit). Move within a radius of 40 or so yards and an option appears to revive. Click on this in a spot where you are safe from the aggro of nearby monsters or PvPers. If you died deep underwater, you have to fully submerge to get in range to revive.

Reviving in this manner has NO penalty toward your character's experience. Also, you are returned to your body with 50% of your maximum health and mana (these return normally after that point). There is no Resurrection Sickness, and you are free to adventure normally.

RESURRECTION (REZ)

If there is an allied person in the area where your body falls, Resurrection may be possible. Shamans, Paladins, Priests, Druids, and Warlocks have various powers to Resurrect characters in some way, shape, or form. In the first three cases, Shamans, Paladins, and Priests cast spells on corpses that call the spirit back to the body. The player in question receives an accept/decline button to let them know that Resurrection is being used on them. This works even if the person has already released and is heading back to their body as a sprit.

When Resurrected your character appears almost instantly in the area, alive, but not well. Depending on the spell used, your character may have as little as 1% of their health and mana.

There are no penalties to accepting a Resurrection. Your characters suffers no experience penalty or long-term attribute harm. Thus, the tradeoff with Resurrection over a release and corpse run is a matter of time only.

DRUID REBIRTH

Druids are able to use a spell called Rebirth to Resurrect a person. This spell has a 30-minute timer and is used in battle to bring someone back to life with a fair portion of their health and mana (it's a set quantity, based on the rank of Rebirth used). This spell allows Druids to save a primary Rezzer in the event that a group or raid is in very bad shape. In raid PvE content and the Battlegrounds, Rebirth is a tremendous advantage to everyone involved.

A Seed reagent is needed for Rebirth. These are purchased in major cities and carry a trivial price compared to their value for preventing catastrophic wipes.

WARLOCKS AND SOULSTONES

Warlocks are able to Resurrect as well, but it's a special case that merits an explanation. Warlocks turn Soul Shards (collected from enemies as the creatures die) into various stones. One of these items is a Soulstone. Warlocks use these on other characters.

If you have a Soulstone, the game immediately asks if you wish to revive when you die. Your character returns to life in the location where you fell. The Soulstone is destroyed in the process (though if you use a different method to Resurrect, the Soulstone is not used).

This power is quite good for use in Instances, where losing a character who has Resurrect might mean the end of a good expedition. Even a total party wipeout can be reversed with these items (almost always give the Soulstone to the group's primary Rezzer).

THE SHAMAN SELF-REZ

A wonderful ability of Shamans is the power to Resurrect themselves. This requires that they have Ankhs in their inventory (purchased from vendors in major cities at a trivial price), and Ankhs can only be used once an hour. This spell is learned at level 30, and after that point Shamans become an incredible tool for groups and raids against total wipeouts. If everyone goes down, the Shaman should wait and find out if anyone is using a Soulstone from a Warlock. If not, the Shaman pops back up and starts Rezzing the rest of the group as soon as they can. A self-Rezzing Rezzer! Who could ask for more? Note that this does not need to be cast ahead of time. Simply having an Ankh in your inventory after the spell is learned is enough to trigger the option after death.

GOBLIN JUMPER CABLES, FOR THE NON-REZZERS

Okay, so we saved one of the secret tricks for last. Even non-Rezzers have a chance to save their buddies if they are Engineers with 165 skill and have Goblin Jumper Cables. This item is used to attempt a Resurrection. There is a 30-minute timer on the Cables, so be sure to use them on a Rezzer. Also, remember that this is a fine piece of Goblin Engineering; that means you very well might end up dead just for trying to use them! They deal 100 damage to you when they fail.

Rogues with Goblin Jumper Cables are especially valued. In the event that a group or raid wipes multiple times and uses its full supply of tricks to Rez itself, the Rogues can run back to the dungeon, stealth past mobs that have respawned, and try to save a Rezzer. Sending several Rogues to do this may mean the difference between a brief wipe or losing an entire raid to bad luck and having to reclear a major raid dungeon.

THE SPIRIT HEALER

Okay, so there had to be a costly method somewhere. People who cannot retrieve their bodies, are too tired or frustrated to try, or who want a VERY fast Rez can choose to Resurrect at the Spirit Healer.

Every Graveyard has a Spirit Healer. These floating figures of death and rebirth return people to life where their spirit stands (thus, you appear at the Graveyard of the nearest allied faction). Even if you make the long run to a farther Graveyard and use their Spirit Healer, your body appears at the yard closest to your corpse.

Do you lose experience? Nope. That doesn't even happen here. However, you do lose more durability than you would for a normal death. Beyond that, Resurrection Sickness hits your character. This debuff lasts for a short time and prevents your character from fighting well. Thus, you take a financial hit in terms of repairs, and you are forced to fight very soft enemies for a while or run the risk of dying again.

Does this mean that the Spirit Healer is a bad deal for most players? Yes, most of the time it does, but in no way is the Spirit Healer a bad thing to consider in special cases. If you are so far away from your corpse that a run would cost major time and frustration, it might be worth a Rez at the Spirit Healer. Or, if you die way out in the ocean somewhere, or at a place that is almost unreachable anyway, it's worth avoiding the trouble.

Keyboard Layouts

PC KEYBOARD

MOVEMENT	
Key	**Action**
clear (Mac)	Auto Run
Num Lock (PC)	Auto Run
W	Move Forward
A	Turn Left
S	Move Backward
D	Turn Right
Q	Strafe Left
E	Strafe Right
Space Bar	Jump
X	Toggle Sit/Stand
Z	Sheathe/ Unsheathe Weapon
NumPad /	Toggle Run/Walk

HOTBAR	
Key	**Action**
1-0, - and +	Hotbar Keys
Alt + Hotbar Key (PC)	Use ability on Self without changing Targets
CTRL + Hotbar Key	Secondary Action Button (Pet Bars)
CTRL + F1-F10	Special Action Button
ESC	Open/Close Game Menu
SHIFT + 1-6	Toggle through Hotbars 1-6
SHIFT + 7	Next Action Bar
SHIFT + 8	Previous Action Bar

TARGETING	
Key	**Action**
F1	Target Self
F2 - F5	Target Party Members 2 - 5
SHIFT + F1 - F5	Target Party Pets 1 - 5
TAB	Select Front Hostile Target Toggle Hostile Targets
G	Select Last Hostile Target
CTRL + TAB	Target Nearest Friend
CTRL + SHIFT + TAB	Target Previous Friend

CHARACTER INFO	
Key	**Action**
C	Character Pane
SHIFT + C	Combat Log
I	Ability Pane
SHIFT + I	Pet Book
K	Skill Pane
L	Quest Log
N	Talent Pane
O	Social Pane
P	Spellbook
U	Reputation Pane
H	Honor Pane

Commands and Macros

It's actually quite easy to start moving around and controlling your character in World of Warcraft; the system is quite intuitive. Still, there are always commands that you won't think of right off the bat. This section explains more about the command system and the macros that can be used during gameplay. Guild commands and aspects are discussed later in the guide.

GENERAL COMMANDS

General commands can be bound to keys or typed out fully. These control a wide array of speech and combat options.

/assist "Name"	Switches your target to that of the person named; If no name is used, your current target is selected as the default for the assist.
/cast	Used in macros to control spell use (automatically initiated when you click on spells or press their equivalent hotkey)
/em [message]	Creates a custom emote
/exit	Leaves the game
/follow	Follows the current character from your faction (great to bind to a hotkey)
/invite [player]	Invites "player" into your current group or starts a group with "player" as the second person
/logout	Exits your current character, cannot be done in combat; takes 20 secs. unless in a city
/party or /p [message]	Puts up text in a different color that is only heard by group members

MAC KEYBOARD

CAMERA

Key	Action
Help (Mac)	Pitch Up
Insert (PC)	Pitch Up
Delete	Pitch Down
Home	Next Camera View
End	Previous Camera View
Y	Flip Camera
Keypad 2	Back
Keypad 4	Rotate Left
Keypad 8	Rotate Right
Right Mouse Button + A	Rotate Left
Right Mouse Button + D	Rotate Right

INVENTORY

Key	Action
B	Open/Close Backpack
F8	Open/Close Bag 1
F9	Open/Close Bag 2
F10	Open/Close Bag 3
F11	Open/Close Bag 4
F12	Open/Close Bag 5
	Close All Bags
SHIFT + B	Open/Close All Bags

CHAT

Key	Action
ENTER	Initiate Chat
/	Initiate Chat Command
R	Reply to a /whisper or /tell
/em	Initiate Emote
/v	Initiate Voice Command
Shift +R	/whisper to last person whispered

DISPLAY

Key	Action
V	Show Name Plates
ALT + Z	Toggle HUD
F13 (Mac)	Capture Screenshot
Print Screen (PC)	Capture Screenshot
M	Opens Map

ATTACKING

Key	Action
T	Attack Target
SHIFT + T	Pet Attack Target
F	Assist Target
Shift +F	Target Last Hostile

SOUND

Key	Action
CTRL + M	Toggle Music
CTRL + S	Toggle Sound
CTRL + +	Master Volume Up
CTRL + -	Master Volume Down

/played	Displays the amount of time you have invested in your current character and the amount of time you have spent in your current level
/pvp	On PvE and RP servers, this flags your character for PvP combat; even if you toggle this by typing PvP again there is a five minute delay before you become unflagged
/r	Replies to the last person who whispered you
/random [X]	Rolls a random number with "X" being the maximum roll (100 is the default)
/say [message]	Speaks out loud; anyone nearby will hear you
/sit	Your character sits down
/stand	Your character stands back up (or move forward to automatically have your character move)

/tell or /t [player] [message]	Sends a private message to "player"
/whisper or /w [player] [message]	Sends a private message to "player"
/ignore "Name"	Places the person named onto a list of people that cannot message you; you also won't hear them /say, /yell, emote, invite, mail, etc.
/who	Used to search for specific people, to list characters of a given level range, or characters found in a specific area (Examples: /who 10-11 for a level search, /who Kayal to see if there are people with that type of name, /who Winterspring to see who is playing in Winterspring)
/yell [message]	Shouts a message that appears in a different color than /say and will be heard over a larger distance (don't spam these)

CHAT CHANNEL COMMANDS

Chat Channels are extremely useful for interactions with both public players and friends. There are default channels, like World Defense and General, that you cannot control (save to leave them or re-enter them), and there are also ones that you can create and moderate on your own.

Some ideas for Chat Channels: if you have close friends who aren't in a guild with you, make a private Chat Channel with a name that all of your buddies can remember. Type /join MidlandHigh (if your friends were from such a high school).

/# (#=Number of Chat Channel)	For channels that you are already in, speaking is a matter of typing /1, /2, etc. So /1 Hi everyone might say Hi everyone in General if that was the first channel in your list
/afk "X"	Lets anyone who messages you know that you are away from keyboard
/dnd "X"	"X" Creates an autoreply so that people who message you get X as a response (Example: We are raiding Molten Core, Talk Later)
/announcements, /ann	Toggles whether a channel displays people entering and leaving
/ban "X"	Bans player X from using the channel
/unban "X"	Unban character "X"
/chathelp	Lists and explains Chat Channel commands
/chatlist "Number" /chatwho "Number"	Lists the characters logged into the channel "Number"
/join "X" /channel "X" /chan "X"	Joins Channel "X"
/kick "Name"	Kicks character "Name" out of the channel
/leave, /chatleave, /chatexit [channel]	Takes you out of the listed channel (you can use the name or number of the channel to do this)
/mod "Name" /moderator "Name"	Makes the named person a moderator for the channel
/unmod "Name" /unmoderator "Name"	Stops the named person from being a moderator
/moderate "Number"	Toggles whether the channel can be moderated
/password, /pass [channel] [password]	Creates a password to protect the channel from unwanted visitors

MACROS

Macros are used to create automatic actions (sometimes entire groups of them) that are used with a single key press.

Creating a Macro

- Click on the text bubble by your chat bar and select Macros from the menu there; this brings up the Create Macros system
- Select whether a macro will be a general macro or a character-specific macro
- Select "New" then use one of the icons available and name your macro
- At the bottom of the screen, type in the text for your macro; any mix of standard commands can be used

Ideas for Macros

- Roleplaying while using abilities
- Used to shift equipment or use several abilities in tandem
- Alert other players to problems or dangers
- Inform people about rules or protocols

Macro Name: Assist

Macro Text Line 1: /assist "Name of Main Assist"

Macro Name: Sap (Rogue)

Macro Text Line 1: /cast Sap(Rank #)—# is the Proper Level of Your Sap Ability
Macro Text Line 2: /p Sapping %t

Macro Name: Bandaging You

Macro Text Line 1: /script SendChatMessage["Hold Still, Bandaging You","Whisper","Language To Be Used", UnitName("target")];—Language Would be Common in Many Cases
Macro Text Line 2: UseContainerItem(#,#);—Where #,# is the Bag You Are Using and Slot Within That Bag
* Bags are (0) Backpack through (4) Far Left and slots are (1) Upper Left to (n) Lower Right

Macro Name: Loot Rules

Macro Text Line 1: /say Group Loot for today will be used
Macro Text Line 2: /say Need can only be rolled for item upgrades that will be used
Macro Text Line 3: /say Greed is rolled for Bind on Equip items OR on Bind on Pickup Items if you are an Enchanter
Macro Text Line 4: /say Pass on Bind on Pickup items if you are not an Enchanter

Macro Name: Raid Conduct

Macro Text Line 1: /ra Do Not post in raid chat unless you are a group leader or the information is VITAL
Macro Text Line 2: /ra Keep chat to private channels or within your group
Macro Text Line 3: /ra Inform your group if/when you go /afk and put /follow on a healer
Macro Text Line 4: /ra Pay extra attention to all attack and cease fire orders

DUN MOROGH

Dwarves and gnomes have been part of the Alliance for quite some time. These industrious folk have also supported each other, and that shows in the way both races live in close proximity without savaging each other every few years. Yet, there are clear differences between these two cultures. The dwarves are strong, courageous, and proud. They produce blades, guns, armor, and great buildings of stone. Gnomes are more inquisitive, building gadgets that are not always of immediate use or even known purpose. Together, the two races make Dun Morogh a land of many trades.

Legend

1	Gnomeregan	5	The Grizzled Den	9	Coldridge Valley	13	Eastern Dun Morogh	17	Far Eastern Dun Morogh	21	South Gate Pass
2	Frostmane Hold	6	Kharanos	10	Anvilmar	14	Misty Pine Refuge	18	Helm's Bed Lake	22	Ironforge (Capital City)
3	Southwest Dun Morogh	7	Steelgrill's Depot	11	Iceflow Lake	15	Amberstill Ranch	19	North Gate Pass		
4	Chill Breeze Valley	8	Coldridge Pass	12	Shimmer Ridge	16	Gol'Bolar Quarry and Mine	20	North Gate Outpost		

Your First Day

Anyone who suddenly appears inside Ironforge or any number of Dwarven Strongholds might think that the land outside was blasted with heat and steam. Yet, Dun Morogh is a cold land, high in the mountains where a biting wind becomes one's frequent companion. Between the rocky crags and icy lakes, the Yetis, Trolls, and beasts find their niche, but there are rewards in this isolated land. Potent herbs find a way to poke through the snows, desperate for light, and metal seems to pour up through the earth as well. For the wary eye, Dun Morogh is a place of great riches!

ANVILMAR

Anvilmar is a place of rest in southern Dun Morogh. Mainly a dwarven site, the merchants, trainers, and travelers who come through are often on their way to more comfortable climates. Luckily, your first steps are quite safe. There is very little danger from the weaker troggs and wolves that dominate the hunting grounds nearby, and people are friendly in Anvilmar, offering many quests and services to those who are willing to work.

Sten Stoutarm has work for you (**Dwarven Outfitters**). He's willing to make you some gloves if you bring him eight pieces of Tough Wolf Meat. Accept his offer and head south to find the wolves. They are weak and do not pose a danger to you.

With the required meat in your backpack, return to Sten for your reward. Now that he knows he can count on you, he has more work for you, as do others in the area. He'll have a message for you from your class trainer and some mail he needs delivered. Accept **Coldridge Valley Mail Delivery** and speak with Balir Frosthammer for more work.

This local toughman is angry at the Troggs for their recent attacks; instead of ignoring the "buggers," he wants to bring them to heel. He asks you to slay five Rockjaw Troggs and five Burly Rockjaw Troggs (**A New Threat**). Both are found in the local fields, though more Burly Troggs can be found in camps west of Anvilmar.

The Spoils of War

Your backpack is nearly full. First, take the time to look through it and see if there is any usable equipment for you. If there is, equip it. Second, become familiar with any recovery items (potions, food, drink, etc.) you've accumulated. Everything else that can be sold to vendors should be.

Head up the path and into Anvilmar. Speak with your trainer to complete your first class quest and to learn your level two abilities. With everything in town accomplished, head south across the wolf fields and engage the Rockjaw Troggs.

The Rockjaw Troggs are fairly easy fights, aren't aggressive, and won't double team you. At most you may need to rest a short while between fights to recover mana and health. There are a few Burly Rockjaw Troggs in the hills, but if they are scarce, head along the path west from Anvilmar.

Traveling the Bloody Way

As you're traveling, consider killing any enemies that are your level or lower. The enemies around Anvilmar are fairly weak and the additional experience and usable equipment make it worth your time.

Take the path west of Anvilmar to Talin Keeneye's camp. Talin is grateful for the mail and lets you know that not all the mail is for him. A letter is for Grelin (**Coldridge Valley Mail Delivery**). Talin makes a living by hunting the boars in the area. Recently, however, there are so many boars that it has become dangerous for him. He'll reward you if you can help him by killing 12 Small Crag Boars (**The Boar Hunter**).

The boars are everywhere around his camp. Head out and start killing. Watch your health and mana; rest between fights if either is low. The boars aren't terribly dangerous, but they're higher level than your targets thus far. Kill the required Small Crag Boars and return to Talin for your reward.

As you only have a single backpack, your inventory is getting full. Make a quick stop back at Anvilmar to sell, search for upgrades, train (if you've gained level 4), and speak with Balir once again for your reward.

Stopping inside Anvilmar reveals that Felix Whindlebolt would like to have a word with you. He tells a story that is common among the Gnomes. In his haste to escape the catastrophe in Gnomeregan, some of his belongings were lost. He's fairing better than most since he knows where they are. He saw trolls taking them to their camps in the southwest. Felix asks you to recover his belongs for him since he isn't an adventurer (**A Refugee's Quandary**).

Now it is time to deal with the letter to Grelin Whitebeard. If you are nosy, you can read it. Wow! It's signed by Magni Bronzebeard, the King of Ironforge. This must be really important and you shouldn't delay its delivery any longer. Head southeast across the snows to the end of the path and Grelin's camp.

Grelin is pleased to receive his mail and tips you for the service. He's also very eager to conscript you into the service of Ironforge. **The Troll Cave** to the south needs to be dealt with before it can become a real threat. He wants you to kill 14 Frostmane Troll Whelps for your reward. Nearby, Nori has a predicament. He's got a delivery of Scalding Mornbrew that needs to get to Anvilmar before it gets cold. He's got a fire to keep it hot and you're going the other way, so avoid the quest for now (it's a timed quest).

To the southwest is the troll cave and inside the trolls you need and Felix's belongings. The Frostmane Troll Whelps are much more aggressive than the enemies you've fought so far. They will attack you if you get close (called ag-gro) and they come to the aid of their friends if you're not careful. The outer trolls are spread out so this isn't as much of a worry. Keep the fights quick and pull back if reinforcements are nearby.

Felix's Bucket of Bolts is near the campfire at the entrance to the cave. Stick to killing the Frostmane Troll Whelps outside the cave as inside is more danger-ous. If there are enough of the trolls outside, you won't even need to venture within the cave just yet. Once you've killed enough Frostmane Troll Whelps, don't delay in returning to Grelin.

While you were attacking the cave, a group of trolls attacked Grelin's camp. Everyone's okay, but the trolls stole Grelin's journal and he wants it back. Grelin got a reasonable look at the troll that took it and wants you to kill Grik'nir the Cold to retrieve it (**The Stolen Journal**). Head back to the troll cave. This time you need to go inside.

While the constant fighting may cause you to rest more often, do not try to sneak past the Frostmane Troll Whelps. Kill everything on your way inside. At the first intersection, take the tunnel going north. Choose your targets carefully and avoid fighting large groups of enemies at the same time. The tunnel opens into a large cavern with Grik'nir at the back. Follow the ledge along the left wall and kill your way down.

Pull the enemies one at a time until Grik'nir stands alone. He's a tough fight and you don't want any of his friends helping. Without friends, kill Grik'nir and recover Grelin's Journal.

Inventory Full?

It's been a good while since you were near a merchant and your inventory shows it. Once your inventory is full you can't pick up any more items, including quest items. Take the time to destroy some of the less lucrative items in your inventory when you need room for quest items.

Less lucrative items are items of lowest quality and lowest armor (symbolized by the grey name). This means grey cloth items are often the first to be dropped. If you don't need the food or drink for recovery purposes, these are also prime candidates.

Exit the cave as quickly as caution allows. Don't try to run past any trolls that have respawned. Take the time to kill each one. Once out of the cave, head east to the next troll camp. You still need to collect Felix's belongings. Felix's Chest is sitting beside the fire at the first camp you come to. Exercise the same caution attacking this camp as you used in the cave. Kill the enemies one at a time until you get to the chest.

Grab Felix's Chest and head northeast to the final troll camp. Felix's Box is just inside the camp. Recover it and head back to Grelin's camp. Grelin rewards you for his journal and asks you to deliver a report to Mountaineer Thalos for him (**Senir's Observa-**

tions). As your next stop is Anvil-mar, speak with Nori Pridedrift for the **Scalding Mornbrew Delivery**. This quest is timed, so don't delay much on your way to Anvilmar.

Durnan Furcutter is in the very back of Anvilmar awaiting his Scalding Mornbrew. He enjoys the mug of Mornbrew and, as a kind soul, asks if you would return to empty mug to Nori (**Bring Back the Mug**). Return Felix's items on your way out of Anvilmar. He's very pleased to have them back and rewards you with some coin. Sell any excess loot and make a quick run to return the mug to Nori.

The work for you in Coldridge Valley is finished. Stop by your trainer in Anvilmar if you've reached level six. Consider spending some time killing if you haven't reached level six yet. Follow the path east from Anvilmar when you're ready to make the trip to Kharanos.

The trail ascends to the tunnel entrance. Mountaineer Thalos warns you of the trogg infestation in the tunnel. At first, Thalos advises you to stay in Anvilmar until the tunnel is cleared, but when you show him Grelin's letter he realizes the import of your trip. He gives you directions to Kharanos and bids you a safe travel to Senir Whitebeard (**Senir's Observations**).

Stranded outside the tunnel entrance is Hands Springsprocket. He has a delivery to make to the inn at Kharanos, but can't get through the tunnel with the troggs in the way. He asks you to make the delivery for him as you're heading through the tunnel already (**Supplies to Tannok**).

Head into the tunnel with your weapon ready. The troggs are very aggressive and do not back down from the fight. Kill them as you move through the tun-

nel and to Dun Morogh proper. It's quite a hike to Kharanos, but follow the stone path and you can't miss it.

KHARANOS AND STEELGRILL'S DEPOT

Standing by a tent at the entrance to town is Senir Whitebeard. Deliver the report to him. He mentions that he'll have work for you later and rewards you for your work thus far. There are others who wish to speak with you, but first head to the inn on the east side of the road. Deliver the supplies to Tannok Frosthammer and speak with Innkeeper Belm. He can set your hearthstone to return you here if you ask him to make this inn your home. Do so.

Head outside and speak with Ragnar Thunderbrew. He's run into a bind. The trapper that used to supply him with crag boar ribs enlisted in the King's Army and was deployed elsewhere. He's willing to give you the recipe to cook **Beer Basted Boar Ribs** and even a sample if you collect six Crag Boar Ribs for him and buy a Rhapsody Malt from the inn. Accept the quest and head across the street.

Tharek Blackstone makes tools and is constantly supplying Steelgrill's Depot. The latest shipment is ready and he asks you to drop it off on your way out (**Tools for Steelgrill**). Head northeast over the hill to Steelgrill's Depot. Kill any boars you come across on the way.

The tanks and mechnostriders are a dead give-away for Steelgrill's. Speak with the pilots and mechanics on your way in. Pilot Bellowfiz needs help **Stocking Jetstream**, his tank. He asks you to get four Chunks of Boar Meat and two Thick Bear Furs. Pilot Stonegear wants to make a rug for the inside of Trollplow. Eight Wendigo Manes should be enough. You can get these from **The Grizzled Den**. Loslor Rudge needs you to recover a lost shipment of **Ammo for Rumbleshot**. The previous courier was frightened off by the wendigo west of Kharanos. Before heading out with all this work, remember to deliver the tools to Steelgrill.

Head southwest through Kharanos, to the Grizzled Den. The wendigo are very aggressive and dangerous. The Young Wendigo outside the cave can drop the manes and the ammo crate is in the camp, so there is little reason to enter the cave at this time.

Kill the boars and bears in the area while killing the wendigo near the cave entrance. Grab the ammo crate when you need a break from fighting to recover. Watch for the snow leopards in the south. They aren't terribly dangerous, but they are aggressive and run around a lot. With Kharanos so close, return to sell excess loot should your inventory fill up. As the boar meat is sellable, be careful about emptying your entire inventory. Keep the items needed for your quests.

With your quests finished, return to Kharanos. Stop at the distillery to purchase the Rhapsody Malt and bring it and the Crag Boar Ribs to Ragnar. Senir now has work for you. Speak with him about **Frostmane Hold**. The trolls near Brewnall Village have been more active of late and he needs you to poke around and kill a few to see what's going on. Accept the quest and head back to Steelgrill's Depot for more rewards.

Bellowfiz appreciates all the hunting you did for him. He pays you for your work, and asks another task of you. He needs something to drink on the road. **Evershine** is his favorite and can only be bought in Brewnall Village. Head back to Kharanos then follow the road south toward Coldridge Valley. Hegnar Rumbleshot is awaiting his ammo shipment along the road. Continue following the road toward Coldridge Valley, but head northwest before entering the tunnel. A short ways through the valley and you come across a trail at the base of Chill Breeze Valley.

CHILL BREEZE VALLEY

Head north up the valley. There are two caves along the valley; one on each side. Give the eastern cave a wide berth and head to the western cave. Follow the path up and speak with Tundra MacGrann. An elite wendigo has stolen his locker of dried meats. Old Icebeard can't open the locker, but Tundra still needs to eat.

Old Icebeard is very powerful and can't be killed alone. There are two ways to accomplish this rather daunting task. If you are alone, hide near the entrance to his cave and wait for him to wander off. When he does, rush in, get the meats from the locker, and run out. If you have a number of friends and feel up to a challenge, engage Old Icebeard directly. Either way, returning the meats to Tundra prompts his appreciation and a reward. Head to the southern end of the valley and follow the path west to Brewnall Village.

BREWNALL VILLAGE

Speak with Rejold to get the cask of **Evershine**. He will give it to you…if you do him a favor. The wildlife has been encroaching on Brewnall Village and the crafters are losing time dealing with them. If you kill eight Elder Crag Boars, eight Snow Leopards, and six Ice Claw Bears, the Evershine is yours (**A Favor for Evershine**). He also has a more personal favor to ask. Rejold wants to create **The Perfect Stout**. He's still searching for the right ingredients and would like to try Shimmerweed. The problem is the Frostmane Seers use it in their rituals. He wants you to swipe six of them for him.

No one has **Bitter Rivals** like crafters. Marleth Barleybrew wants you to swap her Barrel of Barleybrew Scalder with a barrel of Thunder Ale next time you're in Kharanos. Accept the quest and head back to Kharanos. Head east around Iceflow Lake and through Chill Breeze Valley this time. It's shorter and there is wildlife that needs to be thinned.

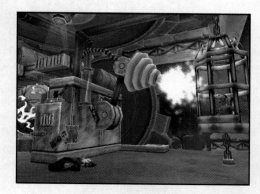

Stop at the small workshop just north of Kharanos. Inside, two gnomes are diligently working on the Gnomeregan problem. Razzle Sprysprocket would like your help with **Operation Recombobulation**. He needs you to collect eight Restabilization Cogs and eight Gyromechanic Gears from the leper gnomes near Gnomeregan. Grab the quest and continue into Kharanos.

Head into the Thunderbrew Distillery. In the lower levels sits the Guarded Thunder Ale Barrel. Jarven Thunderbrew is almost as vigilant a guard as he is a drinker. Buy some Thunder Ale from the Innkeeper and help Jarven quench his thirst. Once Jarven has one, he has to have another. Wait for him to get up the stairs before switching the barrels and making a hasty exit. While you're in the distillery, stop by your trainer and see if you can learn any new abilities.

It's time to return to Brewnall. Take the northern route and trim the wildlife on your way.

GNOMEREGAN, TROLLS, AND BREWNALL REVISITED

Marleth is grateful for the switch you pulled at the Thunderbrew Distillery and gives you some coin to show it. Repair your gear, sell excess loot and head northwest. It isn't far before you can see the green gases spewing from Gnomeregan.

Continue pruning the wildlife as you search for the parts Razzle needs. Whatever happened in Gnomeregan, it's driven the leper gnomes quite mad and they have no problem taking that anger out on you.

The leper gnomes are very dangerous. While clearly loony, they're still intelligent. If they're losing a fight, they run for help. Be ready to finish your enemies off quickly or stop their flight. Allowing one to run guarantees a long walk from the graveyard. They do a lot of damage, so be ready to fully rest after each engagement.

With the required parts and wildlife killed, return to Brewnall. Rejold rewards you for hunting the animals with the cask of Evershine for you to **Return to Bellowfiz**. Sell excess loot and head southwest to Frostmane Hold.

Anyone can sneak up to a camp and observe the enemy. Senir needs you to enter the cave and scout the area. Follow the tunnel west into a large cavern. Continue along the outer edge killing as you go and watching for the patrols. Once you've explored the cave to satisfaction (your quest log will show this), fight your way back out. Hunting the trolls outside is much safer.

Once the quest is complete, return to Brewnall. You don't have anything to turn in, but you should repair and sell excess loot before heading out again. Your next stop is Shimmer Ridge. Be aware, the trolls on Shimmer Ridge are quite dangerous and work together.

The path up to Shimmer Ridge is on the east side of Iceflow Lake. Look around for others heading up the path and join forces if they are willing. Shimmerweed can be obtained from both the Frostmane Seers and the

baskets on the ground. If there are no baskets and all the Frostmane Seers are dead, sit and wait. The camp is very dangerous if it's allowed to spawn fully. Kill the trolls as soon as they spawn to keep the danger to a minimum.

First kill the Frostmane Seers around the edge of the camp. The center is a bit crowded and too much for a single person. The enemies are primarily casters and ranged attackers. This means they are very difficult to pull. Use a ranged attack and run away from them. When you get out of their casting range, they will be forced to come after you. As soon as they are clear of their friends, turn around and show them the mistake they just made.

A good technique for clearing the camp is to attack, kill one, and run away. The keys are being able to kill the first enemy quickly and being able to get away before his friends kill you. Using this technique over and over again slowly clears the camp and makes it much more manageable.

Now it's time for a bit of walking. Return to Brewnall and speak with Rejold for your reward. He asks you to deliver a barrel of the new **Shimmer Stout** to his brother. It'll be some time before you get there, but stout never goes bad, so pick up the quest. Next head back to Kharanos and the gnome house just north of it.

The recombobulator isn't quite working yet. You've collected everything you need for Razzle. Wish him luck in returning Leper Gnomes to sanity, and head to Kharanos to give your report to Senir. With the information you gathered, it's time to make a report to Ironforge. Senir asks you to deliver **The Reports**. Stop by Steelgrill's on your way north and speak with Bellowfiz.

IRONFORGE AND THE ROAD TO LOCH MODAN

Senir's mission is one of importance, but it also gives you a nice break from the constant work. Much of southern and eastern Dun Morogh is calming down (thanks to your good deeds). It's time to see the capital of the dwarves. Take the road north and climb the long ramp to the mighty Gates of Ironforge.

As all classes and professions are represented in Ironforge, it's a good place for training. If you're picking up crafting professions, seek out the trainers while you are delivering the letter for Senir. Senator Barin Redstone is in the High Seat, which sits on the southeast side of the Great Forge.

> ### It's Big!
> Ironforge is a rather impressive town. Exploring all of it would take quite a bit of effort, but you're not the first to get lost in this city. The guards are accustomed to newcomers needing directions and they give them freely. To find things in a hurry, ask a guard and they will plot it on your mini-map.

Ironforge Points of Interest

Location	Useful Stores/NPCs
Main Gate	Inn, Bank, Visitor's Center, General Goods, Auction House
Mystic Ward	Mage/Portal Trainer, Paladin Trainer, Priest Trainer
Forlorn Caverns	Rogue Trainer, Fishing Trainer, Warlock/Demon Trainer
Hall of Explorers	Quest Recipients
Tinker Town	Gnomeregan Quests, Engineering Trainer, Alchemy Trainer, Stormwind/Ironforge Tram
Military Ward	Inn, Warrior Trainer, Hunter Trainer
Great Forge	Griffon Master, Herbalism Trainer, First Aid Trainer, Enchanting Trainer, Mining Trainer, Blacksmith Trainer, Tailoring Trainer, Leatherworking Trainer, Skinning Trainer, Cooking Trainer, High Seat

Further east sits the Gol'Bolar Quarry. Generally a mine dedicated to supplying Ironforge with stone, the quarry has become overridden with troggs. Senator Mehr Stonehallow is asking all adventurers to find **The Public Servant** inside themselves and help. He needs you to kill 10 Rockjaw Bonesnappers before the miners can return to work.

Foreman Stonebrow is standing on the edge of the quarry in frustration. He doesn't have the political power that Stonehallow does, but he wants the troggs dead all the same. He asks you to kill six Rockjaw Skullthumpers to help end the occupation of **Those Blasted Troggs!**

With a group, these two quests are frighteningly easy and fast. If alone, take the quarry very slowly and fight near the walls to avoid as many patrol issues as possible. Be careful of troggs that stand behind the pillars of ice near the cave entrance, and stay well rested in case sudden adds demand more from your hit points and mana.

Becoming More Talented

Every level (starting at level ten), you gain a Talent Point. These can be used to increase your abilities or learn new ones. Open your talent window (defaulted to 'n'). There are three panels in the window. Look at each talent carefully before choosing as once you spend your points, it costs gold to unlearn them. There is more about the benefits of each talent in the class section.

A Crafter's Dream

The Wendigo Cave was good, but the Quarry is an even better location for crafters of all sorts. There is a wealth of copper inside the mine itself, but there are also veins outside of it (in the general Quarry). Beyond that, the troggs are a fine source of Linen and drop money as well. Herbalists will also be pleased with the high concentration of Earthroot, Silverleaf, and Peacebloom nearby.

With the capital explored and many fine quests completed, it's appropriate for you to seek Loch Modan, the beautiful land east of Dun Morogh. There are still some exciting places to see before you leave your homeland, so start making your way east and look for some of the following hotspots.

There is a ranch just a minute or so east of Ironforge. Rudra Amberstill breeds rams there, yet she is beset by troubles caused by a monster named Vagash. She asks you to help her by **Protecting the Herd**. Vagash is found in a cave above the ranch. Climb west and around the bulk of the mountains and bring a friend or two unless you are greatly prepared for an ugly fight! Vagash is level 11 and is an elite wendigo, so take that into consideration before the fight starts. Offer the Fang of Vagash as proof to Rudra that the attacks will stop and claim your reward.

In the far northeast is a short quest that you can finish to ease the mind of a troubled dwarf. Pilot Hammerfoot is guarding some engines in the area, but he won't leave the region until he's convinced that his friend Mori is either alive and well, or dead and lost. **The Lost Pilot** charged off into the hills some time back, and you can help out by discovering his fate. Move farther north along the road until you can break west. The body of Mori lies in a pile of bloody snow.

Though slain, Mori was able to account for his fate before his death. In his journal the dwarf wrote of a powerful bear named Mangeclaw. Vengeance was the pilot's final wish, and it would further aid his companion to know that this was done. Look slightly south and scour the area for the bear, then slay the beast. Tell Pilot Hammerfoot when the mission of vengeance is complete.

The road east leads directly through South Gate Outpost where Mountaineer Barleybrew works; give him his brother's barrel of Shimmer Stout. The dwarf also wants one of his friends to try the mixture, and he passes the brew along with a request that it be sent to Mountaineer Kadrell of Loch Modan (one of the Thelsamar guards). Because you were on your way to Loch Modan already, this offers no expense of time or energy.

Congratulations on your success in Dun Morogh. Rams are breeding happily, the dwarves have raised a fine toast in your name, and even the snow seems to have receded a bit because of such fine efforts. New challenges wait in Loch Modan and in lands such as Westfall to the south and Darkshore across the ocean, but those are adventures for another day.

ELWYNN FOREST

Elwynn Forest is the pleasant home of Stormwind City and the basket of human civilization in the east. Surrounded by settled farms, lumber mills, and mines, it's no wonder where the Humans get their grand ideas of a peaceful future.

Legend

1	Westbrook Garrison	5	The Stonefield Farm	9	Crystal Lake	13	Jasperlode Mine	17	Stone Cairn Lake and Hero's Vigil
2	Forest's Edge	6	The Maclure Vineyards	10	Northshire Valley	14	Southern Elwynn Forest	18	Eastvale Logging Camp
3	Mirror Lake Orchard	7	Jerod's Landing	11	Echo Ridge Mine	15	Brackwell Pumpkin Patch	19	Ridgepoint Tower
4	Fargodeep Mine	8	Goldshire	12	Northshire Vineyards	16	Tower of Azora	20	Stormwind (Capital City)

YOUR FIRST DAY

A light breeze blows through the trees. The smells of freshly cut wood and baked goods drift from just through the woods. The sun is shining and it's just warm enough for a refreshing glass of water or lemonade. Such is life at the heart of the human lands where the guards patrol the roads and train daily.

NORTHSHIRE

Northshire is one of the first places adventurers are sent to train. In the abbey are veterans of many trades and walks of life to help you grow. The merchants outside understand who they are dealing with and sell many weapons and armor designed for the newly enlisted. Few of the problems here are terribly dangerous and most make for good practice of skills that keep you alive elsewhere.

Report to Deputy Willem to begin your training. As you are here answering the call about **A Threat Within**, he directs you to Marshal McBride inside the abbey. McBride's first orders are for you to assist in a **Kobold Camp Cleanup**. He wants you to kill ten Kobold Vermin and return. The kobolds are just northwest of the abbey, but head around the right side of the building first.

Eagan Peltskinner has more work for the willing. With so many **Wolves Across the Border**, Eagan is hiring people to hunt them. He wants eight pieces of Tough Wolf Meat to cook. He rewards you for your time, so accept the quest and head north to hunt the wolves.

The kobolds aren't terribly bright and don't much like each other. You can kill them with impunity and those nearby do not assist. Avoid going into the mine as your targets are around the campfires outside and the enemies in the mine are more dangerous. With both quests done, return for your rewards.

McBride has more work for you now that you've proven a willing hand. He has a message for you from your trainer and needs you to help **Investigate Echo Ridge**. To remove the kobold infestation, he wants ten Kobold Workers killed.

Take a moment to visit your trainer and learn any new abilities before heading out of the abbey. Deputy Willem has more work for you. The Defias Brotherhood has been seen in the area. This **Brotherhood of Thieves** must be put down before they can become a problem. He asks you to collect 12 Red Burlap Bandanas as proof of your commitment to the safety of Northshire.

First head north to the kobold camps. The Kobold workers are at the campfires with the Kobold Vermin. Do your part to aid in the investigation and return McBride for more work. McBride outranks Willem and thus his work comes first.

Your work has shown that the kobold infestation is worse than expected and a **Skirmish at Echo Ridge** may be unavoidable. McBride asks you to penetrate the kobold defenses around the mine and kill 12 Kobold Laborers to bring their digging to a halt. Head north and carry out his orders.

Traveling the Bloody Way

As you are traveling, consider killing any enemies that are your level or lower. The enemies in Northshire Valley are fairly weak and the additional experience and usable equipment make it worth your time.

McBride is pleased with your work and gives you leave to **Report to Goldshire**. Accept the documents, but don't head out of Northshire just yet. Deputy Willem needs your assistance and there is more to do. Visit your class trainer again to check for new abilities to learn.

Young Wolf

The Spoils of War

Your backpack is nearly full. First, take the time to look through it and see if there is any usable equipment for you. If so, equip it. Second, become familiar with any recovery items (potions, food, drink, etc.) you've accumulated. Everything else that can be sold to vendors should be.

When you are ready, head across the creek to the Northshire Vineyards. The thieves are everywhere and more intelligent than the wolves and kobolds you've fought so far. They will attack you on sight, and assist their friends.

With proof of your deeds, return to Willem for your reward. While you were killing the brigands, there have been other developments. There's a **Bounty on Garrick Padfoot** for harassing the farmers and leading the local thieves. Willem is authorized to pay well for Garrick's Head. **Milly Osworth**, a friend of Willem's, also needs a hand. Milly stands behind the abbey.

Milly was harvesting in the vineyards when the Defias moved in. **Milly's Harvest** was left in several crates. She's worried they'll either be stolen or damaged and wants you to recover eight of them. Head across the bridge again and kill the enemies around Milly's Harvest. When you've recovered all you need, head further east to find Garrick.

Milly is very pleased to have the harvest saved. While she still rewards you, someone else would like to reward hard work. Take the **Grape Manifest** to Brother Neals in the bell tower to show the work you've done.

Both Brother Neals and Deputy Willem reward you. With so much accomplished in Northshire, it's time to head to Goldshire.

GOLDSHIRE

The south road from Northshire takes you through a well-guarded set of walls. Falkhaan Isenstrider is relaxing at a beautiful fountain advertising the Lion's Pride Inn at Goldshire. His friend owns the establishment and Falkhaan suggests stopping by for some **Rest and Relaxation**.

Follow the road south to Goldshire. Make a quick stop at the Lion's Pride Inn for some free food or water. Speak with Innkeeper Farley about how to make this inn your home. This resets your hearthstone to this location and is a good habit to get into. William Pestle stands off to one side of the inn looking troubled. He's looking to gather wax, but the best source of it is **Kobold Candles**. He's no adventurer, so he'll pay if you bring him eight Large Candles.

Now that you've taken a moment to rest from your travels, deliver your papers to Marshal Dughan. He doesn't waste any time putting you to work and wants you to explore **The Fargodeep Mine** and report back on the kobold presence. Remy "Two Times" runs the local **Gold Dust Exchange**. Bring him ten Gold Dust from kobolds and he pays handsomely.

Pretty much everything people are asking of you so far involves the kobolds at Fargodeep Mine but it's a bit too dangerous to go in without having a better understanding of the area. Follow the road west until you can cut south to the Stonefield Farm. "Auntie" Bernice Stonefield is upset about a **Lost Necklace**. She believes Billy Maclure took it and wants it back. Find and question Billy Maclure at the Maclure Vineyards to the east.

Billy Maclure claims he knows who took it, but he's smarter than he looks and wants some pie for the information. Bernice makes a good Pork Belly Pie, but she needs four Chunks of Boar Meat to make the **Pie for Billy**. Luckily, the boars in the vineyards have the meat you need. Hunt them and return to Bernice.

Bernice isn't happy about being blackmailed to get her necklace back, but she'll do whatever it takes. Bernice makes the pie and asks you to take it **Back to Billy**. Ma Stonefield has work for you as well. The Brackwells have a prize-winning pig that has a habit of sneaking over and eating the veggies from the Stonefield Farm. Ma has decided that **Princess Must Die!** Bring Princess' collar to Ma and she rewards you.

With the pie in hand, return to the Maclure Vineyard and speak with Billy. Billy saw a kobold making off with Bernice's Necklace. The kobold ran into the Fargodeep Mine and had a huge **Goldtooth**. Before you run into the mine, speak with Maybell Maclure. She's having some real trouble as her one and true love is…a Stonefield. The rivalry between the two families is terrible, but these **Young Lovers** are determined to find a way to happiness. Take Maybell's Love Letter to Tommy Joe Stonefield, who is moping at the river west of Stonefield Farm.

Tommy Joe is so caught up in his love for Maybell that he can't think straight. He asks you to **Speak with Gramma** to find a way for the two to be together. Gramma has seen a number of things in her life and knows that a potion can fix anything. Take her **Note to William** in Goldshire next time you're in the area. For now, prepare to enter Fargodeep Mine.

The kobolds in the mine are very aggressive. Take it slow and kill everything near you. There are two entrances: one to the upper level and the other to the lower level. Goldtooth stands in the corridor that joins the levels, but you'll be in here long enough you're bound to see him.

The Marshals haven't been lax about recruiting people to clear the mine and you won't be alone. Consider joining forces with others already there. These quests take longer to do in a group, but your survivability is much higher with friends. Be extra careful to pull enemies to you when entering the larger chambers as several of the kobolds may attack from different sides.

Inventory Full?

It's been a good while since you were near a merchant and your inventory shows it. Once your inventory is full you can't pick up any more items, including quest items. Take the time to destroy some of the less lucrative items in your inventory when you need room for quest items.

Less lucrative items are items of lowest quality and lowest armor (they are grey in name). This means grey cloth items are often the first to be dropped. If you don't need the food or drink for recovery purposes, these are also prime candidates.

Keep your health and mana full as you clear out the mine. When you've finished with the quests, return to Bernice at the Stonefield Farm. She's very happy to have her necklace back and frees you to return to Goldshire. Use your hearthstone for a quick trip back or simply leg it.

William Pestle packages the candles and asks you to take the **Shipment to Stormwind**. This isn't a time sensitive quest and you can deliver them when you visit the capital. Accept the quest and give him the note from Gramma Stonefield. William has a way to help them, but he needs help **Collecting Kelp** for the potion. He needs four Crystal Kelp Fronds. Crystal Lake is patrolled by nasty Murlocs. They are VERY social, so adds are very common.

Report to Marshal Dughan next. He's very pleased with your exploration of the Fargodeep Mine. He's so pleased he asks you to explore **The Jasperlode Mine** as well. Accept his assignment and speak to Remy about your gold dust. True to his word, he pays you for the dust. He also asks you to speak with Dughan about **A Fishy Peril** elsewhere in Elwynn Forest.

Dughan has spoken with Remy before and his hands are tied until he gets an official call for aid to combat the murloc menace. He doesn't have the manpower to check the situation…you've been his eyes and ears already. If you have **Further Concerns** about the matter, he suggests you speak with Guard Thomas along the east road. Accept the quest and take a moment to visit your trainer before heading out.

Head east following the lake. There are murlocs on the islands of the lake; they have the kelp you need. Pull them back and be ready to finish them off quickly. They're aggressive, don't like to fight alone, and run for help when wounded. Once you have the required kelp, retreat to the road and continue east.

THE EASTVALE LOGGING CAMP

Follow the road east until it crosses the river. Guard Thomas is standing here. Speak with him about the murloc threat in the area. Two guards were sent to investigate the matter further, but they haven't returned. Thomas needs you to **Find the Lost Guards** so he can complete his report. They were looking around where the river meets the lake.

Murlocs are not the only threat to the logging camp. The bears and wolves in the area are becoming more numerous and more brazen as the loggers become the only food source in the area. Thomas asks you to join in the effort to **Protect the Frontier** by killing eight Prowlers and five Young Forest Bears. Accept both his quests and follow the river north.

Watch for the bears as you move north to the lake. There aren't any Prowlers on the west side of the river, but the remains of Footman Malaki Stone are lying where the river drains from Stone Cairn Lake. This solves the fate of one soldier, but you still need to **Discover Rolf's Fate**. Webbed footprints lead east from the corpse and you can see a murloc village on the edge of the lake. Follow the lake edge east.

The murlocs are very aggressive and attack if they catch the slightest hint you are in the area. Look for others hunting the murlocs and join forces. If there is no one to join forces with, continue to Eastvale Logging Camp and speak with Supervisor Raelen. You'll be in the area for awhile and you can investigate the camp when it's safer.

Raelen is in **A Bundle of Trouble**. Because of all the attacks, her loggers haven't been able to gather the required lumber. They've felled the trees but the wood is in small piles. She needs you to bring eight Bundles of Wood back. Head out of the camp and search near the base of the nearby trees.

Watch for the Prowlers and Young Forest Bears. These are the reason the loggers had to flee. They need to be killed. As you hunt through the trees, keep an eye on the murloc camp. If someone else is hunting them or in the area, join together or sneak in before the murlocs respawn. Rolf's remains are easier to get to from a southern approach.

With the fate of both guards revealed, **Report to Thomas**. The murlocs are a greater threat than previously believed. **Deliver Thomas' Report** to Marshal Dughan. But first, head back to the logging camp. Sara Timberlain is a kind person and will make you clothes if you bring her the materials she needs. She prefers to work with **Red Linen Goods**. Bring six Red Linen Bandanas from gang members in Elwynn Forest.

Drop off your wood and sell excess loot before crossing the river west. Travel northwest to the Jasperlode Mine. Without even setting foot in the mine, the kobold presence can be seen. Marshal Dughan needs to know the strength of the infestation though.

The kobolds here are more dangerous than the ones in Fargodeep. They don't travel alone often, and the ones wearing blue shirts understand magic. The casting kobolds can do a lot of damage quickly, but don't last long in a fight. Target them first if you are engaged by more than one kobold.

Deeper in, the tunnel walls are covered with web, and kobolds hang from the ceiling in silky cocoons. You've seen what you needed and now it's time to get out. If your Hearthstone is ready, port back to Goldshire. Should your Hearthstone be on cooldown, exit the mine as quickly as caution allows and head back to town.

William uses the kelp to make an Invisibility Liquor that helps with **The Escape**. Hold onto it until you see Maybell Maclure next. Marshal Dughan is eager to hear your reports. He doesn't like what's happening, but he rewards you as promised. He gives you a Stormwind Armor Marker to give to Sara Timberlain. She'll craft **Cloth and Leather Armor** for you to use in the defense of Elwynn Forest.

As one of the commanding officers in charge of Elwynn's defense, Dughan always has more work for you. He asks you to **Report to Gryan Stoutmantle** in Westfall when Elwynn is under control, and alerts you that the **Westbrook Garrison Needs Help!**

Smith Argus has work for you if you're willing. He's been asked to send people to Grimand Elmore in Stormwind. **Elmore's Task** is one of several that are sending you to the capital.

STORMWIND CITY AND BACK TO EASTVALE LOGGING CAMP

Now is a good time to see the glorious city of Stormwind. Follow the northwest road to the city of light and the center of the human armies.

As all classes and professions are represented in Stormwind, it's a good place for training. If you're picking up crafting professions, seek out the trainers while you are delivering the shipment for William and speaking with Grimand. Morgan Pestle is in his apothecary just inside the gates while Grimand is in the Dwarven District.

Stop by and listen to Renato Gallina, who is standing on a large crate on the west side of the street. He's advertising the Gallina Winery and gives you a ticket to prove you were sent by the **Wine Shop Advert** and garner a free Bottle of Pinot Noir.

It's Big!

Stormwind is a rather impressive city. Exploring all of it would take quite a bit of effort, but you're not the first to get lost in this city. The guards are accustomed to newcomers needing directions and they give them freely. To find things in a hurry, ask a guard and they will plot it on your mini-map.

Stormwind Points of Interest

Location	Useful Stores/NPCs
Trade District	Griffon Master, Inn, Bank, Weapon Trainer, Auction House, Visitor's Center
Mage Quarter	Alchemy Trainer, Enchanting Trainer, Herbalism Trainer, Tailoring Trainer, Mage/Portal Trainer
Park	Hunter Trainer, Stable Master, Druid Trainer, Herbalism Trainer
Cathedral Square	Paladin Trainer, Priest Trainer
Dwarven District	Blacksmithing Trainer, Engineering Trainer, Mining Trainer, Forge, Anvil, Tram to Ironforge
Old Town	Cooking Trainer, Leatherworking Trainer, Skinning Trainer, Warrior Trainer, Rogue Trainer
Canal District	Fishing Trainer

Stormpike's Delivery is given to you by Grimand. He wants the supplies sent to Loch Modan in the Dwarven Lands. These lands are far away, but accept the quest now so you have it when you venture there. If you've reached level ten, speak with your trainer for a class specific quest before heading back to Goldshire.

There's still more to do in the east. Take the road from Goldshire to the Eastvale Logging Camp. Guard Thomas has another mission for you. With the information you've brought, the Stormwind Army has placed a **Bounty on Murlocs**. Thomas is authorized to reward you if you bring eight Torn Murloc Fins as proof of the kills. Continue east to Eastvale Logging Camp.

Turn your armor marker in to Sara Timberlain for your armor, then head south across the road. East of Ridgepoint Tower is a small Defias camp. Kill them for their Red Linen Bandanas. When you've acquired enough for Sara, return to Eastvale. Sell your excess loot before heading north to the murloc camps.

The murlocs are a bit easier now that you've gained a level or two. Do the lower level characters a favor and kill the enemies near Rolf's Remains first. Clear the murlocs slowly as they are still very aggressive. With the fins in hand, follow the river south to Guard Thomas and your reward.

Break off the road and head southwest to the Brackwall Pumpkin Patch. The outer edges are guarded by brigands, but between the pumpkins a

beast moves. Princess and her entourage move about the patch with a royal bearing. To attack one is to gain the wrath of all three. Check for other players in the area that are willing to help you before attempting the kill.

Take the Brass Collar and return to the Maclure Vineyard to the west. Give the Invisibility Liquor to Maybell and help the two lovers break free of the oppression of the hate between their families. Your next stop is the Stonefield Farm. Ma Stonefield is rather pleased to have her veggies safe from the monster and rewards you accordingly. Sell any excess loot to Homer Stonefield and head north to the road, and west to the Westbrook Garrison.

WESTBROOK GARRISON

On the path from the road to the garrison is a large wanted poster. **Wanted: "Hogger"** doesn't leave much to the imagination. The Stormwind Army has placed a bounty on the savage gnoll and empowered Marshal Dughan to reward anyone bringing his Huge Gnoll Claw as proof of the deed.

Report to Deputy Rainer at the garrison for your assignment. The gnolls in to the south have grown in number to become a significant threat. The guard tower doesn't have the numbers to clear the vermin out, so adventurers are being recruited for the **Riverpaw Gnoll Bounty**. Bring back eight Painted Gnoll Armbands for your reward.

Head south across the road. Many of the gnolls stay in camps where their numbers offer protection. If you are in a larger group, attack these camps carefully. Solo adventurers should avoid these camps entirely as they are nothing more than a fast trip to the graveyard. Instead, look for the few gnolls that patrol between the camps alone. Ambush these for the armbands.

Keep a watchful eye for Hogger. He is very dangerous and can be the doom of you or your party if he attacks while you are engaged with other gnolls. When you see Hogger, rest to full and wait for him to be away from other gnolls. He is an elite enemy, shown by the gold dragon encircling his portrait, and has many more hitpoints and does much more damage than most enemies his level.

Collect the armbands and return to Deputy Rainer. As promised, he rewards your service to king and country. With little else to be done at Westbrook Garrison, hearthstone back to Goldshire and turn the Huge Gnoll Claw in to Dughan.

Congratulations on your success in Elwynn Forest. Farmers are back at work, the local merchants tell stories of you to customers, and the roads are just a little bit safer. The call for aid has come from the land of Westfall and the allies in the dwarven land of Loch Modan and the Elven land of Darkshore could certainly use a skilled hand, but those are adventures for another day.

TELDRASSIL

Teldrassil is the new home of the brave night elves, a people who have taken arms and magic to battle against demons and restore the balance of their spirits. With the former capital of Elven power nearly destroyed by the fighting against the demons, the refuge has grown in prominence. Those ancient and animated trees that remain to protect the forest have gathered here to stop any final advance from the evil remnants. Now the night elves are shaking off their suffering and readying themselves for the next chapter in their history.

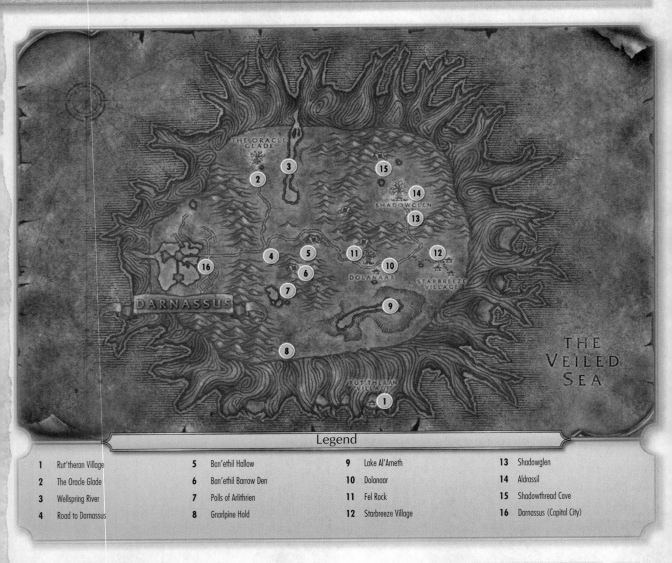

Legend

1	Rut'theran Village	5	Ban'ethil Hallow	9	Lake Al'Ameth	13	Shadowglen
2	The Oracle Glade	6	Ban'ethil Barrow Den	10	Dolanaar	14	Aldrassil
3	Wellspring River	7	Polls of Arlithrien	11	Fel Rock	15	Shadowthread Cave
4	Road to Darnassus	8	Gnarlpine Hold	12	Starbreeze Village	16	Darnassus (Capital City)

YOUR FIRST DAY

Teldrassil is a tree the size of a large island off the coast of Kalimdor. Isolated from the effects of many recent troubles, the land itself is free from some of the greater taint that plagues many of Kalimdor's forests. Yet even here, there are the stirrings of disease and corruption.

The greatest problems that exist in Teldrassil involve the tainting of natural creatures and beasts by a force of evil. Your duties often involve seeking out this taint in an attempt to isolate it, redeeming those corrupted, or, when all else fails, to destroy the creatures who are beyond salvation.

Speak with Ilthalaine and get the next step of restoring **The Balance of Nature**. Now you need to kill seven Mangy Nightsabres and the same amount of Thistle Boars. He also has a message from your class trainer. Accept both the quests and head to your trainer. Most of the trainers are inside the main hall of the building, but the nature-based class trainers (such as the Druid trainer) are in the higher branches of the building. Get your character any new skills, then find Tarindella just north of Ilthalaine.

ALDRASSIL

Aldrassil is the starting town, in the north-east of Teldrassil, where your character begins the journey into greatness. As with all new character areas, the majority of the creatures are neutral and won't attack unless engaged directly. A single large building at the center of this forested valley holds trainers, vendors, and the leaders of Aldrassil.

Speak to a nearby night elf after watching the introduction to Teldrassil. Conservator Ilthalaine stands a few feet from you. He tells you of **The Balance of Nature** and how Shadowglen has become unbalanced with the rapid growth of the boar and nightsabre populations. He asks you to kill seven Young Nightsabres and four Young Thistle Boars to begin trimming the populations. Accept his quest and move east as you kill.

At the entrance to the main building in Aldrassil is Melithar Staghelm. Tarindella, **The Woodland Protector**, has been seen in Shadowglen. Melithar asks you to find out why she is here and aid her in any work. Continue east into a field plentiful with Young Nightsabres and Young Thistle Boars. Kill them

until your quest is complete and you've gained level two. On your way back to Conservator Ilthalaine, speak with Dirania Silvershine at the cooking pot. Iverron, **A Good Friend** of Dirania, hasn't been seen since he headed up to the spider cave. Dirania would like you to find him for her.

Tarindella is in the area fighting the corruption. The Grells in the area are collecting Fel Moss (which spreads the corruption). She asks you to collect eight pieces of Fel Moss. The Grells have been driven quite made by the Fel Moss and won't give it up without a fight. Travel north to the Grell camps and kill them until you have the Fel Moss and have gained level three. If you finish the Fel Moss before gaining the next level, kill a few more…it's the only way to be sure.

Your bags are likely full by now. Return to Tarindella and give her the Fel Moss. With her gratitude stop at the merchants in Aldrassil and sell any excess loot. Remember to equip any extra bags you've found and head north once again. Gilshalan Windwalker stands at the bottom of the ramp nearby. He's studying the spiders in the area and needs ten **Webwood Venom** sacs from the spiders. As you have other quests near the spider cave, accept his and continue north to Shadowthread Cave.

Look to the west of Shadowthread Cave, in a small valley, a wounded night elf male named Iverron waits. He was bitten by the largest of the foul spiders and is too weak to return to Aldrassil. His condition is worsening as the poison runs its course. He asks you to help **A Friend in Need** by telling Dirania Silvershine of his plight. He's a strong man and can survive a bit longer, so finish your other quests before heading back.

When you've collected the venom sacs, head southeast. There are more Mangy Nightsabres and Thistle Boars if you return this route. With the animal populations successfully thinned, speak with Dirania about Iverron's situation. She can make **Iverron's Antidote**, but needs some ingredients.

She needs seven Hyacinth Mushrooms which grow near the trees in the area but you must fight the grells that wander nearby. Look around the northern ponds for the four Moonpetal Lily, while the Webwood Ichor is easily obtained from the spiders you are already fighting.

Stop at the merchants to sell excess loot and speak to your trainer about learning new abilities before heading out again. Get your reward from Ilthalaine and give the venom sacs to Gilshalan. With the venom specimens, he has set his sights higher. He wants a live spider to observe. As capturing a full grown spider is a daunting task, he wants you instead to bring him a **Webwood Egg**. Accept his quest and head north to collect the ingredients for the antidote. With the ingredients collected, head into Shadowthread Cave.

Inventory Full?

It's been a good while since you were near a merchant and your inventory shows it. Once your inventory is full you can't pick up any more items, including quest items. Take the time to destroy some of the less lucrative items in your inventory when you need room for quest items.

Less lucrative items are items of lowest quality and lowest armor (grey named). This means grey cloth items are often the first to be dropped. If you don't need the food or drink for recovery purposes, these are also prime candidates.

There are said to be hundreds of the eggs inside Shadowthread Cave, so the only worry comes from fighting past all of the poisonous beasts. The eggs are on the top level of the cave. The center path takes you through a narrow passage as it climbs up to the eggs. Only one of the spiders is as high as fifth level, so even a solo character can move through the cave safely (just don't try to fight more than one enemy at a time). Grab the Webwood Egg and return to town triumphant. The spiders might have respawned by now. Fight your way out or use your Hearthstone for a fast trip back.

After you give Gilshalan the egg, he asks you to answer **Tenaron's Summons**. This accomplished night elf won't take much of your time. He merely asks that you fill a Crystal Phial with the waters of the Moonwell just north of town as payment for learning of the **Crown of the Earth**. Head down the tree and give the ingredients to Dirania to make the antidote. It won't stay potent for long (it is a timed quest), so immediately head north to the Moonwell.

Filling the Phial

To fill the Phial, stand in the Moonwell and open your inventory (defaulted to 'i'). Right click on the Empty Phial to get the Filled Crystal Phial.

With the Filled Crystal Phial, turn west and fight through the spiders to Iverron. He rewards you for giving him the antidote. With things just about done here, return to Tenaron atop Aldrassil for your reward.

Tenaron informs you that your time in Aldrassil is at an end and hands you a vessel with the Moonwell water to take to Dolanaar, a large town near the center of Teldrassil.

ENTERING DOLANAAR

Following Tenaron's bidding, it's time to seek the greater town of Dolanaar. Finish selling extra items to the vendors below, and make sure to train with the masters that specialize in your class. With that done, take the southern road away from Aldrassil and into the greater wilds of this majestic land.

At the entrance to Shadowglen, Porthannius stands. He has a **Dolanaar Delivery** he'd like you to help with. As you were already heading that way, it costs you nothing and is worth your while. Accept his quest and continue south.

Stick to the road, and fight creatures nearby if you wish. A lone Satyr, Zenn Foulhoof, stands on the right side of the path, by a tree. He seems friendly, and is willing to award you a simple quest. Return items from the Nightsabres, Strigid Owls, and Webwood Spiders to complete **Zenn's Bidding**. It takes a number of kills to collect everything, so this is best accomplished while you are busy with other quests.

Press on to Dolanaar and talk to everyone in town. Standing at the ramp to the north building is Syral Bladeleaf. She has a delivery she would like you to finish for her. She gives you **Denalan's Earth** and directions to find him at the lake to the south. At the entrance stands Athridas Bearmantle, who wants you to enter the Firbolg village to the east. Athridas feels **A Troubling Breeze** and there is another night elf there who he is worried about. Promise to help him and head to the top of the building.

Tallonkai Swiftroot is in the highest room and has a few problems you can help with. First, he lost **The Emerald Dreamcatcher**. It was held at Starbreeze Village to the east and he can't retrieve it himself. Accept this quest and ask him about his other problem. Tallonkai Swiftroot wants to see the head of Melenas, minus the body. Melenas is a dark Satyr who lives in a cave called Fel Rock, just north of Dolanaar. The **Twisted Hatred** Melenas feels toward all things healthy must be stopped.

There is yet more to do before heading out of town. Head into the building just south of the road and speak with Innkeeper Keldamyr.

Dolanaar, A Good Home

Talk to Innkeeper Kaldamyr in Dolanaar to set your home point. With all the running back and forth that needs to be done, especially for some of the later quests, it's nice to have the option of getting back quickly.

After getting your reward, continue south out of the building and deliver the Partially Filled Vessel to Corithras Moonrage. He accepts the delivery and asks you to continue working on the **Crown of the Earth** by collecting water from the Moonwell near Starbreeze Village. Accept his quest and look to the east.

Zarrin is a cook who works well with odd dishes. If you have taken Cooking as one of your secondary professions, seek this teacher for the quest to learn the **Recipe of the Kaldorei** (a fine piece of spider-cuisine).

With your quest log nearly bursting, head out of town. Run east, mostly following the road and kill any owls, nightsabres, or spiders nearby until you see the outskirts of Starbreeze Village and the Moonwell. Jump into the Moonwell and fill the phial.

Next, move slowly into the village but beware of the Furbolgs (they have become quite feral and attack almost anything they see). The first large building on the right has two floors, and Gaerolas Talvethren is on the top floor. Fight the few Firbolg in the way and head upstairs. Gaerolas isn't in great shape, but he tells you what has happened and asks you to tell Athridas in Dolanaar of the **Gnarlpine Corruption**. Before leaving, move to the south-eastern cottage of Starbreeze and search the dresser for the Emerald Dreamcatcher.

Return to Dolanaar, fighting the beasts for Zenn along the way, to turn in the quests you have completed. Corithras gives you another phial to fill, while Athridas asks you to collect the **Relics of Wakening**. After returning the dreamcatcher to Tallonkai, he realizes that part of it is missing. He asks you to get it from **Ferocitas the Dream Eater** and slay some of the Firbolg Mystics in the area. Take a companion or two if you are uncertain of victory. Tallonkai's Jewel isn't immediately apparent on the corpse of Ferocitas. Take the Gnarlpine Necklace and right click to reveal the jewel. Return to Zenn (if you have completed his quest) and to Tallonkai Swiftroot.

Investing in Your Future

With so much time spent outside of town and so much killing being done, your backpack tends to fill up quickly. Consider speaking with the General Supplies merchant in Dolanaar. He sells bags. These aren't inexpensive, but they allow you to carry more loot home. More loot sold means more money. The bag will pay for itself quick enough to warrant the purchase.

RECOVER AND CLEAR THE LAKE

By now, it's probably time to train again and sell a few things. Talk to any of the craft trainers in town if you want to learn Cooking, First Aid, Alchemy, or Herbalism (three are on the south side; look to the north to find the First Aid trainer). There are a fair number of quests to grab now. Talk to everyone but focus on getting **Seek Redemption** from Syral Bladeleaf. To make things right with her, leave town and walk south until you reach Lake Al'Ameth. First, speak with Denalan, on the eastern edge of the lake. Then, while walking around the Lake, collect the Fel Cones on the ground near the trees.

After putting the soil you brought him in a nearby planter, Denalan has two quests that can be completed while looking for more Fel Cones. He too wants to find out what is harming the land, but he's not a fighter. Collect the **Timberling Sprouts**, and **Timberling Seeds** for him. The sprouts are found all around the lake (and other bodies of water in Teldrassil). Right-click on these growing plants while moving around. Fight the aggressive Timberlings you come across to gain the seeds. If your eyes are sharp and can spot the steaming Fel Cones, all three quests can be done in a single pass around the lake!

Turn in everything to Denalan and receive his shipment to Rellian Greenspyre. Rellian is in Darnassus (do not head out to Darnassus yet), the capital, and can be found on either the east side of town, just outside Warrior's Terrace, or north of the bridges (before reaching the Druid's Grove).

It's time to bring an end to Melenas. Seek a small group on the same quest. There are many aggressive Grells in the cave, and having a few friends can make a huge difference. Stop at Zenn on the way over to give him the Fel Cones and get a good laugh. Search the cave while killing the nasty monsters and look for the wandering Melenas; though he stands in the north-western corner atop a ledge, he also patrols from time to time. Target Melanas first and bring him down to make sure the quest is a success. Even if you die, return to the body and loot it for victory.

With that done, there are several quests west of town that can be done in a loop. If you still have a group, it is even easier, since one of the small dungeons is on the list and can be quite challenging.

WEST OF TOWN:
HOME OF THE DRUIDS

Athridas Bearmantle has been patiently waiting for you to gather **The Relics of Wakening**. With a small group in tow, head out west of town. A Sentinel tells you **The Road to Darnassus** is dangerous to travel. Tell him you will help and move west, toward the mountains ahead. Look for the Gnarlpine Ambushers south of the road. The quest for these is very fast, as you only need to kill six. Follow the hill that rises to the south, beyond the Ambushers, and notice the slightly stronger Furbolgs.

At the top of the hill is Ban'ethil Barrow Den. Below are the relics that you are seeking, but dozens of Firbolg patrol the corridors and make life difficult for anyone who tries to enter. Move slowly with your group, taking on only one or two Firbolg at a time, and search the rooms of the dungeon for the four artifacts. They are held in grey chests (usually in alcoves). This is not your only goal in the dungeon. A restless spirit resides in a room on the second tier of the dungeon. Oben Rageclaw was trapped in slumber when the Firbolg found a way to separate his body and spirit. They now use it to attack people. Oben's spirit wants this to end. Slay the Shamans for **The Sleeping Druid** until you find the Shaman Voodoo Charm. Return this to Oben, then agree to slay his body. Seek the animated body at the lowest level of the dungeon, fight it, then use the Charm to give this druid a final, lasting rest.

Speak with Oben again, then return the artifacts to town. Athridas is ready to have you go after **Ursal the Mauler**, the very Firbolg who began this war against the Druids of Teldrassil. Move to Gnarlpine Hold in the south-west, at the very base of Teldrassil. While getting into position, fill your phial at the next Moonwell (completing another portion of **Crown of the Earth**), and steal a piece of fruit from the glowing tree south of the Moonwell. Denalan rewards you for bringing him the **Glowing Fruit**.

Ursal is somewhat easy to kill, yet the many Furbolgs around him offer moderate resistance. Hopefully you can carry the group from the last dungeon onward and plow through Ursal's allies without trouble. Be wary of the Avengers and casters, since these enemies pack a wicked punch.

Avengers are *EVIL!*

Avengers are a troublesome class of enemies. The Furbolgs are one of the races that have Avengers, and there are a number of them out in the forests of Teldrassil. When you slay another Firbolg near an Avenger, the Avenger bursts into a rage and starts to attack very quickly with devastating results. Try to slay the Avengers first.

If there are casters around, they need to be brought down quickly as well. To solve this conundrum, have one person attack a caster to interrupt their spells while the other party members beat on the Avenger. This way, both enemies are limited in their ability. It's not optimal, but fighting both casters and Avengers at the same time never is.

DARNASSUS AND
THE NORTHERN QUESTS

Return to town and rejoice. All of the substantially challenging quests are done in Teldrassil, and the remaining ones are much easier with the skills you are already beginning to master. The next part for **Crown of the Earth** takes you up to the Oracle Glade, in the north-eastern section of Teldrassil. Sell, train, and grab that final quest before moving out.

The house on the side of the road as you head toward Darnassus has a Skinner and Leatherworking trainer. Stop there for a second if you are interested, then it's on to the capital. Before striking out to the Oracle Glade, complete Denalan's dropoff to Rellian; better late then never, eh? Rellian wants you to collect **Tumors** from the larger Timberlings that live along the

Wellspring River, east of Oracle Glade. Accept that quest and visit the temple on the south side of town for **Tears of the Moon**. Priestess A'moora gives you that quest, and she is on the upper tier of the temple.

Darnassus is a rather impressive city. Exploring all of it would take quite a bit of effort, but you're not the first to get lost in this city. The guards are accustomed to newcomers needing directions and they give them freely. To find things in a hurry, ask a guard and they will plot it on your mini-map.

Darnassus Points of Interest

Location	Useful Stores/NPCs
Cenarion Enclave	Druid Trainer, Hunter Trainer, Rogue Trainers; Arch Druid Fandral Staghelm, Night Elf Mount Vendor
Craftsmen's Terrace	Alchemy Trainer, Tailoring Trainer, Leatherworking Trainer, Enchanting Trainer, Cooking Trainer, Inn
Warrior's Terrace	Warrior Trainer, Weapon Master
Tradesmen's Terrace	Auction House, Merchants
Temple Gardens	Bank, Mailbox, Teleporter to Ruth'theran Village
Temple of the Moon	Priest Trainer, Herbalism Trainer, Chief Archaeologist Greywisker, Priestess A'moora

Now that you are loaded up with quests for the northern area, head out from town and walk to the Wellspring River. Fight the Timberlings as you plod north along the banks, and keep your eyes peeled for a dark-colored Timbering named **Blackmoss the Fetid**. Kill him if you see him (his heart can be turned into Denalan for additional experience, and you soon shall see Denalan for other rewards, so it's win-win).

Once the tumors are yours, walk along the north side of the area and search for the spider, Lady Sathrah. This magnificent spider has been tainted, like so many things in the land, and you need to slay her. Take the Spinneretes from

her body after the deed is done. Also, continue just west of her usual location to find a second glowing tree (another piece of fruit can be picked there). Denalan will reward you for bringing him **The Shimmering Frond**.

Steer toward the center of the region and talk to the night elves who live there and fill up your phial at the Moonwell. Recently, a messenger to Darnassus was murdered by the Harpies while carrying a report from **The Enchanted Glade**. Sentinel Arynia Cloudsbreak needs to see their numbers beaten back, and she asks you to take up the challenge. Agree. West and slightly to the north, between the western wall and the trees, is where you find the harpies. Not only do these kills help to rake in the Bloodfeather Belts, that you need but there is also a trapped tiger named Mist. Talk to the wounded beast and escort it back to the Glade safely. Turn in the belts and

receive the reward for that and saving Mist. Return to Darnassus to receive rewards from the temple and from Rellian. Only one thing is left to do for Sathrah to rest. Place her silvery spinnerets in the fountain inside the temple to complete **Sathrah's Sacrifice**.

Every level (starting at level ten), you gain a Talent Point. These can be used to increase your abilities or learn new ones. Open your talent window (defaulted to 'n'). There are three panels in the window. Look at each talent carefully before choosing as once you spend your points, it costs gold to unlearn them. There is more about the benefits of each talent in the class section.

With Teldrassil almost done, it's time to wrap up a few loose ends. Return to Dolanaar using your Hearthstone, if it's available, or your feet if it is not. Give the phial to Corithras. The next step of **Crown of the Earth** involves Darkshore, so tuck the Empty Phial into a bag and head south. Talk to Denalan and give him the final few goodies you found in the north. Take the time to examine the results of Denalan's experiments.

With the tumors to examine, he'll ask that you destroy the Timberling with the most Gargantuan Tumor that he has seen. This is certainly one that has the power to damage the land further because it has been tainted so badly. **Oakenscowl** is the Timberling's name, and he is undoubtedly the most powerful monster in the vicinity. Bring several allies to attack Oakenscowl, who lives south-west of the lake, just inside a small cave.

Bid Denalan farewell after receiving your reward, sell and train in Darnassus. The mists of Darkshore beckon. To reach the foreign coast, look for a glowing pagoda on the western end of Darnassus that teleports users to Rut'theran Village. Here a boat can send you across the seas. Once you arrive in Darkshore, be sure to speak to the Hippogriff Master to open up a flight path between Darkshore and Rut'theran.

Elune be praised!

DUROTAR

Durotar is the new homeland of the Orcs and Trolls on the continent of Kalimdor. It was Thrall who led the Orcs to this new desolate land and began to rebuild what his people had lost. Thrall rescued the Trolls as well and the remnants of the Darkspear tribe have also taken up residence in Durotar. Though chosen for its desolate and arid climate, enemies still lurk in the crags and caves of Durotar.

Legend

1	The Valley of Trials	5	Echo Isles	9	Drygulch Ravine	13	Rocktusk Farm	17	Southfury River
2	Burning Blade Coven	6	Tiragarde Keep	10	Margoz' Camp	14	Jaggedswine Farm	18	Razormane Grounds
3	Kolkar Crag	7	Scuttle Coast	11	Skull Rock	15	Zeppelin Tower	19	Thunder Ridge
4	Darkspear Strand	8	Dustwind Cave	12	Dead Eye Shore	16	Bladefist Bay	20	Orgrimmar (Capital City)

YOUR FIRST DAY

Durotar is mostly a desert region with the capital city of Orgrimmar to the North, the river to the west, and ocean to the east and south. Caverns and crags wind their way through the rocky terrain creating havens for those seeking to strike at the newcomers. Even the lush island chain to the southeast houses ill intent.

VALLEY OF TRIALS

Kaltunk has been assigned to greet all upcoming additions to the Horde armies. His primary duty is to set you on the path to finding **Your Place In The World**. He decides you should start by speaking with Gornek and working in the immediate area.

Gornek is just west in The Den. Gornek isn't terribly friendly or charismatic, but that isn't his duty. He's here **Cutting Teeth** with the new recruits. He wants you to kill ten Mottled Boars before he gives you a more difficult assignment. Head out of The Den and north.

You don't need to go far to find the troublesome creatures. There are many scavenging the arid grounds. Kill them, but don't stray too far from The Den as you return shortly.

Mottled Boar

The Spoils of War

Your backpack is nearly full. First, take the time to look through it and see if there is any usable equipment for you. If so, equip it. Second, become familiar with any recovery items (potions, food, drink, etc.) you've accumulated. Everything else that can be sold to vendors should be.

Return to Gornek for your next mission. The scorpids in the area have a nasty poison so the army keeps antidote on hand for accidents. Their supply is running low and the scorpids are a good way to prove yourself in battle. Bring ten Scorpid Worker Tails to Gornek to resupply antidote for the **Sting of the Scorpid**.

Gornek also has a message for you from your class trainer. Take the message to your trainer for a small amount of experience. Speak to them to train new abilities. Leave The Den and immediately turn north. Duokna is a General Goods merchant that buys any excess loot you have and Galgar will cook you some food if you bring him ten Cactus Apples. **Galgar's Cactus Apple Surprise** is very good…just don't ask what the surprise is!

South of the entrance to The Den, Zureetha Fargaze is recruiting aid. She has found a group of the Burning Blade residing in the Valley of Trials. These beasts must be brought to justice. The first step is to slay 12 of their **Vile Familiars**. Accept her quest and head to the east side of the valley (travel first north through the boars, then turn east).

Traveling the Bloody Way

As you're traveling, consider killing any enemies that are your level or lower. The enemies in the Valley of Trials are fairly weak and the additional experience and usable equipment make it worth your time.

The Cactus Apples can be found growing on many of the cacti in the valley. Gather these as you move east and keep an eye out for them as you harvest the scorpid tails. Lying in the shade of a tree is Hana'zua. He was stung badly by a particularly aggressive scorpid named **Sarkoth**. Before he can seek aid, his honor must be upheld. He asks you to find and slay this beast. Turn south hunting the scorpids as you climb the narrow slope.

Sarkoth is surrounded by other scorpids, but these beasts understand nothing of teamwork and do not aid him. If there are any other people in the area, recruit them to help you before bringing an end to this monster. Return to Hana'zua with Sarkoth's Mangled Claw as proof of its demise. With his honor protected, Hana'zua asks you to tell Gornek of the attack by **Sarkoth**. Report to Gornek of Hana'zua and to give him the scorpid stingers.

True to his word, Galgar gives you an entire stack of his Cactus Apple Surprise for your hard work. Gornek has no more work for you, but others do. Take a quick visit to your trainer before speaking with Foreman Thazz'ril to the east of The Den. He's having trouble keeping the Lazy Peons working. He gives you a Foreman's Blackjack to use on any peons you find sleeping. Between the two of you, the work will get done.

Follow the mountain edge north looking for sleeping peons and Vile Familiars. The familiars are aggressive and have some ranged capabilities, so engage them quickly. Return to The Den when the demon forces outside the cave are weakened and when your arm gets sore from blackjacking peons.

Thazz'ril appreciates your hard work and efficiency enough that he's willing to pay you for another task. **Thazz'ril's Pick** was left in the northern cave last time he was surveying and he'd like you to retrieve it for him. Visit Zureetha before heading out as she has sensed a leader in the cave to the north who possesses the **Burning Blade Medallion** that is calling the demons there.

The cave is filled with demons that are not only aggressive, but determined to end your life. Take the enemies one at a time and stick to the right tunnel as you ascend through the cave. Yarrog Baneshadow walks along a ledge at the back of the cave. Destroy this worshipper of dark magic and take the medallion from his corpse. Thazz'ril's Pick is in the center room by the waterfall. Grab it on your way out.

SOUTHERN DUROTAR

With your work in the Valley of Trials finished, Zureetha asks you to **Report to Sen'jin Village**. Sell you excess loot and head east past the gates and into greater Durotar.

Standing on the road is Ukor. He brought food to the valley without knowing they didn't need it and is afraid to take it back to Razor Hill. Though this delivery is **A Peon's Burden**, accept his quest. Razor Hill is to the north, but you have business in the south, so take the path off the road toward Sen'jin Village.

Watch for Lar Prowltusk south of the path. He doesn't stay in one place too long because he's watching the Kolkar. He's working hard, but he needs your help with **Thwarting Kolkar Aggression**. He snuck into their camp last night and found they are planning on an organized attack. He needs you to break into their camps and destroy the attack plans. Gather fellow warriors and head southeast toward Kolkar Crag to do your duty as a member of the Horde.

The male centaur are purely melee attackers and can be pulled to avoid fighting several at once. The female centaur use bows and do not move to you, so the fight must be taken to them. No matter who you're fighting, be ready to kill them quickly. They are not stupid and run for help when they get low on health. Find the attack plans in their three camps, destroy them, and return to Lar.

Now that you've gained level 6, it's time for a bit of walking. Only mages have a class trainer in Sen'jin Village, so follow the road north to Razor Hill. The fights on Echo Islands are tougher and you need all the abilities you can get. Speak with the Innkeeper to complete **A Peon's Burden**, but don't reset your hearthstone. Visit your class trainer and speak with Cook Torka at the east exit of town. He needs you to **Break a Few Eggs**. Accept his quest and use your hearthstone to return to Valley of Trials and walk to Sen'jin Village.

Report to Master Gadrin and collect the other quests before heading to the beach. Master Gadrin is in charge of the defense of Sen'jin and is recruiting adventurers to deal with **Zalazane.** Zalazane's Head must be brought back as along with the deaths of eight of the Hexed and Voodoo Trolls that have joined him. One of Zalazane's first victims was Gadrin's brother Mishina. **Mishina's Skull** has been enchanted by Zalazane to hold Mishina's spirit forever. Bring the skull back to Gadrin so it can be destroyed properly. Master Vornal needs four Intact Makura Eyes and eight Crawler Mucus for **A Solvent Spirit**. Vel'rin Fang asks you to hunt more **Practical Prey** for more practical reasons. He asks you to bring four Durotar Tiger Furs to stock his supplies.

There's a great deal to do. Start by hunting the crawlers and makura on your way to the islands. There will be plenty of time to get them, so don't worry about finishing it just yet. Head to the islands and search for the tigers and raptor nests. Stay on the smaller islands until you finish Practical Prey and Break a Few Eggs. This gives you time to get some experience and look for adventurers to join in attacking Zalazane's island.

Swimming With The Fishes

Crawlers and makura are underwater creatures. As such they have no need for air and can move much faster than you in the water. Pull them to the surface to avoid suffocating during a long fight and have ranged attacks ready if they run from you.

Once you have a couple adventurers with you, strike out to the largest island. On the southeast side, there is a camp near a small hill. Zalazane patrols this camp, protected by the Hexed and Voodoo Trolls. He guards the skulls on the hill. Pull the trolls one at a time until you can pull Zalazane to your party and his doom. Decapitate the monster and collect Mishina's Skull from the circle of power on the hill. Continue killing the trolls on the island until your quest is complete.

Inventory Full?

It's been a good while since you were near a merchant and your inventory shows it. Once your inventory is full you can't pick up any more items, including quest items. Take the time to destroy some of the less lucrative items in your inventory when you need room for quest items.

Less lucrative items are items of lowest quality and lowest armor (grey colored). This means grey cloth items are often the first to be dropped. If you don't need the food or drink for recovery purposes, these are also prime candidates.

Once the more difficult quests are complete, take the time to finish hunting the less intelligent enemies before returning to Sen'jin Village with swelled bags and pride. Gather the rewards for all your hard work and head north once again to **Report to Orgnil** in Razorhill.

CENTRAL DUROTAR

Razor Hill is built in the center of Durotar. The road north leads to Orgrimmar, the road west leads to The Barrens, the road south leads to The Valley of Trials, while east…well, there really isn't anything east.

Give the eggs to the cook, and report to Orgnil. Orgnil is rather upset and immediately orders the death of Fizzle, the one causing these **Dark Storms**. Gar'thok, on the second floor of the bunker, has quests for you. He asks you to **Vanquish the Betrayers**, and slow the quilboar **Encroachment**. Accept his quests, take care of in-town errands, and head out the south gates to Tiragarde Keep.

Investing in Your Future

With so much time spent between towns and so much killing being done, your backpack tends to fill up quickly. Consider speaking with the General Supplies merchant in the Razor Hill Barracks. He sells bags as well. These aren't inexpensive, but they allow you to carry more loot home. More loot sold means more money. The bag will more than make up the cost.

Show the Kul Tiras that their treachery will not go unpunished by slaying ten Sailors, eight Marines, and Lieutenant Benedict, their leader. Kill your way into the keep and climb the stairs. While in the open, the humans running is of little consequence, it can mean your death inside the keep. Reinforcements aren't far off and you must stop them quickly or face a fight against several opponents.

Once in the hallway atop the stairs, turn left and take the ramp up to the highest room. Lieutenant Benedict stands guarded by several marines. Pull the marines near the doorway one at a time before engaging Benedict and his final guard. Loot the body for his key and take the right path and head to the roof. Open Benedict's Chest and examine the aged envelope within. Take **The Admiral's Orders** to Gar'Thok.

With the leadership of Tiragarde Keep dead, it's time to pick up the pieces **From The Wreckage…** Garthok wants you to recover three Gnomish Tools from the shipwrecks off the coast of Tiragarde Keep and deliver **The Admiral's Orders** to Nazgrel in Orgrimmar. Sell your excess loot and head east to the ocean, gather the tools, then return.

Take the east road out of Razor Hill. To the south are camps of Razormane Quilboars and Scouts. To the north are Razormane Dustrunners and Battleguards. Kill four of each before returning to Gar'Thok for your reward.

NORTHERN DUROTAR

With work at Razor Hill done, continue north toward Orgrimmar. Follow the road through the canyons until you find a goblin on the side of the road beside a cart. Rezlak is upset with the harpies in the area. These **Winds of the Desert** keep attacking the caravans and stealing the supplies. He needs you to retrieve five Sacks of supplies from the harpies. Head southwest and visit the Tor'kren Farm. Misha's son Kron has been **Lost But Not Forgotten**. She asks you to look for some sign of him along the river. Assure her you will and travel directly west to the harpy canyon. Collect the sacks, then speak with Rezlak again.

With the supplies recovered, Rezlak employs you in **Securing the Lines**. He wants you to kill 12 Dustwind Savages and 8 Dustwind Storm Witches. Accept his quest and travel south to Drygulch Ravine. Travel through the tunnel and begin your killing spree. Return to Rezlak when the deed is done.

Gather a force and head to Thunder Ridge. It's time to stop Fizzle once and for all. Take your party to the southern entrance to Thunder Ridge. Fight your way past the lizards slowly until you are looking into the small alcove the Burning Blade have taken as their own. Pull Fizzle's guards one at a time and kill them outside the alcove. When Fizzle is alone, teach him the meaning of fear and take his claw from his dead body. Take the claw to Orgnil in Razor Hill and learn of **Margoz**.

ORGRIMMAR AND PREPARING FOR RAGEFIRE CHASM

Take the road north and complete your journey to Orgrimmar. Take the time to set your hearthstone here, visit your class trainer, and sell excess loot before heading to Thrall's Chambers in the Valley of Wisdom.

Orgrimmar Points of Interest

Location	Useful Stores/NPCs
Valley of Spirits	Mage/Portal Trainer, Priest Trainer, First Aid Trainer
Valley of Strength	Windrider Master, Reagent Vendor, Inn, Auction House, Mailbox
The Drag	Leatherworking Trainer, Skinning Trainer, Tailoring Trainer, Herbalism Trainer, Enchanting Trainer, Alchemy Trainer, Cooking Trainer, Mailbox
Cleft of Shadows	Rogue Trainer, Warlock Trainer, Demon Trainer, Poison Vendor, Reagent Vendor, Ragefire Chasm Entrance
Valley of Wisdom	Shaman Trainer, Thrall
Valley of Honor	Warrior Trainer, Hunter Trainer, Blacksmithing Trainer, Engineering Trainer, Mining Trainer, Fishing Trainer, Weaponmaster

Deliver the Admiral's Orders and speak with Thrall. He asks you to help him uncover **Hidden Enemies** within Orgrimmar itself. To begin, you need to get a Lieutenant's Insignia from Skull Rock. Accept the mission and leave Orgrimmar.

Travel southeast and speak with Margoz, who has work for you in **Skull Rock** as well. He wants you to gather six Searing Collars from the cultists inside and bring them to him. Travel to the northeast and enter the cave. If there are others around, recruit their assistance.

Take the cave slowly and avoid fights with more than one enemy when you can. Many of the cultists have mastered the ability to control demons and have them at their beck and call. Kill the cultist before focusing on the pet. Work you way to the back collecting collars. A dark painted orc named Gazz'uz who has been leading the Burning Blade. Kill him and take the Burning Eye of Shadow from him. Take it to Neeru Fireblade in Orgrimmar who knows more about **Burning Shadows**.

Return to Thrall with the insignia to receive your next task. Thrall needs you to deceive Neeru Fireblade into believing you are a member of the Burning Blade. Gather as much information as you can about the **Hidden Enemies** before returning to Thrall.

Neeru takes the Eye of Burning Shadow from you and rewards you for its collection. Speak to him about **Slaying the Beast** within Ragefire Chasm. He wants you to bring him the heart of Taragaman the Hungerer. With all the formalities finished, tell Neeru that he may speak frankly and listen to him. Continue pumping him for information until you've found what Thrall wanted you to. High-tail it back to Thrall to squeal on Neeru.

With the new information, your role as a spy is at an end. Thrall tasks you with the destruction of the **Hidden Enemies** beneath Orgrimmar. He wants Bazzalan and Jergosh the Invoker dead.

Congratulations on your success in Durotar. Peons are taking fewer naps, the Trolls have some peace of mind returned to them, and even the glare of the sun seems less burdensome. There is still more to do to the west in The Barrens or across the seas in the Silverpine Forest. But what of the Burning Blade and the Shadow Council? Treachery directly beneath the capital of the Horde can not go unchallenged, but those are adventures for another day.

MULGORE

The Tauren, once a nomadic people hunted by the centaur, have taken up residence within the grassy meadows of Mulgore. They walk paths closely intertwined with the Earth Mother and the way of the hunt is a right of passage for all Tauren. Through hunting the beasts of the land and making a place for themselves in the cycle of life, the Tauren gain a greater understanding of the world around them. With the help of Thrall, the Tauren were able to drive the centaur out of Mulgore. The Tauren have gained a home where they can raise their children in safety and they seek to repay the favor.

Legend

1	Lift	6	Stonebull Lake	11	Winterhoof Water Well	16	Wildmane Water Well	21	Spirit Rise
2	Camp Narache	7	Palemane Camps	12	The Venture Co. Mine	17	The Golden Plains	22	Elder Rise
3	Well	8	Palemane Rock	13	Ravaged Caravan	18	Windfury Ridge	23	Hunter Rise
4	Seer Graytongue	9	The Rolling Plains	14	Thunderhorn Water Well	19	Red Rocks		
5	Brambleblade Ravine	10	Bloodhoof Village	15	Bael'Dun Digsite	20	Thunder Bluff		

YOUR FIRST DAY

The Tauren have built their home in harmony with Mulgore. The gentle breeze make some think of paradise and relaxation, but the Tauren are constantly on a path of both betterment and enlightenment. The Tauren stewardship of this land can be seen in the lush fields of grass, prevalence of herbs, and the roaming herds of kodo, but there are those that seek to pillage this rich land. dwarves and Venture Company alike dig deep into the earth to steal the copper.

CAMP NARACHE AND THE RITE OF STRENGTH

Camp Narache is where all who seek citizenship in Thunder Bluff begin. The teachers help you take your first steps in the Rites of the Earthmother and teach you how to learn from the world around you.

Grull Hawkwind stands before you and wastes no time with meaningless chatter. As **The Hunt Begins**, Grull wants you to collect seven Plainstrider Feathers and Plainstrider meat. This begins your training and helps restock the village supplies. Accept his quest and move northwest to Chief Hawkwind's tent. Chief Hawkwind asks **A Humble Task** of you. His mother set out this morning to fetch water from the well, and he would like you to check on her. Assure him you will and leave the village to the southeast.

There are many Plainstriders on the way to the well and around it. Kill these as you move to speak with Greatmother Hawkwind. The Greatmother has arrived safely at the well and even drawn the water, she is just resting

before making the trip back up the hill to the village. She asks you to take a pitcher from the well and take it to her son. The pitchers are sitting on the edge of the well and can be picked up by right-clicking them.

Hunt the Plainstriders until you have enough meat and feathers. Avoid going far to the east as the Battle Boars are aggressive and attack you on sight. With the supplies collected, head back to the village.

Grull is pleased with your prowess and **The Hunt Continues**. He wants you to hunt the Mountain Cougars to the south and collect ten of their pelts for clothing and tents. He also has a message from your class trainer. Accept both quests and take a moment to visit your trainer as you've gained level 2 and have new abilities waiting for you.

Chief Hawkwind is impressed with your kindness and begins the **Rites of the Earthmother**. First you must seek out Seer Graytongue to the south. Accept his quest and head south.

Hunt the Mountain Cougars as you move up the hill toward Seer Graytongue's camp. Graytongue sets you on the first rite, the **Rite of Strength**. To gain respect, you must slay the enemies of the tribe. Bring 12 Bristleback Belts to Chief Hawkwind from the quilboars in Brambleblade Ravine to the east. Accept the quest and finish hunting the cougars.

With the pelts received, Grull asks you to trim some of **The Battleboars** from the hunting grounds and bring back the parts for some food. Brave Windfeather patrols nearby and has a task for you. The quilboars have been waging a war against the Tauren for some time and Brave Windfeather wants it to end. She charges you with bringing her the head of their leader—she asks you to **Break Sharptusk!**

58

As you're traveling, consider killing any enemies that are your level or lower. The enemies around Camp Narache are fairly weak and the additional experience and usable equipment make it worth your time.

Prepare yourself, then travel east. Slay the Battleboars for their flanks and snouts as you enter the Brambleblade Ravine. Once inside, slay the quilboars and take their belts as proof. Fight your way east to the very heart of their land. Make them pay for the suffering they have caused. Heal this scar upon the land.

Most of the quilboars in the area know only how to attack with their fists and their weapons, but there are ones that are more intelligent. The Bristleback Shamans have learned the use of magic and attack from range, if allowed. These can be easily spotted by their blue robes and should be killed quickly as they can do quite a bit of damage.

Atop a rise in the heart of the Bristleback lands, stands a large tent. From here Chief Sharptusk Thornmantle leads the war against the Tauren. Slay first his guards, then remove his head. Much work has been done this day, but there is more to do. Leave the tent and head south to a cave in the mountain.

Inventory Full?

It's been a good while since you were near a merchant and your inventory shows it. Once your inventory is full you can't pick up any more items, including quest items. Take the time to destroy some of the less lucrative items in your inventory when you need room for quest items.

Less lucrative items are items of lowest quality and lowest armor (grey colored). This means grey cloth items are often the first to be dropped. If you don't need the food or drink for recovery purposes, these are also prime candidates.

Sharptusk's younger sibling, Squealer Thornmantle, sits in the cave guarding the plans his chief has drafted. Kill Squealer and take the plans from the floor. Continue hunting until all your quests are complete, then use your hearthstone to return to the village triumphant.

Speak with your teachers and be rewarded for your hard work. Once you have room in your inventory, right-click the Dirt-Stained Map and learn of the **Attack on Camp Narache**. Take your findings to Chief Hawkwind. He gives you a totem to take to Baine Bloodhoof so that you may continue the **Rites of the Earthmother**.

BLOODHOOF VILLAGE AND THE RITE OF VISION

Your time at Camp Narache is at an end. You have the Totem of Hawkwind to show your progress. Follow the path south and east until you come to the border of Red Cloud Mesa. Antur Fallow stands nervously. She has **A Task Unfinished** as she is working on the Rite of Strength. As you are already heading to Bloodhoof Village, take the Bundle of Furs there for her.

Deliver the furs to Innkeeper Kauth and ask him to make this inn your home. This sets your hearthstone to return you here. Next Speak with Baine Bloodhoof. He tells you of the **Rite of Vision** and asks you to help him deal with the gnolls in the area. The gnolls have moved into Mulgore, but have not respected the Tauren attempts at **Sharing the Land**. He asks you to kill ten Palemane Tanners, eight Palemane Skinners, and five Palemane Poachers.

There are many people with tasks for you. Wander the village and collect all the quests. Mull Thunderhorn asks you to help him with a **Poison Water** problem, Harken Windtotem speaks of **Swoop Hunting**, while Zarlman Two-Moons continues your **Rite of Vision**, Maur Raincaller was attacked and poisoned by **Mazzranache** and Ruul Eagletalon teaches of the **Dangers of the Windfury**.

Taking Up Skinning?

Only a few of the professions are represented in Bloodhoof Village. If you intend to become adept at the art of skinning, now is a good time to start. Speak with the Skinning Trainer and purchase a skinning knife.

Collect the plethora of quests and head south out of the village. Keep your eyes open for the Ambercorns as you move about. They are small pinecone-like objects usually found near trees.

The gnolls have their camps against the cliffs to the south. They are very aggressive and have many ranged attackers. Kill them one at a time and don't be afraid to rest between fights. Kill the gnolls at the first camp and move east to the next. You need parts from all the animals out here, so kill everything in your path.

With the required number of gnolls dead, move north to the Winterhoof Water Well. The Venture Company has taken residence around it, but you need two Wellstones. Kill the hirelings around the edge until you can reach the wellstones. Collect what you need and return to Bloodhoof Village killing everything along the way.

Visit your trainer and learn any new abilities possible and speak with Baine Bloodhoof about the gnoll situation. He rewards you and asks for additional assistance. A **Dwarven Digging** group has been recklessly harvesting metal in the west. Accept the quest and speak with Zarlman Two-Moons. He gives you the Water of the Seers to consume at the bonfire to produce a vision. Do so, but don't follow the visionary wolf. The wolf leads you to a cave in the north that you will be visiting soon enough to complete your **Rite of Vision**.

Investing in Your Future

With so much time spent between towns and so much killing being done, your backpack tends to fill up quickly. Consider speaking with the General Goods merchant in Bloodhoof Village. He sells bags as well. These aren't inexpensive, but they allow you to carry more loot home. More loot sold means more money. The bag pays for itself fast.

Sell any excess loot and head southeast toward the Windfury Harpies. As you complete the quests, keep track of which enemies you still need to kill. A good policy, however, is to kill everything in your path. You can always use the money and experience after all.

The enemies on the way to the harpies are higher level than any you've fought so far and most are aggressive. Take care to only engage them one at a time and only after you've recovered your health and mana.

Collect the Windfury Talons until you have all eight of them. Keep fighting on the edge of the cliffs as the wolves below are much higher level then

the harpies. When the quest is complete, use your hearthstone to return to Bloodhoof Village and speak to Ruul and Mull.

With the items you've gathered, Mull creates a totem for the **Winterhoof Cleansing**. Take the totem and head to the water well to end the poisoning. Start by killing the hirelings around the edge, then slowly kill your way to the water well. Use the totem to cleanse the well and return to Mull. There are other water wells that need cleansing and he needs materials for each. He needs six Stalker and Cougar Claws to craft the **Thunderhorn Totem** next.

Your next target is the Bael'Dun Digsite. Cross the river and head northwest. Kill any targets you still need for quests (swoops are likely one) as you move to the cliffs. The dwarves present a new problem for you. While you've fought aggressive enemies that run for help before, the Bael'dun Appraisers are healers and can draw fights out. Pull the diggers away from the healers one at a time and dispatch them. When a healer is alone, throw everything you have at it as quickly as possible. If you have abilities that interrupt casting, be prepared to use them.

Watch for other adventurers in the area and group together as this quest is made easier with more hands. Gather the Prospector's Picks from the dwarves as you kill them. When you have five, move to the forge at the back of the camp. Use each of the tools to break them. Exit the camp and turn north.

Thunder Bluff can be seen in the distance, but that is not your current destination. Move north past another area of harpies and watch for a cave in the eastern cliffs. Seer Wiserunner has been waiting for you since the lupine vision arrived. He is here to set you upon the **Rite of Wisdom**. Accept his quest and travel east, across the road, to hunt the Prairie Stalkers and Flatland Cougars on your way back to Bloodhoof Village.

Turn in your quests, get your rewards, repair, sell excess loot, train if you need to, then follow the road east. Morin Cloudstalker patrols the road and has a task for you. He needs you to search **The Ravaged Caravan** near the lake and find why the Venture Company are trying to salvage it. The caravan sits smoldering on the northeast edge of Stonebull Lake. Kill any cougars and stalkers you need to finish **Thunderhorn Totem** while you're in the area.

Clear out the Venture Company workers and open the Sealed Supply Crate near the center fire. Return to Morin with what you've found. After examining the evidence you recovered, Morin has more work for you. **The Venture Co.** must be stopped and the best way to do that is to kill **Supervisor Fizsprocket** and many of the workers. Morin wants 14 Venture Co. Workers and 6 Venture Co. Supervisors killed and Fizsprocket's Clipboard pried from his cold, dead hands. Move to the Venture Co. Mine.

The enemies inside the mine are very dangerous as they are close together and it's difficult to get fights with only one enemy. Gather any adventurers you see in the area and venture in as a group. Make sure everyone in your party is rested before starting each engagement.

Every level (starting at level ten), you gain a Talent Point. These can be used to increase your abilities or learn new ones. Open your talent window (defaulted to 'n'). There are three panels in the window. Look at each talent carefully before choosing as once you spend your points, it costs gold to unlearn them. There is more about the benefits of each talent in the class section.

Thunder Bluff is a rather impressive town. Exploring all of it would take quite a bit of effort, but you're not the first to get lost in this city. The guards are accustomed to newcomers needing directions and they give them freely. To find things in a hurry, ask a guard and they will plot it on your mini-map.

When you have his clipboard and have killed the help, return to Morin for your rewards. Make a quick trip to Bloodhoof to sell, train, repair, and speak with Mull. With the totem complete the time for the **Thunderhorn Cleansing** is at hand. Skorn Whitecloud talks of **The Hunter's Way** and suggests you gather four Flatland Prowler Claws and present them to Melor Stonehoof as a gesture of willingness to learn.

Cross the river to the north and begin clearing the Thunderhorn Water Well. Kill the Venture Co. workers and cleanse the water well and return for your reward and a list of ingredients for the **Wildmane Totem**. Take care of any final errands and head north to Red Rock.

Thunder Bluff Points of Interest

Location	Useful Stores/NPCs
Bottom Central Rise	Weaponmaster, Auction House, Bank, Mail Box, Blacksmithing Trainer, Mining Trainer, Inn
Middle Central Rise	Tailoring Trainer, Leatherworking Trainer, Skinning Trainer, Herbalism Trainer, Alchemy Trainer, Enchanting Trainer
Top Central Rise	Cairn Bloodhoof, Cooking Trainer, Fishing Trainer
Hunter Rise	Warrior Trainer, Hunter Trainer, Pet Trainer
Elder Rise	Druid Trainer, Magatha Grimtotem
Spirit Rise	Shaman Trainer, First Aid Trainer
Tower	Windrider Master

THUNDER BLUFF AND THE RITE OF WISDOM

Once you cross into the Golden Plains, begin hunting the Flatland Prowlers and Prairie Wolf Alphas as you move northeast. Lorekeeper Raintotem sits by a fire south of Red Rocks. He charges you with removing the interlopers from **A Sacred Burial**.

Move north and clear your way through the vagabonds to the Ancestral Spirit. Your Rites of the Earthmother are now complete. The spirit informs you that it is time to **Journey Into Thunder Bluff**. Return to Lorekeeper Raintotem south of here for your reward.

Turn downhill and head deeper into the Golden Plains. Hunt the wolves and cougars until you've finished **The Hunter's Way** and the **Wildmane Totem**. Once both quests are complete, hearthstone back to Bloodhoof Village and speak with Mull about the **Wildmane Cleansing**.

Take the road north to Thunder Bluff. The road ends at a set of lifts that take people far above the plains of Mulgore and to the majestic mesas of the Tauren capital.

As all Tauren classes and professions are represented in Thunder Bluff, it's a good place for training. If you're picking up crafting professions, seek out the trainers while you Speak with Cairn Bloodhoof and Melor Stonehoof. Cairn is on the highest level of the central rise and Melor is on Hunter Rise.

Eyahn Eagletalon stands at the lifts with a problem. He's behind in his **Preparation for Ceremony** and needs you to collect six Azure Feathers and six Bronze Feathers from the harpies northwest of Thunder Bluff. Accept his quest and continue on to speak with Melor and Cairn. Cairn has one last task for you to complete your **Rites of the Earthmother**. He wants you to hunt the mighty Arra'chea.

Take the western lifts down to Mulgore and head northwest to the harpies. Hunt them for their feathers before moving northeast to the Wildmane Well. All the harpies are casters, so have your interrupt abilities ready.

With the well cleansed, there are only a few things left to do. Travel east and hunt Arra'chea. She wanders a great deal, but is usually found within the Golden Plains. When you find her, clear any aggressive animals first or wait until she moves away from them. Engage Arra'chea and prove yourself to Cairn.

Take her horn and complete your **Rites of the Earthmother**. Return to Thunder Bluff to turn in your quests and pick up any you find before traveling to Bloodhoof. Tell Mull of the cleansing of the final well before following the road east to the Barrens.

Congratulations on your success in Mulgore. Kodo are breeding happily, the Tauren of Thunder Bluff recognize your name, and the spirits know you. New challenges wait in the Barrens and even in the Ragefire Chasm beneath Orgrimmar, but those are adventures for another day.

TIRISFAL GLADES

Tirisfal Glades has seen better days. The mighty city of Lordaeron has fallen, demons encroach, and the last vestige of humanity has declared war on anything that isn't part of the Scarlet Crusade. What keeps this land to succumbing to anarchy? From below the ruins of Lordaeron, the Banshee Queen commands the Forsaken. Though killed by the plague and never granted death, the Forsaken have rebelled. They have chosen to reclaim Tirisfal Glades and halt the advance of the Scourge.

Legend

1	Deathknell	5	Stillwater Pond	9	Garren's Haunt	13	Balnir Farmstead
2	Night Web's Hollow	6	Agamand Mills	10	Ruins of Lordaeron	14	The Bulwark
3	Solliden Farmstead	7	Cold Hearth Manor	11	Undercity (Capital City)	15	Crusader Outpost
4	Nightmare Vale	8	Brill	12	Brightwater Lake	16	Venomweb Vale

17	Faol's Rest	20	Zeppelin Tower
18	Whispering Gardens- The Scarlet Monastery	21	The North Coast
19	Scarlet Watch Post	22	Gunther's Retreat

YOUR FIRST DAY

Lordaeron and the other establishments within Tirisfal Glades had been sacked, burned, and forgotten. The land was assumed to be a stronghold of the Scourge, but the will of Sylvanas Windrunner shattered the plans of the Scourge and brought a major player to the table. The Forsaken have chosen to ally with the Horde in an attempt to stave off their destruction. While the Forsaken are a power to be reckoned with, there are many that wish them nothing short of a final rest.

The Bulwark holds the plagued wildlife and forces of the Scourge from seeping in from the Plaguelands, but the war with the living isn't far off. A bastion of the Scarlet Crusade has survived against the Scourge, and now survives against the Forsaken.

A COLD AWAKENING

You awaken much like all undead…in a crypt. You not only took ill, but you died and were buried. The flesh has rotted from parts of your body, but you are still mobile. Ascend the stairs and speak with Undertaker Mordo about your **Rude Awakening**.

Mordo stands at the opening to the crypt and directs the newly awakened to Shadow Priest Sarvis in Deathknell. Accept his quest and follow the stone path into what's left of town. Once through the gate, turn left, then enter the remains of the town church to find Sarvis.

Sarvis tells you more about what's happening. He relates how not everyone who was killed by the plagues awoke as Forsaken. Many became **Mindless Ones**. These poor souls have no will of their own and are merely tools of the Lich King. They must be destroyed. Sarvis tasks you with destroying eight Mindless Zombies and just as many Wretched Zombies.

Exit the building and turn north. Just down the street, guards are keeping the zombies at bay, but are terribly outnumbered by the shambling forces. There is so little left in the minds of these enemies that they do not attack you until you attack them. Engage and kill the zombies before returning to Sarvis for your reward.

Sarvis congratulates you on your decision to take up the banner of the Banshee Queen and fight for the Forsaken. There is more to do, however. He wants you to join the others **Rattling the Rattlecages**. The skeletons are tougher than the zombies, but need to be removed from Tirisfal all the same. Sarvis also has a message from your class trainer. Accept both of these quests and seek your trainer for new abilities and speak with Novice Elreth.

Elreth spends her unlife helping those enlisting in the military. She is willing to make you some armor if you bring her parts of **The Damned** in the area. Six Scavenger Paws and Duskbat Wings net you some experience and a piece of armor. The bats and dogs can be found in abundance to the northwest.

Traveling the Bloody Way

As you are traveling, consider killing any enemies that are your level or lower. The enemies around Deathknell are fairly weak and the additional experience and usable equipment make it worth your time.

Kill the skeletons as you exit town to the north, then hunt the dogs and bats. When you've harvested enough parts, return to town and finish killing the skeletons. With both quests complete and your bags full, return to the ruined church and speak with Sarvis and Elreth for your rewards.

Elreth had a friend named Marla who was murdered by her husband after he succumbed to the plague and joined the Lich King's forces. Though now Forsaken, Elreth wants help granting **Marla's Last Wish** which was to be buried beside her husband. She's buried in the cemetery, but her husband still roams as a slave to the Lich King. Elreth wants you to destroy him and bury his remains with Marla.

Inventory Full?

It's been a good while since you were near a merchant and your inventory shows it. Once your inventory is full you can't pick up any more items, including quest items. Take the time to destroy some of the less lucrative items in your inventory when you need room for quest items.

Less lucrative items are items of lowest quality and lowest armor (grey in color). This means grey cloth items are often the first to be dropped. If you don't need the food or drink for recovery purposes, these are also prime candidates.

With the mine being brought under control, it's time to use your talents elsewhere. **The Scarlet Crusade** has set up a camp to the southeast. There is little doubt in anyone's mind that they intend to attack Deathknell. Take the fight to them first by collecting 12 Scarlet Armbands from their corpses.

Leave town to the east and look for the tents. The Scarlet Crusade attack on sight, so be watchful as you approach the camp. Pull the enemies one at a time and avoid entering the camp as they also help each other. The Scarlet Initiates are mages and will be reluctant to come to you. Be ready to kill them quickly. With the required armbands, return to Arren for your reward and your next assignment.

The numbers at the Scarlet camp have been lessened. Now you have a chance to strike at **The Red Messenger**. Meven Korgal is in possession of the Scarlet Documents. While unsure of the contents of the documents, Arren knows that it's better to have them then allow Meven to keep them. Find Meven near the tent at the southern edge of the camp. Pry the documents from his cold, dead fingers.

After reading through the documents, Arren finds some **Vital Intelligence** that must be taken to Brill. He can find more work for you here, but getting this information to Brill is more important. Take a moment to visit your trainer and sell any excess loot before taking the road north.

Take a moment to stop at the merchant in the house across the street to sell your excess loot and speak with Executor Arren. He is recruiting aid in clearing the spiders from **Night Web's Hollow** so the gold mining can be restarted. He rewards you if you kill ten Young Night Web Spiders and eight Night Web Spiders. Remember to equip any extra bags you've found and head north to speak with Deathguard Saltain.

Saltain's attitude might be a bit rough, but his goals are in tune with the Banshee Queen's. He's organizing the recruits in **Scavenging Deathknell** for equipment for the newly risen. He wants you to collect six Scavenged Goods from the ruined town and return. With several quests in your log, it's time to head out. Search the buildings of Deathknell for the boxes as you head north.

Follow the road as it bends east. At a northern turn of the road, there is a ruined camp and several named skeletons and zombies shambling about. Find Samuel Fipps and give him the final rest so many have been denied by the Lich King. Carefully collect his remains and store them in your pack before turning northwest and traveling to Night Web's Hollow.

The Young Night Web Spiders are plentiful outside the mine and are still fairly docile. They won't attack you until you strike first. The Night Web Spiders, however, stay inside the mine and are quite aggressive. They attack without any provocation and care must be exercised as you move through

the mine. At the very back of the cave sits the Night Web Matriarch. Though you have no specific quest to slay her, she has a cloak that would be very nice to have. With the spiders trimmed back, use your hearthstone to teleport back to the crypt.

Run back to Deathknell and speak to Arren and Saltain for your rewards. Directly behind Arren is the graveyard. In the first row is Marla's grave. Place Samuel's Remains there to fulfill Marla's Last Wish and speak with Elreth for your reward. Take a moment to speak with your trainer before Arren gives you more work.

GUARDING WHAT'S LEFT

Calvin Montague stands at the palisade along the road. He has a letter to be delivered to Brill. Accept his quest and continue along the road until you find Deathguard Simmer. Simmer wants you to steal ten pumpkins from a nearby farm. It sounds easy, but don't do it just yet. Accept the quest and continue to Brill. Watch for aggressive enemies near the road as you travel.

Gordo, an abomination, patrols the road. Accept **Gordo's Task**. He needs three Gloom Weeds picked up and taken to Brill. The weeds are near the road, so take the time to pick them before continuing to Brill. Watch for the aggressive demon dogs nearby and avoid venturing too far into the woods.

There are a number of people to speak with in Brill. Junior Apothecary Holland, in the graveyard, should be your first. It seems Gordo isn't very bright, Holland needs you to collect ten **Doom Weed**. Speak with Deathguard Dillinger to receive **A Putrid Task**. Inside the first building on your right, Apothecary Johaan has work for you as well. He's working on **A New Plague** and tells you to collect five Darkhound Blood. Continue speaking with people in Brill and collecting all the quests. The Wanted sign behind Executor Zygand shouldn't be ignored as it offers a reward for killing Maggot Eye.

Talk with Innkeeper Renee and have her make this inn your home. This allows you to teleport here using your hearthstone. If it is in your plan, pick up First Aid from the rather striking undead female near the entrance. With all your errands done and many quests in your log, leave town and head north toward Garren's Haunt.

Follow the fork in the road as it bends west. The **Graverobbers**, Rot Hide Gnolls, have been stealing the corpses from the mass graves to bolster the Scourge's armies. Kill eight Rot Hide Graverobbers, five Rot Hide Mongrels, and collect eight of their Embalming Ichor.

Once you've killed the graverobbers, continue north to Garren's Haunt. As you move through the woods, watch for **Doom Weed** near the bases of the trees. Patroling the field are Rot Hide Gnolls and Mongrels. Enter the field carefully as the gnolls are very aggressive and attack at even the slightest hint of your presence. Kill the mongrels as you move north across the field. In a small building stands Maggot Eye. He is far too powerful for you to attack alone, so look for other adventurers in the area and form a group to kill him.

With Maggot Eye's Paw, the Embalming Ichor, and the Doom Weed, return to Brill. There are several people you should talk for your rewards. Sell any excess loot, pick up any new quests, and head west toward Solliden's Farmstead.

At the bridge, some of the Scourge have made their way into Tirisfal Glades. Take a few moments to kill the Rotting Dead and Ravaged Corpses. It's **A Putrid Task**, but someone's got to do it. Collect seven Putrid Claws from the bodies before continuing to Solliden's Farmstead.

Farmers guard the field while soldiers patrol the road. Kill the farmers as you harvest the pumpkins. Turn the farmstead into **Fields of Grief** by stealing ten Tirisfal Pumpkins. Continue west and show that you are **At War With The Scarlet Crusade** by slaying ten Scarlet Warriors.

Use your hearthstone or your feet to return to Brill and turn in your quests. Pick up any quests that become available, and visit your trainer if you've gained a level. See a merchant before heading to the bottom floor of the inn and giving the pumpkin to the Scarlet Zealot.

With so much in town taken care of, head southwest toward the Nightmare Vale. Hunt the darkhounds for samples of **A New Plague** and the duskbats to stave off **The Chill of Death**. The darkhounds attack from a great distance, so be watchful of them and avoid fighting more than one enemy at a time.

The Scarlet Crusade have taken the ruined tower and turned it into a bastion of zealotry. This cannot go on. Slay the guards outside the tower one at a time as you make your way closer. Take ten Scarlet Insignia Rings from their corpses as **Proof of Demise**.

Captain Perrine stands inside the tower with a bodyguard. Slay them both to show them the Forsaken are, and will always be, **At War With The Scarlet Crusade**. Finish killing the humans around the tower before heading back to Brill. Take the time to collect the Darkhound Blood and Duskbat Pelts before returning.

Stop at Abigail Shiel, by the wagon, to buy a single Coarse Thread and sell loot before turning in all your quests.

BURYING THE PAST

A number of the dead in Tirisfal have risen as servants of the Scourge. **The Mills Overrun** with mindless undead. Head west to grant them final rest. Collect five Notched Ribs and three Blackened Skulls as you destroy the servants of the Scourge.

Watch for Devlin Agamand as you travel **The Haunted Mills**. He patrols near the road approaching the mill and is slightly higher level than the enemies around him. Grab his remains and continue north. Certainly everyone has **Deaths in the Family**, but you are about to be the Agamand's personal reaper. Nissa is just inside the first house on the right side of the road. Take your time pulling the enemies out front as they can all attack at the same time.

Thurman and Gregor wander the mills long the path to the northwest. Collect all their remains and hunt for the ribs and skulls. When all is collected, hearthstone or walk back to Brill.

A Letter to Yvette

As you loot all the skeletons, watch for A Letter to Yvette. Right-click on it to start a quest that sends you back to Brill. How convenient!

UNDERCITY AND BUILDING A NEW FUTURE

Follow the road southeast from Brill. At the intersection, take the east road far enough to speak with Deathguard Linnea. Accept her quests and continue south to Undercity. Bethor is in the Magic Quarter waiting for you.

It's Big!

Undercity is rather impressive. Exploring all of it would take quite a bit of effort, but you're not the first to get lost in this city. The abominations are accustomed to newcomers needing directions and they give them freely. To find things in a hurry, ask a guard and they will plot it on your mini-map.

Undercity Points of Interest

Location	Useful Stores/NPCs
Trade Quarter	Auction House, Bank, Inn, Mailbox, Merchants, Bat Handler
Magic Quarter	Tailoring Trainer, Reagent Vendor, Mage Trainer, Portal Trainer, Warlock Trainer, Demon Trainer, Fishing Trainer
Rogues' Quarter	Poison Vendor, First Aid Trainer, Skinning Trainer, Leatherworking Trainer, Engineering Trainer, Forge, Anvil, Rogue Trainer
Apothecarium	Alchemy Trainer, Herbalism Trainer, Enchanting Trainer
Royal Quarter	Varimathras, Lady Sylvanas Windrunner
War Quarter	Mining Trainer, Weapon Master, Blacksmithing Trainer, Forge, Anvil, Warrior Trainer, Priest Trainer

You have a number of quests for eastern and northern Tirisfal Glades. Take the elevators back to the surface and follow the road east toward the Balnir Farmstead.

The Bulwark stops most of the Scourge from entering Tirisfal, but some slip past. Destory eight Bleeding Horrors and eight Wandering Spirits for the **Rear Guard Patrol**. The horrors don't move much, but the spirits wander a good bit so watch your back to avoid having one attack when you're already engaged.

Becoming More Talented

Every level (starting at level ten), you gain a Talent Point. These can be used to increase your abilities or learn new ones. Open your talent window (defaulted to 'n'). There are three panels in the window. Look at each talent carefully before choosing as once you spend your points, it costs gold to unlearn them. There is more about the benefits of each talent in the class section.

Once you've done your part to keep the Scrouge from Tirisfal, climb the cliff to the north and engage the Scarlet Crusade. Until these religious zealots are destroyed, the Forsaken are **At War With The Scarlet Crusade** and you are their favorite soldier. Kill the friars as you make your way to the tower. Captain Vachon is inside and needs to be shown the error of his ways.

The Scarlet Friars heal themselves and their compatriots. They must be killed quickly or interrupted to avoid long fights. Watch for others in the area and form a party to make this quest easier. With the leadership of another Scarlet outpost dead, head northwest to Brightwater Lake.

The Prodigal Lich lives on an island in Brightwater Lake surrounded by his own mindless protectors. Search through Gunther's books until you find his spellbook. Now it's north to the coast to work on **A New Plague**.

If one had never been to Tirisfal Glades, you might expect the coastline to be in better shape. The ocean is very large and the waves always tearing away at the plague that is gripping the land. It's a nice thought, but the beach is just as diseased as the rest of the land. It appears that even the ocean is powerless against such terrible magic.

Tear the fins off the murlocs you find. Watch for the oracles as they have mastered lightning magic and make your time at the beach difficult.

You Can't Fight Just One

Murlocs are notorious for their ability to bring an army to a one-on-one fight. When engaged, they immediately call any of their nearby friends to aid them. Pull the murlocs carefully and be ready to kill them quickly. At the first sign of losing the fight, they make tracks back for help.

If you weren't able to get a group to kill Maggot Eye earlier, stop by his shack now. You've gained a number of levels while he hasn't. With the five Vile Fin Scale samples, walk or hearthstone back to Brill to turn in your quests.

Begin another circuit by heading to Undercity. Speak with Bethor Iceshard again, then take the road east to speak with Linnea. Follow the path north from Linnea toward the Scarlet Monastery. When the path turns north, break east. Do not approach the Monastery, as the seat of the Scarlet Crusade is beyond your reach for quite some time. Enter the Venomweb Vale to continue gathering reagents for **A New Plague**. You need four Vicious Night Web Spider Venom and the spiders aren't likely to give it freely.

Venom in hand, follow the path north until it forks. Take the west fork toward the Scarlet Watch Post. Watch for other adventurers to join as you approach the Scarlet Watch Post.

Kill the guards as you approach the tower. Watch for the caster that patrols around the tower. Wait for her to come into range and eliminate her before engaging Captain Melrache and the Scarlet Bodyguards. The bodyguards are much lower level and can be killed quickly while Melrache is held by a warrior or combat controlled. Finish this portion of **At War With The Scarlet Crusade** and head southwest to Gunther's Retreat.

Gunther is grateful when you **Return the Book**, but he doesn't fully trust you. He gives you the task of **Proving Allegiance**. Grab a candle from the box at his feet and head to the south edge of the island. On a smaller island sits Lillith's Dinner Table. Place the candle on the table to summon Lillith Nefara and slay her. Return to Gunther to show that you are an enemy of the Scourge just as you've been telling him.

Return to Brill and help Johaan test **A New Plague** by giving it to the Captured Mountaineer in the inn. There is little else to be done in Brill. Head west to Agamand Mills and **The Family Crypt.**

Follow the path past the mills and over the bridge. The crypt is on the north side of the area. Kill the Wailing and Rotting Ancestors as you approach the crypt and descend into the depths. Take the crypt slowly as there are many wandering enemies and not a lot of space. Fights of two are almost guaranteed with fights of three or more being possible if you get careless or unlucky.

At the lowest room, Dargol stands with several ancestors. Pull the ancestors one at a time until Dargol stands alone. Collect Dargol's Skull and rest a

moment. There are likely to be enemies respawned behind you. If your hearthstone is up, teleport back to Brill. If not, fight your way out of the crypt and return by foot.

Congratulations on your success in Tirisfal Glades. The dead are waking safely, a new plague designed to threaten all life is in the works, and even the Scarlet Crusade seems to have receded a bit because of such fine efforts. New challenges wait in Silverpine Forest to the south, in the Ragefire Chasm beneath Orgrimmar, and in the Barrens across the ocean, but those are adventures for another day.

Learning About the World

A Glimpse of the World

Setting foot into unknown lands is a dangerous prospect. The lands of Azeroth have been ravaged by wars and plagues, but peace is finding footholds and the land is healing…in places.

This section gives a brief description of each of the areas. While role-players gain the greatest use, even general gamers will find the information useful as it influences quest lines, ongoing wars, and other matters of import.

THE EASTERN KINGDOMS

Long past are the days of Lordaeron standing proud and strong. Deadly plagues have divided the population into the infected and those who fear infection. Caught between religious zealotry, and mindless undead, the races living here do so only through constant vigilance.

LORDAERON

Based under the ruins of Lordaeron, the Forsaken have thrown off the shackles of the Scourge and retained their own will. The Forsaken have tossed their lot in with the Horde…for now. This gives them aid as Dwarves and Humans are constantly seeking to take Hillsbrad to the south. This war has seen many shifts in power and is unlikely to be resolved anytime soon.

A threat even closer to home shows itself in the Scarlet Crusade. Many of this religious order have declared war on anyone and anything that is not a member. While their methods are disdainful, their fear is echoed by the Forsaken. How does one defend themselves from the mindless undead legions of the Scourge?

With only the Bulwark outpost between Tirisfal Glades and the Plaguelands, Lordaeron is infested with wildlife that has succumbed to one plague or another. The previously gentle wildlife has turned bloodthirsty and violent. The constant threat of their surroundings makes it more difficult for the Forsaken to concentrate on malevolent intelligent dangers. The forces of Dalaran across the lake and the mage Arugal in Silverpine are threats far more dangerous than any set of poisoned fangs.

KHAZ MODAN

The Dwarves of Ironforge patrol the lands of Khaz Modan devoutly, but their numbers are spread thin. Incursions of Ogres and Troggs slip past and are allowed to fester while the army is busy elsewhere. Word of attacks comes from all over the Dwarven lands. Even the outpost of Dun Algaz has been attacked and communications have been lost.

Perhaps this is a fitting view of the Dwarves themselves. The Dark Iron Dwarves, having split off hundreds of years ago in an event known as the War of the Three Hammers, have become a considerable threat to Ironforge and the Alliance.

After fleeing from their home of Gnomeregan, the Gnomes have been taken in by the Dwarves. Release of dangerous toxins researched for the war against the Troggs have made Gnomeregan unlivable and any Gnomes unfortunate to be caught inside…quite insane. Though exiled from their home, the Gnomes continue to fight at the side of the Dwarves. An underground tram connecting Stormwind and Ironforge has been completed and makes movement between the cities much easier.

Azeroth

The glimmering white walls of Stormwind stand proud and tall, but its military is scattered and worn. The Defias Brotherhood, a group of thieves and brigands, has grown to such strength that many wonder why the king has been absent on the matter. Combined with the Orcs, Gnolls, and walking dead, the armies of

Stormwind are kept from mobilizing due to Lady Katrana Prestor's influence.

The coast of Westfall has come under attack. Defias have taken Moonbrook while an army of Gnolls slowly threatens the common peoples. The local militia has pulled back to try and hold Sentinel Hill, but they are vastly outnumbered. Word has been sent to the capital, but no more troops have arrived.

The peaceful land of Elwynn Forest is no longer. The guards of Stormwind keep the road safe, but much of Westfall lacks adequate protection. The nuisances of Kobolds, Murloc, and brigands have become full dangers.

Signs of trouble are stirring in both Stormwind and Duskwood. With so many Defias thrown into the Stockades so quickly, the guards find themselves outnumbered and out-muscled. The guards that made it to the surface have erected a chokepoint at the exit, but the Stockades are in the hands of the Defias now.

Something stirs in Duskwood. The dead of Ravenhill Cemetery are no longer content to lie buried. The Worgen have taken several farms and attack any who draw near. The Night Watch is comprised of concerned citizens, but without the help of the Stormwind guards, can these warriors keep Darkshire safe?

Kalimdor

Many races have made Kalimdor home. The Orcs, Trolls, and Tauren have carved a home from the rock, but peace escapes them still. Night Elves, Ogres, and Demons all threaten the homelands of the Horde.

Central Kalimdor

Most of the Horde have carved homes out of Central Kalimdor. Built within in the canyons on northern Durotar stands Orgrimmar. The Orcs and Darkspear Trolls have made a home in the red sands and thrived. Centaur infestations and even the cult of the Burning Blade are small dangers to the unity Orgrimmar symbolizes.

To the west lies Mulgore; a lush and rich land. Thrall helped the Tauren claim this land from the centaur and that aid will be repaid for generations to come. While still active in Thousand Needles and Desolace, the centaurs have no presence in Mulgore and only small camps in the Barrens.

At first sight, the Barrens seem a dangerous land and Crossroads a village about to be blown away by the wind. While the peace of Crossroads is fragile and often broken, it is permanent. The Barrens is a success story of the cooperation of the Horde. Once a land where only the most stalwart adventurer would go, the combined forces of the Horde are slowly bringing peace to the land.

The task is not yet done. Harpies and the Venture Company still terrorize the northern Barrens while the Quilboar are firmly entrenched in the south. Even the Dwarves are trying to carve out a piece of this potent land by excavating near the border to Dustwallow Marsh.

SOUTHERN KALIMDOR

The wilderness is as varied and untamed as the races living there. Small outposts are the only glimpse of civilization and those are few and far between.

Thousand Needles is largely controlled by the centaur, but even they are kept in check by the harpies and other more dangerous creatures of the wild. The desolate silence of Thousand Needles is broken by the thunderous crashes from the Shimmering Flats. Though far from civilization, the salt flats provide the perfect track for the Gnomes and Goblins to race their most recent inventions. They pay good money for people to keep their track clear.

West of Thousand Needles the land is much more lush. The forest of Feralas is quite beautiful to behold. Were it not for the Ogres infesting the ancient ruins and the Gnolls camped throughout the valleys, this land would be quite a place to visit.

Venturing further south from Thousand Needles leads into the desert of Tanaris. Gadgetzan and Steamwheedle Port are the only signs of friendly civilization. The Goblins put a city anywhere there is profit to be had. The gates of Ahn'Qiraj have been opened in the far south, but their reach is ever expanding. The Silithid desert on the other side of the crater is a place of epic danger and glory untold.

NORTHERN KALIMDOR

Much of Northern Kalimdor shows the touch of the Night Elves. Though pushed to Teldrassil, the Elves have returned to repair the damage done to the land.

Just across the sea from Teldrassil, Auberdine has become a haven for crafters and those wishing to help heal the land. While the threat of Naga is strong and the spirits of the ruins in the north are angry, demonic corruption has tainted the Furbolg and wildlife populations.

South of Darkshore lays Ashenvale. The Horde have erected a camp on the beach just outside some ruins and deeper in the woods at Warsong Lumber Camp, but they are the least of the problems in the forest. Naga patrol the coastline and large tribes of aggressive Furbolg have taken residence in Ashenvale. The land is, for the most part, healthy. Felwood to the northeast is not so lucky. Corrupted animals and twisted trees are the hallmark of this terrible place.

A bridge across the Southfury River leads to Azshara. Though the land is beautiful, there are many powers at work. Naga and Satyr have claimed many of the ruins in central Azshara while Furbolg and Dragonkin roam the southeast.

TELDRASSIL

The Night Elves moved to Teldrassil in an attempt to unite the Night Elves in a single city. Teldrassil, created to restore the waning power of the Night Elves, is beginning to show signs of corruption.

ALTERAC MOUNTAINS

The Alterac Mountains are home to many powerful Ogres and to the Dalaran. While standing on the northwest shores of the area, a person can see over to the grim canopy of Silverpine Forest, a land filled with the walking dead. Yeti hold many of the high, snow-filled areas of Alterac, while the mages of Dalaran and the dangerous Syndicate control the lowlands.

Alterac Mountains Legend

1 Lordamere Internment Camp
Alina 33 Quest Target
Dalaran Shield Guard 31-32
Dalaran Theurgist 32-33
Dermot 34 Quest Target
Elder Gray Bear 25-26
Giant Moss Creeper 24-25
Mountain Lion 32-33
Ricter 33 Quest Target

2 Dalaran
Archmage Ansirem Runeweaver 40
Dalaran Shield Guard 32
Dalaran Summoner 34-35
Dalaran Theurgist 33
Dalaran Worker 33-34

Elder Gray Bear 25-26
Elemental Slave 33-34
Gavin's Naze
Giant Moss Creeper 25-26
Giant Moss Creeper 25-26
Hulking Mountain Lion 33-34
Mountain Lion 32-33
Snapjaw 30-31

3 The Headland
Mountain Lion 32-33

4 Corrahn's Dagger
Hulking Mountain Lion 33-34
Mountain Lion 32-33
Syndicate Footpad 33
Syndicate Thief 33-34

5 Growless Cave
Giant Yeti 33-34
Mountian Yeti 32-33

6 Ruins of Alterac
Bro'kin 49 Speciality Alchemist
Crushridge Enforcer 38-39 Elite
Crushridge Mage 37-38 Elite
Crushridge Mauler 37-38 Elite
Crushridge Warmonger 39-40 Elite
Mudrake 40 Elite

7 The Uplands
Argus Shadow Mage 36
Giant Yeti 33-34
Grandpa Vishas 34 Elite
Hulking Mountain Lion 33-34
Nancy Vishas 33 Elite

Syndicate Saboteur 37-38
Syndicate Sentry 36-37

8 Misty Shore
Snapjaw 30-31

9 Dandred's Ford
Hulking Mountain Lion 33-34
Snapjaw 30-31
Syndicate Assassin 38-39
Syndicate Enforcer 39-40

10 Slaughter Hollow
Crushridge Brute 35-36
Crushridge Ogre 34-35

11 Crushridge Hold
Crushridge Brute 35-36
Crushridge Ogre 34-35

12 Gallows' Corner
Crushridge Brute 35
Crushridge Ogre 35

13 Strahnbad
Syndicate Spy 35
Syndicate Wizard 35

14 Chillwind Point
Bath'rah the Windcatcher 35 Quest
Hulking Mountain Lion 33-34
Mountain Lion 32-33
Snapjaw 30-31
Stonefury 37

15 Sofera's Naze
Henchman Valik 30
Syndicate Footpad 32
Syndicate Thief 33-34

ARATHI HIGHLANDS

A fragrant wind of pollen, grass, and other living things blows over those who enter the Highlands of Arathi. People from both the Horde and Alliance settle here, trying to farm the arable land of the north and struggle against the many natural dangers of the land. Raptors walk across the flatlands, hunting for prey, and there are many aggressive Ogres and Trolls out in the wild as well. Beware the deadly elementals that spawn near old and forgotten shrines, for they have tremendous power. Seek Hammerfall in the northeast for safety (as the Horde), or walk into the small gorge of Refuge Pointe (as Alliance) in the center of the Highlands.

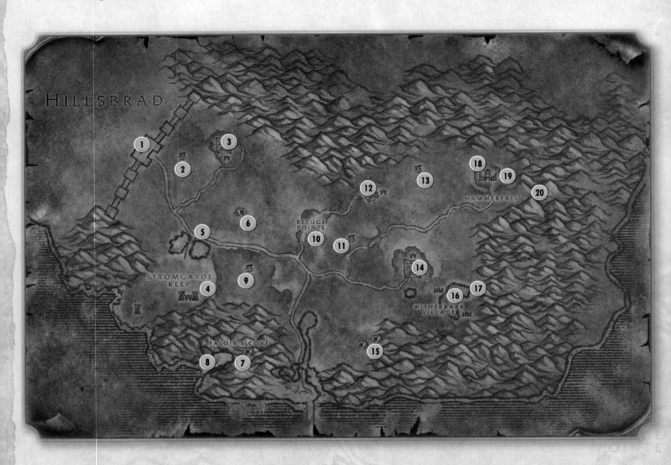

Arathi Highlands Legend

1 Thoradin's Wall
Highland Strider 30-31
Plains Creeper 32-33
Young Mesa Buzzard 31-32

2 Circle of West Binding
Burning Exile 38-39

3 Northfold Manor
Plains Creeper 32-33
Syndicate Highwayman 30-31
Syndicate Mercenary 31-32
Syndicate Pathstalker 32-33
Young Mesa Buzzard 21-32

4 Stromgarde Keep
Boulderfist Lord 39-40 Elite
Boulderfist Mauler 37-38 Elite
Boulderfist Shaman 38-39 Elite
Lord Falconcrest 40 Elite
Otto 38 Elite
Prince Galen Trollbane 44 Elite
Stromgarde Defender 38-39 Elite
Stromgarde Troll Hunter 37-38 Elite
Stromgarde Vindicator 40 Elite
Syndicate Conjurer 36 Elite
Syndicate Magus 38 Elite
Syndicate Prowler 36 Elite

5 Arathi Highway
Forsaken Courier 35
Forsaken Bodyguard 35
Lieutenant Valorcall 38 Elite
Stromgarde Cavalryman 37-38 Elite

5 Boulder'gor
Boulderfist Ogre 32-33
Highland Thrasher 33-34
Witherbark Troll 31-30

6 Boulderfist Outpost
Boulderfist Enforcer 33-34
Witherbark Witch Doctor 33

7 Faldir's Cove
Lolo the Lookout 39 Quest
Shakes O'Breen 40 Quest

8 The Drowned Reef
Daggerspine Raider 38-39
Daggerspine Sorceress 39-40

9 Circle of Inner Binding
Highland Thrasher 33-34
Mesa Buzzard 34-35
Rumbling Exile 38-39

10 Refuge Pointe
Apprentice Kryten 30 Quest
Captain Nials 41 Quest
Cedric Prose 55 Gryphon Master

Highland Strider 30-31
Young Mesa Buzzard 31-32

11 Circle of Outer Binding
Thundering Exile 38-39

12 Dabyrie's Farmstead
Dabyrie Laborer 30-31
Dabyrie's Militia 31-32
Fardel Dabyrie 33 Quest Target
Marcel Dabyrie 34 Quest Target

13 Circle of East Binding
Shards of Myzrael
Cresting Exiles 38-39

14 Go'Shek Farm
Kinelory 38 Quest
Quae 38 Quest
Giant Plains Creeper 35-36
Hammerfall Grunt 34-35
Hammerfall Peon 33-34
Mesa Buzzard 34-35

15 Boulderfist Hall
Boulderfist Brute 35-36
Boulderfist Magus 37
Highland Fleshstalker 36-37
Kor'gresh
Mesa Buzzard 34-35
Witherbark Berserker 36-37 Elite

16 Witherbark Village
Giant Plains Creeper 35-36
Witherbark Axe Thrower 32-33
Witherbark Head Hunter 34-35
Witherbark Witchdoctor 33-34

17 Witherbark Cave
Witherbark Headhunter 34-35
Witherbark Shadow Hunter 35-36

18 Hammerfall
Drum Fel 30 Quest
Gor'mul 40 Quest
Innkeeper Adegwa 30 Innkeeper
Slagg 38 Superior Butcher
Tharlidun 30 Stable Master
Tor'gan 40 Quest
Urda 55 Wind Rider Master
Zaruk 60 Quest
Zengu 40 Quest
Highland Strider 30-31

19 Drywhisker Gorge
Drywhisker Kobold 35-36

20 Drywhisker Cave
Drywhisker Digger 36-37
Drywhisker Surveyor 37-38

ASHENVALE

Ashenvale is a lush and vibrant area of forests, meadows and lakes. Today Demons, Elementals, Furbolgs and many more supernatural creatures rule this land. The Night Elves, inherently attuned to nature, have started to cleanse this land, but it will take many years before it is safe for travelers to roam freely through this land.

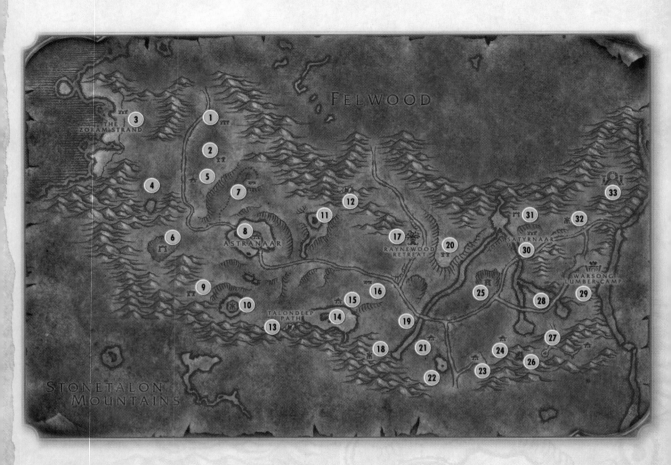

Ashenvale Legend

1 Bathran's Haunt
Forsaken Seeker 18-19
Forsaken Herbalist 18-19
Forsaken Thug 20

2 The Ruins of Ordil'
Dark Strand Cultist 18-19
Imp (Minion) 18-19
Dark Strand Adept 18-19
Voidwalker Minion 18-19

3 The Zoram Strand
Andruk 55 Wind Rider Master
Clattering Crawler 19-20
Mystlash Hydra 20
Spined Crawler 20-21
Wrathtail Sorceress 18-19
Wrathtail WaveRider 18-19
Ghostpaw Runner 19-20
Wild Buck 18-19
Entrance to Blackfathom Deeps
     World Dungeon

3A Fishing Village
Talen 17 QuestAndruk 55 Elite Wind Rider Master

4 Lake Falathim
Ghostpaw Runner 19-20
Mugglefin 23+
Saltspittle Muckdweller 20-21
Salthspittle Oracle 20-21
Saltspittle Puddlejumper 19-20
Wild Buck 18-19

5 Maestra's Post
Feero Ironhand 20 Quest
Delgren the Purifier 19 Quest
Orendil Broadleaf 27 Quest
Liladris Moonriver 42 Quest
Sentinel Onaeya 20 Quest
Wild Buck 18-19

6 The Shrine of Aessina
Illiyana 24 Quest
Therysil 17 Quest
Sentinel Melyria Frostshadow Quest
Lilyn Darkriver Quest

7 Thistlefur Village
Dal Bloodclaw 25
Thistlefur Shaman 22-23
Thistlefur Avenger 22-23
Thistlefur Pathfinder 22-23

8 Astranaar
Pelturas Whitemoon 21 Quest
Nantar 21 Baker
Maluression 30 Stable Master
Raene Wolfrunner 25 Quest
Dagri 23 Raene Wolfrunner's Pet
Fahran Silentblade 28 Tools and Supplies
Maliynn 19 Grocer
Korra 20 Tiger
Haljan Oakheart 26 General Goods
Kimlya 30 Innkeeper
Dalria 24 Trade Goods
Xai'ander 35 Weaponsmith
Aayndia Floralwind 37 Leatherworker
Faldreas Goeth'shael 19 Quest
Sentinel Thenysil 23 Quest
Shindrell Swiftfire 25
Daelyshia 55 Hippogriff Master
Lardan 25 Leatherworking
Llana 25 Reageant Supplies
Tandaan Lightmane 23 Leather Armor Merchant
Aeolynn 22 Clothier
Astranaar Sentinenl 40

9 Fire Scar Shrine
Felslayer 22-23
Burning Legionnaire 23-24

10 Ruins of Stardust
Shadethicket Raincaller 23-24
Shadethicket Woodshaper 23-24

11 Iris Lake
Shadethicket Moss Eater 21-23

12 The Howling Vale
Terrorwulf Fleshripper 28-29
Terrorwulf Shadow Weaver 29-30

13 Talondeep Path
Shadowhorn Stag 21-22
Ashenvale Bear 21-22

14 Mystral Lake
Befouled Water Elementals 23-25

15 Silverwind Refuge
Harklan Moongrove 24 Alchemy Supplies
Shandrina 24 Trade Goods
Ulthaan 26 Butcher
Danlaar Nightstride 35 Hunter Trainer
Jayla 23 Skinner Trainer
Bhaldaran Ravenshade 34 Bowyer
Cylania Rootstalker 24 Herbalist
Kylanna 31 Alchemist
Sentinel Velene Starstrike 25 Quest

16 Greenpaw Village
Foulweald Totemic 23-24
Foulweald Ursa 23-24
Foulweald Shaman 23-24
Foulweald Warrior 23-24
Foulweald Den Watcher 23-24
Foulweald Pathfinder 23-24

17 Raynewood Retreat
Keeper Ordanus 29
Laughing Sister 24-25
Cenarion Protector 25-26
Cenarion Vindicator 26-27

18 Bloodtooth Camp
Ran Bloodtooth 30
Bloodtooth Guard 27-28
Ghostpaw Runner 19-20
Ashenvale Bear 21-22

19 Moonwell
Blink Dragon 26
Ghostpaw Howler 23
Wildthorn Venomspitter 24

20 Night Run
Wildthorn Venomspitter 24-25
Elder Ashenvale Bear 24-25
Felmusk Satyr 25-26
Felmusk Rogue 26-27
Felmusk Felsworn 27-28
Felmusk Shadowstalker 26-27

21 Silverwing Outpost
Ashenvale Sentinel 40
Ashenvale Warriror 40

22 Fallen Sky Lake
Shadethicket Stone Mover 25-26
Shadethicket Bark Ripper 26-27
Wildthorn Stalker 20-21

23 Nightsong Woods
Wildthorn Stalker 20-21
Warsong Shredder 27
Rotting Slime 20-22
Ghostpaw Runner 19-20
Horde Shaman 28-29
Horde Grunt 29-30

**24 The Dor'Danil
     Barrow Den**
Uthil Mooncaller 32
Rotting Slime (Outside) 21-22
Forsaken Infiltrator 28-29
Forsaken Intruder 28-29
Forsaken Stalker 28-29

Forsaken Assasin 28-29
Severed Druid 28-29
Severed Dreamer 29-30
Severed Keeper 29-30
Severed Sleeper 29-30

25 Splintertree Post

**26 Monument to
     Grom Hellscream**
Felguard 29-31
Legion Hound 29-31
Searing Infernal 29-31

27 Demon Fall Canyon
Legion Hound 29-30
Mannoroc Lasher 29-30
Searing Infernal 29-30
Felguard 29-30

28 Felfire Hill
Mannoroc Lasher 29-30
Searing Infernal 29-30
Felguard 29-30

29 Warsong Lumber Camp
Loruk Foreststrider 44 Banker
Horde Grunt 29-30
Horde Shaman 28-29
Warsong Shredder 27-28
Horde Scout 26-27
Horde Peon 26-27

30 Satyrnaar
Bleakheart Trickster 26-28
Bleakheart Shadowstalker 26-28
Bleakheart Saytr 26-28
Bleakheart Hellcaller 26-28

31 Xavian
Galtharis 32
Xavian Felsworn 28-30
Xavian Betrayer 28-30
Xavian Hellcaller 28-30
Xavian Rogue 28-30

32 Forest Song
Kayneth Stillwind 31 Quest
Giant Ashenvale Bear 29-30
Wildthorn Lurker 29-30

33 Bough Shadow
Dreamstalker 62
Emeraldon Tree Warders 60
Emeraldon Oracles 61

75

AZSHARA

Azshara is located to the east of Ashenvale. Named after Queen Azshar, the Naga still roam this land. This zone has progressive level increases as you travel to the edges of the land.

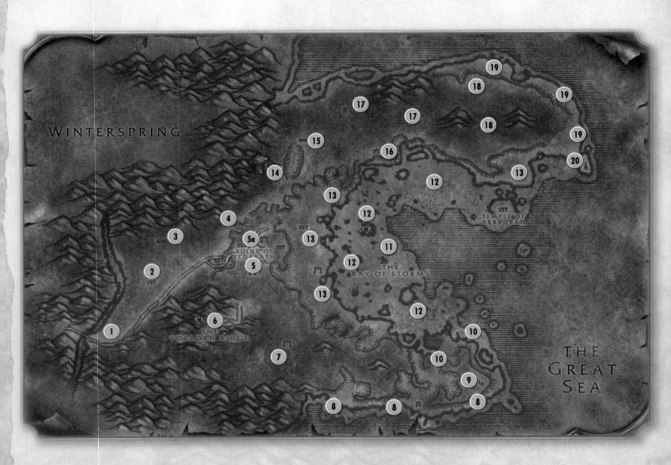

Azshara Legend

1 Shadowsong Shrine
Highborn Apparition 45-47
Highborn Lichling 45-57
Mosshoof Runner 45-46

2 Haldarr Encampment
Cliff Walker 53-54 Elite
Haldarr Felsworn 45-46
Haldar Satyr 45-46
Haldarr Trickster 45-46
Mosshoof Runner 45-47
Sentinel Keldara Sunblade 45
Thunderhead Hippogryph 46-48

3 Valormok
Ag'Tor Bloodfist 45 Quest
Haggrum Bloodfist 45
Jediga 49 Quest
Kroum 55 Elite Flight Master
Mosshoff Runner 45-46

4 Bear's Head
Cliff Walker 53 Elite
Timbermaw Pathfinder 47-48
Timberweb Recluse 47-48
Timbermaw Totemic 47-48
Timbermaw Warrior 47-48

5 Ruins of Eldarath
Lady Sesspira 51 Elite
Lingering Highborne 48-50
Spitelash Screamer 46-48
Spitelash Siren 51-52
Spitelash Serpent Guard 48-49
Spitelash Warrior 46-48
Thunderhead Stagwing 49-60
Timberweb Recluse 47-48

5A Temple of Zin-Malor
Spitelash Serpent Guard 48-49
Spitelash Siren 51-52
Spitelash Siren 51-52
Warlord Krellian 55

6 Forlorn Ridge
Forest ooze 52-53
Mosshoof Courser 53-54

7 Lake Minnar
Blue Dragon Spawn 50-51
Blue Scalebane 52-53
Draconic Magelord 53-54
Draconic Mageweaver 51-52
Mosshoof Courser 52-53
Azuregos

8 The Ruined Reaches
Horizon Scout Crewman 42
Jubie GadgetSpring 44 Engineer Supplier, Rare Schematics
Coralshell Lurker 53-54
Great Wavethrasher 53-54
Makrinni Razorclaw 54-55
Storm Bay Oracle 54-55

9 Ravencrest Monument
Spitelash Battlemaster 53-54
Spitelash Enchantress 54-55

10 South Ridge Beach
Coralshell Lurker 53-54
Makrinni Razorclaw 54-55
Great Wavethrasher 53-54
Storm Bay Oracle 54-55

11 Hetaera's Clutch
Servant of Arkkoroc 53-55 Elite

12 Bay of Storms
Lormus Thalipedes 60 Quest
Rataf 50 Elite Lormus' pet

Shatllar 50 Elite Lormus' pet
Zaman 50 Elite Lormus' pet
Servant of Arkkoroc 53-55 Elite

13 The Shattered Strand
Coralshell Lurker 53-54
Great Wavethrasher 53-54
Makrinni Razorclaw 54-55
Spitelash Myrmidon 50-51
Spitelash Siren 51-52
Arkkoran Clacker 53-54
Arkkoran Muckdweller 53-54
Arkkoran Oracle 53-54

14 Timbermaw Hold
Cliff Walker 53-54Elite
Timberweb Recluse 47-48
Timbermaw Pathfinder 46-47
Timbermaw Shaman 50-51
Thunderhead Stagwing 49-50
Timbermaw Watcher 49-50
Timbermaw Warrior 47-48

15 Ursolan
Timbermaw Shaman 50-51
Thunderhead Skystormer 51-52
Timbermaw Ursa 51-52
Timbermaw Watcher 49-50

16 Thalassian Base Camp
Blood Elf Reclaimer 52-53
Blood Elf Surveyor 51-52
Thunderhead Skystormer 51-52

17 Legash Encampment
Cliff Breaker 54-55 Elite
Cliff Walker 52-53 Elite
Forest Ooze 52-53
Legashi Hellcaller 52-53
Legashi Rogue 52-53

Legashi Satyr 51-52
Mosshoof Courser 51-52
Thunderhead Consort 53-54
Thunderhead Skystormer 51-52

18 Bitter Reaches
Cliff Breaker 54-55 Elite
Cliff Thunderer 54-55 Elite
Cliff Walker 52-53 Elite
Forest Ooze 52-53
Mistwalker Ravager 52-53
Mosshoof Courser 51-52
Thunderhead Skystormer 51-52
Thunderhead Consort 53-54
Thunderhead Patriarch 54-55

19 Jagged Reaches
Coralshell Lurker 53-54
Makrinni Scrabbler 52-53
Storm Bay Warrior 51-52
Wavethrasher 52-53

20 Tower of Elpara
Coralshell Lurker 53-54
Makrinni Scrabbler 52-53
Storm Bay Warrior 51-52
Wavethrasher 52-53

21 Temple of Arkkoran
Arkkoran Clacker 53-54
Arkkoran Oracle 54-55
Arkkoran Pincer 54-55
Arkkoran Muckdweller 53-54
Lord Arkkoran 60 Elite

THE
BAY OF STORMS

Badlands

South of Loch Modan is an area of open sand and rock known as the Badlands. Many natural predators hunt here, but there are also rare and fierce creatures as well. Dragon Whelps of considerable size grow in the eastern part of the region, near Uldaman (a place with quite a reputation for danger and adventure). To the west is a Horde town, barely more than a well-staffed building to show for itself, but offering what little civilization holds out in this rugged place.

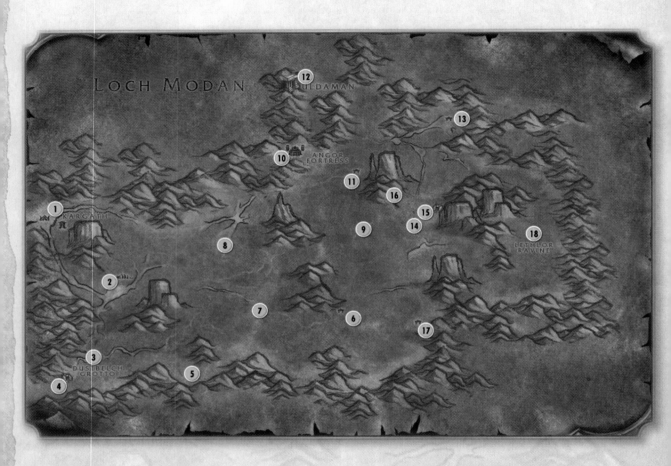

Badlands Legend

1 Kargath
Gorrick 55 Wind Rider Master
Greth 30 Stable Master
Grunt Gargal 52 Quest
Initiate Amakkar 52 Quest
Innkeeper Shul'kar 30 Innkeeper
Razal'blade 52 Quest
Shadowmage Vivian Lagrave 60 Quest
Thal'trak Proudtusk 55 Quest
Thunderheart 52 Quest

2 Apocryphan's Rest
Elder Crag Coyote 39-40
Giant Buzzard 39-40
Ridge Stalker Patriarch 40-41

3 Camp Cagg
Boss Tho'grun 41 Quest Target
Dustbelcher Mauler 41-42
Dustbelcher Mystic 37
Dustbelcher Shaman 41-42
Dustbelcher Wyrmhunter 40-41
Greater Rock Elemental 42-44

4 Dustbelch Grotto
Dustbelcher Lord 44
Dustbelcher Ogre Mage 44

5 Mirage Flats
Elder Crag Coyote 39-40
Giant Buzzard 39-40
Ridge Stalker Patriarch 40-41
Zaricotl 55 Elite

6 Agmond's End
Agmond's Body Quest
Theldurin the Lost 30 Quest
Buzzard 37-38
Feral Crag Coyote 37-38
Murdaloc 42 Quest Target
Ridge Huntress 39
Rock Elemental 39-40
Stonevault Shaman 40-41
Stonevault Stonesnapper 39-40

7 Camp Wurg
Dustbelcher Brute 39
Dustbelcher Ogre 38-39
Elder Crag Coyote 39-40
Ridge Stalker Patriarch 41

8 The Dustbowl
Lotwil Veriatus 36 Quest
Lucien Tosselwrench 31 Quest
Elder Crag Coyote 39-40
Giant Buzzard 39-40
Lesser Rock Elementals 37-39
Ridge Stalker Patriarch 41

9 Valley of Fangs
Jazzrik 38 Vendor
Martek the Exiled 42 Quest
Rigglefuzz 37 Quest
Crag Coyote 35-36
Ridge Huntress 38-39

10 Angor Fortress
Crag Coyote 35
Ridge Stalker 36-37
Shadowforge Chanter 38-39
Shadowforge Warrior 38
Stone Golem 38-39

11 Hammertoe's Digsite
Prospector Ryedol 35 Quest
Sigrun Ironhew 40 Quest
Crag Coyote 35-36
Ridge Stalker 35-36
Shadowforge Darkweaver 36-37
Shadowforge Tunneler 35-36
Starving Buzzard 35-36

12 The Maker's Terrace
Primary Entrance to Uldaman
  World Dungeon
Shadowforge Digger 35-36 Elite
Shadowforge Ruffian 36-37 Elite
Shadowforge Surveyor 35-36 Elite

13 Camp Kosh
Dustbelcher Mystic 37
Dustbelcher Warrior 36-37

14 Dustwind Gulch
Garek 50 Quest
Thorkaf Dragoneye 50 Master Dragonscale
  Leatherworker
Buzzard 37-38
Feral Crag Coyote 37-38

Ridge Stalker 35-36
Starving Buzzard 35-36

15 Dustwind Gulch Cave
Secondary Entrance to Uldaman World Dungeon
Stonevault Basher 40 Elite
Stonevault Seer 39-40 Elite

16 Crypt

17 Camp Boff
Dustbelcher Brute 39-40
Dustbelcher Ogre 38-39
Feral Crag Coyote 37-38

18 Lethlor Ravine
Large Gray Pillar
Pillar of Amethyst
Pillar of Diamond
Blacklash 50 Elite
Hematus 50 Elite
Scalding Whelp 42-43
Scorched Guardian 43-45 Elite

The Barrens

The Barrens are one of the largest zones and a central hub for travel between regions. Savannah Prowlers roam the land and remain hidden from younger adventurers, while Raptors, Centaurs, Harpies and all sorts of other wildlife can be seen hunting or foraging. This provides plenty of skinning opportunities. Ore and herbs are also all across the landscape. Three dungeons are within the zone: The Wailing Caverns, Razorfen Downs, and Razorfen Kraul. The Barrens offers access to many other zones including Stonetalon, Thousand Needles, Durotar, and Dustwallow Marsh; of course, that doesn't mention the Wyvern paths or the port town of Ratchet where adventurers can book passage on a ship.

Barrens Legend

1 Bael Modan
Bael'dun Excavator 21-22
Bael'dun Foreman 22-23
Bael'dun Officer 26
Bael'dun Rifleman 24,25
Bael'dun Soldier 23,24
Digger Flameforge 24
General Twinbraid 30
Lord Cyrik Blackforge 23
Malgin Barleybrew 25
Prospector Khazgorm 26
Captain Gerogg Hammertoe 27 Elite

2 Blackthorn Ridge
Razormane Pathfinder 20,21
Razormane Seer 23,24
Razormane Stalker 22,23
Razormane Warfrenzy 24,25
Kuz Orcbane 21
Nak Orcbane 23

Lok Orcbane 25
Hagg Taurenbane 26 Elite

3 Southern Barrens
Gann Stonespire 18 Quest
Hannah Bladeleaf 24 Elite
Marcus Bel 24 Elite
Thora Feathermoon 25 Elite
Brontus 27 Elite
Barrens Kodo 19,20
Greater Barrens Kodo 24,25
Wooly Kodo 25,26
Greater Thunderhawk 23,24
Hecklefang Stalker 22,23
Stormhide 22,23
Thunderstomp 24
Washte Pawne 25

4 Silithid Mounds 18-24
Hannah Bladeleaf 24 Elite
Marcus Bel 24 Elite

Thora Feathermoon 25 Elite
Brontus 27 Elite
Silithid Creeper 20,21
Silithid Grub 20
Silithid Harvester 24
Silithid Protector 18,19
Silithid Swarmer 21,22
Barrens Kodo 19,20
Wooly Kodo 25,26
Greater Barrens Kodo 24,25

5 Field of Giants
Azzere the Skyblade 25
Owatanka 24
Brontus 27 Elite
Hannah Bladeleaf 24 Elite
Marcus Bel 24 Elite
Thora Feathermoon 25 Elite
Thunderhead 20-21
Wooly Kodo 25-26

Zhevra Courser 20-21
Thunderhawk Cloudscraper 20-21
Greater Barrens Kodo 24-25
Gazelle 2
Barrens Kodo 19120
Zhevra Courser 20-21

6 Camp Taurajo
Kelsuwa 30 Stablemaster
Innkeeper Byula 30 Innkeeper
Dranh 15 Skinner
Jorn Skyseer 32 Quest
Yonada 25 Tailoring & Leatherworking
  Supplies
Mahani 31 Expert Tailor
Krulmoo Fullmoon 42 Expert
  Leatherworker
Gahroot 25 Butcher
Ruga Ragetotem 30 Quest
Grunt Logmar 20 Quest

Grunt Dogran 20 Quest
Mangletooth 17 Quest
Kirge Sternhorn 22
Tatternack Steelforge 14
Takar the Seer 45 Quest

7 Bramblescar
Bristleback Geomancer 19-20
Bristleback Hunter 18-19
Bristleback Thornweaver 17-18

8 Raptor Grounds
Sunscale Scytheclaw 15-16
Sunscale Screecher 13-15
Sunscale Lashtail 11-13
Fleeting Plainstrider 12-13
Hecklefang Hyena 15-16
Ornery Plainstrider 16-17
Zhevra Charger 17-18

9 Middle Barrens
Hannah Bladeleaf- 24 Elite
Marcus Bel 24 Elite
Thora Feathermoon 25 Elite
Barrens Giraffe 15-16
Wandering Barrens Giraffe 18-19
Barrens Kodo 19-20
Hecklefang Snarler 18-19
Thunderhawk Hatchling 18-20
Gazelle 2
Stormsnout 18-19

10 Agama'gor
Bristleback Geomancer 19-20
Bristleback Hunter 18-19
Bristleback Thornweaver 17-18
Bristleback Water Seeker 16-17
Geopriest Gukk'rok 19
Swinegart Spearhide 22 Elite

11 Northwatch Hold
Gilthares Firebough 17 Quest
Theramore Marine 15-16
Theramore Preserver 16-17
Cannoneer Smythe 19
Cannoneer Whessan 19
Captain Fairmount 20

12 The Merchant Coast
Klannoc Macleod 65 The Islander, Quest
Islen Waterseer 37 Quest
Mahren Skyseer 32 Quest
Southsea Brigand 12-13
Southsea Cannoneer 13-14
Southsea Cutthroat 24-15
Southsea Privateer 14-15
Polly 18
Tazan 13
Baron Longshore 16
Slimeshell Makrura 18-19
Isha Awak 27

13 Ratchet
Brewmaster Drohn 9 Quest
Captain Thalo'thas Brightsun 25 Quest
Wrenix the Wretched 20 Quest
Vazario Linkgrease 40 Master Goblin
    Engineer, Quest Giver
Tinkerwiz 25 Journeyman Engineer
Gagsprocket 20 Engineering Goods
Gazlowe 60 Quest Giver
Sputtervalve 15 Tinkers' Union,
    Quest Giver

Crane Operator Bigglefuzz 18 Quest Giver
Zikkel 30 Banker
Fuzruckie 27 Banker
Mebok Mizzyrix 17 Quest Giver
Ironzar 23 Weaponsmith
Wharfmaster Dizzywig 15 Quest Giver
Shipmaster Grimble 45 Shipmaster
Kilxx 24 Fisherman
Liv Rizzlefix 17 Workshop Assistant
Grazlix 25 Armorer & Shieldcrafter
Vexspindle 24 Cloth & Leather Armor
    Merchant
Ranik 22 Trade Supplies
Jazzik 22 General Supplies
Zizzek 22 Fisherman
Reggifuz 35 Stablemaster
Innkeeper Wiley 35 Innkeeper
Menara Voidrender 50 Quest Giver
Strahad Farsan 60 Quest Giver
Acolyte Magaz 20 Quest Giver
Acolyte Fenrick 20 Quest Giver
Acolyte Wytula 20 Quest Giver

14 North Ratchet Plain
Thun'grim Firegaze 29 Quest
Ornery Plainstrider 16,17
Savannah Matriarch 17,18
Sunscale Scytheclaw 15,16
Zhevra Charger 17,18
Ishamuhale 19
Swiftmane 21 Elite
Humar the Pridelord 23 Elite

15 Stagnant Oasis
Kolkar Marauder 15-16
Kolkar Pack Runner 14-15
Kolkar Packhound 13
Kolkar Stormer 13-14
Kolkar Wrangler 12-13
Oasis Snapjaw 15-16
Brokespear 17
Verog the Dervish 18
Rocklance 17 Elite

16 Lushwater Oasis/Wailing
    Caverns
Falla Sagewind 25 Quest
Kalldan Felmoon 27 Specialist
    Leatherworking Supplies
Nalpak 14 Disciple of Naralex, Quest
Ebru 14 Disciple of Naralex, Quest
Waldar 28 Journeyman Leatherworker

Deviate Coiler 15,16 Elite
Deviate Creeper 15,16 Elite
Deviate Lurker 16,17 Elite
Deviate Slayer 16,17 Elite
Deviate Stalker 15,16,17 Elite
Deviate Stinglash 17 Elite
Devouring Ectoplasm 16,17 Elite
Cloned Ectoplasm 16,17 Elite
Mad Magglish 18 Elite
Kolkar Marauder 15-16
Kolkar Pack Runner 14-15
Kolkar Packhound 13
Kolkar Stormer 13-14
Kolkar Wrangler 12-13
Oasis Snapjaw 15-16
Hezrul Bloodmark 19
Gesharahan 20 Elite

17 Crossroads
Innkeeper Boorand Plainswind 30
    Innkeeper
Larhka 18 Beverage Merchant
Zargh 16 Butcher
Moorane Hearthgrain 18 Baker
Lizzarik 19 Weapon Dealer
Sergra Darkthorn 34 Quest Giver
Kil'hala 25 Journeyman Tailor
Wrahk 18 Tailoring Supplies
Halija Whitestrider 19 Clothier
Tonga Runetotem 22 Quest
Kaltimah Stormcloud 23 Bags and Sacks
Mankrik 15 Quest
Thork 42 Quest
Devrak 55 Wind Rider Master
Hula'mahi 30 Reagents and Herbs
Korran 12 Quest
Uthrok 16 Bowyer and Gunsmith
Johan Hawkwing 21 Leather & Mail
    Armor Merchant
Nargal Deatheye 35 Weaponsmith
Traugh 31 Expert Blacksmith
Sikwa 30 Stable Master
Barg 14 General Goods Vendor
Tari'Qa 14 Trade Supplies
Gazrog 25 Quest
Apothecary Helbrim 22 Quest
Tarban Hearthgrain 22 Baker
Grub 13 Quest Giver
Duhng 18 Cook
Kranal Fiss 15 Quest Giver

18 Orc Rampart
Lanti'gah 4
Regthar Deathgate 28 Quest
Kolkar Invader 16-17
Kolkar Storm Seer 15-16
Warlord Krom'zar 20

19 Central Barrens
Barrens Giraffe 15-16
Gazelle 2
Hecklefang Hyena 15-16
Lost Barrens Kodo 14-15
Ornery Plainstrider 16-17
Savannah Prowler 14-15
Sunscale Screecher 13-15
Zhevra Charger 17-18
Snort the Heckler 17

20 Honor's Stand
Ornery Plainstrider 16-17
Sunscale Scytheclaw 15-16
Zhevra Charger 17-18

21 The Forgotten Pools
Kolkar Stormer 13,14
Kolkar Wrangler 12,13
Barak Kodobane 16
Stonearm 15

22 Thorn Hill
Razormane Defender 12,13
Razormane Geomancer 12,13
Razormane Hunter 11,12
Razormane Mystic 13,14
Razormane Thornweaver 10,11
Razormane Water Seeker 10,11
Kreenig Snarlsnout 15
Elder Mystic Razorsnout 15 Elite

23 Far Watch Post
Ak'Zeloth 22 Quest
Kargal Battlescar 15 Quest
Uzzek 20 Quest

24 Kodo Bones
Savannah Huntress 11-12
Savannah Prowler 14-15
Echeyakee 14

25 Dreadmist Peak
Burning Blade Acolyte 11-12
Burning Blade Bruiser 10-11
Rathorian 15

26 The Mor'shan Rampart
Vrang Wildgore 48 Weaponsmith &
    Armorcrafter
Wenikee Boltbucket 19
Ornery Plainstrider 16-17
Savannah Patriarch 15-16
Sunscale Scytheclaw 15-16
Zhevra Charger 17-18

27 The Dry Hills
Witchwing Ambusher 17,18
Witchwing Harpy 14,15
Witchwing Roguefeather 15,16
Witchwing Slayer 16,17
Witchwing Windcaller 17,18
Sister Rathtalon 19 Elite

28 Northern Barrens
Barrens Giraffe 15,16
Fleeting Plainstrider 12,13
Hecklefang Hyena 15,16
Lost Barrens Kodo 14,15
Savannah Prowler 14,15
Sunscale Screecher 13,14,15
Zhevra Runner 13,14
Gazelle 2

29 Venture Company Operations
Taskmaster Fizzule 35 Elite Quest
Venture Co. Peon 13-14
Venture Co. Drudger 14-15
Tinkerer Sniggles 16

30 Sludge Fens
Venture Co. Mercenary 15-16
Venture Co. Drudger 14-15
Engineer Whirleygig 19
Foreman Grills" 19
Formeman Silixiz 25
Overseer Glibby 16
Grand Foreman Puzik Gallywix 26 Elite

31 Northern Plain
Ornery Plainstrider 16-17
Sunscale Scytheclaw 15-16
Zhevra Charger 17-18
Takk the Leaper 19 Elite

32 Boulder Lode Mine
Venture Co. Enforcer 16-17
Venture Co. Overseer 17-18
Boss Copperplug 19

33 Southfury River
Dreadmaw Crocolisk 9-11

Blasted Lands

The Dark Portal sits here, ominous in its presence and guarded for unknown purposes. Ogres, cultists, and warped beasts walk through the Blasted Lands almost unchecked, save for an Alliance stronghold, Nethergarde Keep. Though well stocked with people and provisions, this outpost of Humans and their allies is scarcely enough to hold back the tide of danger from the rest of the southern lands. Who can say what would happen if enough Warlocks gathered at the portal one day?

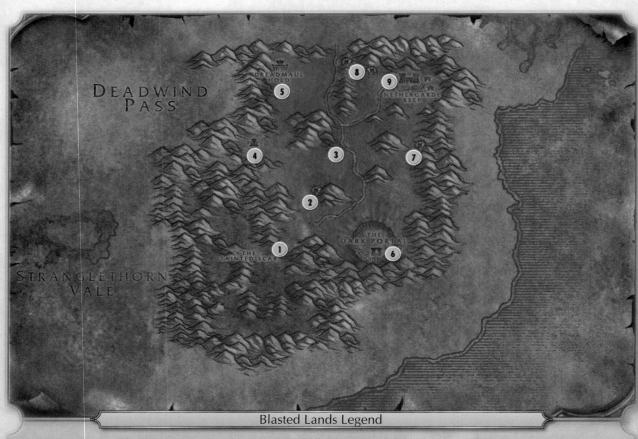

Blasted Lands Legend

1 The Tainted Scar
Felguard Elite 60
Doomguard Commander 61
Manahound 60
Lord Kazzak

2 Dreadmaul Post
Dreadmaul Mauler 53-54
Dreadmaul Warlock 53-54
Servant of Grol 53-54

3 Rise of the Defiler/Central Blasted Lands
Kum'isha the Collector Quest
Black Slayer 47-48
Felbeast 50-51
Hellboar 52-53
Portal Seeker 52-53
Redstone Basilisk 47-48
Redstone Crystalhide 50-51

Scorpok Stinger 51
Starving Snickerfang 46

4 Altar of Storms
Lady Sevine 59 Elite
Servant of Sevine 56
Shadowsworn Dreadweaver 53-55
Shadowsworn Enforcer 54
Shadowsworn Warlock 53-55

5 Dreadmaul Hold
Dreadmaul Brute 46-47
Dreadmaul Ogre Mage 46-47
Grol the Destroyer 58 Quest Target
Scorpok Stinger 50-51
Servant of Grol 53
Starving Snickerfang 45-46
Wretched Lost One 46

6 The Dark Portal
Felguard Elite 60 Elite
Felguard Sentry 55
Felhound 55
Hellboar 52-53
Manahound 60 Elite
Redstone Crystalhide 51
Scorpok Stinger 50-51
Servant of Razelikh 57
Razelikh the Defiler 60

7 Serpent's Coil
Ashmane Boar 47-49
Black Slayer 48
Redstone Basilisk 47-48
Servant of Allistarj 54
Shadowsworn Adept 52-53
Shadowsworn Cultist 52
Shadowsworn Thug 52-53

8 Nethergarde Armory
Nethergarde Engineer 47-48
Nethergarde Forman 46-48
Nethergarde Miner 47-48

9 Nethergarde Keep
Alexandra Constantine 55 Elite Gryphon Master
Ambassador Ardalan 55 Quest
Enohar Thunderbrew 50 Quest
Watcher Mahar Ba 45
Nethergarde Analyst 50
Nethergarde Cleric 49-51
Nethergarde Elite 55 Elite
Nethergarde Officer 50
Nethergarde Riftwatcher 49-51
Nethergarde Soldier 49-51
Quartermaster Lungertz 54

Burning Steppes

The Burning Steppes are more dangerous than almost any realm in the east, save perhaps for the Plaguelands, where the Scourge is located. In the Burning Steppes, massive Drakes, Whelps, and Dragonkin thrive in the heat, ash, and shadow of Blackrock Mountain, and other great mountains that line the area's perimeter. Passage into the Steppes is mainly possible through the road up from Lakeshire, in Redridge, but the creatures are so terrible in this land that few dare to approach.

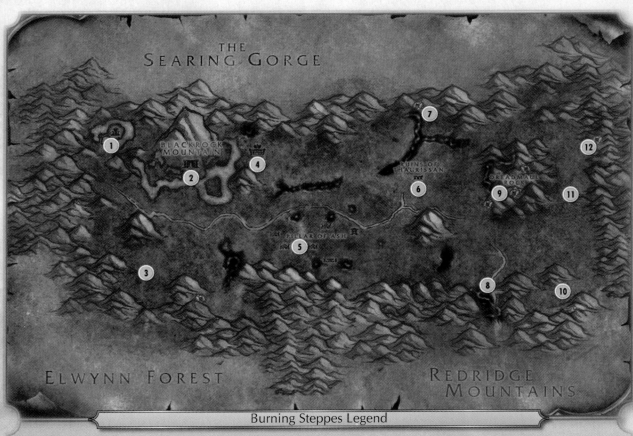

Burning Steppes Legend

1 Altar of Storms
Blackrock Warlock 55-57

2 Blackrock Mountain
Black Wyrmkin 51-54

3 Draco'dar
Firetail Scorpid 56-57
Flamescale Broodling 55-56
Flamescale Dragonspawn 56-57 Elite
Flamescale Wyrmkin 57-58 Elite
Giant Ember Worg 55-56
Scalding Broodling 51-54
Scalding Drake 52-55 Elite
Searscale Drake 55-58 Elite

4 Blackrock Stronghold
Grark Lorkrub 56 Elite Quest
Blackrock Slayer 54-57
Blackrock Soldier 53-56

Blackrock Sorcerer 53-56
Blackrock Warlock 55-57

5 Pillar of Ash
Blackrock Slayer 54-57
Blackrock Soldier 53-56
Blackrock Sorcerer 53-56
Blackrock Warlock 55—57
Deathlash Scorpid 53-55
Flamekin Rager 54-56
Flamekin Spitter 50-53
Flamekin Sprite 51-53
Flamekin Torcher 54-56
Greater Obsidian Elemental 55-57
Obsidian Elemental 50-53
Slavering Ember Worg 53-54

6 Ruins of Thaurissan
Black Broodling 48-52
Black Dragonspawn 50-53 Elite
Black Drake 48-52 Elite

Black Wyrmkin 51-54 Elite
Flamekin Rager 54-56
Flamekin Spitter 50-53
Flamekin Sprite 51-53
Flamekin Torcher 54-56
Greater Obsidian Elemental 55-57
Obsidian Elemental 50-53
Thaurisan Agent 54-55
Thaurisan Firewalker 53-55
Thaurisan Spy 53-54
War Reaver 53-55

7 Flame Crest
Kibler 56 Quest
Mathredis Firestar 60 Quest
Maxwort Umberglint 42 Quest
Ragged Jon 57 Quest
Tinkee Steambail 53 Quest
Yuka Screwspigot 53 Quest
Deathlash Scorpid 53-55

8 Blackrock Pass
Venomtip Scorpid 50-53

9 Dreadmaul Rock
Remains of Sha'ni Proudtusks Quest
Firegut Brute 50-53
Firegut Ogre Mage 48-52
Firegut Ogre 48-51

10 Morgan's Vigil
Helendis Riverhorn 55 Quest
Marshal Maxwell 55 Quest
Mayara Brightwing 55 Quest
Oralius 55 Quest

11 Terror Wing Path
Ember Worg 49-52
Venomtip Scorpid 50-53

12 Slither Rock
Cyrus Therepantous 52 Quest
Flamescale Wyrmkin 57-58 Elite

Darkshore

Darkshore is the first port of call for Night Elves leaving their beloved Darnassus behind. This zone can easily support those characters wishing to create a home until they gain a bit of experience. As a zone on the sea, it has many beaches and the perils to go with them. While it's not as large a metropolis as Stormwind or Ironforge, Auberdine does a good job of supporting the adventurers and boasts a fine dock in which ships ferry travelers into more dangerous territories.

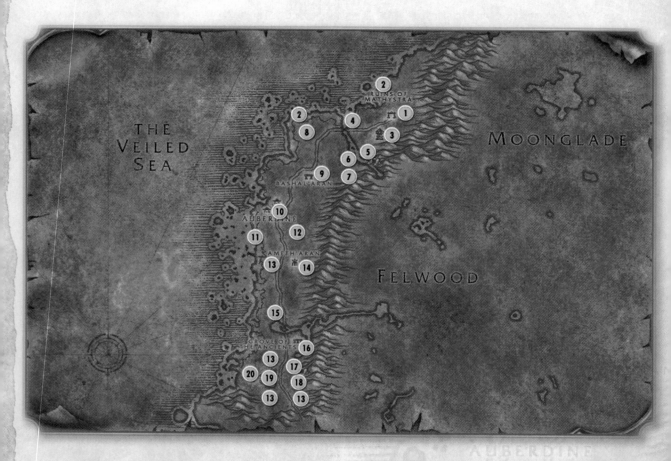

Darkshore Legend

1 Ruins of Mathystra
Giant Forestrider 17-19
Moonstalker Matriarch 19-20
Moonstalker Sire 18-19
Moonstalker Runt 16 Moonstalker Matriarch's Minion
Stormscale Myrmidon 18-19
Stormscale Sorceress 19-20
Stormscale Warrior 20-21

2 Mysts Edge
Gelkak Gyromist 18 Quest
Raging Reef Crawler 20-21
Greymist Tidehunter 19
Greymist Oracle 18-19
Elder Darkshore Thresher 16-17

3 Tower of Althalaxx
Dark Strand Fanatic 16-17
Delmanis the Hated 17
Dark Strand Voidcaller 28-29
Dark Strand Voidcaller's Minion 28-29
Balthule Shadowstrike 15

4 Cliffspring River
Encrusted Tide Crawler 18-20
Reef Crawler 15-17
Moonstalker 14-15
Rabid Thistle Bear 13-15
Forestrider 14-16

5 Cliffspring Falls
Stormscale Wave Rider 15-16
Stormscale Siren 16-17

6 Blackwood Village
Blackwood Warrior 16-17
Blackwood Totemic 18

7 Thistle Bear Den
Thistle Cub 10
Den Mother 18

8 Darkshore General
Thistle Bear 11-12
Rabid Thistle Bear 13-14
Moonstalker Runt 10-11
Moonstalker 14-15
Forestrider Fledgling 11-13

9 Bashal'Aran
Asterion 15 Quest
Vile Sprite 10-11
Wild Grell 11-12
Deth'ryll Satyr 12-13

10 Auberdine
Auberdine Sentinel 40
Thornarian Treetender 18 Quest
Terenthis 15 Quest
Grimclaw 13 Quest
Sentinel Elissa Starbreeze 20 Quest
Gershala Nightwhisper 20 Quest
Thelgrum Stonehammer 30 Mining Supplier
Jenna Lemkenilli 26 Journeyman Engineer
Kurdram Stonehammer 35 Mining Trainer
Delfrum Flintbeard 25 Journeyman Blacksmith
Elisa Steelhand 30 Blacksmithing Supplier
Gorbold Steelhand 30 General Trade Supplier
Valdaron 14 Tailoring Supplies
Grondal Moonbreeze 29 Journeyman Tailor
Shaldyn 15 Clothier
Alanndarian 22
Dalmond 17 General Goods
Naram Longclaw 20 Weaponsmith

Thundris Windreaver 15
Mavralyn 18 Leather Armor and Leatherworking
   Supplies
Harlon Thornguard 25 Armorer & Shieldsmith
Archeologist Hollee 12 Explorer's League Quest
Sentinel Glynda Nal'Shea 45 Quest
Barithras Moonshade 14 Quest
Allyndia 15 Grocer
Taldan 16 Drink Vendor
Innkeeper Shaussiy 30 Innkeeper
Kyndri 13 Baker
Laird 14 Fish Vendor
Wizbang Cranktoggle 15 Quest
Cerellean Whiteclaw 15 Quest
Boats to Teldrassil and Menethil
Gwennyth Bly'Leggonde 21
Caylais Moonfeather 55 Elite Hippogryph Master
Yalda 51
Jaelysa 30 Stable Master
Gubber Blump 15 Quest

11 The Long Wash
Pygmy Tide Crawler 9-10
Greymist Raider 11-12
Greymist Coast Runner 12-13
Young Reef Crawler 10-11
Darkshore Thresher 13

12 Moonkin Cave
Moonkin 12-13
Young Moonkin 11-12

13 Twilight Vale
Blackwood Windtalker 13-14
Blackwood Pathfinder 12-13
Moonstalker 14-15

Rabid Thistle Bear 13-14
Grizzled Thistle Bear 16-17
Forestrider 15
Blackwood Warrior 16-17
Blackwood Totemic 17-18
Giant Forestrider 17-19
Moonstalker Sire 18-19
Moonstalker Matriarch 19-20
Moonstalker Runt 16 Moonstalker Matriarch's Minion

14 Ameth'Aran
Anaya Dawnrunner 16 Quest
Cursed Highborn 10-11
Writhing Highborn 11-12
Wailing Highborn 12-13

15 Wildbend River

16 Grove of the Ancients
Onu 55 Ancient of Lore Quest
Tiyana 15 Grocer
Ullana 15 Trade Supplies

17 Grimclaw 13 Quest

18 Blackwood Den
Blackwood Ursa 18-19
Blackwood Shaman 19-20

19 The Master's Glaive
Twilight Disciple 16-17
Twilight Thug 17-18

20 Remtravel's Excavation
Prospector Remtravel 16 Explorer's League Quest
Cracked Golem 18-19
Sentinel Aynasha 20 Quest

FELWOOD

DESOLACE

Appropriately named, Desolace is a land where there is little growth, joy, or hope. In the south, demons move about the hills, poisoning the territory and attacking anything that comes near. (They are thankfully lacking in greater demons or leadership.) Because the territory is so poorly held by any concentrated force, the Horde and Alliance both have a foothold here, with the Alliance in the north and the Horde farther down. Warring Centaur tribes stay of opposite sides of the lower central areas, east and west. It is possible to join with one of these and turn the tides against the other, improving relations with the first. In a land so unrelenting, perhaps war is the only means of survival.

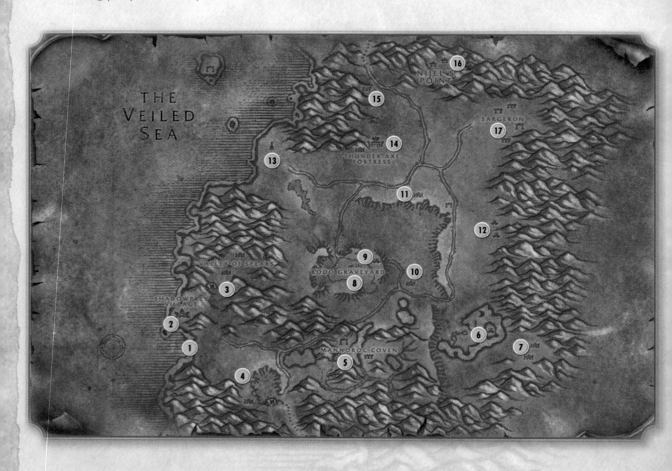

Desolace Legend

1 Sar'theris Strand
Drysnap Crawler 33-34
Drysnap Pincer 34-35
Elder Thunder Lizard 34-38
Dread Ripper 37-40
Scorpashi Lasher 34-35
Scorpashi Snapper 30-32

2 Shadowsprey Village
Thalon 55+ Wind Rider Master
Jinar'Zillen 40 Quest
Roon Wildmane 45 Quest
Innkeeper Sikewa 30 Innkeeper
Aboda 30 Stable Master
Taiga Wiseman 60 Quest

3 Valley of Spears
Maraudine Bonepaw 37-38+
Maraudine Khan Advisor 38-39+
Maraudine Khan Guard 39-40+
Maraudine Marauder 39-40+
Maraudine Mauler 38-39+
Maraudine Pack Runner 39+
Maraudine Scout 37-38
Maraudine Windchaser 38-39
Maraudine Wrangler 37-38

4 Gelkis Village
Gelkis Earthcaller 34-35
Gelkis Marauder 35-36
Gelkis Mauler 35-36
Gelkis Outrunner 32-33
Gelkis Scout 32-33
Gelkis Stamper 33-34
Gelkis Windchaser 33-34
Dread Ripper 37-40
Elder Thunder Lizard 34-38

5 Mannoroc Coven
Scorpashi Lasher 34-35
Scorpashi Snapper 30-32
Elder Thunder Lizard 34-38
Ley Hunter 39-40
Doomwarder 37-38
Doomwarder Captain 38-39
Doomwarder Lord 39-40
Lesser Infernal 36-37
Nether Maiden 37-38
Mage Hunter 38-39

6 Magram Village
Warug 44 Quest
Magram Bonepaw 37-38
Magram Marauder 35-36
Elder Thunder Lizard 34-38
Dread Ripper 37-40
Whirlwind Shredder 32-34

7 Shadowbreak Ravine
Burning Blade Invoker 40
Burning Blade Summoner 38-39
Ley Hunter 40
Imp Minion 38-39
Burning Blade Nightmare 40

8 Kodo Graveyard
Aged Kodo 33-35
Ancient Kodo 37-38
Dying Kodo 37
Carrion Horror 35-38

9 Ghost Walker Post
Gurda Wildmane 35 Quest
Felgur Twocuts 44 Quest
Superior Macecrafter 40
Nataka Longhorn 40 Quest
Narv Hidecrafter 42 Expert Leathercrafter
Takata Steelblade 40 Quest

Maurin Bonesplitter 35 Quest
Harnor 40 Food & Drink
Kireena 41 Trade Goods
Ghost Walker Brave 50

10 Scrabblescrews Camp
Smeed Scrabblescrews 45
Gizelton Caravan Kodo 35
Tamed Kodo 34-35

11 Kormek's Hut
Bibbly F'utzbuckle 45 Quest
Cork Gizelton 38 Quest
Rigger Gizelton 36 Quest
Gizelton Caravan Kodo 35
Hulking Gritjaw Basilisk 37-38
Elder Thunder Lizard 34-38
Bonepaw Hyena 30-32
Whirlwind Stormwalker 36-38
Dread Flyer 34-38
Scorpashi Lasher 34-35
Scorpashi Snapper 30-32

12 Kolkar Village
Elder Thunder Lizard 34-38
Raging Thunder Lizard 31-34
Dread Swoop 31-33
Kolkar Battle Lord 32-33
Kolkar Centaur 30-31
Kolkar Destroyer 32-33
Kolkar Mauler 31-32
Kolkar Scout 30-31
Kolkar Windchaser 31-32

13 Ethel Rethor
Azore Aldamort 60 Quest
Scorpashi Lasher 34-35
Scorpashi Snapper 30-32
Hulking Gritjaw Basilisk 37-38
Whirlwind Stormwalker 35-37
Whirlwind Ripper 32-34

Dread Swoop 30-33
Slitherblade Myrmidon 34-35
Slitherblade Naga 32-33
Slitherblade Oracle 34-35
Slitherblade Razortail 35-36
Slitherblade Sea Witch 35-36
Slitherblade Tidehunter 36-37
Slitherblade Warrior 33-34

14 Thunder Axe Fortress
Burning Blade Adept 31-32
Burning Blade Augur 30-31
Burning Blade Felsworn 31-32
Burning Blade Invoker 38-39
Burning Blade Reaver 30-31
Burning Blade Shadowmage 32-33
Burning Blade Summoner 38-39

15 Tethris Aran
Gritjaw Basilisk 32
Dread Swoop 32-33
Scorpashi Snapper 30-31

16 Nijel's Point
Vahlarriel Demonslayer 37 Quest
Corporal Melkins 39
Captain Pentigast 42
Kreldig Ungar 35 Reclaimers Inc. Quest
Innkeeper Lyshaera 30 Innkeeper
Janet Hommers 40 Food & Drink
Shelgrson 30 Stable Master
Baritanas Skyriver 55 Hyppogryph Master
Nijel's Point Guard 45

17 Sargeron
Hatefury Betrayer 32-33
Hatefury Felsworn 30-32
Hatefury Hellcaller 31-33
Hatefury Rogue 30-32
Hatefury Shadowstalker 32-33
Hatefury Trickster 31-32

DUN MOROGH

Dun Morogh rests in the highlands between the Wetlands and the Searing Gorge. Blocked from reaching either because of the impassable cliffs of stone and ice that surround it, Dun Morogh is only traversable over land via the route through Loch Modan. This is the home of the dwarven capitol, Ironforge. Though Wolves, Troggs, and a small pocket of resistance from Dark Iron Dwarves are found here, few greater threats exist. The most dangerous part of Dun Morogh is located in the north-west, where the Gnome capitol of Gnomeregan once bustled with activity. A failed experiment in weaponry has altered the capitol into a nightmare of disease and poison, avoided by many.

Dun Morogh Legend

1 Gnomeregan
Entrance to Gnomeregan Instance
Elder Crag Boars 7-8
Ice Claw Bear 7-8
Leper Gnome 8-10
Snow Leopard 7-8

2 Frostmane Hold
Elder Crag Boars 7-8
Frostmane Headhunter 8-9
Frostmane Snowstrider 8-9
Frostmane Troll 7-8
Ice Claw Bear 7-8
Snow Leopard 7-8

3 Southwestern Dun Morogh
Crag Boar 5-6
Juvenile Snow Leopard 5-6
Young Black Bear 5-6

4 Chill Breeze Valley
Tundra MacGrann 20 Quest
Large Crag Boar 6-7
Old Icebeard 11+

5 The Grizzled Den
Wendigo 6-7
Young Wendigo 5

6 Kharanos
Golom Frostbeard 10 Vendor
Gremlock Pilsnor 10 Cook
Innkeeper Belm 30 Innkeeper
Jarven Thunderbrew 15 Quest
Ozzie Togglevolt 10 Quest
Ragnar Thunderbrew 30 Quest
Razzle Sprysprocket 20 Quest
Senir Whitebeard 12 Quest
Shelby Stoneflint 30 Stable Master
Thammer Pol 11 Physician
Tharek Blackstone 12 Quest
Tognus Flintfire 30 Blacksmith

7 Steelgrill's Depot
Beldin Steelgrill 12 Quest
Bronk Guzzlegear 24 Engineer
Milli Featherwhistle 50 Mechanostrider Merchant
Pilot Bellowfiz 18 Quest
Pilot Stonegear 20 Quest
Yarr Hammerstone 10 Miner

8 Coldridge Pass
Rockjaw Raider 3-4

9 Coldridge Valley
Grelin Whitebeard 5 Quest
Talin Keeneye 5 Quest
Burly Rockjaw Trogg 2
Frostmane Novice 3-4
Frostmane Troll Whelps 3-4

Grik'nir the Cold 5 Quest Target
Ragged Young Wolf 1-2
Rockjaw Troggs 1-2
Small Crag Boar 3

10 Anvilmar
Adlin Pridedrift 5 Quest
Felix Whindlebolt 2 Quest
Sten Stoutarm 5 Quest

11 Iceflow Lake
Elder Crag Boars 7-8
Ice Claw Bear 7-8
Snow Leopard 7-8

12 Shimmer Ridge
Frostmane Headhunter 8-9
Frostmane Seer 8
Frostmane Snowstrider 8-9
Frostmane Troll 7-8

13 Eastern Dun Morogh
Elder Crag Boar 7-8
Snow Tracker Wolf 6-7

14 Misty Pine Refuge
Father Gavin 15 Argent Dawn

15 Amberstill Ranch
Rudra Amberstill 10 Quest
Turuk Amberstill 10 Vendor
Vagash 12+ Quest Target

16 Gol'Bolar Quarry and Mine
Foreman Stonebrow 12 Quest
Senator Mehr Stonehallow 50 Quest
Rockjaw Bonesnapper 8-9
Rockjaw Skullthumper 8-9

17 Far Eastern Dun Morogh
Elder Crag Boars 8-9
Rockjaw Ambusher 9-10
Scarred Crag Boar 9-10

18 Helm's Bed Lake
Captain Beld 11 Quest Target
Dark Iron Spy 9-10
Rockjaw Backbreaker 11-12
Rockjaw Bonesnapper 8-9
Scarred Crag Boar 9-10

19 North Gate Pass
Elder Crag Boars 8-9
Ice Claw Bears 8-9
Scarred Crag Boar 9-10

20 North Gate Outpost
Pilot Hammerfoot 17 Quest
Snow Leopard 8
Mangeclaw 11 Quest Target

21 South Gate Outpost

22 Ironforge

DUROTAR

Some of Azeroth's Orcs and Trolls call Durotar their home. The Valley of Trials begins to temper the characters with its rugged and demanding landscape. Sen'jin is to the south and Razor Hill lies to the north. Orgrimmar, the capitol city of the Orcs, is at the exteme northern edge of the region. A new dungeon was recently discovered within Orgrimmar itself and adventurers trying to prove themselves often venture there before even leaving Durotar for far off lands.

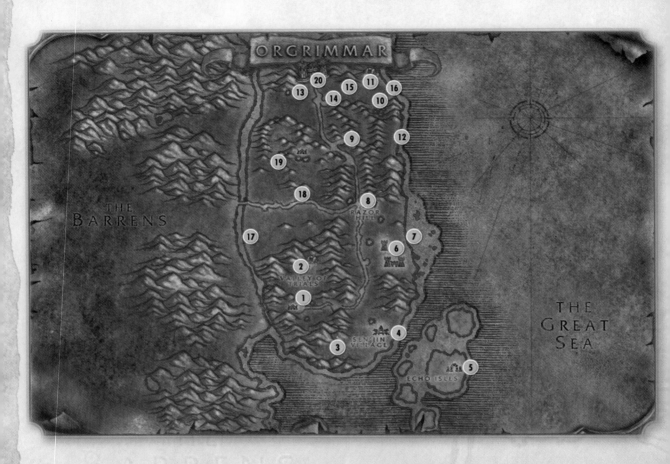

Durotar Legend

1 The Valley of Trials
Kzan Thornslash 34 Weaponsmith
Rarc 10 Armorer & Shieldcrafter
Huklah 11 Cloth & Leather Armor
Rwag 8 Rogue Trainer
Gornek 5 Quest
Den Grunt 75
Ken'Jai 10 Priest Trainer
Shikrik 10 Shaman Trainer
Canoga Earthcaller 8 Quest
Mai'ah 10 Mage Trainer
Ruzan 10 Quest
Zureetha Fargaze 12 Quest
Jen'shan 8 Hunter Trainer
Frang 11 Warrior Trainer
Magga 5
Duokna 10 General Goods
Zlagk 9 Butcher
Galgar 8
Kaltunk 20
Mottled Boar 1-2
Sarkoth 4
Scorpid Worker 3
Vile Familiar 3-4
Felstalker 3-4

2 Burning Blade Cove
Yarrog Baneshadow 5
Vile Familiar 3-4
Felstalker 3-4

3 Kolkar Crag
Kolkar Drudge 6-7
Kolkar Outrunner 7-8

**4 Sen'jin Village/
     Darkspear Strand**
Ukor 4 Quest
Sen'jin Watcher 25-30
Miao'zan 25 Journeyman Alchemist
Hai'zan 14 Butcher
Vel'rin Fang 7 Quest
Master Vornal 11 Quest
Master Gadrin 12
K'waii 11 General Goods

Tai'tasi 12 Trade Supplies
Xur'gyl 40 Axe Trainer
Trayexir 40 Bow Trainer
Zansoa 14 Fishing Supplies
Xar'Ti 50 Raptor Rider Trainer
Zjolnir 45 Raptor handler
Un'Thuwa 14 Mage Trainer
Bom'bay 8 Witch Doctor in Training
Mishiki 14 Herbalist
Clattering Scorpid 5-6
Dire Mottled Boar 6-7
Pygmy Surf Crawler 5-8
Makura Clacker 6-7
Makura Shellhide 6-7

5 Echo Isles
Zalazane 10
Durotar Tiger 5-8
Bloodtalon Taillasher 6-8
Makura Clacker 5-8
Surf Crawler 7-8
Hexed Troll 8-9
Voodoo Troll 8-9

6 Tiragarde Keep
Lieutenant Benedict 8
Kul Tiras Marine 6-7
Kul Tiras Sailor 5-6

7 Scuttle Coast
Pygmy Surf Crawler 5-6
Makura Clacker 6-7
Makura Shellhide 6-7

8 Razor Hill
Razor Hill Grunt 28-32
Orgnil Soulscar 18 Quest
Thotar 16 Hunter Trainer
Gar'Thok 10 Quest
Kaplak 14 Rogue Trainer
Takrin Pathseeker 30 Quest
Grimtak 14 Butcher
Cook Torka 6 Quest
Showja'my 30 Stable Master
Innkeeper Grosk 30 Innkeeper
Yelnagi Blackarm 16

Wuark 16 Armorer & Shieldcrafter
Krunn 16 Miner
Dwukk 27 Journeyman Blacksmith
Uhgar 15 Weaponsmith
Ghrawt 13 Bowyer
Cutac 14 Cloth & Leather Armor Merchant
Dhugru Gorelust 37 Warlock Trainer
Ophek 10
Kitha 17 Demon Trainer
Voidwalker 17 Kitha's Minion
Flakk 15 Trade Supplies
Rawrk 15 First Aid Trainer
Jark 14 General Goods
Swart 15 Shaman Trainer
Tai'jin 18 Priest Trainer
Tarshaw Jaggedscar 43 Warrior Trainer
Furl Scornbrow 6 Quest

9 Drygulch Ravine
Dustwind Harpy 7-8
Dustwind Pillager 7-8
Dustwind Savage 9-10
Dustwind Storm Witch 10-11

10 Margoz' Camp
Margoz 18 Quest

11 Skull Rock
Gazz'uz 14
Burning Blade Thug 8-9
Burning Blade Apprentice 10-11
Rezlak 5 Tinker's Union

12 Dead Eye Shore
Makrura Snapclaw 8-9
Encrusted Surf Crawler 7-10
Corrupted Surf Crawler 10-11
Elder Mottled Boar 8-9
Venomtail Scorpid 9-10
Bloodtalon Scythemaw 8

13 Rocktusk Farm
Swine 3
Elder Mottled Boar 8-9
Venomtail Scorpid 9-10
Bloodtalon Scythemaw 8

14 Jaggedswine Farm
Swine 3
Elder Mottled Boar 8-9
Venomtail Scorpid 9-10
Bloodtalon Scythemaw 8-10

**15 Zeppelin to Grom'gol Base camp and
      Undercity**

16 Bladefist Bay
Makrura Snapclaw 8-9
Encrusted Surf Crawler 7-10
Corrupted Surf Crawler 10-11
Elder Mottled Boar 8-9
Venomtail Scorpid 9-10
Bloodtalon Scythemaw 8

17 Southfury River
Bloodtalon Scythemaw 8-10
Bloodtalon Taillasher 5-10
Armored Scorpid 8-10
Corrupted Bloodtalon
     Scythemaw 10-11
Dreadmaw Crockilisk 9-11
Elder Mottled Boar 8-9
Misha Tor'kren 5 Quest

18 Razormane Grounds
Dire Mottled Boar 6-7
Razormane Dustrunner 8-9
Razormane Battleguard 9-10
Razormane Scout 7-8
Razormane Quillboar 6-7
Bloodtalon Taillasher 6-8
Armored Scorpid 7

19 Thunder Ridge
Fizzle Darkstorm 12
Voidwalker Minion 10
Lightning Hide 10-11
Thunder Lizard 9-10
Burning Blade Apprentice 10-11
Burning Blade Fanatic 9-10

20 Orgimmar

THE
GREAT

91

DUSKWOOD

Duskwood has become quiet; the silent dead now wander through this once tranquil forest, slaying the living and threatening to overwhelm the town of Darkshire. People of that town speak of Raven Hill, a western town whose people have all but disappeared. And through it all, a force of great power wanders the road to Darkshire, calling to the people of Duskwood, "I hunger!"

Duskwood Legend

1   The Hushed Bank
Sven Yorgen 20 Quest
Green Recluse 21-22
Pygmy Venom Web Spider 18-19
Rabid Dire Wolf 20-21
Starving Dire Wolf 19-20
Venom Web Spider 19-20

2   Addle's Stead
Defias Enchanter 26-27
Defias Night Blade 25-26
Defias Night Runner 25-26
Pygmy Venom Web Spider 18-19
Rabid Dire Wolf 20-21
Venom Web Spider 19-20

3   Raven Hill
Jitters 25 Quest

4   Raven Hill Cemetery
Abercrombie 35 Quest
Bone Chewer 26-27
Carrion Recluse 25-26
Flesh Eater 24-25
Mor'ladrim 35 Elite Quest Target
Rotted One 25-26
Skeletal Fiend 24-25
Skeletal Raider 27-28

5   Dawning Woods Catacombs
Brain Eater 28-29
Plague Spreader 27-28
Skeletal Warder 28-29

6   Forlorn Rowe
Brain Eater 28-29
Morbent Fel 35 Elite Quest Target
Plague Spreader 28
Skeletal Healer 26-27
Skeletal Raider 27-28

7   The Darkened Bank
Black Widow Hatchling 24-25
Green Recluse 21-22
Pygmy Venom Web Spider 18-19
Rabid Dire Wolf 20-21
Starving Dire Wolf 19-20

8   Vul'Gor Ogre Mound
Splinter Fist Enslaver 30-31
Splinter Fist Firemonger 28-29
Splinter Fist Taskmaster 27-28
Splinter Fist Warrior 29-30

9   Crossroad
Watcher Dodds 29 Quest
Black Ravager Mastiff 25-26
Black Ravager 25-26
Stitches 35 Elite
Young Black Ravager 23-24

10   Yorgen Farmstead
Defias Enchanter 26-27
Defias Night Blade 25-26
Defias Night Runner 24-25
Young Black Ravager 23-24

11   Twilight Grove

12   The Rotting Orchard
Nightbane Shadow Weaver 27-28
Nightbane Dark Runner 28-29

13   Brightwood Grove
Black Ravager Mastiff 25-26
Black Ravager 25-26
Nightbane Dark Runner 28-29
Nightbane Shadow Weaver 27-28
Nightbane Worgen 26-27
Young Black Ravager 23-24

14   Manor Mistmantle
Fetid Corpse 29-30
Stalven Mistmantle 35 Elite Quest Target

15   Darkshire
Ambassador Berrybuck 30 Quest
Calor 20 Quest
Chef Grual 30 Quest
Clarise Gnarltree 31 Expert Blacksmith
Clerk Daltry 31 Quest
Commander Althea Ebonlocke 45 Quest
Councilman Millstipe 28 Quest

Danielle Zipstitch 27 Specialty Tailor
Felicia Maline 55 Gryphon Master
Finbus Geargrind 31 Expert Engineer
Innkeeper Trelayne 30 Innkeeper
Jonathon Carevin 25 Quest
Lord Ello Ebonlocke 30 Quest
Madame Eva 25 Quest
Sirra Von'Indi 24 Quest
Steven Black 30 Stable Master
Tavernkeeper Smitts 22 Quest
Viktori Prism'Antras 28 Quest
Watcher Backus 42 Quest

16   Spider Cave
Black Widow Hatchling 24-25

17   Blind Mary's Haunt
Blind Mary 40 Quest
Black Widow Hatchling 24-25
Skeletal Horror 23-24

18   Tranquil Gardens Cemetery
Insane Ghoul 26 Quest Target
Skeletal Mage 22-23
Skeletal Warrior 21-22

19   Roland's Doom
Gutspill 32
Nightbane Tainted One 30-31
Nightbane Vile Fang 29-30

DUSTWALLOW MARSH

Watery murky pools scattered among the land are the biggest indication that you're in Dustwallow Marsh. Theramore, an Alliance City, has a few trainers and vendors and there are many travel options including a flight path and a boat going to Menethil on the Eastern Kingdoms continent. This is a dangerous area and only adventurers reaching the mid to highest levels of their training can wander here in safety. There are plenty of quests for either faction to take part in, but be careful. The creatures in the marsh tend to attack in packs, so be cautious while you travel through.

Dustwallow Marsh Legend

1 Brackenwall Village
Mudcrush Durtfeet 42 Quest
Brackenwall Enforcer 55
Nazeer Bloodpike 48 Quest
Ghok'ka 43 Tailoring Supplies
Shardi 55 Elite Wind Rider Master
Zanara 43 Bowyer
Zulrg 43 Weaponsmith
Overlord Mok'Morokk Quest
Krog 40 Quest
Krak 43 Armorer
Do'gol 30
Ogg'mar 40 Butcher
Draz'Zilb 40 Quest
Tharg 44 Quest

2 Dark Mist Cavern
Darkmist Recluse 36-37
Darkmist Spider 35-36

3 Bluefen
Drywallow Crocolisk 35-36
Bloodfen Raptor 35-36
Drywallow Vicejaw 36-37
Darkfang Spider 35-36
Darkfang Lurker 36
Withervine Bark Ripper 36-37 Elemental
Theramore Infiltrator 36
Withervine Creeper 35-36

4 North Sentry Point
Theramore Sentry 35-36

5 Witch Hill
'Swamp Eye' Jarl 42 Quest
Drywallow Crocolisk 35-36
Bloodfen Raptor 35-36
Bloodfen Screecher 36-37
Drywallow Vicejaw 36-37
Withervine Creeper 35-36

6 Sentry Point
Sentry Point Guard 32-33

7 Dreadmurk Shore
Mirefin Coastrunner 36-37
Mirefin Muckdweller 36-
Murdrock Spikeshell 37-38
Murdrock Tortoise 37

8 Theramore Isle
Theramore Guard 53-57
Theramore Lieutenant 52
Michael 30 Stable Master
Morgan Stern 36
Fiora Longears 26
Innkeeper Janene 30 Innkeeper
Bartender Lillian 45 Bartender
Craig Nollward 32 Cook
Ingo Woolybush 39 Explorer's League
Guard Byron 40

Medic Tamberlyn 51
Captain Thomas 53
 Blue Team Captain
Guard Kahill 50
Guard Narrisha 50
Combat Master Szigeti 55
Combat Master Criton 55
Medic Helaina 51
Guard Jarad 50
Captain Andrews 53
 Red Team Captain
Guard Tark 50
Spot 35
Theramore Practicing Guard 48-49
Brother Karman 45 Paladin Trainer
Dwane Wertle 28 Chef
Piter Verance 41 Weaponsmith & Armorer
Clerk Lendry 20
Captain Evencane 45 Warrior Trainer
Command Samaul 40
Captain Garran Vimes 50
Adjutant Tesoran 35
Alchemist Narett 37 Expert Alchemist
Uma Bartulm 37 Herbalism & Alchemy Supplies
Marie Holdston 37 Weaponsmith
Hans Weston 37 Armorer & Shieldsmith

Caz Twosprocket 35
Gregor MacVince 35 Horse Breeder
Helenia Olden 34 Trade Supplies
Timothy Worthington 51 Master Tailor
Baldruc 55 Elite Gryphon Master

9 Alcaz Island
Strashaz Hydra 59-60 Elite
Strashaz Siren 59 Elite
Strashaz Sorceress 61 Elite

10 Dust Wallow Bay
Mottled Drywallow Crocolisk 38-39
Drywallow Snapper 37
Drywallow Daggermaw 40-41 Elite

11 The Quagmire
Darkfang Creeper 38
Tabetha quest npc

12 The Dragonmurk
Mottled Drywallow Crocolisk 38-39
Drywallow Snapper 37
Drywallow Daggermaw 40-41 Elite
Searing Whelp 42

13 The Wyrmbog
Firemane Scalebane 43-44 Elite
Searing Hatchling 41-42
Firemane Flamecaller 44 Elite
Giant Darkfang Spider 41
Entrance to Onyxia's Lair World Dungeon

14 Stonemaul Ruins
Firemane Ashe Tail 42-43 Elite
Firemane Scout 41-42 Elite
Searing Hatchling 41-42

15 Bloodfen Burrow
Bloodfen Lashtail 40-41

16 The Den of Flame
Firemane Ash Tail 42-43 Elite
Firemane Scout 41-42 Elite

17 Lost Point
Theramore Deserter 37
Swamp Ooze 38
Bloodfen Scytheclaw 37
Darkfang Venomspitter 38
Mottled Drywallow Crocolisk 38-39

18 Shady Rest Inn

19 Tidefury Cove
Muckshell Pincer 42
Muckshell Scrabbler 42

20 Beezil's Wreck
Acidic Swamp Ooze 39-41
Corrosive Swamp Ooze 38

The Eastern Plaguelands

Beyond Darrowmere Lake are the Eastern Plaguelands, home of disease, sorrow, and some of the Scourge's greatest troops. Poison fills the air and the water is dangerous. Only the Scarlet Crusaders and the Argent Dawn are brave (or foolish) enough to stay here and fight against impossible odds. All wise adventurers avoid the Scarlet Crusade, who see the taint in everything, but the Argent Dawn camp, in the east, is a safe haven for the Alliance.

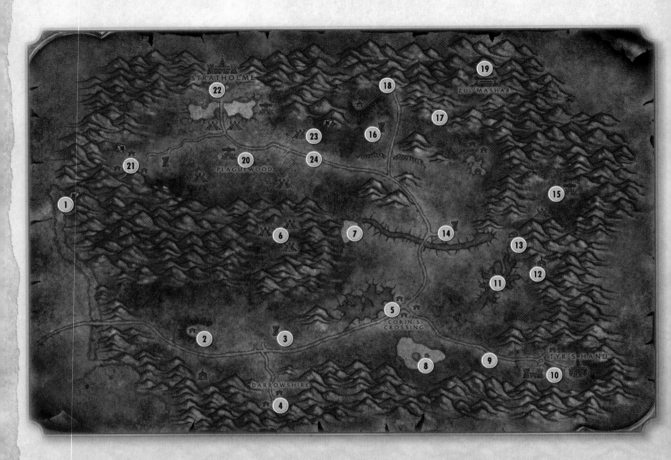

Eastern Plaguelands Legend

1 Thondroril River
Tirion Fordring 61 Quest
Carrion Grub 54-55
Plaguebat 54
Plaguehound Runt 53-54

2 The Marris Stead
Abomination 59-60
Death Singer 57-59
Diseased Flayer 59
Duskwing 60 Elite
Eyeless Watcher 58
Scourge Champion 60

3 Crown Guard Tower
Carrion Grub 55
Noxious Plaguebat 55-56
Plaguehound 55-56

4 Darrowshire
Carrion Grub 55
Plaguebat 53
Plaguehound Runt 53-54
Putrid Gargoyle 56

5 Corin's Crossing
Dark Caster 56
Gibbering Ghoul 57
Hate Shrieker 55-57
Scourge Warder 56
Stitched Horror 58
Unseen Servant 55
Vile Tutor 56-57

6 The Fungal Vale
Abomination 59-60
Crypt Slayer 58-59
Dark Adept 57
Death Singer 59
Diseased Flayer 59
Eyeless Watcher 58
Scourge Champion 59-60
Shadowmage 59-60

7 Blackwood Lake
Blighted Horror 56-57
Plague Monstrosity 58

8 Lake Mereldar
Plague Ravager 55-56

9 Scarlet Base Camp
Scarlet Cleric 54 Elite
Scarlet Enchanter 55 Elite
Scarlet Warder 53-54 Elite

10 Tyr's Hand
Scarlet Archmage 55-57 Elite
Scarlet Cleric 54-55 Elite
Scarlet Curate 55-56 Elite
Scarlet Enchanter 53-55 Elite
Scarlet Praetorian 56-57 Elite
Scarlet Warder 53-54 Elite

11 Pestilent Scar
Living Decay 55-56
Rotting Sludge 54-55

12 Light's Hope Chapel
Archmage Angela Dosantos 60
Argent Guard 55
Argent Medic 57
Argent Rider 60
Argent Sentry 60
Betina Bigglezink 57
Carlin Redpath 58
Commander Eligor Dawnbringer 60
Craftsman Wilhelm 59
Dispatch Commander Metz 60
Duke Nicholas Zuerenhoff 60
Emmissary Gormok 55
Emmissary Whitebeard 55
Father Inigo Montoy 60
Georgia 55 gryphon master
Huntsman Leopold 60
Jase Farlane 56
Jessica Chambers 52, Innkeeper
Khaelyn Steelwing 55 gryphon master
Korfax, Champion of the Light 60
Leonid Barthalomew the Revered 60
Lord Maxwell Tyrosus 62
Matous the Wrathcaster 60
Pack Mule 1-2
Packmaster Stonebruiser 59

Quartermaster Miranda
 Breechlock 60
Rimbalt Earthshatter 60
Rohan the Assassin 60
Smokey LaRue 55
Scarlet Commander Marjhan 60

13 Browman Mill
Death Singer 58-59
Diseased Flayer 58
Dread Weaver 58-59
Scourge Champion 59-60

14 Eastwall Tower
Borelgore 61 Elite
Carrion Grub 55
Crypt Horror 57-58
Diseased Flayer 59
Noxious Plaguebat 55-56
Plaguehound 55-56
Scourge Guard 57-58

15 The Noxious Glade
Crypt Slayer 58-59
Death Singer 59
Diseased Flayer 59
Dread Weaver 59
Scourge Champion 59

16 Northpass Tower
Aurora Skycaller 62
Kriss Goldenlight 60
Carrion Grub 55
Noxious Plaguebat 55-56
Plaguehound 55-56

17 Northdale
Death Singer 57-59
Eyeless Watcher 57-58
Frenzied Plaguehound 57
Plague Monstrosity 58

18 Quel'Lithien Lodge
Pathstrider 57-58
Ranger 59-60
Ranger Lord Hawkspear 60 Elite
Woodsman 58-59

19 Zul'Mashar
Mossflayer Cannibal 57-59
Mossflayer Scout 57-58
Mossflayer Shadowhunter 58-59

20 Plaguewood
Cannibal Ghoul 54
Cursed Mage 54-55
Putrid Gargoyle 56
Scourge Soldier 53-54
Scourge Warder 56
Stitched Horror 57

21 Terrordale
Carrion Devourer 56
Crypt Fiend 53-54
Crypt Walker 55-56
Dark Caster 56
Gibbering Ghoul 57
Hate Shrieker 55-57
Scourge Soldier 53
Scourge Warder 56
Stitched Horror 57-58
Stitched Horror 58
Torn Screamer 53-55
Unseen Servant 55
Vile Tutor 56-57

22 Stratholme
Entrance to Stratholme World Dungeon
Hate Shrieker 55-56
Necromancer 54
Stitched Horror 58
Torn Screamer 53-55

23 Stratholme
Secondary Entrance to Stratholme World Dungeon

24 Naxxramas

ELWYNN FOREST

Elwynn Forest has been a quiet land for some time, but pressing attacks from the Defias Brotherhood and nearby Gnolls have made the Humans here nervous. It seems that the times of peace are over, because only the mighty city of Stormwind seems immune to the presence of foul beasts and aggressive bandits. The once great copper mines of Elwynn are plagued with Kobolds now, and the people of Goldshire have had to arm themselves against the wild beasts of the valley.

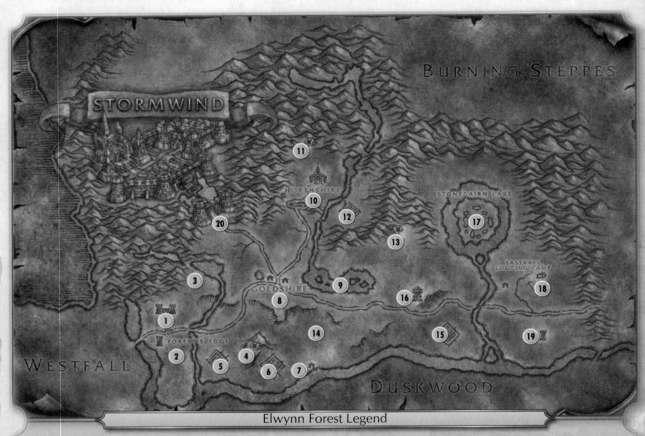

Elwynn Forest Legend

1 Westbrook Garrison
Deputy Rainer 10 Quest

2 Forest's Edge
Hogger 11+ Quest Target
Longsnout 10-11
Riverpaw Outrunner 9-10
Riverpaw Runt 8-9
Young Forest Bear 9

3 Mirror Lake Orchard
Defias Bandit 8-9
Defias Cutpurse 6
Defias Rogue Wizard 9
Mangy Wolf 5

4 Fargodeep Mine
Goldtooth 8
Kobold Miner 7
Kobold Taskmaster 10 Rare
Kobold Tunneler 5-6

5 The Stonefield Farm
"Auntie" Bernice Stonefield
  6 Quest
Gramma Stonefield 3 Quest
Ma Stonefield 3 Quest
Tommy Joe Stonefield 2 Quest
Stonetusk Boar 5-6
Young Forest Bear 8-9

6 The Maclure Vineyards
Billy Maclure 1 Quest
Joshua Maclure 5 Vendor
Maybell Maclure 2 Quest
Stonetusk Boar 5-6
Rockhide Boar 8

7 Jerod's Landing
Defias Dockmaster 10
Rockhide Boar 8

8 Goldshire
Adele Fielder 22 Leatherworker
Helene Peltskinner 12 Skinner
Innkeeper Farley 30 Innkeeper
Marshal Dughan 25 Quest
Michelle Belle 11 Physician
Remy "Two Times" 5 Quest
Smith Argus 24 Blacksmith
  Quest
Tomas 10 Cook
William Pestle 6 Quest

9 Crystal Lake
Lee Brown 8 Fisher
Defias Bandit 8-9
Grey Forest Wolf 7-8
Mangy Wolf 5-6
Murloc Steamrunner 6-7
Murloc 7

10 Northshire Valley
Deputy Willem 18 Quest
Eagan Peltskinner 3 Quest
Falkhaan Isenstrider 10 Quest
Marshal McBride 20 Quest
Milly Oswroth 2 Quest
Young Wolf 1-2

11 Echo Ridge Mine
Kobold Laborer 4
Kobold Vermin 1-2
Kobold Worker 3

12 Northshire Vineyards
Defias Thug 3-4
Garrick Padfoot 5 Quest Target

13 Jasperlode Mine
Kobold Geomancer 7-8
Kobold Miner 6-7
Mine Spider 9

14 Southern Elwynn Forest
Rockhide Boar 7-8
Young Forest Bear 8

15 Brackwell Pumpkin Patch
Ripe Pumpkin (Ground Spawn)
Defias Bandit 8-9
Erlan Drudgemoor 8
Morgan the Collector 10
Porcine Entourage 7
Princess 9
Rockhide Boar 7-8
Surena Caledon 9

T16ower of Azora
Dawn Brightstar 35 Arcane
  Goods
Kitta Firewind 44 Enchanter
Morley Eberlein 10 Vendor
Servant of Azora 8-9
Theocritus 24 Quest

17 Stone Cairn Lake and Hero's Vigil
Defias Rogue Wizard 9-10
Murloc Lurker 9-10

18 Eastvale Logging Camp
Katie Hunter 10 Vendor
Marshal Haggard 20 Quest
Sara Timberlain 5 Quest
Supervisor Raelen 15 Quest
Terry Palin 11 Vendor
Prowler 9-10

19 Ridgepoint Tower
Dead-tooth Jack 11 Quest
  Target
Defias Bandit 8-9
Prowler 9-10
Young Forest Bear 8-9

20 Stormwind

FELWOOD

Felwood is rife with corruption. The once green of the land is now filled predominantly with shades of ominous brown. The Emerald Circle works hard to push out the corruption that has taken over this land however, their efforts seem miniscule compared to the sheer devastation that surrounds them. This zone is located to the north of Ashenvale and serves as a passageway to both Moonglade and Winterspring. This area is a higher-level region best for those from Level 45 and up.

Felwood Legend

1 Morlos'Aran
- Arathandris Silversky 60 Emerald Circle
- Angerclaw Bear 47-48
- Ironbeak Owl 48-49
- Felpaw Wolf 47-48

2 Deadwood Village
- Felpaw Wolf 47-48
- Deadwood Warrior 48-49
- Deadwood Pathfinder 49-50
- Deadwood Gardener 48-49
- Ironbeak Owl 48-49

3 Emerald Circle
- Jessir Moonbow 50
- Della 49 Jessir's Pet
- Greta Mosshoof 59 Emerald Circle
- Tenell Leafrunner 62 Emerald Circle
- Kelek Skysweeper 57 Emerald Circle
- Eriden Bluewind 57 Emerald Circle
- Taronn Redfeather 50 Emerald Circle
- Ivy Leafrunner 63 Emerald Circle
- Ironbeak Owl 48-49

- Angerclaw Bear 47-48
- Felpaw Wolf 47-48

4 Maybess Riverbreeze 60 Emerald Circle

5 Jadefire Glen
- Jadefire Satyr 49-50
- Jadefire Felsworn 49-51
- Felpaw Wolf 47-48

6 Ruins of Constellas
- Xavathras 54
- Cursed Ooze 49-50
- Felpaw Wolf 47-48
- Angerclaw Bear 47-48
- Jadefire Shadowstalker 51-52
- Jadefire Rogue 50
- Jadefire Felsworn 50-51

7 Felwood (General)
- Felpaw Wolf 47-48
- Angerclaw Bear 47-48
- Angerclaw Mauler 49-50

- Ironbeak Hunter 50-51
- Felpaw Scavenger 49-50

8 Jaedenar
- Tainted Ooze 51-52
- Jaedenar Hound 50-51
- Jaedenar Guardian 50-51
- Jaedenar Adept 51-52
- Ironbeak Hunter 50-51
- Jaedenar Cultist 51-52

9 Bloodvenom Post
- Bloodvenom Post Brave 65
- Storm Shadowhoof 60 Quest
- Trull Failbane 55 Quest
- Bale 55 General Goods
- Brakkar 55 Elite Wind Rider Master

10 Bloodvenom Falls
- Tainted Ooze 51-52
- Angerclaw Mauler 49-50
- Ironbeak Hunter 50-51

11 Shatter Scar Vale
- Entropic Horror 54
- Entropic Beast 51-52
- Infernal Bodyguard 54 Elite
- Infernal Sentry 52-53 Elite

12 Jadefire Run
- Jadefire Trickster 52-53
- Jadefire Betrayer 52
- Jadefire Hellcaller 53-54
- Felpaw Scavenger 49-50
- Angerclaw Mauler 49-50

13 Irontree Woods
- Arei 56 Quest
- Irontree Stomper 52-53
- Toxic Horror 54

14 Irontree Cavern
- Warped Shredder 53
- Warpwood Moss Flayer 52-53

15 Felpaw Village
- Felpaw Ravager 51-53
- Deadwood Den Watcher 53-54
- Deadwood Shaman 53-54
- Deadwood Avenger 54-55
- Winterfall Runner 57
- Chieftain Bloodpaw 56

16 Talonbranch Glade
- Galhine the Hooded 60 Druid Trainer
- Kaerbrus 57 Hunter Trainer
- Shi'alune 56 Kaerbrus' Pet
- Malygen 55 General Goods
- Ironbeak Screecher 53

17 Timbermaw Hold/Passage to Winterspring and Moonglade
- Grazle 55 Quest

Feralas

Feralas is a tropical region filled with plenty of vegetation where various creatures hide. It's located south of Desolace and west of Thousand Needles and is a contrast to their stark landscapes. This is a region for mid-level adventurers and has many great soloing opportunities within it as well as some great grouping regions. There are also Horde and Alliance towns within this region. Skinners find this region to offer abundant targets for their trade and, for those looking for good experience at relatively low risk, this could be the place for which you're looking.

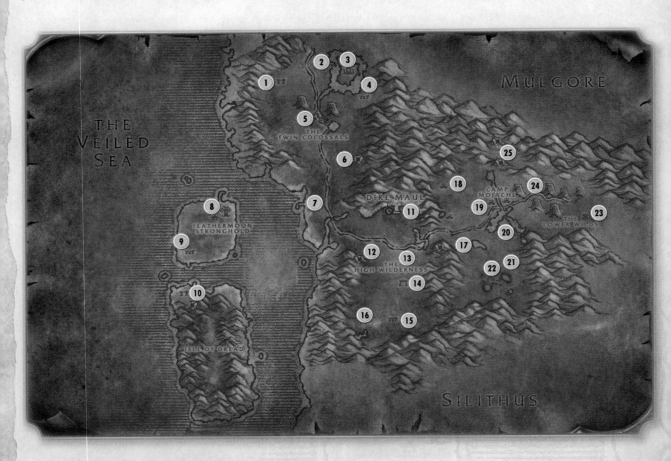

Feralas Legend

1 Ruins of Ravenwind
Northspring Roguefeather 48-49
Northspring Windcaller 49-50
Northspring Slayer 49-50

2 Jademir lake
Jademir Dragonspawn 60 elite

3 Dream Bough
Jademir Dragonspawn 60 elite

4 Oneiros
Jademir Dragonspawn 60 elite

5 The Twin Colossals
Milbon Snarltooth 50
Ironfur Patriarch 48-49
Rabid Longtooth 47-48
Groddoc Thunderer 49-50
Sprite Dragon 48-50
Rockbiter 45
Land Walker 48-49 elite
Cliff Giant 49-50 elite
Wandering Forest Walker 45 elite

6 Rage Scar Hold
Ferocious Rage Scar 47-48
Rage Scar yeti 46-47
Elder rage Scar 48-49

7 The Forgotten Coast
Rogue Vale Screecher 44-46
Sea Elelmental 48-49
Deep Strider 47 elite
Shore Strider 48-48 elite
Wave Strider 48
Sea Spray 47-48

**8 Feathermoon Stronghold-Alliance
     camp (Sardor isle)**
Innkeeper Shyria 30
Feathermoon Sentinel 65
Fyldren Moonfeather 55 elite
Pratt McGrubben Leatherworker 55
Brannock 52 fisherman
Antarius 30 stablemaster

Logannas 52 alchemy supplier
Vivianna 52 trade supplies
Madrack Greenwell 54 food and drink
Faralorn 53 General supplies

9 Ruins of Solarsal
Hatecrest Warrior 42-43
Hatecrest Screamer 41-42
Hatecrest Siren 42
Hatecrest Waverider 41-42

10 Isle of Dread
Hatecrest Myrmidon 43-44
Hatecrest Sorceress 43-44
Hatecrest Serpentguard 44-45
Lord Shalzaru 47

11 Entrance to Dire Maul World Dungeon
Arcane Chimaerok 61-62
Chimaerok 60-61
Gordok Brute 60 elite
Grizzled Ironfur Bear 44-45
Longtooth Howler 44
Lord Lakmaeran 63
Rogue vale Screecher 45

12 Feral Scar Vale
Feral Scar Yeti 43-44
Enraged Feral Scar 44-45
Hulking Feral Scar 46
Lurking Feral Scar 46
Vale Screecher 42

13 High Wilderness
Grizzled Ironfur Bear 44
Rogue Vale Screecher 46
Longtooth Howler 44

14 Ruins of Isildien-North
Gordunni Brute 42-43
Gordunni Mauler 43
Gordunni Warlock 43-44
Vale Screecher 41
Ironfur Bear 41-42
Groddoc Ape 42-43

15 Ruins of Isildien-South
Gordunni Mauler 43-44
Gordunni Warlock 43-44
Gordunni Shaman 45
Gordunni Mage-lord 45-46
Gordunni Warlord 46-47
Gordunni Battlemaster 45-45

16 Frayfeather Highlands
Frayfeather Stagwing 44-45
Frayfeather Hippogryph 43
Frayfeather Skystormer 45-46
Cursed Sycamore 45 elite
Frayfeather Patriarch 46-47

17 Lower Wilds-west
Grimtotem Shaman 43-44
Sprite Darter 44-45
Ironfur Bear 42
Grimtotem Naturalist 41-42
Grimtotem Raider 42-43
Longtooth Runner 40

18 Grimtotem Compound
Grimtotetm Naturalist 41-42
Grimtotem Shaman 43-44
Grimtotem Raider 42-43

19 Camp Mojache
Rok Orhan 40
Witch Doctor Uzer'l 50
Shyrka Wolfrunner 30 stablemaster
Kulleg Stonehorn 41 skinning trainer
Hahrana Ironhide 55 Master Leatherworker
Worb Strongstitch 46 leatehrworking supplies
Sheendra Tallgrass 52 trade supplies
Hodoken Swiftstrider 45
Sage Palerunner 44
Ruw 44 herbalism trainer
Bronk 45 alchemy trainer
Jannos Lighthoof 43 druid trainer
Camp Mojache Brave 65
Orik'andi 42
Talo thornhoof 50

Loorana 43 food and drink
Orwin Gizzmick 50
Shyn 55 elite wind rider master
Blaise Montgomery 47
Innkeeper Gruel 30
Cawind Trueaim 46 gunsmith and Bowyer

20 Wildwind Lake

21 Woodpaw Hills
Woodpaw Brute 41-42
Woodpaw trapper 40-41
Woodpaw Mongrel lvl 40-41
Woodpaw Alpha 43-44
Woodpaw Reaver 42-43
Woodpaw Mystic 42-43

22 The Writhing Deep
Grizzled Ironfur Bear 44-45
Longtooth Howler 43-44
Zukk'ash Wasp 44-45
Zukk'ash Worker 44-45

23 Lower Wilds
Longtooth Howler 44
Groddoc Ape 41-43
Ironfur Bear 42
Longtooth runner 41
Woodpaw Trapper 41-42
Woodpaw Brute 41-42
Woodpaw Mongrel 40-41

24 Lariss Pavilion
Ironfur Bear 41-42
Longtooth Runner 41

25 Gordunni Outpost
Gordunni Brute 41-43
Gordunni Ogre 40-41
Gordunni Ogre-mage 41-42

Hillsbrad Foothills

The gentle foothills around Hillsbrad would have stayed peaceful if not for the fall of Lordaeron. Now, these farmlands have become the frontlines for the war between the Alliance and the Undead of the Forsaken. Tarren Mill is a Horde town in the northeast with strong connections to the Undercity. Southshore, loyal to the Alliance, is settled in the south, along the river. Tension is high in Hillsbrad itself, to the northwest, and its people are constantly under attack by Horde troops. There is no escape from this by land, and neither does the sea offer salvation (Sirens and Murlocs wander the strands, settling freely while their enemies fight amongst themselves).

Hillsbrad Foothills Legend

1 Southpoint Tower
Deathstalker Lesh 32
Elder Gray Bear 25-26
Forest Moss Creeper 20-21

2 Azurelode Mine
Elder Gray Bear 25-26
Giant Moss Creeper 25-26
Hillsbrad Foreman 28
Hillsbrad Miner 26-27
Hillsbrad Sentry 27-28
Miner Hackett 29 Quest target

3 Western Strand
Torn Fin Coastrunner 29-30
Torn Fin Muckdweller 28-29
Torn Fin Oracle 30-31
Torn Fin Tidehunter 31-32

4 Hillsbrad Fields
Hillsbrad Tailor 24 Tailor (Alliance)
Blacksmith Verrington 26 Quest
Target Blacksmith (Alliance)
Clerk Horace Whitesteed 26 Quest Target
Farmer Ray 23 Quest Target
Forest Moss Creeper 20-21
Gray Bear 21-22
Hillsbrad Apprentice Blacksmith 24-25
Hillsbrad Councilman 25-26

Hillsbrad Farmer 23-24
Hillsbrad Farmhand 22-23
Hillsbrad Footman 25-26
Hillsbrad Peasant 24-25
Magistrate Burnside 30
Starving Mountain Lion 23-24
Vicious Gray Bear 23-24

5 Darrow Hill
Cave Yeti 30-31
Starving Mountain Lion 23-24
Vicious Gray Bear 22-23

6 Yeti Cave
Cave Yeti 30-31

7 Southshore
Bartolo Ginsetti 32 Quest
Chef Jessen 35 Quest
Darren Malvew 30 Quest
Innkeeper Anderson 30 Innkeeper
Lieutenant Farren Orinelle 25 Quest
Loremaster Dibbs 30 Quest
Magistrate Henry Maleb 30 Quest
Marshal Redpath 41 Quest
Merideth Carlson 32 Horse Trainer
Phin Odelic 36 Quest
Wesley 30 Stable Master
Snapjaw 30-31

Starving Mountain Lion 23-24
Vicious Gray Bear 22-23

8 Tarren Mill
Apothecary Lydon 35 Quest
Arachne Venomblood 29 Herbalist
Daryl Stock 56 Master Tailor
Deathguard Humbert 32 Quest
Deathguard Samsa 32 Quest
High Executor Darthalia 50 Quest
Innkeeper Shay 30 Innkeeper
Kayren Soothsallow 30
Keeper Bel'varil 34 Quest
Krusk 25 Quest
Magus Wordeen Voidglare 42 Quest
Melisara 25 Quest
Novice Thaivand 30 Quest
Serge Hinnot 32 Expert Alchemist
Tallow 27 Quest
Theodore Mon Claire 30 Stable Master
Zarise 55 Bat Handler
Elder Gray Bear 25-26
Forest Moss Creeper 20-21
Giant Moss Creeper 24-25
Gray Bear 21-22
Snapjaw 30-31

9 Durnholde Keep
Elder Gray Bear 25-26
Forest Moss Creeper 20-21
Giant Moss Creeper 24-25
Syndicate Rogue 21-22
Syndicate Shadow Mage 21-22
Syndicate Watchman 20-21
Vicious Gray Bear 22-23

10 Thoradin's Wall
Elder Gray Bear 25-26
Elder Moss Creeper 26-27
Giant Moss Creeper 24-25

11 Nethander Stead
Elder Gray Bear 25-26
Elder Moss Creeper 26-27
Feral Mountain Lion 27-28
Giant Moss Creeper 24-25
Mudsnout Gnoll 26-28
Mudsnout Shaman 27-28
Snapjaw 30-31
Syndicate Rogue 21-22
Syndicate Shadow Mage 21-22
Syndicate Watchman 20-21

12 Dun Garok
Dun Garok Mountaineer 28-29 Elite
Dun Garok Priest 29-30 Elite

Dun Garok Rifleman 29-30 Elite
Elder Moss Creeper 26-27
Feral Mountain Lion 27-28

13 Eastern Strand
Daggerspine Screamer 29-30
Daggerspine Shorehunter 30-31
Daggerspine Shorestalker 29-30
Daggerspine Siren 30

14 Purgation Isle
Arados the Damned 35 Quest Target
Condemned Acolyte 57
Condemned Cleric 31-32
Condemned Cleric 59-60
Condemned Monk 31-32
Condemned Monk 58
Cursed Acolyte 30-31
Cursed Justicar 33
Cursed Justicar 59-60
Cursed Paladin 30-31
Cursed Paladin 57-58
Judge Thelgram 34 Friendly to Alliance
Writhing Mage 31-32
Writhing Mage 58-59

The Hinterlands

In the far northeast is a land that is almost forgotten by those who fight for survival throughout the Eastern Kingdoms. The Hinterlands is an expanse of trees and valleys where Wolves, Owlbeasts, and even Dragonkin live. On the southern ridgeline are many outposts of the Vilebranch and Witherbark Trolls, all powerful and very much steeped in a bloody philosophy that even divides them from the Horde's Trolls. Along the northwest end are Dwarves and Elves. Hunting up in Hinterlands is usually safe and quiet, making it a place beloved by crafters throughout the world.

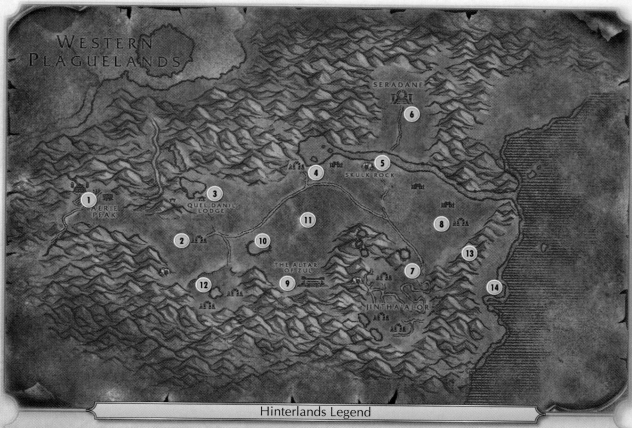

Hinterlands Legend

1 Aerie Peak
High Thane Falstad Wildhammer 50
Killium Bouldertug 50 Stable Master
Wildhammer Sentry 55
Mangy Silvermane 41-42
Razorbeak Gryphon 45
Trained Razorbeak 40-41

2 Hiri'watha
Witherbark Hideskinner 42-43
Witherbark Venomblood 43

3 Quel'Danil Lodge
Highvale Marksman 45-46
Highvale Outrunner 43-44
Highvale Ranger 46-47
Highvale Scout 44-45

4 Agol'watha
Cerulean Dragonspawn 48-49
Green Sludge 46-47
Jade Ooze 48
Primitive Owlbeast 44

5 Skulk Rock
Green Sludge 46-47
Jade Ooze 47-48
Savage Owlbeast 46-47

6 Seradane
Dreamtracker 62
Verdantine Boughguard 62
Verdantine Oracle 61
Verdantine Tree Warder 60
This is also one of the four spawn points of the
    Emerald Dragon world bosses.

7 Jintha'Alor
Hitah'ya the Keeper 51
Jade Sludge 47-48
Silvermane Stalker 47-48
Vile Priestess Hexx 51
Vilebranch Aman'zasi Guard 50-51
Vilebranch Berserker 47-48
Vilebranch Blood Drinker 49-50
Vilebranch Headhunter 46-47

Vilebranch Hideskinner 48-49
Voidwalker Minion 47-48
Vilebranch Raiding Wolf 50-51
Vilebranch Shadowcaster 47-48
Vilebranch Shadowhunter 48-49
Vilebranch Soul Eater 49-50
Vilebranch Warrior 45-46
Vilebranch Warrior 46 Elite
Vilebranch Witch Doctor 46-47
Vilebranch Witch Doctor 46-47 Elite
Vilebranch Wolf Pup 46 Beast

8 Shaol'watha
Silvermane Stalker 47-48

9 The Temple of Zul
Morta'Gya The Keeper 50 Elite
Qiaga The Keeper 52 Elite Quest Target
Vilebranch Soothsayer 47
Vilebranch Axe Thrower 46
Vilebranch Scalper 47
Vilebranch Wolf Pup 46-47

10 Valorwind lake
Primitive Owlbeast 44-45
Razorbeak Gryphon 45
Silvermane Howler 46

11 The Creeping Ruin
Green Sludge 46-47
Jade Ooze 48

12 Shadra'Alor
Atal'ai Exile 45 Quest
Witherbark Broodguard 44-45
Witherbark Caller 45-46
Witherbark Sadist 44-45

13 The Overlook Cliffs
Gammerita 48 Elite Quest Target
Saltwater Snapjaw 49-50

14 Revantusk Village

101

Loch Modan

Loch Modan is a large lake, created by the presence of the Stonewrought Dam and large meltoffs from the surrounding cliffs. Offering a blast of color and warmer weather to the Dwarves coming from Dun Morogh, this is a place of comfort. Yet, the presence of many militant Troggs and the recent ingress of Orc tribes to the north has put things on edge in Loch Modan. The Dwarves have concentrated more of their efforts here, and hope to fight the good fight against these enemies (and perhaps the dangerous Ogres in the northeast as well), but setbacks occur at every angle. Could there be traitors in the ranks?

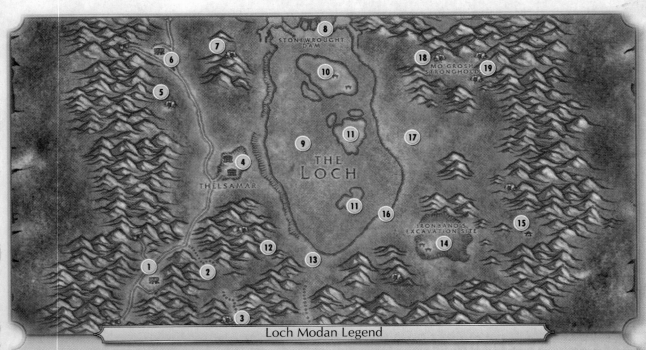

Loch Modan Legend

1 Valley of Kings
Captain Rugelfuss 40 Quest
Mountaineer Cobbleflint 30 Quest
Mountaineer Gravelgaw 30 Quest
Mountaineer Pebblebitty 44 Quest
Elder Black Bear 11-12
Forest Lurker 10-11

2 Stonesplinter Valley
Stonesplinter Bonesnapper 15-16
Stonesplinter Scout 11-12
Stonesplinter Seer 13-14
Stonesplinter Shaman 15-16
Stonesplinter Skullthumper 13-14
Stonesplinter Trogg 11-12

3 Stonesplinter Caves
Brawler 16
Gnasher 16
Grawmug 17 Quest Target
Stonesplinter Bonesnapper 15-16
Stonesplinter Seer 13-14
Stonesplinter Shaman 15-16
Stonesplinter Skullthumper 13-14

4 Thelsamar
Brock Stoneseeker 15 Mining Trainer
Dakk Blunderblast 15 Quest
Ghak Healtouch 25 Quest
Innkeeper Hearthstove 30 Innkeeper
Kali Healtouch 14 Herbalism Trainer
Lina Hearthstove 30 Stable Master
Magistrate Bluntnose 20 Quest
Mountaineer Kadrell 30 Quest
Mountaineer Langarr 30 Quest
Mountaineer Stenn 30 Quest
Thorgrum Borrelson 55 Gryphon Master
Torren Squarejaw 15 Quest
Vidra Hearthstove 10 Quest
Elder Black Bear 11-12
Forest Lurker 10-11
Mountain Boar 10-11
Stonesplinter Scout 11-12
Stonesplinter Trogg 11-12

5 Tunnel Rat Cave
Tunnel Rat Scout 10-11
Tunnel Rat Vermin 10-11

6 Algaz Station
Mountaineer Stormpike 30 Quest
Elder Black Bear 11-12

Forest Lurker 10-11
Mountain Boar 10-11

7 Silver Stream Mine
Elder Black Bear 11-12
Forest Lurker 10-11
Mountain Boar 10-11
Tunnel Rat Digger 12-13
Tunnel Rat Forager 11-12
Tunnel Rat Geomancer 12-13
Tunnel Rat Kobold 11-12
Tunnel Rat Vermin 10-11

8 Stonewrought Dam
Chief Enginneer Hinderweir VII 40 Quest
Deek Fizzlebizz 27 Journeyman Engineer
Dark Iron Insurgent 18
Dark Iron Sapper 17

9 The Loch
Cliff Lurker 13-14
Loch Frenzy 12-13
Mangy Mountain Boar 14-15
Young Threshadon 19-20

10 Trogg Islands
Bingles' Tools (Ground Spawn)
Stonesplinter Bonesnapper 15-16

Forest Lurker 10-11
Stonesplinter Bonesnapper 15-16
Stonesplinter Seer 13-14
Stonesplinter Shaman 15-16
Stonesplinter Skullthumper 13-14

11 Crocolisk Islands
Loch Crocolisk 14-15

12 Grizzlepaw Ridge
Black Bear Patriarch 16-17
Grizzled Black Bear 13-14
Mangy Mountain Boar 14-15
Ol' Sooty 20 Elite Quest Target

13 Caravan
Huldar 15 Quest
Miran 15 Quest
Dark Iron Ambusher 10
Saean 10

14 Ironband's Excavation Site
Prospector Ironband 15 Quest
Berserk Trogg 19-20
Grizzled Black Bear 13-14
Mangy Mountain Boar 14-15
Stonesplinter Digger 18-19
Stonesplinter Geomancer 18-19

15 Farstrider Lodge
Daryl the Youngling 15 Quest
Vyrin Swiftwind 15 Quest
Cliff Hadin 15 Bowyer Vendor
Irene Sureshot 15 Gunsmith Vendor
Grizzled Black Bear 13-14
Mangy Mountain Boar 14-15
Mountain Buzzard 15-16

16 Bingles' Crash Site
Bingles Blastenheimer 20 Quest

17 Hunting Grounds
Black Bear Patriarch 16-17
Elder Mountain Boar 16-17
Wood Lurker 17-18

18 Mo'grosh Stronghold
Mo'grosh Enforcer 18-19 Elite
Mo'grosh Orge 18-19 Elite
Mo'grosh Shaman 18-19 Elite

19 Mo'grosh Cavern
Chok'sul 22 Elite Quest Target
Mo'grosh Brute 19-20 Elite
Mo'grosh Mystic 19-20 Elite

Moonglade

Moonglade is a peaceful and serene setting with a small village named Nighthaven looking down on it. There isn't much here as of yet, but the way in is dangerous if you aren't friendly with the Timbermaws that guard the way in. The Lunar Festival takes place here. Brave souls can also find Malfurion Stormrage resting in the Stormrage Barrow Dens.

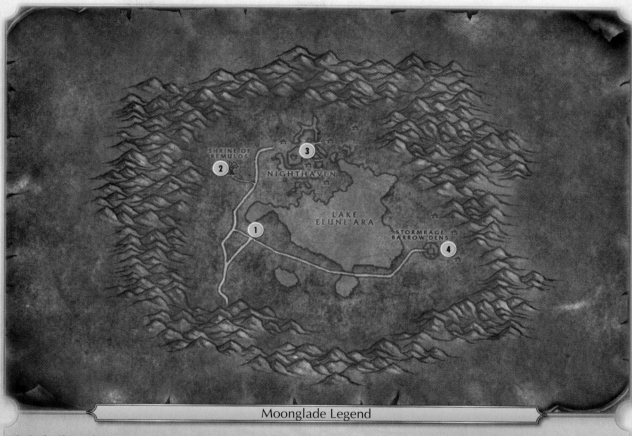

Moonglade Legend

1 Bunthen Plainswind 60	**3 Nighthaven**	Dendrite Starblaze 60	Celes Earthborn 60
2 Shrine of Remulos	Bessany Plainswind 60	Moren Riverbend 60	Tajarri 60
Keeper Remulos 62 Quest	Genia Sunshadow 51 Specialty Dress Maker	Keeper Remulos 62	**4 Stormrage Barrow Den**
	Darnall 53 Tailoring Supplies	Rabine Saturna 60	
	Mylentha Riverbend 60	Silva Fil'naveth 60	

MULGORE

Mulgore is the starting region for the Tauren. The largest portion of the land is made up of open plains ringed by mountains and the mesas that make up the capitol city of Thunder Bluff to the north. Wild Kodo Beasts roam the land and there is a rumor that a massive patriarch walks among them. Harpies have taken residence along the hillsides and the Venture Co. is trying to strip the land around Thunder Bluff and Bloodhoof Village. However, among even those dangerous adversaries, there are heroes. Cairne Bloodhoof sits in Thunder Bluff waiting for those willing to defend the land to join him.

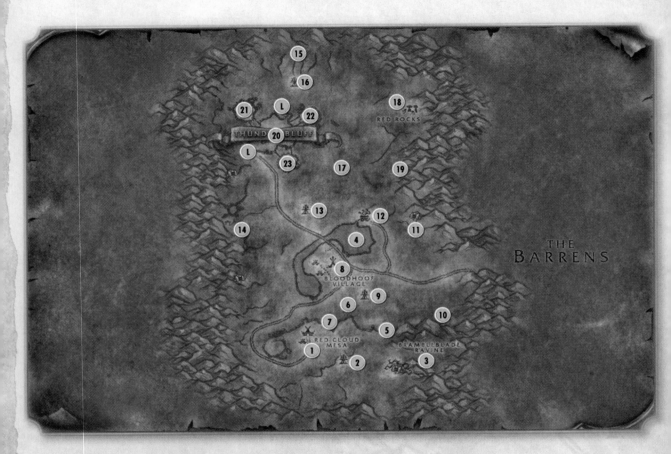

Mulgore Legend

L   Lift

1   Camp Narache
Moodan Sungrain 11 Baker
Brave Windfeather 13 Quest NPC
Vorn Skyseer 5
Bronk Stoolrage 10 Armorer and Shieldcrafter
Marjak Keenblade 9 Weaponsmith
Varia Hardhide 7 Leather Armor Merchant
Grull Hawkwind 4 Quest
Chief Hawkwind 36 Quest
Harutt Thunderhorn 10 Warrior Trainer
Lanka Farshot 11 Hunter Trainer
Seer Ravenfeather 10
Meela Dawnstrider 10 Shaman Trainer
Gart Mistrunner 9 Druid Trainer
Hawnie Softbreeze 8 General Goods
Brave Lightning Horn 15
Brave Proudsnout 16
Brave Greathoof 13
Brave Running Wolf 12

2   Well/Red Cloud Mesa
Antur Fallow 3 Quest
GreatMother Hawkwind 9 Quest
Mountain Cougar 3
Plainstrider 1-2
Battleboar 3-4
Seer Graytongue 8 Quest

3   Brambleblade Ravine
Chief Sharptusk 5
Bristleback Quilboar 3-4
Bristleback Battleboar 4-5
Bristleback Shaman 4

4   Stonebull Lake

5   Palemane Camps
Palemane Tanner 5-6
Palemane Skinner 6-7
Palemane Poacher 7-8

6   The Rolling Plains
Prairie Wolf 5-10
Taloned Swoop 8-9

Elder Plainstrider 8- 9
Golak Centaur 10
Golak Outrunner 9
Flatland Cougar 7-8
Prairie Stalker 7-8
Swoop 7-9
Adult Plainstrider 6-7
Flatland Prowler 9

7   Palemane Rock
Palemane Tanner 5-6
Palemane Skinner 6-7
Palemane Poacher 7-8

8   Bloodhoof Village
Brave Rainchaser 14
Krang Stonehoof 14 Warrior Trainer
Gennia Runetotem 12 Druid trainer
Narm Skychaser 13 Shaman Trainer
Horken Windtotem 21 Quest
Zarlman Two-Moons 7
Brave Wildrunner 14
Brave Strongbash 14
Brave Ironhorn 14
Brave Cloudmane 14
Brave Dawneagle 14
Yaw Sharpmane 11 Hunter Trainer
Harn Longcast 9 Fishing Supplies
Wunna Darkmane 10 Trade Goods
Moorat Longstride 12 General Goods
Yonn Deepcut 8 Skinner Trainer
Chaw Stronghide 23 Leatherworking Trainer
Pyall Silentstride 12 Cooking Trainer
Kennah Hawkeye 10 Gunsmith Supplier
Mahnott Roughwound 11 Weaponsmith
Harant Ironbrace 13 Armorer and Shieldcrafter
Skorn Whitecloud 21 Story Teller
Seikwa 30 Stable Master
Magrin Rivermane 6
Innkeeper Kauth 30
Vira Younghoof 13 First Aid Trainer
Varg Windwhisper 14 Leather Armor Merchant
Ruul Eagletalon 9 Quest

Jhawna Oatwind 13 Baker
Morin Cloudstalker 10 Quest

9   Winterhoof Waterwell
Venture Co. Hireling 5-6
Vencure Co. Laborer 6

10   Windfury Harpies
Windfury Harpy 7-8
Windfury Wind Witch 9
Windfury Matriarch 10-11
Windfury Sorceress 9-10

11   The Venture Co. Mine
Venture Co. Worker 8-9
Venture Co. Supervisor 9-10

12   Ravaged Caravan
Flatland Cougar 7-8
Adult Plainstrider 6-7
Prairie Stalker 7-8
Venture Co. Laborer 7
Venture Co. Taskmaster 7-8
Swoop 7-9

13   Thunderhorn Water Well
Flatland Cougar 7-8
Elder Plainstrider 8-9
Adult Plainstrider 6-7
Swoop 7-9
Praire Stalker 7-8
Venture Co. Laborer 6-7
Venture Co. Taskmaster 8

14   Bael'Dun Digsite
Bael'dun Digger 7-8
Bael'dun Appraiser 8-9

15   Windfury Ridge
Seer Wiserunner

16   Wildmane Water Well
Prairie Wolf Alpha 9-10
Flatland Prowler 9
Elder Plainstrider 8-9
Venture Co. Worker 8-9
Venture Co. Supervisor 9

Windfury Matriarch 10-11
Windfury Sorceress 9-10
Taloned Swoop 8-10

17   The Golden Plains
Kodo Calf 7
Kodo Bull 7-11
Kodo Matriarch 11-12
Prairie Stalker 7-8
Swoop 7-9
Taloned Swoop 8-10
Adult Plainstrider 6-7
Elder Plainstrider 8-9
Flatland Prowler 9
Prairie Wolf Alpha 9-10
Flatland Cougar 7-8
The Rake 10
Windfury Matriarch 10-11
Windfury Sorceress 9-10

18   Red Rocks:
     Sacred Burial Ground
Lorekeeper Raintotem 8 Quest
Ancestral Spirit 9 Quest
Flatland Prowler 9
Taloned Swoop 8-10
Prairie Wolf Alpha 9-10
Elder Plainstrider 8-9
Kodo Matriarch 11-12
Kodo Bull 10
Bristleback Interloper 9-10

19   Venture Co. Buildings
Enforcer Emilgund 11
Venture Co. Worker 8-9

20   Thunder Bluff

21   Spirit Rise

22   Elder Rise

23   Hunter Rise

REDRIDGE MOUNTAINS

East of Stormwind and Elwynn Forest is the town of Lakeshire, placed in the middle of the Redridge Mountains. Under siege by eastern Orc clans and hassled by Gnolls, things aren't simple for the people of Lakeshire currently. A great bridge that spans Lake Everstill is under repairs, even as enemy catapults lie in ruins along the southern ridgeline. To the north are Orcish Champions, known for their power and bravery, while the eastern groups have even greater leadership. Stonewatch Keep, on the far side of Lake Everstill sits as a constant reminder that peace has collapsed into a drawn-out war in Redridge.

Redridge Mountains Legend

1 Three Corners
Guard Parker 30 Quest
Black Dragon Whelp 17-18
Great Goretusk 16-17
Redridge Mongrel 15-16
Redridge Thrasher 14-15
Tarantula 15-16

2 Lakeshire
Alma Jainrose 20 Herbalism Trainer
Ariena Stormfeather 55 Gryphon Master
Chef Breanna 19 Quest
Crystal Boughman 22 Cooking Trainer
Darcy 15 Quest
Deputy Feldon 33 Quest
Foreman Oslow 20 Quest
Innkeeper Brianna 30 Innkeeper
Magistrate Solomon 36 Quest
Marshal Marris 35 Quest
Martie Jainrose 20 Quest
Verner Osgood 25 Quest

Bellygrub 24
Blackrock Outrunner 20-21
Great Goretusk 16-17

3 Lake Everstill
Great Goretusk 16-17
Murloc Flesheater 18-19
Murloc Minor Tidecaller 17-18
Murloc Scout 18-19
Murloc Shorestriker 16-17
Murloc Tidecaller 19-20

4 Lakeridge Highway
Black Dragon Whelp 17-18
Dire Condor 18-19
Great Goretusk 16-17
Murloc Minor Tidecaller 17-18
Murloc Shorestriker 16-17
Redridge Mongrel 16-17
Redridge Poacher 16-17

5 Redridge Canyons
Great Goretusk 16-17

Redridge Alpha 21-22
Redridge Basher 19-20
Redridge Brute 17-18
Redridge Mystic 18-19
Yowler 25 Quest Target

6 Rethban Caverns
Redridge Basher 19-20
Redridge Drudger 20-21

7 Render's Camp
Corporal Keeshan 25 Elite
Blackrock Champion 24-25
Blackrock Outrunner 20-21
Blackrock Renegade 21-22
Blackrock Summoner 22-23
Blackrock Tracker 23-24

8 Render's Rock
Blackrock Champion 24-25
Blackrock Summoner 22-23
Blackrock Tracker 23-24

9 Alther's Mill
Black Dragon Whelp 17-18
Dire Condor 18-19
Great Goretusk 16-17
Greater Tarantula 19-20

10 Stonewatch Tower
Blackrock Grunt 19-20
Blackrock Outrunner 19-20
Blackrock Scout 20 Elite
Blackrock Sentry 21-22 Elite
Blackrock Shadowcaster 22-23 Elite

11 Stonewatch Keep
Blackrock Gladiator 25 Elite
Blackrock Hunter 24 Elite
Blackrock Shadowcaster 22-23 Elite
Gath'Ilzogg 26 Elite Quest Target
Tharil'zun 24 Elite Quest Target

12 Galardell Valley
Rabid Shadowhide Gnoll 21-22
Shadowhide Brute 23-23

Shadowhide Darkweaver 25-26
Shadowhide Gnoll 22-23
Shadowhide Slayer 25-26
Shadowhide Warrior 24-25

13 Tower of Ilgalar
Shadowhide Darkweaver 25-26
Shadowhide Slayer 25-26
Shadowhide Warrior 24-25
Morganth

14 Stonewatch Falls
Murloc Nightcrawler 21
Murloc Tidecaller 19-20
Shadowhide Darkweaver 25-26
Shadowhide Slayer 25-26
Shadowhide Warrior 24-25

15 Render's Valley
Blackrock Outrunner 21
Blackrock Renegade 21-22

Searing Gorge

West from the Badlands is the Searing Gorge, fed by lava flows. There are Dark Iron Dwarves and Elementals building up their forces to move on Nefarian and the Alliance. The Twilight Hammer lives in the northwest, holding true to ceremonies and beliefs of the old gods, and these people are not interested in making friends with any who draw near. Those who seek fame, fortune, mithril, and thorium are drawn here as moths to the flame.

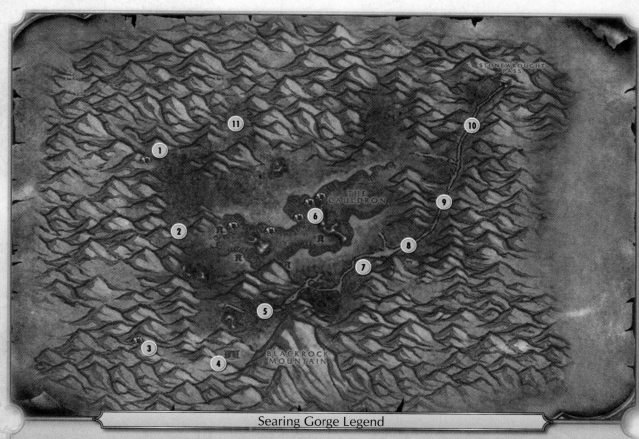

Searing Gorge Legend

1 Firewatch Ridge
Twilight Dark Shaman 47-48 Elite
Twilight Fire Guard 48-49 Elite
Twilight Geomancer 50 Elite
Twilight Idolater 50 Elite

2 Western Searing Gorge
Greater Lava Spider 47-48
Inferno Elemental 49
Magma Elemental 46-47

3 Blackchar Cave
Greater Lava Spider 48-49

4 Blackrock Mountain
Entrance to Blackrock World Dungeon

5 SW Sear Gorge
Craw Cornerstone 58 Vendor
Craw Cornerstone's Guardian 48
Greater Lava Spider 47-48
Magma Elemental 46-48
Searing Elemental 49

6 The Cauldron
Blazing Elemental 45-47
Dark Iron Slaver 45-46
Dark Iron Taskmaster 47
Heavy War Golem 48-49
Magma Elemental 47-48
Shadowsilk Poachers 47-48
Slaved Worker 45-47

7 The Sea of Cinders
Magma Elemental 47-48
Searing Lava Spider 45-47

8 Tanner Camp
Sarah Tanner 50 Master Elemental
  Leatherworker
Glassweb Spider 43-45

9 Grimsilt Dig Site
Dark Iron Geologist 43
Dark Iron Watchman 44
Glassweb Spider 43-35
Tempered War Golem 45-46

10 Dustfire Valley
Locked Door to Loch Modan
Dark Iron Geologist 43
Dark Iron Watchman 44
Glassweb Spider 43-35
Tempered War Golem 45-46

11 Thorium Point

SILITHUS

Climbing west, out of the steam of Un'Goro Crater, lies Silithus. This desert land is in a state of flux. The Cenarion Circle has bravely taken up arms to defend Azeroth from the inhabitants of Ahn'Qiraj, and the host of insect-monsters that call the various Hives home. Among the larger more visible dangers a thread of discord is sewn from the followers of the Twilight Hammer. Many dangers lurk in this mysterious land, but there is much to gain.

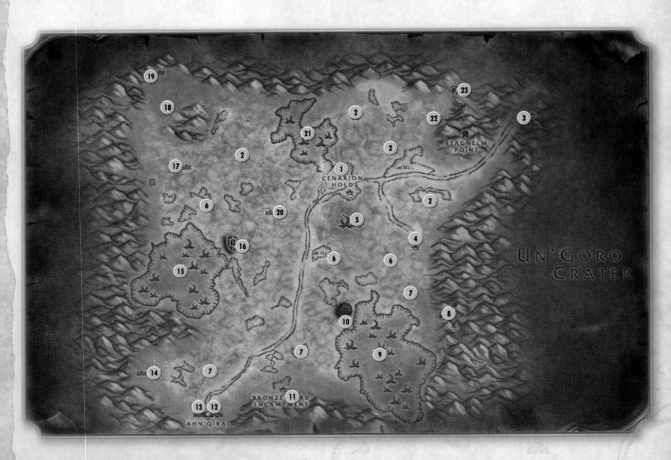

SilithusLegend

1 Cenarion Hold
Runk Windtamer 55 Wind Rider Master
Scout Bloodfist 55 Quest
Squire Leoren Mal'derath 60 Stable Master
Baristolth of the Shifting Sands 60 Quest
Commander Mar'alith 62 Quest
Mishta 58 General Trade Goods Vendor
Windcaller Kaldon 60 Quest
Cloud Skydancer 55 Hippogryph Master
Rifleman Torrig 55 Quest
Vish Kozus 61 Quest
Garon Hutchins 60 Quest
Windcaller Yessendra 55 Quest
Aurel Goldleaf 60 Quest
Dirk Thunderwood 60 Quest
Calandrath 54 Innkeeper
Keyl Swiftclaw 60 Quest
Beetix Ficklespragg 57 Quest
Noggle Ficklespragg 55 Quest
Kania 54 Enchanting Supplier
Vargus 57 Quest/Blacksmith
Warden Haro 58 Quest
Geologist Larksbane 60 Quest
Bor Wildmane 57 Quest
Huum Wildmane 60 Quest
Khur Hornstriker 57 Reagent Vendor

2 Northern Desert
Stonelash Scorpid 54-55
Sand Skitterer 55-56
Dredge Striker 55-56
Dust Stormer 55-56

3 Valor's Rest
Zannok Hidepiercer 59 Leatherworking Supplies
Jarund Stoutstrider 55 Quest
Layo Starstrike 55 Quest

4 Southwind Village
Tortured Druid 55-56
Tortured Sentinel 57
Aendel Windspear 60 Recipe Vendor
Hive'Ashi Drone 57-58

5 The Swarming Pillar
Hive'Ashi Swarmer 57-58 Elite

6 Central Desert
Stonelash Pincer 56
Dredge Crusher 57-58
Desert Rumbler 58
Twilight Marauder 58
Twilight Marauder Morna 58 Elite Boss

7 Southern Desert
Stonelash Flayer 57-58
Rock Stalker 57-58
Cyclone Warrior 57-58
Twilight Marauder 58
Twilight Marauder Morna 58 Elite Boss

8 Ortell's Hideout
Hermit Ortell 58 Quest

9 Hive'Regal
Hive'Regal Spitfire 59-60 Elite
Hive'Regal Hive Lord 59-62 Elite
Hive'Regal Ambusher 59-60 Elite
Hive'Regal Burrower 59-60 Elite
Hive'Regal Slavemaker 59-60 Elite
Mistress Natalia Mar'alith 62 Elite Boss
Cenarion Scout Landion 60 Quest

10 Horde Encampment
Krug Skullsplit 60 Quest
Merok Longstride 60 Quest
Shadow Priestess Shal 60 Quest

Apothecary Quinard 55 Quest
General Kirika 60 Quest

11 Bronzebeard Encampment
Rutgar Glyphshaper 60 Quest
Frankal Stonebridge 60 Quest
Deathclasp 59 Elite Boss

12 The Scarab Wall

13 The Scarab Dias
Jonathan the Revelator 61 Quest

14 Southern Twilight Camp
Twilight Geolord 59-60
Twilight Avenger 58-59
Twilight Master 60
Twilight Stonecaller 59-60
Twilight Keeper Exeter 60
Nelson the Nice 60 Elite

15 Hive'Zora
Hive'Zora Reaver 59-60 Elite
Hive'Zora Waywatcher 59 Elite
Hive'Zora Wasp 58-59
Hive'Zora Hive Sister 59-60 Elite
Hive'Zora Tunneler 58 Elite
Cenarion Scout Azenel 60 Quest

16 Alliance Encampment
Janela Stouthammer 60 Quest
Marshal Bluewall 60 Quest
Captain Blackanvil 60 Quest
Arcanist Nozzlespring 60 Quest
Sergeant Carnes 60 Quest

17 Eastern Twilight Camp
Twilight Geolord 59-60
Twilight Avenger 58-59
Twilight Stonecaller 59-60

Twilight Keeper Mayna 60
Twilight Prophet 60 Elite

18 The Crystal Vale
Dust Stormer 55-57
Desert Rumbler 57-58

19 Ravaged Twilight Camp
Desert Rumbler 57-58
Highlord Demitrian 62 Quest

20 Central Twilight Camp
Twilight Geolord 59-60
Twilight Avenger 58-59
Twilight Stonecaller 59-60
Twilight Keeper Havunth 60
Twilight Prophet 60 Elite

21 Hive'Ashi
Hive'Ashi Worker 57-58 Elite
Hive'Ashi Swarmer 57-58 Elite
Hive'Ashi Defender 58-59 Elite
Hive'Ashi Sandstalker 58-59 Elite
Hive'Ashi Stinger 57 Elite
Cenarion Scout Jalia 60 Quest

22 Staghelm Point
Twilight Overlord 60-61
Twilight Avenger 59
Dust Stormer 55
Ralo'shan the Eternal Watcher 60 Quest

23 Twilight's Run
Twilight Flamereaver 60
Twilight Overlord 60-61
Vyral the Vile 61

Silverpine Forest

The gloom of Silverpine is now a calming force for many of the area's residents. The Scourge control this area with a loose and rotting hand, and there are only a couple of areas that are hotly contested. Over on the east, in the middle of Lordamere Lake is a fortress where many Gnolls resist the attacks of the Forsaken. On the southern front, there are a number of mages of Dalaran who maintain a keep from which to launch strikes against their eternal foes. Apart from these enemies, the various elements of Worgen and disloyal Undead are dangerous forces for unwary travelers. Heroes from both the Horde and Alliance sometimes come here to battle Arugal, the lord and master of Shadowfang Keep.

Silverpine Forest Legend

1 North Tide's Hollow
Moonrage Darksoul 13-14
Moonrage Glutton 12-13

2 North Tide's Run
Moonrage Darksoul 13-14
Moonrage Glutton 12-13

3 The Skittering Dark
Giant Grizzled Bear 12-13
Moss Stalker 12-13

4 Skittering Dark Cave
Mist Creeper 13-14
Moss Stalker 12-13

5 The Dead Field
Ferocious Grizzled Bear 11-12
Giant Grizzled Bear 12-13
Moonrage Glutton 12-13
Mottled Worg 11-12
Nightsalk 14 Quest Target
Rothide Gladerunner 11-12
Rothide Mystic 12-13

6 The Ivar Patch
Quinn Yorick 14 Quest
Rane Yorick 15 Quest

Mottled Worg 11-12
Ravenclaw Slave 11-12

7 Maiden's Orchard
Deathstalker Erland 11 Quest
Mottled Worg 11-12
Worg 10-11

8 The Shining Strand
Vile Fin Shredder 12-13
Vile Fin Tidehunter 13-14

9 Lordamere Lake
Vile Fin Lakestalker 18-19
Vile Fin Oracle 19-20

10 Fenris Isle
Elder Lake Skulker 16-17
Lake Skulker 15-16
Rot Hide Brute 16-17
Rot Hide Plague Weaver 17
Rot Hide Savage 18-19
Vile Fin Lakestalker 18-19
Vile Fin Oracle 19-20

11 Fenris Keep
Raging Rot Hide 18-19
Rot Hide Savage 18-19

12 The Dawning Isles
Elder Lake Creeper 18-19
Elder Lake Skulker 16-17
Lake Creeper 17-18
Lake Skulker 15-16
Vile Fin Shorecreeper 16-17
Vile Fin Tidecaller 17-18

13 The Decrepit Ferry
Fenwick Thatros 16
Hand of Ravenclaw 15-16
Ravenclaw Champion 14-15
Ravenclaw Servant 13-14

14 The Sepulcher
Apothecary Renferrel 14 Quest
Dalar Dawnweaver 21 Quest
Guillaume Sorouy 28 Journeyman
  Blacksmith
High Executor Hadrec 30 Quest
Innkeeper Bates 30 Innkeeper
Johan Focht 19 Miner Trainer
Karos Razok 55 Bat Handler
Sarah Goode 30 Stable Master
Shadow Priest Allistar 20 Quest
Yuriv's Tombstone Quest Target

Ferocious Grizzled Bear 11-12
Moonrage Whitescalp 10-11

15 Deep Elm Mine
Ferocious Grizzled Bear 11-12
Grimson the Pale 15 Quest Target
Moonrage Darksoul 13-14
Moonrage Glutton 12-13

16 Deep Elm Canyons
Dalaran Wizard 19-20
Moonrage Bloodhowler 15-16
Moonrage Darksoul 13-14
Vile Fin Lakestalker 18-19
Vile Fin Oracle 19-20

17 Olsen's Farthing
Ravenclaw Raider 12-13
Ravenclaw Slave 11-12

18 Shadowfang Keep
Entrance to Shadowfang Keep World
  Dungeon

19 Pyrewood Village
Dalaran Apprentice 13-14
Giant Grizzled Bear 12-13
Pyrewood Elder 14-15 Elite

Pyrewood Sentry 15 Elite
Pyrewood Watcher 14 Elite

20 Greymane Wall
Bloodsnout Worg 16-17
Haggard Refugee 18-19
Moonrage Bloodhowler 15-16
Sickly Refugee 19-29
Valdred Moray 21 Quest Target

21 Ambermill
Archmage Arateic 18 Quest Target
Dalaran Conjurer 17-18
Dalaran Protector 14-15
Dalaran Warder 16-17
Dalaran Watcher 18-19
Dalaran Wizard 19-20

22 Beren's Peril
Dalaran Watcher 18-19
Dalaran Wizard 18-19
Ravenclaw Drudger 19-20
Ravenclaw Guardian 20-21

Stonetalon Mountains

Stonetalon Mountains can be found in the mountains between the Barrens and Desolace. The Tauren outpost of Sun Rock Retreat lies off the beaten path near the middle of the mountain and provides the Horde with the only local inn. The Peak itself houses an Alliance flight path and an Alliance vendor. Though home to many beasts, the wilderness is constantly being cut back by expanding goblin deforesters. In addition to the Barrens and Desolace, explorers can travel to and from Ashenvale forest via a secret tunnel that burrows through the foothills.

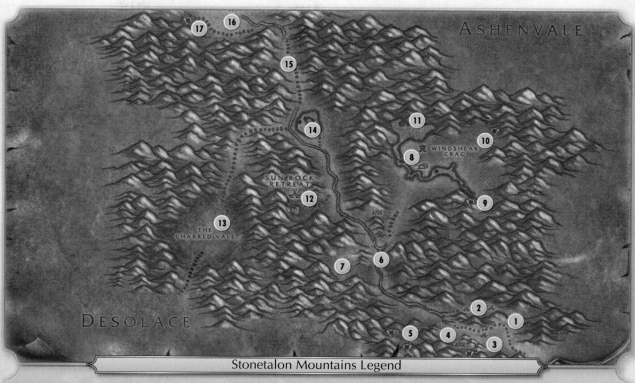

Stonetalon Mountains Legend

1 Camp Aparaje
Grimtotem Mercenary 15
Grimtotem Ruffian 15

2 Grimtotem Post
Cliff Stormer 17
Gorehoof the Black 17
Grimtotem Brute 15-16
Grimtotem Sorcerer 15-16
Kaya Flathoof 15

3 Greatwood Vale
Grimtotem Mercenary 15
Grimtotem Ruffian 15

4 Malaka'jin
Witch Doctor Jin'Zil 25 Quest
Ken'Zigla 20 Quest
Borand 30 Bowyer

5 Boulderslide Ravine

6 Web Winder Path
Gaxim Rustfizzle 30 Quest
Kaela Shadowspear 23 Quest
Deepmoss Creeper 17-18
Deepmoss Venomspitter 18-19

7 Sishir Canyon

8 Windshear Crag
Ziz Fizziks 20 Quest
Cliff Stormer 18-19
Raging Cliff Stormer 19-20
Deepmoss Venomspitter 18-19
Deepmoss Webspinner 20-21
Young Pridewing 19
Venture Company Logger 19-20
Venture Company Deforester 20
Venture Company Operator 20,21
XT:4 23
XT:9 23

9 Windshear Mine
Piznik 20 Quest
Windshear Digger 21-22
Windshear Geomancer 21-22
Windshear Overlord 22-23
Windshear Tunnelrat 21

10 Talondeep Path
Braug Dimspirit 35 Quest

11 Cragpool Lake
Nizzik 24 Vendor
Venture Company Builder 22
Venture Company Engineer 21-22
Venture Company Machine Smith 22-23
Gerenzo Wrenchwhistle 27
Compact Harvest Reaper 22

12 Sun Rock Retreat
Innkeeper Jayka 30 Innkeeper
Tharm 55 Wind Ride Master
Gereck Stable Master
Jeeda 24 Vendor
Krond 27 Butcher
Grawnal 32 General Goods
Stonetalon Grunt

13 The Charred Vale
Blackened Basilisk 24
Scorched Basilisk 28
Singed Basilisk 25
Rogue Flame Spirit 24
Burning Ravager 24-25
Burning Destroyer 25-26
Charred Ancient 25

Blackened Ancient 28
Furious Stone Spirit 24-27
Young Chimaera 24
Fledgling Chimaera 25-27
Chimaera Matriarch 28
Bloodfury Harpy 23-24
Bloodfury Ambusher 23-24
Bloodfury Slayer 25-26
Bloodfury Rogue Feather 25-26
Bloodfury Windcaller 24
Bloodfury Storm Witch 26-27

14 Mirkfallon Lake
Pridewing Wyvern 21-22
Pridewing Consort 22-23
Pridewing Skyhunter 23-24
Deepmoss Venomspitter 18-19
Raging Cliff Stormer 19-20
Antlered Courser 22
Blackened Basilisk 24
Rogue Flame Spirit 23

15 Stonetalon Mountain
Braelyn Firehand 30 Quest
Antlered Courser 22-23

16 Stonetalon Peak
Teloren Hippogryph Master
Chylina 24 Vendor
Keeper Albagorm 30 Quest
Sap Beast 22-23
Corrosive Sap Beast 25
Antlered Courser 22-23
Great Courser 25
Fey Dragon 24
Wily Fey Dragon 26
Twilight Hunter 23-24
Son of Cenarius 25
Daughter of Cenarius 23-25
Cenarion Botanist 23-24
Treant Ally 23

17 The Talon Den
Cenarion Druid 26-27 Elite
Cenarion Caretaker 25-26 Elite
Mirkfallon Dryad 25 Elite
Gatekeeper Kordurus 25 Elite

Stranglethorn Vale

At the southern end of the Eastern Kingdoms is an area of rivers, jungle, and coastline known as Stranglethorn Vale. This gigantic section of the continent is home to many beasts, and it is also a place where Goblins have and pirates are found in great numbers. The Horde settlement of Grom'Gol is here, along the western coast (accessed via Blimps from Orgrimmar and Undercity). To the south is Booty Bay, a neutral town that is truly a place where anything goes. Some of the finest hunters of big game in all of Azeroth come to Stranglethorn in hope of fighting the rarest of felines, apes, and raptors.

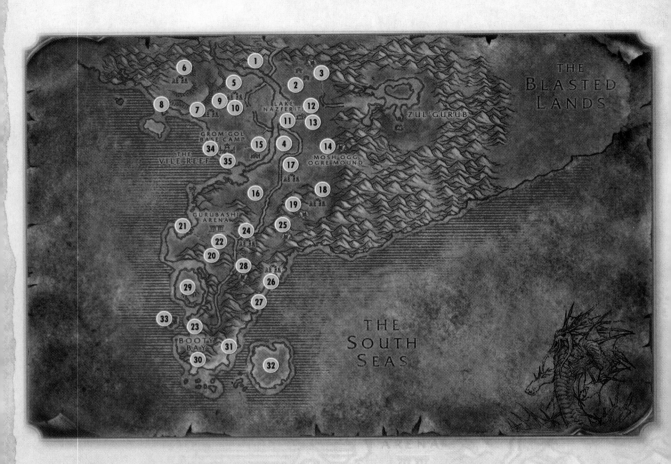

Stranglethorn Vale Legend

1 Rebel Camp
Brother Nimetz 40 Quest
Corporal Bluth 40 Vendor
Corporal Kaleb 40 Quest
Lieutenant Doren 40 Quest

2 Kurzen's Compound
Kurzen Commando 34
Kurzen Jungle Fighter 32-33
Kurzen Medicine Man 32-33
Kurzen War Panther 32-33
Kurzen War Tiger 32
Kurzen Wrangler 34

3 The Stockpile
Colonel Kurzen 40 Elite Quest Target
Kurzen Commando 34-35
Kurzen Elite 36-37
Kurzen Headshrinker 34-35
Kurzen Shadow Hunter 38
Kurzen Subchief 38
Kurzen Witch Doctor 36

4 Northern Stranglethorn Vale
Galvan the Ancient 60 Quest
Bhag'thera 40 Quest Target
Bloodscalp Beastmaster 34
Bloodscalp Hunter 35
Bloodscalp Scavenger 33
Elder Stranglethorn Tiger 34-35
Lashtail Raptor 35
Mistvale Gorilla 32-33
Panther 32-33
River Crocolisk 31
Shadowmaw Panther 38
Sharptooth Frenzy 31
Stone Maw Basilisk 32
Stranglethorn Tiger 33
Stranglethorn Tigress 37-38
Venture Company Mechanic 34
Venture Company Miner 34-35
Young Panther 30-31
Young Stranglethorn Tiger 30-31

5 Nesingwary's Expedition
Ajeck Rouack 40 Quest
Barnil Stonepot 40 Quest
Hemet Nesingwary 40 Quest
Jaquilina Dramet 39 Axe Vendor
Sir S. J. Erigadin 40 Quest
River Crocolisk 30-31
Young Stranglethorn Tiger 30-31

6 Ruins of Zul'Kunda
Bloodscalp Beastmaster 34-35
Bloodscalp Berserker 36-37
Bloodscalp Headhunter 36-37
Bloodscalp Hunter 34-35
Bloodscalp Mystic 35
Bloodscalp Scout 34-35
Bloodscalp Tiger 35

Bloodscalp Witch Doctor 37
Nezzliok the Dire 40 Quest Target

7 Zuuldaia Ruins
Bloodscalp Berserker 36-37
Bloodscalp Headhunter 36-37
Bloodscalp Witch Doctor 37

8 The Savage Coast
Bloodscalp Axethrower 33
Bloodscalp Shaman 34
Crystal Spine Basilisk 34
Elder Saltwater Crocolisk 38
Lashtail Raptor 35
Saltwater Crocolisk 35-36

9 Bal'lal Ruins
Bloodscalp Axe Thrower 33
Bloodscalp Shaman 33-34
Bloodscalp Warrior 33-34

10 Tkashi Ruins
Bloodscalp Axe Thrower 34
Bloodscalp Shaman 33-34
Bloodscalp Warrior 33-34

11 Lake Nazferiti
Snapjaw Crocolisk 35-36
Sharptooth Frenzy 31-32

12 Venture Company Operations Center
Foreman Cozzle 38 Quest Target
Venture Company Geologist 35-36
Venture Company Mechanic 35

13 Venture Company Base Camp
Venture Company Geologist 35-36
Venture Company Mechanic 34
Venture Company Shredder 37

14 Mosh'Ogg Ogre Mound
Mosh'Ogg Lord 45 Elite
Mosh'Ogg Mauler 43 Elite
Mosh'Ogg Shaman 43 Elite
Mosh'Ogg Spellcrafter 43-44 Elite
Mosh'Ogg Wormonger 41-42 Elite

15 Mizjah Ruins
Mosh'Ogg Brute 36-37
Mosh'Ogg Witchdoctor 37

16 Southern Stranglethorn
Se'Jib 50 Tribal Leatherworker
Cold Eye Basilisk 39
Jungle Thunderer 37-38
Shadowmaw Panther 37
Sharptooth Frenzy 32
Stranglethorn Tigress 37-38

17 Balia'mah Ruins
Skullsplitter Mystic 39
Skullsplitter Axe Thrower 39-40
Skullsplitter Warrior 39-40

18 Ruins of Zul'Mamwe
Ana'thek the Cruel 45

Kurzen Mindslave 44
Mogh the Undying 44 Elite
Skullsplitter Axe Thrower 39-40
Skullsplitter Beastmaster 42
Skullsplitter Berserker 43-44
Skullsplitter Headhunter 43-44
Skullsplitter Hunter 41-42
Skullsplitter Mystic 39-40
Skullsplitter Panther 41-42
Skullsplitter Scout 41-42
Skullsplitter Spiritchaster 44
Skullsplitter Warrior 39-40
Skullsplitter Witch Doctor 41-42

19 Venture Company Mine
Venture Company Foreman 42
Venture Company Strip Miner 40-41
Venture Company Tinkerer 41

20 The Cape of Stranglethorn
Jungle Stalker 40-41
Shadowmaw Panther 37
Thrashtail Basilisk 41-42

21 Southern Savage Coast
Bloodsail Mage 40-41
Bloodsail Raider 40-41
Cold Eye Basilisk 39-40
Jungle Stalker 40-41
Naga Explorer 43-44

22 Gurubashi Arena
Jungle Stalker 40-41

23 Bloodsail Compound
Bloodsail Swashbuckler 42
Bloodsail Warlock 42-43
Jungle Stalker 40-41

24 Ruins of Jubuwal
Jon-Jon the Crow 44
Zanzil Hunter 44
Zanzil Zombie 44

25 Crystalvein Mine
Ironjaw Basilisk 43-44

26 Ruins of Aboraz
Yenniku 41 Quest
Chucky "Ten Thumbs" 43
Zanzil Hunter 44
Zanzil Naga 44
Zanzil Witch Doctor 44
Zanzil Zombie 43

27 The Crystal Shore
Silverback Patriarch 43

28 Mistvale Valley
Witch Doctor Unbagwa 50 Quest
Elder Mistvale Gorilla 40-41
Gorlash 47 Elite Quest Target

29 Nek'mani Wellspring
Naga Explorer 43-44

30 Booty Bay
"Sea Wolf" MacKinley 44 Quest
"Shaky" Phillips 44 Quest
Baron Revilgaz 60 Quest
Brikk Keencraft 54 Blacksmith
Captain Hecklebury Smotts 37 Quest
Crank Fizzlebub 34 Quest
Drizzlik 45 Quest
First Mate Crazz 44 Quest
Flora Silverwind 44 Herbalist
Gramik Goodstitch 34 Tailor
Gringer 55 Wind Rider Master
Gyll 55 Gryphon Master
Innkeeper Skindle 46 Innkeeper
Kebok 35 Quest
Krazek 35 Quest
Narkk 42 Pet Vendor
Oglethorpe Obnoticus 50 Gnome Engineer/Quest
Rikqiz 43 Leatherworker
Xizk Goodstitch 43 Tailor

31 Wild Shore
Bloodsail Deckhand 43-44
Bloodsail Elder Magus 44
Bloodsail Mage 40-41
Bloodsail Seadog 44-45
Bloodsail Swabby 44
Bloodsail Swashbuckler 42-43
Bloodsail Warlock 42-43
Brutus 43
Captain Keelhaul 47
Fleet Master Firallon 48
Garr Salthoof 43
Ironpatch 43
Southern Sand Crawler 40-41

32 Jaguero Isle
Princess Poobah 50 Quest
Jaguero Stalker 50
King Mukla 55 Quest Target
Skymane Gorilla 50

33 Janeiro's Point
Mok'rash 50 Elite Quest Target

34 Kal'al Ruins
Murkgill Forager 35
Murkgill Hunter 35-36
Murkgill Lord 37
Murkgill Warrior 35-36

35 Grom'gol Base Camp
Angrun 40 Herbalist
Brawn 35 Leatherworker
Commander Aggro'gosh 55 Quest
Far Seer Mok'thardin 45 Quest
Kin'weelay 39 Quest
Mudduk 40 Cook
Nimboya 41 Quest
Thysta 55 Wind Rider Master
Zeppelin Master Nez'raz 60 Zeppelin Master

Swamp of Sorrows

Through Deadwind Pass, east from Duskwood, is the Swamp of Sorrows. Dragonkin dominate the eastern swamps, destroying any interlopers, while Murlocs, Spiders, and Horde patrols hold the south. Fortified and reinforced frequently is a Horde outpost in the south, in a spot where the Alliance simply has no control or ability to oust their troops. To the north many lost ones are found, though some are mad and aggressive to all, a few have wisdom to share.

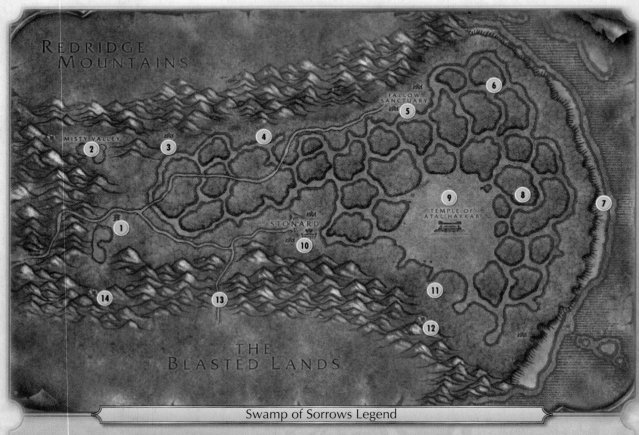

Swamp of Sorrows Legend

1 Splinterspear Junction
Sorrow Spinner 36
Stonard Scout 37
Swamp Jaguar 36

2 Misty Valley
Mire Lord 42
Swampwalker Elder 39-40
Swampwalker 38-39
Tangled Horror 40-41

3 The Harborage
Magtoor 42 Quest
Mosct T'andr 44 Vendor
Draenel Exile 42
Swamp Jaguar 37
Young Sawtooth Crocolisk 35-36

4 The Shifting Mire
Lost One Fisherman 36
Lost One Muckdweller 36-37
Lost One Mudlurker 34
Naboru the Cudgel 39 Quest Target
Sawtooth Crocolisk 38
Sorrow Spinner 36-37
Swamp Jaguar 36-37
Swampwalker 39
Tangled Horror 40

5 Fallow Sanctuary
Galen Goodward 37 Quest
Lost One Chieftain 39
Lost One Cook 37
Lost One Fisherman 36
Lost One Hunter 36-37
Lost One Muckdweller 36-37

Lost One Riftseeker 37-38
Lost One Seer 38
Stonard Explorer 37-38

6 Northern Swamp of Sorrows
Sawtooth Crocolisk 38-39
Shadow Panther 39-40
Tangled Horror 40

7 Misty Reed Strand
Marsh Flesheater 43-44
Marsh Inkspewer 42-43
Marsh Murloc 41
Monstrous Crawler 43
Sawtooth Snapper 42
Silt Crawler 40-41
Stonard Explorer 38

8 Sorrowmurk
Elder Dragonkin 45 Elite
Sawtooth Snapper 41-42
Scalebane Captain 43-44 Elite

9 Pool of Tears
Green Scalebane 42 Elite
Green Wyrmkin 42 Elite
Scalebane Captain 43-44 Elite

10 Stonard
Breyk 55 Wind Rider Master
Dispatch Commander Ruag 60 Quest
Fel'zerul 60 Quest
Grunt Tharlok 55 Quest
Grunt Zuul 55 Quest
Helgrum the Swift 60 Quest
Rogvar 53 Alchemist
Stonard Cartographer 52

Stonard Grunt 55
Stonard Orc 50
Stonard Wayfinder 50-51
Zun'dartha 60 Quest

11 Stagalbog
Deathstrike Tarantula 40-41
Marsh Flesheater 43
Marsh Inkspewer 42-43

12 Stagalbog Cave
Marsh Flesheater 43
Marsh Inkspewer 42-43
Marsh Oracle 45

13 Pass to Blasted Lands
Fallen Hero of the Horde 60 Quest

14 Itharius' Cave
Itharius 45 Quest

Tanaris

Gadgetzan is one big desert with all the desert creatures you have come to expect by now. It has lizards, buzzards, elementals and more. There are also Dragons, Ogres and humans along with an instanced dungeon to test the mighty. If that's not enough, head north and check out the pirates, they always put on a good show. It's a good place to solo - especially to farm things you need like leather or cloth. Some great rare items drop here (Julie's Dagger). Beyond that, the zone is huge and easily shareable with others. There's a place right by the crater where the mobs drop herbs, so you can kill for the herbs instead of looking for them.

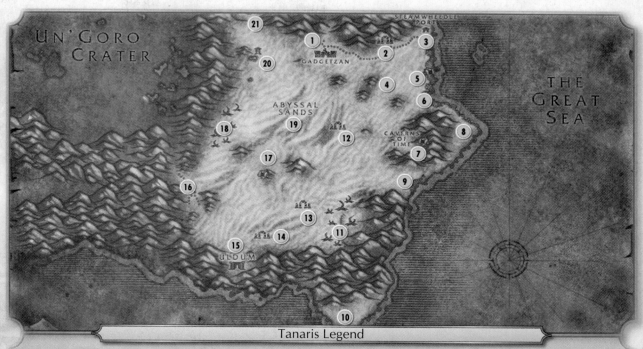

Tanaris Legend

1 Gadgetzan
Senior Surveyor Fizzledowser 50 Quest
Tran'rek 45 Quest
Nixx Sprocketspring 55 Goblin Engineer
Buzzek Bracketswing 55 Master
Engineer
Spigot Operator Luglunket 40 Quest
Trenton Lighthammer 55 Quest
Pikkle 45 Mining Trainer

2 Noonshade Ruins
Wastewander Bandit 41-42
Wastewander Thief 40-41

3 Steamwheedle Port
Yeh'ikinya 40 Quest
Prospector Ironboot 45 Quest
Stoley 30 Quest
Torta 45 Quest

4 Waterspring Field
Wastewander Bandit 41-43
Caliph Scorpidsting 46
Wastewander Thief 40-42
Wastewander Shadow Mage 40-43
Wastewander Rogue 42-44
Wastewander Assassin 43-46
Scorpid Tail Lasher 44-45 Fire Roc 43-44

Blisterpaw Hyena 43-45
Glasshide Gazer 44-46

5 Zalashji's Den
Zalashji 45

6 Wavestrider Beach

7 Caverns of Time
Anachronos
Chronalis
Occulus 50 Elite
Tick

8 Lost Rigger Cove
Southsea Pirate 44-46
Southsea Freebooter 43-45
Andre Firebeard 45
Southsea Dock Worker 44-46
Southsea Swashbuckler 44-45

9 South Break Shore
Coast Strider 48 Elite Giant
Surf Glider 48-50

10 Lands End Beach
Giant Surf Glider 48-50 Elite

11 The Gaping Chasm
Glasshide Glazer 45
Hazzali Sandreaver 49-51

Hazzali Stinger 49
Hazzali Stormer 49-50
Hazzali Tunneler 48-49
Hazzali Wasp 48
Hazzali Worker 47-49

12 Broken Pillar
Marvon Rivetseeker Quest NPC
Blisterpaw Hyena 43-46
Fire Roc 44-45
Glasshide Gazer 43-45
Scorpid Tail Lasher 43-46
Scorpid Dunestalker 45-47
Gusting Vortex 44-46

13 East Moon Ruins
Rabid Blisterpaw 45-48
Dunemaul Ogre 45-47
Dunemaul Brute 45-48
Dunemaul Enforcer 45-47
Dunemaul Ogre Mage 45-48
Dunemaul Warlock 45-48
Glasshide Gazer 44-47
Glasshide Petrifier 48-49

14 South Moon Ruins
Dunemaul Enforcer 45-47
Dunemaul Ogre Mage 45-48

Dunemaul Warlock 45-48
Dune Smasher 48-49
Glasshide Petrifier 47-49
Searing Roc 47-48
Scorpid Dunestalker 46-47

15 Valley of the Watchers
Prospector Gunston 45 Explorers'
League Quest
Dune Smasher 48-49 Elite Giant
Raging Dune Smasher 50 Elite
Blisterpaw Hyena 43-46
Glasshides Petrifier 47-49

16 Thistleshrub Valley
Glasshide Petrifier 47-49
Scorpid Dunestalker 46-47
Thistleshrub Rootshaper 49-50
Thistleshrub Dew Collector 48-49
Gnarled Thistleshrub 48-50

17 Dunemaul Compound
Rabid Blisterpaw 45-48
Dunemaul Ogre 45-47
Dunemaul Brute 45-48
Dunemaul Enforcer 45-47
Dunemaul Ogre Mage 45-48
Dunemaul Warlock 45-48
Glasshide Gazer 44-47

18 The Noxious Lair
Centipaar Stinger 48-50
Centipaar Swarmer 49-50
Centipaar Wasp 47-49

19 Abyssal Sands
Blisterpaw Hyena 44-46
Scorpid Tail Lasher 43-44
Fire Roc 43-45
Glasshide Basilisk 43-
Scorpid Dunecrawler 46-47
Glasshide Gazer 45-46
Land Rager 45-46

20 Sandsorrow Watch
Ground Pounder 41-42
Glasshide Basilisk 42-43
Starving Blisterpaw 41-42
Sandfury Hideskinner 42-43 Elite
Sandfury Axe Thrower 42-44 Elite
Sandfury Firecaller 43-44 Elite
Sandfury Shadowcaster 43-44 Elite

21 Entrance to Zul'Farrak
World Dungeon

Teldrassil

Teldrassil is the new home of the Night Elves. This distant homeland is far away from the safety of the Alliance lands, yet they are free from the focus of many enemies. Undead are not tolerated in this forest of life and beauty, and the Night Elves have many protectors that guard the land from any demonic taint. Beware though; the Firbolg and Timberlings who once existed in perfect balance with this land, have grown aggressive of late. The Druids of Teldrassil seek answers before the beasts and people of the land suffer their own madness.

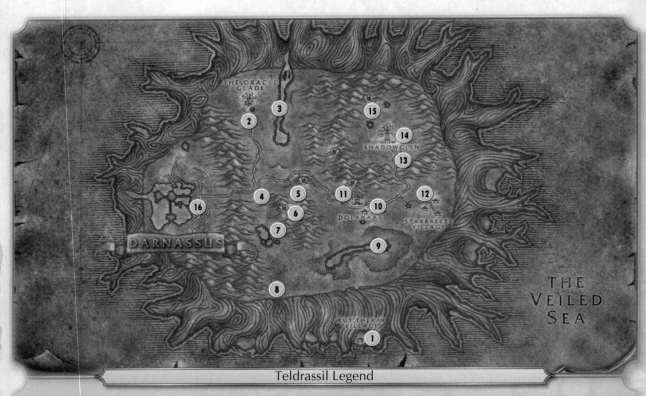

Teldrassil Legend

1 Rut'theran Village
Boat to Auberdine
Daryn Lightwind 30 Quest
Erelas Ambersky 30 Quest
Vesprystus 55 Hippogryph
  Master

2 The Oracle Glade
Alanna Raveneye 29 Enchanter
Mist 10 Quest
Sentinel Arynia Cloudsbreak
  10 Quest
Strange-Leafed Plant
Bloodfeather Fury 9-10
Bloodfeather Harpy 8-9
Bloodfeather Matriarch 11
Bloodfeather Rogue 9
Bloodfeather Sorceress 9
Elder Nightsaber 8-9
Feral Nightsaber 11
Lady Sarthrah 12

Minion of Sethir 10
Sethir the Ancient 13 Quest
  Target
Strigid Hunter 8-9
Strigid Screecher 7-8
Webwood Silkspinner 9

3 Wellspring River
Blackmoss the Fetid 13 Quest
  Target
Elder Timberling 11
Timberling Mire Beast 9

4 Road to Darnassus
Nadyia Maneweaver 30
  Leatherworker
Radnaal Maneweaver 19
  Skinner
Nightsaber Stalker 7-8
Strigid Screecher 7-8
Webwood Venomfang 7-8

5 Ban'ethil Hollow
Agal 8 Quest Target
Gnarlpine Ambusher 6-7
Gnarlpine Defender 7
Gnarlpine Shaman 8
Webwood Venomfang 7-8

6 Ban'ethil Barrow Den
Oben Rageclaw 40 Quest
Gnarlpine Augur 9
Gnarlpine Defender 7
Gnarlpine Shaman 8
Rageclaw 10 Quest Target

7 Pools of Arlithrien
Nightsaber Stalker 7-8
Strigid Screecher 7-8
Webwood Venomfang 7-8

8 Gnarlpine Hold
Strange-Fruited Plant
Gnarlpine Avenger 10

Gnarlpine Pathfinder 9-10
Ursal the Mauler 12 Quest
  Target

9 Lake Al'Ameth
Denalan 11 Quest
Fel Cone (Ground Spawns)
Timberling Seed (Ground
  Spawns)
Oakenscowl 9+ Quest Target
Timberling Bark Ripper 7-8
Timberling Tramplers 8-9
Timberling 5-6

10 Dolanaar
Arthridas Bearmantle 11 Quest
Byancie 22 First Aid
Corithras Moonrage 10 Quest
Cyndra Kindwhisper 28
  Alchemist
Innkeeper Keldamyr 30
  Innkeeper
Malorne Bladeleaf 17 Herbalist

Sentinel Kyra Starsong
  12 Quest
Syral Bladeleaf 12 Quest
Tallonkai Swiftroot 11 Quest
Zarrin 13 Cook

11 Fel Rock
Dark Sprite 6-7
Lord Melenas 8 Quest Target
Rascal Sprite 5-6
Shadow Sprite 5-6
Vicious Grell 7

12 Starbreeze Village
Gaerolas Talvethren 7 Quest
Zenn Foulhoof 7 Quest
Ferocitas Dream Eater 8
  Quest Target
Gnarlpine Gardener 5
Gnarlpine Mystic 6-7
Gnarlpine Ursa 5-6
Gnarlpine Warrior 6-7

13 Shadowglen
Iverron 5 Quest
Tarindrella 7 Quest
Grell 2-3
Grellkin 3-4
Mangy Nightsaber 2-3
Thistle Boar 2-3
Webwood Spider 3-4
Young Nightsaber 1-2
Young Thistleboar 1-2

14 Aldrassil
Conservator Ilthalaine 4 Quest
Dirania Silvershine 8 Quest
Gilshalan Windwalker 9 Quest
Tenaron Stormgrip 10 Quest

15 Shadowthread Cave
Webwood Egg (Ground Spawn)
Githyliss the Vile 5 Quest Target
Webwood Spider 3-4

16 Darnassus

THOUSAND NEEDLES

This region is located beyond the Barrens in southern Kalimdor. It's a large, winding valley dotted with tall mesas all around, save for the area to the south-east. It's completely flat down there and perfect for some questing. High atop the mesas, the Tauren have built a network of rope bridges and lifts to convey customers to vendors and quest givers. There are no guardrails to keep you safe; you can easily fall over the edge while taking a peek.

Thousand Needles

1 Camp E'Thok
Galak Mauler 27-28
Galak Marauder 26-27
Galak Stormer 26-28
Pesterhide Snarler 28-29
Needles Cougar 28-29

2 Highperch
Highperch Wyvern 28-29

3 Whitereach Post
Wizlo Bearingshiner 31 Quest
Laer Steprunner 42 Food and drink
Pesterhide Snarler 28-29
Motega Fireman 28

4 Darkcloud Pinnacle (bottom area)
Boiling Elemental 27-28
Scaulding Elemental 28-29

5 Darkcloud Pinnacle (Entrance to top)
Grimtotem Bandit 25-26
Grimtotem Stomper 26-27
Grimtotem Geomancer 25-27
Grimtotem Reaver 28

6 The Screeching Canyon
Screeching Roguefeather 29-30
Screeching Harpy 28-29

7 Roguefeather Den
Screeching Roguefeather 29-30
Screeching Harpy 28-29
Screeching Windcaller 30
Grenka Bloodscreech 31

8 Splithoof Crag
Galak Wrangler 25-26
Galak Windchaser 24-25
Galak Packrunner 26
Galak Packhound 24-25
Galak Scout 24-25

9 Splithoof Hold
Galak Scout 24-25
Galak Mauler 27-28
Galak Stormer 26-27
Galak Marauder 27-28
Galak Flame Guard 30

10 Freewind Post Entrance (Horde town)
Freewind Brave 45
Nyse 55 Elite Flight Master
Elv 28 Quest
Inkeeper Abeqwa 30 Innkeeper
Dandia 37 Trade supplies
Rau Cliffrunner 30
Thalia Aberhide 30
Jawn Highmesa 35 General Goods
Awenasa 30 Stable Master
Turhaw 40 Butcher Food & Water

11 Windbreaker Canyon
Elder Cloud Serpent 27-29
Pesterhide Snarler 28-29
Needles Cougar 28-29

12 The Weathered Nook
Prate Cloudseeker 37
Dorn Plainstalker 29 Quest

13 An Orc Camp Quests
Krueg Skullsplitter 37
Tarkrev Shadowstalker 35
Nag'Zhen 35
Mortkar Krin 35
Bok'Zhen 35
War Party Kobo 29-20

14 Snapper Spawns
Sparkshell Snapper 34-35
Sparkshell Tortoise 31-32

Guard Wachabe 45
Montarr Lorkeeper 45 Rare Items
Starn 37 Gunsmith and Bower

15 Scavenger Spawns
Salt Flat Scavenger 30-31

16 Saltstone Spawns
Saltstone Grazer 34-35
Saltstone Crystalhide 32-33

17 The Rustmaul Dig Site
Silithid Hive Drone 33-34
Silithid Invader 34-35
Silithid Searcher 32-33

18 Scorpid Spawns
Scorpid Terror 33-34
Scorpid Reaver 32-33

19 Mirage Raceway
Brivelthwerp 35 Ice Cream Vendor
Gnome Pit Boss 35
Gnome Pit Crewman 30
Crazzle Sprysprocket 35 Gnome Ticket Vendor
Jinky Twizzlefixxit 30 Engineer Supplier

Kravel Koalbeard 29 Quest
Fizzle Brassbolts 30 Quest
Wizzle Brassbolts 31 Quest
Daisy 15 Race Start Girl
Goblin Pit Crewman 30
Goblin Pit Boss 35
Rugfizzle 35 Goblin Ticket Vendor
Razzeric 30
Pozzik 30
Riznek 35 Drink vendor
Drag Master Miglen
Track Master Zherin 30est
Zuzubeb 35 Race Announcer
Rizzlle Brassbolts 31
Magus Tirth 51 Chicken Vendor
Quenting 40
Zamek 30

Tirisfal Glades

Tirisfal Glades has seen the ravages of plague and the Scourge. The once vibrant villages and grand city of Lordaeron lay in ruins. Remnants of the Scourge still roam the land and the Forsaken who have awakened of their own free will are hunted by the Scarlet Crusade. Murlocs infect the northern shore and Rothide Gnolls have been seen taking over a farmstead just south of it. It is a land in constant turmoil.

Legend Tirisfal Glades

1 Deathknell
Undertaker Mordo 5 Quest
Executor Arren 5 Quest
Deathguard Saltain 75 Quest
Duskbat 1-2
Young Scavenger 1-2
Wretched Zombie 1-2
Mindless Zombie 1-2
Rattlecage Skeleton 2-3
Mangy Duskbat 3-4
Ragged Scavenger 2-3
Scarlet Convert 3
Mevin Korgal 5
Calvin Montague 5 Quest

2 Night Web's Hollow
Young Night Web Spider 2-3
Night Web Spider 3-4

3 Solliden Farmstead
Deathguard Simmer 23 Quest
Greater Duskbat 6-7
Decrepit Darkhound 5-6
Tirisfal Farmhand 5-6
Tirisfal Farmer 7
Scarlet Warrior 6-7

4 Nightmare Vale
Decrepit Hound 5-6
Greater Duskbat 6-7
Cursed Darkhound 7-8

Scarlet Zealot 8-9
Scarlet Missionary 7-8
Captain Perrine 9

5 Stillwater Pond
Decrepit Darkhound 5-6
Cursed Darkhound 7-8
Greater Duskbat 6-7
Rotting Dead 5- 6
Ravaged Corpse 6-7

6 Agamand Mills
Cursed Darkhound 7-8
Rattlecage Soldier 6-7
Lost Soul 6
Devlin Agamand 9
Darkbone Caster 7-8
Cracked Skull Soldier 8-9
Nissa Agamand 10
Thurman Agamand 10
Gregor Agamand 10
Rotting Ancestor 10-11
Wailing Ancestor 9-11

7 Cold Hearth Manor
Bowen Brisboi 24 Journeyman Tailor
Ravaged Corpse 6-7
Rotting Dead 5-6
Vampiric Duskbat 8-9
Cursed Darkhound 7-8
Greater Duskbat 6-7

8 Brill
Deathguard Dillinger 22 Quest
Junior Apothecary Holland 20 Quest
Faruza 5 Apprentice Herbalist
Morganus 30 Stable Master
Zochariah Post 30 Undead Horse Merchant
Velma Warnam 30 Undead Horse Riding Instructor
Executor Zygand 14 Quest
Eliza Callen 12 Leather Armor Merchant
Abigail Shiel 9 Trade Supplies
Mrs. Winters 10 General Supplies
Selina Weston 12 Alchemy & Herbalism Supplies

9 Garren's Haunt
Rot Hide Gnoll 6-7
Rot Hide Graverobber 6-7
Rot Hide Mongrel 7-8
Maggot Eye 10

10 Ruins of Lordaeron

11 Undercity

12 Brightwater Lake
Clyde Kellen 16 Fisherman
Cursed Darkhound 7-8
Vampiric Duskbat 8-9

13 Balnir Farmstead
Cursed Darkhound 7-8
Vampiric Bat 8-9
Bleeding Horror 9-11
Wandering Spirit 10-11

14 The Bulwark
Argent Quartermaster Hasana 58 Quest
Argent Officer Garush 60 Quest
High Executor Derrington 61 Quest
Apothecary Dithers 58 Quest
Shadow Priestess Vandis 60 Quest
Alexi Barov 60 Quest

15 Crusader Outpost
Scarlet Zealot 8-9
Scarlet Friar 9-10
Captain Vachon 11

16 Venomweb Vale
Vampiric Duskbat 8-9
Ravenous Darkhound 9-10
Vicious Nightweb Spider 9-10

17 Faol's Rest
Ravenous Darkhound 9-10

18 Whispering Gardens
Entrance to Scarlet Monastery World Dungeon
Scarlet Scout 29-30+
Scarlet Magician 29-30+
Scarlet Preserver 29-30+

19 Scarlet Watch Post
Scarlet Friar 9-10
Scarlet Vanguard 10-11
Scarlet Bodyguard 10-11
Scarlet Neophyte 10-11
Captain Melrache 12

20 Zepplin to Orgrimmar and Grom'Gol-Outpost
Deathguard Linnea 22 Quest
Shelene Rhobart 25 Jouneyman Leatherworker
Rand Rhobart 13 Skinner
Martine Tramblay 15 Fishing Supplies

21 North Coast
Vile Fin Minor Oracle 9-9
Vile Fin Puddlejumper 7-8
Vile Fin Muckdweller 9-10

22 Gunther's Retreat
Gunther Arcanus 53 Quest
Shambling Horror 7-8
Hungering Dead 7-8
Gunther's Minion 7-8

Un'Goro Crater

Un'Goro Crater is the blast from the past. The land is loaded with dinosaurs, walking plants, big bugs and elementals. As often happens in lands with such menacing flora and fauna, adventurers that have managed to get stuck there wish for your help and frequently offer quests. Targets are abundant and that helps with the kill quests. There is some collecting to be done, and there are some incredible quests that balance the whole mix out. It's not the biggest zone which is another plus. There's not an overwhelming amount of running for the quests, and that always helps.

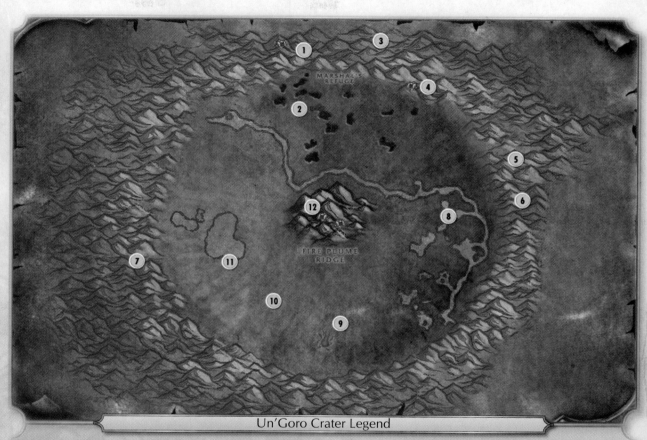

Un'Goro Crater Legend

1 Marshal's Refuge
Shizzle 40 Quest
Quixxil 40 Quest
Muigin 51 Quest
Petra Grossen 46 Quest
Dadanga 45 Quest
Hol'Anyee Marshal 45 Quest
Williden Marshal 48 Quest
Linken 40 Quest
Bloodpetal Pests 30-35

2 Lakkari Tar Pits
Karna Remtravel 45 Quest
Mor'Vek 60 "Ravasaur Trainer"
Tar Lurker 53-54
Tar Lord 53-54
Tar Beast 51-52

Tar Creeper 51-52
Primal ooze 50-51
Bloodpetal Flayer 51-52
Pterrordax 51-52
Stone Guardian 59-50 Elite
Young Diemetradon 50-51

3 Northern Crystal Pylon
Pterrordax 50-51

4 Fungal Rock
A-Me 01 48 Quest
Un'Goro Gorilla 50-51
Un'Goro Stomper 51-52
Un'Goro Thunderer 52-53
U'Cha 55

5 Ironstone Plateau
Fledgling Pterrordax 50

6 Eastern Stone Pylon
Fledgling Pterrordax 50
Pterrordax 50-52
Pterrordax 50-52

7 Western Crystal Pylon
Frenzied Pterrordax 52-53
Frenzied Pterrordax 52-53
Frenzied Pterrordax 52-53

8 The Marshlands
Ravasaur 48-49
Ravasaur Runner 49-50
Venomhide Ravasaur 50-51
Tyannodon 55Elite
Bloodpetal Lasher 49-50

9 The Slithering Scar
Gorishi Wasp 51-52
Gorishi Worker 51-52
Gorishi Reaver 52-53
Gorishi Stinger 52-53
Gorishi Tunneler 52-53

10 Terror Run
Glutinous Ooze 53-54
Bloodpetal Trapper 53-54
Elder Diemetradon 54-55
Spike Stegodon 53 Elite
Thunderstomp Stegodon 55 Elite
Plated Stegodon 53 Elite

11 Golakka Hot Springs
Elder Diemetradon 54-55
Bloodpetal Trapper 53-54

Glutinous Ooze 52-54
Krakle 60 Quest
Spiked Stegodon 52-54 Elite
Stegodon 53 Elite

12 Fire Plume Ridge
Scorching Elemental 53-54
Living Blaze 54-55
Blazerunner 56 Elite
Ironhide DevilSaur 55 Elite

THE WESTERN PLAGUELANDS

Above the Alterac Mountains is the entrance to the Western Plaguelands. Tainted beasts, vicious Humans from the Scarlet Crusade, and a number of Scourge Undead live there. Cauldrons of bubbling liquids are guarded by the mindless dead. The Horde and the Alliance, so seldom to agree on matters, are both at war with the dangers posed by the Scourge, and this is the frontline of that battle. To the east is Darrowmere Lake, where Scholomance sits quietly in a deserted town. Walk here not, lest your group face trials of epic and deadly proportions.

Western Plaguelands Legend

1 The Bulwark
Carrion Vultures 52-53
Diseased Black Bears 51-52
Venom Mist Lurkers 51-52

2 Felstone Fields
Scarlet Hound 52-54
Scarlet Hunter 52-54
Scarlet Ivoker 52-54
Scarlet Medic 52-54
Skeletal Flayer 50-52
Skeletal Sorcerer 50-52
Slavering Ghoul 50-52

3 Dalson's Tears
Blighted Zombie 52-54
Carrion Lurker 53-54
Diseased Wolf 53-54
Rotting Cadaver 52-54
Skeletal Terror 52-54

4 Northridge Lumber
Carrion Lurker 56-57
Scarlet Knight 54-56
Scarlet Lumberjack 54-56

5 Hearthglen
Foreman Jerris 62 Elite
High Protector Lorik 61 Elite
Scarlet Paladin 55-56 Elite
Scarlet Priest 56-57 Elite
Scarlet Sentinel 55-56 Elite
Scarlet Worker 55-57 Elite

6 Scarlet Tower
High Clerist 63 Elite
Scarlet Avenger 56-57
Scarlet Knight 54-55
Scarlet Mage 55-56
Scarlet Spellbinder 57-58

7 The Weeping Cave
Decaying Horror 55-56
Devouring Ooze 55-56
Plague Lurker 54-55
Rotting Behemoth 55-56
Vile Slime 54-55

8 Gahrron's Withering
Hungering Wraith 56-58
Plague Lurkers 54-55
Taunting Vision 56-58
Waling Death 56-58

9 The Writhing Haunt
Fetid Zombie 55-56
Freezing Ghoul 55-56
Plague Lurker 54-55
Rotting Ghoul 55-56

10 Ruins of Anderhol
Cold Wraith 54-56 Elite

Decrepit Guardian 56-57 Elite
Flesh Golem 56-57 Elite
Screaming Haunt 54-56 Elite
Searing Ghoul 54-56 Elite
Skeletal Acolyte 54-56 Elite
Skeletal Executioner 55-56 Elite
Skeletal Warlord 55-56 Elite
Soulless Ghoul 54-56 Elite

11 Sorrow Hill
Skeletal Flayers 50-51
Slavering Ghouls 50-51

12 Uther's Tomb
High Priest Thel'Danis 65

13 Sorrow Hill (Crypt)
Lord Maldazzar
Skeletal Flayers 50-51
Skeletal Sorcerer 51-52
Slavering Ghouls 50-51

14 Darrowmere Lake

15 Caer Darrow
Artist Renfray 12
Baker Masterson 37
Caer Darrow Cannoneer
Caer Darrow Citizen
Caer Darrow Guardsman 54
Caer Darrow Horseman 52-56
Eva Sarkhoff 54
Joseph Dirte 31
Lucien Sarkhoff 55
Magistrate Marduke 57
Magnus Frostwake 50
Melia 1
Rory 35
Sammy 1

16 Entrance to Scholomance
World Dungeon

WESTFALL

Westfall is the bread basket of the southern lands. Once home to hundreds of the best farmers, the area is now sparsely populated; attacks from a huge band of Gnolls and increased activity by the Defias have almost driven everyone out of Westfall. Moonbrook is now a ghost town, save for the wandering of foul bandits, and none of the mines in the area are in the hands of good or honest folk. A militia of the people has formed and rallied around Sentinel Hill, one of the remaining bastions of resistance by the locals. Calling for help from Stormwind, they hold out and work to protect the remaining farms of Westfall.

Westfall Legend

1 Longshore
Crawler 11-12
Greater Fleshripper 16-17
Murloc Coastrunner 12-13
Murloc Hunter 16-17
Murloc Minor Oracle 13-14
Murloc Netter 14-15
Murloc Oracle 17-18
Murloc Raider 11-12
Murloc Tidehunter 17-19
Murloc Warrior 15-16
Old Murk-Eye 20 Elite Quest Target
Riverpaw Herbalist 14-15
Riverpaw Mongrel 13-14
Sand Crawler 13-14
Sea Crawler 15-16
Shore Crawler 17-18

2 Westfall Lighthouse
Captain Grayson 30 Quest

3 Gold Coast Quarry
Coyote Packleader 12-13
Coyote 10-11
Defias Looter 13-14

Defias Looter 13-14
Defias Pillager 14-15
Defias Trapper 12-13
Fleshripper 13
Goretusk 14-15
Harvest Golem 11-12
Riverpaw Miner 14-15
Young Goretusk 12-13

4 The Dagger Hills
Grimbooze Thunderbrew 20 Quest
Defias Highwayman 17-18
Defias Knuckleduster 16-17
Defias Pathstalker 15-16

5 Demont's Place
Defias Knuckleduster 16-17
Defias Pathstalker 15-16
Defias Pillager 14-15
Fleshripper 13-14
Goretusk 14-15
Riverpaw Brute 15-16
Riverpaw Herbalist 14-15

6 Alexston Farmstead
Defias Looter 13-14
Defias Pillager 14-15
Defias Smuggler 11-12
Defias Trapper 13
Dust Devil 18-19
Foe Reaper 4000 20
Harvest Golem 11-12
Harvest Watcher 14-15

7 Moonbrook
Entrance to Deadmines Instance
Defias Looter 13-14
Defias Pillager 14-15
Fleshripper 13-14
Harvest Golem 11-12

8 Jangolode Mine
Coyote Packleader 12
Coyote 10-11
Defias Smuggler 11-12
Defias Trapper 12-13
Kobold Digger 12-13
Young Fleshripper 10-11

9 Furlbrow's Pumpkin Farm
Benny Blaanco 15
Coyote 10-11
Defias Looter 13-14
Defias Pillager 14-15
Defias Smuggler 11-12
Defias Trapper 12-13
Fleshripper 13-14
Harvest Watcher 14-15
Young Fleshripper 10-11
Young Goretusk 12-13

10 The Molsen Farm
Coyote 10-11
Harvest Golem 11-12
Harvest Watcher 14-15
Young Fleshripper 10-11

11 Saldean's Farm
Farmer Saldean 20 Quest
Salma Saldean 20 Quest
Coyote 10-11
Harvest Golem 11-12
Harvest Watcher 14-15

Young Fleshripper 10-11
Young Goretusk 12-13

12 The Jansen Stead
Farmer Furlbrow 20 Quest
Verna Furlbrow 20 Quest
Coyote 10-11
Defias Footpad 10-11
Riverpaw Gnoll 11-12
Rusty Harvest Golem 9-10
Young Fleshripper 11-12
Young Goretusk 12-13

13 Sentinel Hill
Captain Danuvin 33 Quest
Defias Traitor 15 Quest
Gryan Stoutmantle 35 Quest
Innkeeper Heather 30 Innkeeper
Kirk Maxwell 30 Stable Master
Protector Bialon 30 Quest
Scout Galiaan 30 Quest
Thor 55 Griffon Master
Defias Looter 13-14
Defias Pillager 14-15
Fleshripper 13-14

Goretusk 14-15
Great Goretusk 16-17
Greater Fleshripper 16-17
Young Fleshripper 10-11
Young Goretusk 12-13

14 The Dead Acre
Defias Knuckleduster 16-17
Great Goretusk 16-17
Greater Fleshripper 16-17
Harvest Reaper 17-18

15 The Dust Plains
Defias Tower Patroller 24
Defias Tower Sentry 24-25
Dust Devil 18-19
Great Goretusk 16-17
Klaven Mortwake 26 Elite Quest target
Riverpaw Bandit 16-17
Riverpaw Mystic 18-19
Riverpaw Taskmaster 17-18
Venture Co. Drone 22

16 Stilwell Farm
Daphne Stilwell 20

WETLANDS

Sodden with moisure pouring off of the mountains and drifting in from sea, the Wetlands region is swamped with Slimes, Fen Dwellers, and a number of dangerous Humanoids. Gnolls, Orcs, and Dark Iron Dwarves hold various points in the south, east, and northern sections of the area. Out Menethil Harbor and most of the roads are safe from these troubles. For people interested in archeology, a large excavation site is located in the mountains just a tad east from Menethil. At the town itself, ships head out to Auberdine (in Darkshore), and Theramore (in the Dustwallow Marsh).

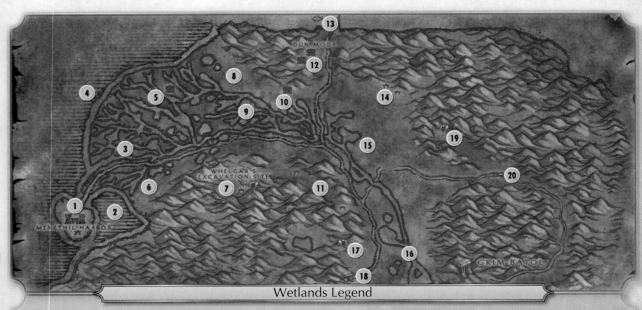

Wetlands Legend

1 Menethil
Archaeologist Flagongut
   44 Quest
Bethaine Flinthammer 30
   Stable Master
Captain Stoutfist 35 Quest
First Mate Fitzsimmons
   30 Quest
Fremal Doohickey 30 First Aid
Glorin Steelbrow 25 Quest
Harlo Barnaby 25 Quest
Harold Riggs 25 Fishing
James Halloran 25 Quest
Junder Brokk 20 Quest
Mikhail 30 Quest
Red Jack Flint 22 Quest
Shellei Brondir 55 Gryphon
   Master
Sida 20 Quest
Tapoke "Slim" John 34 Quest
Telurinon Moonshadow 25
   Herbalism
Unger Statforth 25 Horse
   Vendor
Vincent Hyal 30 Quest

2 Menethil Bay
Bluegill Raider 28-29
Fen Dweller 20
Giant Wetlands Crocolisk 25-26

Wetlands Crocolisk 23-24
Young Wetlands Crocolisk
   21-22

3 Bluegill Marsh
Bluegill Forager 22
Bluegill Muckdweller 23-24
Bluegill Murloc 20-21
Bluegill Oracle 26
Bluegill Puddlejumper 21-22
Bluegill Warrior 24-25
Fen Creeper 24-25
Fen Dweller 20-21
Giant Welands Crocolisk 25-26
Gobbler 22 Quest Target

4 The Lost Fleet
Captain Halyndor 30 Quest
   Target
Cursed Marine 27-28
Cursed Sailor 26-27
First Mate Snellig 29 Quest
   Target

5 Sundown Marsh
Fradd Swiftgear 24 Engineer
   Vendor
Wenno Silkbeard 29 Recipe
   Vendor
Fen Creeper 24-25
Giant Wetlands Crocolisk 25-26
Mosshide Alpha 27

Mosshide Brute 24-25
Mosshide Fenrunner 22
Mosshide Mystic 25-26
Mosshide Trapper 23-24
Wetlands Crocolisk 23-24
Young Wetlands Crocolisk
   21-22

6 Black Channel Marsh
Black Ooze 23
Mottled Raptor 22-23
Mottled Screecher 24-25

**7 Whelgar's Excavation
Site**
Merrin Rockweaver 30 Quest
Ormer Ironbraid 25 Quest
Prospector Whelgar 30 Quest
Mottled Razormaw 25-26
Mottled Scytheclaw 25-26
Saritooth 29 Quest Target

8 Saltspray Glen
Elder Razormaw 29
Fen Creeper 24
Fen Dweller 21
Fen Lord 26
Giant Wetlands Crocolisk 25-26
Highland Lashtail 24-25
Highland Raptor 23-24
Highland Razormaw 27-28
Highland Scytheclaw 25-26
Wetlands Crocolisk 23-24

9 Central Wetlands
Kixxie 25 Vendor
Black Slime 20
Fen Creeper 24
Fen Dweller 21
Fen Lord 26
Giant Wetlands Crocolisk 25-26
Mosshide Alpha 27
Mosshide Brute 24-25
Mosshide Fenrunner 22
Mosshide Mystic 25-26
Mosshide Trapper 23-24
Wetlands Crocolisk 23-24
Young Wetlands Crocolisk
   21-22

10 Ironbeard's Tomb
Black Ooze 23-24
Crimson Ooze 24-25

**11 Angerfang
Encampment**
Chieftain Nek'rosh 32 Elite
Dragonmaw Battlemaster 30
Dragonmaw Boneworder 27-28
Dragonmaw Centurion 29
Dragonmaw Raider 26-27
Dragonmaw Shadoworder 29
Dragonmaw Swamprunner 28

12 Dun Modr
Dark Iron Entrepreneur 30
   Vendor
Longbraid the Grim 35 Quest
Rhag Garmason 25 Quest
Dark Iron Demolitionist
   30-31 Elite
Dark Iron Dwarf 27-28 Elite
Dark Iron Rifleman 27-28 Elite
Dark Iron Saboteur 28-29 Elite
Dark Iron Tunneler 29-30 Elite

13 Thandol Span
Comar Villard 22 Quest

14 Direforge Hill
Balgaras the Foul 34 Elite
   Quest Target
Black Ooze 24
Dark Iron Demolitionist 31 Elite
Dark Iron Dwarf 27-28 Elite
Dark Iron Saboteur 28-29 Elite
Dark Iron Tunneler 29-30 Elite
Highland Lashtail 25
Highland Raptor 24
Highland Scytheclaw 26

15 The Green Belt
Rethiel the Greenwarden
   30 Quest
Black Ooze 24
Crimson Whelp 25-26
Highland Raptor 23-24

Last Whelp 24-25
Red Whelp 24

16 Mosshide Fen
Black Ooze 23
Black Slime 21
Dark Iron Insurgent 18-19
Fen Dweller 20
Mosshide Fenrunner 22-23
Mosshide Gnoll 20-21
Mosshide Mistweaver 22
Mosshide Mongrel 22
Young Wetlands Crocolisk
   21-22

17 Thelgen Rock
Cave Stalker 21-22
Leech Stalker 21

18 Dun Algaz
Dragonmaw Scout 19-20
Dragonmaw Grunt 20-21
Ma'ruk Wyrmscale 23

19 Raptor Ridge
Elder Razormaw 29
Highland Razormaw 27-28

20 Dragonmaw Gates
Red Dragonspawn 47-48
Red Scalebane 49
Red Wyrmkin 48-49
Scalebane Lieutenant 51-52
Scalebane Royal Guard 53-54
Wyrmkin Firebrand 52

WINTERSPRING

The northern land of Winterspring is reached through a dangerous tunnel out of Felwood. The Furbolg who live there are hard to befriend. On the other side of the tunnel is Winterspring itself, where snow falls, geysers blast into the sky, and some of the greatest Yetis in all of Azeroth dwell. To escape from the cold and the monsters of Winterspring, look toward the center of the valley and speak with the Goblins who hold a neutral town there.

Winterspring Legend

1 Frostfire Hot Springs
Fledgling Chillwind 54-55
Ragged Owlbeast 53-55
Rogue Ice Thistle 53-54
Shardtooth Bear 53-54
Winterfall Totemic 54-55
Winterfall Pathfinder 53-54
Winterfall Den Watcher 55-56

2 Timbermaw Post
Winterfall Totemic 54-55
Winterfall Pathfinder 53-54
Winterfall Den Watcher 55-56

3 The ruins of Kel'Theril
Anguished Highborn 55-56
Suffering Highborn 54-55

4 Lake Kel'Theril
Anguished Highborn 55-56
Suffering Highborn 54-55

5 Mazthoril
Brumeran 58 Elite
Chillwind Chimera 55

Cobalt Broodlings 55-56
Cobalt Scalebane 56-57 Elite
Cobalt Mageweaver 57-58 Elite
Cobalt Welps 54
Cobalt Wyrmkin 55-56 Elite
Shardtooth Mauler 55
Spell Eater 55-56
Spellmaw 56 Elite
Manaclaw 58 Elite
Scryer 59 Elite
Winterspring Owl 54-56

6 Dun Mandarr
Berserker Owlbeast 57-58
Crazed Owlbeast 58
Elder Shardtooth 57-58
Moontouched Owlbeast 58
Winterspring Screecher 57-58

7 Frostwhisper Gorge
Frostmaul Preserver 59-60 Elite
Frostmaul Giant 59-60 Elite

8 Darkwhisper Gorge
Hederine Initiate 59-60
Hederine Manstalker 59-60 Elite
Hedereine Slayer 59-60 Elite
Vi'el 60

9 Owlwing Thicket
Ranshalla 58
Berserk Owl Beast 58-59
Chillwind Ravager 59
Crazed Owl Beast 56-57
Moontouched Owlbeast 57-58

10 Ice Thistle Hills
Chillwing Chimaera 55-57
Ice Thistle Yeti 55-56
Ice Thistle Patriarch 57-58
Ice Thistle Matriarch 56-57
Shardtooth Mauler 55-56
Winterspring Owl 55-56

11 Winterfall Village
Shardtooth 54-55

Winterspring Owl 54-55
Winterfall Ursa 57-58
Winterfall Shaman 56-57
Winterfall Den Watcher 55-56

12 Everlook
Everlook Bruiser 65
Maethrya 55 Elite Alliance Flight Master
Yaugrek 55 Elite Horde Flight Master
Meggi Peppinrocker 60
Malyfous Darkhammer 55 The Thorium Brotherhood Quest
Evie Whitbrew 58 Alchemy Supplies Rare recipes
Umi Rumplesnicker 57 Quest
Azzleby 30 Stable Master
Seril Scourbane 57
Lilith the Lithe 55
Qia Trade good supplies Rare Patterns
Kilram 58

Blixxrak 55 Light Armor Merchant
Nixxrak 54 Heavy Armor Merchant
Wixxrap 55 Weaponsmith And Gunsmith
Jack Sterling 50
Umaron Stragarelm 42
Lunnix Sprocketslip 54 Mining supplier
Felnok Steelspring 54
Legacki 57
Himmik 60 Food and Drink
Jessica Redpath 50
Gregor Greystone 55 Argent Dawn
Innkeeper Vizzie 30
Gogo 58
Harco Wigglesworth 54
Xizzer Fizzbolt 55 Engineer Supplier
Chillwind Chimaera 57
Shardtooth Mauler 56

13 The Hidden Grove
Berserk Owl Beast 58-59
Crazed Owl beast 56-57
Moontouch Owl Beast 57-58

14 Frostsaber Rock
Frostsaber Stalker 59-60
Frostsaber Huntress 58-59
Frostsaber Pride Watcher 60
Frostsaber Cub 55-56
Frostsaber 55-56

15 Starfall Village
Syvrana 55 Trade Goods
Lyranne Feathersong 56 Food and Drink
Wynd Nightchaser 62
Jaron Stoneshapper 55 Explorers' Club
Natheril Raincaller 57 General Goods

The Cities of Azeroth

A History

The wars and plagues have claimed many cities throughout the history of Azeroth. While sand and vines bury and break the cities of the past, the people constantly rebuild new ones. These stand as beacons of light and civilization in times of trial.

Darnassus

At first glance Darnassus seems a tranquil refuge for the night elves and fitting replacement for their lost home in Ashenvale. However, Darnassus was created without nature's blessing and the creatures around this fair city suffer greatly for it. The great tree was planted for the most selfish of reasons, to regain their lost immortality by creating a tree that would bind their souls to the eternal world.

"Opulent" is the first word that may spring to mind when gazing around this grand city. It's a city alive and breathing with brightly colored foliage and softly glowing lights. Wisps float serenely along the pathways and large Ancient Protectors cast their gaze about them looking for any sign of danger.

The Tradesman's Terrace is in the southwestern section of the city. Buildings of pagoda inspired architecture line the pathways with their signs prominently announcing the weapons and armor they are selling. One the west side of the city, the Temple of the Moon sits with a large welcoming walkway leading into the moonlit and mystical alcove within. A large alabaster statue stands proudly in the center of a pool of water. Trainers surround the lower ring around the pool and, at the top of the ramps, the Lady Tyrande Whisperwind herself stands.

To the east of the Temple, and in the center of the city surrounded by water, stands a large tree in the shape of a bear. Inside lies no heart, but the treasures of its citizens are kept here in the bank. Just slightly northwest of the bank sites the rune surrounded portal to Rut'theran Village on the sea. In the northern region of the city, small Protectors make their rounds, their woody creaking blends in with the sounds of the smaller creatures as they patrol through the Cenarion Enclave.

The eastern portion of the city contains the Craftsman's Terrace. Herein the various craftsmen sell their wares and train the next to carry on their traditions. So traveling crafters need not walk far, an Inn and Mailbox are also found here. It is a visually beautiful city and one worth making the trip to if you don't happen to be on the wrong side of the way.

Ironforge

The first dwarves came up from the depths of the earth and founded Khaz Modan, naming the mountain range after the Titan Khaz'goroth. Constructing an altar for their Titan father, the dwarves crafted a mighty forge within the heart of the mountain. Thus city that grew around the forge would be called "Ironforge" ever after.

With the loss of their beloved Gnomeregan to invaders, what was left of the gnomish people took residence within the safe halls of their friends and neighbors. The entrance to Ironforge can be imposing to any newcomer. It's large, stony façade and heavy metal portcullis look ready to shut out even the most powerful of the Titans.

Within the city, the sounds of hammers falling rings out through the hustle and bustle. Large openings run through the center of the pathways. Gazing beneath your feet may reveal the source of the heat. Grated catwalks sit about hot molten metal guarding any from a clumsy and costly mistake of falling in.

Following the outer ring of the great city leads past the Military Quarter and toward Tinkertown. This is the gnomish region of the city made quite evident by the technological marvels even intertwined within their architecture. Overlarge gears rotate around walkways as you pass underneath. The King of gnomes, High Tinker Mekkatorque, stands watch over his people and watches as everyone comes and goes from the latest of innovations, the tram to and from Stormwind.

The library of Ironforge sits in the outer ring in the northeastern section of the city. The Explorer's League keeps watch over the many volumes of research and history they have managed to gather. Even with their love of the forge, dwarves have switched their focus to searching for their very own origins and embracing archaeology.

Perhaps the darkest of the areas are the Forlorn Caverns. Strangely enough, there seems to be some decent fishing for those looking for a break from the usual monotony of work. The northwestern area of the city houses the Mystic Ward. The vibrancy of the architecture is a striking contrast after emerging from the Forlorn Caverns. Within the very heart of the city is the Great Forge itself. Oversized anvils are worked on diligently by craftsmen that barely break a sweat although the heat is nearly unbearable. It is worth taking the time to walk through and get to know. There are always new surprises around every corner and it is a fitting home.

Stormwind

Stormwind is the last of the great human cities. With Lordaeron in the hands of the Forsaken and many of the cities that once housed the great kingdoms of humanity in ruins, Stormwind remains the center of commerce and safety.

The entrance to Stormwind itself is a testament to the legacy of heroes lost in time to the horrors of war. Each one bears a plague with the name of

the honoree. It is rightly called the Valley of Heroes and all that enter it can't help but feel their chest swell in pride at the legacy of the Alliance.

Once passing through the Valley of Heroes, you enter the Trade District. Shops crowd against the cobblestone walkways and citizens bustle about from place to place hocking their wares while children scamper between

the legs of passerby's. Word has it that Stormwind may just have the best cheese in all of Azeroth. There is plenty of shopping to be found throughout the city.

To the right of the Trade District is Old Town. As you move in that direction, you'll notice the large canals that run through the city and more small shops line the waterways. Old Town is a smaller, more compact version of the Trade District. It has a cozy charm to it. North of Old Town lays the Dwarven District. It's a haze-covered area of the city as the pollution of the many fires settles over it. Large beast-like machines sit around the region of the city as if waiting to snatch up some imaginary creature for a snack.

Stormwind Keep lies between Old Town and the Dwarven District. The boy king, Anduin Wrynn, stands at court with his advisors, Lady Katrana Prestor and Lord Bolvar Fordragon, at his side. Few stop by to pay their respects. At the northernmost area of the city lies Cathedral Square. The tall spires of the Citadel of Light itself loom protectively over this portion of the city. Its beauty is unmatched and even children are brought by to tour and view where the great Paladins and Priests train.

The west is the Park where Druids go to find their center and train. The night elves have managed to bring a piece of Darnassus here by placing their own small torches on this green oasis among the clean white stones of Stormwind. Soldiers are lined up on the outer edges of receiving medical care from the wounds they received from riots that broke out among the Defias prisoners.

Within the Mage Quarter, a tall tower stands with a spiraling ramp twisting about it. It is truly one of the grandest wizard towers any could possibly hope to see. At the top lies a strange portal that swirls in luminescent green as if to peer out into the cosmos itself. Passing through leads deeper into the Wizard's Sanctum. There is plenty to explore throughout this great city and should you gain a thirst for doing so, stop by the Blue Recluse. They advertise a free drink and you can send out a postcard at the mailbox as well.

Orgrimmar

Named in honor of the legendary Orgrim Doomhammer, Orgrimmar was founded to be the capital of the orcs' new homeland. Built within a large, winding canyon in the harsh land of Durotar, Orgrimmar stands as one of the mightiest cities in the world.

After freeing his people from captivity among the humans, Thrall set out to brave the sea and bring his people to a new land to start a new society for the orcs. They named the land itself "Durotar" after his deceased father, the for-mer chieftain of the Frostwolves. It is in Orgrimmar that the new seat of power resides for all of the orcs that survive to this day. No longer are the clans fractured and now they stand united as one nation.

The entrance to Orgrimmar yawns widely as the orc guards stand by. To the east of it stands the zeppelin Tower. The architecture is crude and yet speaks volumes of the craftsmen that built this city. Although different from conventionally accepted cities, none can say that there isn't a complex and harsh beauty invoked by the sight of Orgrimmar. Bonfires burn high atop the rocks and throughout the city, leaving a faint smoky haze.

The distinctive tile roofs of the city intermingle with the red rock of the terrain; wooden carvings shaped like horns, give off a menacing air as tanned hides are stretched over rooftops and across the rocks to filter out the relentless desert sun. After entering the city, the first region is the Valley of Strength. It serves as the central hub for banking and the buying and selling of all sorts of goods and services.

Just up the tower and across the rope bridge to the west lie the Valley of Spirits and the passageway to the western exit of the city. It is here fewer orcs are seen and more Trolls are apparent. In the Valley of Spirits the Trolls, who have also made a home in Durotar, teach some of the more mystic practices. North of the Valley of Strength is the shadier end of town: the Cleft of Shadow. From the area emanates a purple glow and within are the Warlocks and Rogues among some few vendors that serve their purpose.

Wrapping around the Cleft of Shadow is the Drag; it's filled with shops and trainers. This area is well-shaded from the ravages of the desert sun

and a good place to cool off. The desert breeze can be heard blowing through the rocks. To the northeast, through the Drag, is the Valley of Honor where the orcs work their ways with metal and train their Warriors. There is even a small pond for a little fishing after a hard workout.

Out through the Drag once more, and following the curve of the path to the north, you'll find the Valley of Wisdom and the seat of power for Warchief Thrall. Even more impressive than the Grommash Hold, are the monolithic demon plates out front. It is the demon armor of Mannoroth himself set there to remind the orcs of the grand sacrifice made to defeat the beast and begin the path of reclaiming their honor. Even as crude as the city seems, it is a marvel of orc ingenuity and determination to live off a harsh land and thrive despite all odds.

THUNDER BLUFF

The great city of Thunder Bluff lies atop a series of mesas that overlook the verdant grasslands of Mulgore. The once nomadic Tauren recently established the city as a center for trade caravans, traveling craftsmen, and artisans of every kind. The proud city also stands as a refuge for the brave adventurers who stalk their dangerous prey through the plains of Mulgore and its surrounding areas. Long bridges of rope and wood span the chasms between the mesas, topped with tents, longhouses, colorfully painted totems, and spirit lodges. The mighty chief, Cairne Bloodhoof, watches over the bustling city, ensuring that the united Tauren tribes live in peace and

security. Thunder Bluff sits high above the plains of Mulgore. The only means of arrival are by using the lifts from the plains below or flying in on one of the Wyverns that serve the area.

Brightly painted totems and tents made with stretched animal skins and wood struts lasted together sit atop the mesa giving the true feeling of being a part of a tribal community. The strong Tauren do much of their trade and banking on the main mesa. The winds are strong high atop the mesas and the Tauren capture this energy with brightly colored windmills atop the buildings. A series of rope bridges and towers interlink the varying levels and mesas into one continuous city.

Cairne Bloodhoof, leader of the Tauren, sits at the top level. All Tauren seeking his favor and the way of the hunter that is so precious to their very culture carry out his will.

To the southeast of the central bluff, connected by rope bridges, is the Hunter's Rise. Aspiring Hunters and Warriors train in the Hunter's Hall. Standing on the edge of the mesa here will give way to an amazing vista to the southeast. Watch your step however. There are no guardrails to keep you from falling to your death. The Tauren are more surefooted than that to care for such things. On the northern most mesa, the Elder Rise can be found where the wisest of Tauren reside. Druids can seek their council and learn more of their path in the Hall of Elders. The Spirit Rise lies to the west. The large head of a Kodo is fastened to the side of the building housing the Shaman trainers as if in silent watch and granting its power to those who train here.

Along the side of the mesa is a path leading down into a cavern that resounds of dripping pools of water and quietly spoken conversation. Large yellow mushrooms surround the edges of the pools. The Priest and Mage trainers sit and patiently give their knowledge to those seeking their counsel. The mists of the pools rise ever so silently giving the already eerily glowing cavern a more surreal appearance.

Despite the simple nature of their city, the Tauren have all that is necessary for their people. They put their efforts into their accomplishments and leave their city simple and functional.

UNDERCITY

Far beneath the ruined capital city of Lordaeron, the royal crypts have been turned into a bastion of power and undeath. Originally intended by Prince Arthas to be the Scourge's seat of power, the budding "Undercity" was abandoned when Arthas was recalled to aid the Lich King in distant Northrend. In Arthas' absence, the Dark Lady, Sylvannas Windrunner, led the rebel Forsaken to the Undercity, and claimed it as their own. Since taking up residence, the Forsaken have worked to complete the Undercity's construction by dredging the twisted maze of catacombs, tombs, and dungeons that Arthas began.

Once the seat of power for the humans, Lordaeron fell to the plague released by the Cult of the Damned. The new Lich King Arthas sought to make it his new home but found his conquest had been taken over by Lady Sylvannas. She has finished carving out what Arthas began building and claimed it for the Forsaken. While much of humanity has given up ever reclaiming Tirisfal Glades from the Scourge and Forsaken, a small band of Scarlet Crusaders still attempt to wrest back the cursed land from them. To the naked eye, the Ruins of Lordaeron look empty and uninhabitable. A Warlock will tell you otherwise. With a quick cast they can aid you in seeing the ghostly inhabitants that wander what appears to be an empty ruin.

Deeper in, the throne room sits bare and empty. The throne of a king destroyed by his own son is but a hollow shell of the greatness it once possessed. Swift moving elevators take you below the ruins. Undercity Guardians stand just outside the elevators; their large hulking forms past decay and oozing the remnants of the plague. The Trade Quarter is the heart of this city. Shops surround it on all levels and the bank sits prominently in the center. The grim décor of skulls and horns reflects the tastes of the denizens, all backlit by a constant green glowing pool of slime.

Taking the stairs down past the bank leads past auctioneers to an outer circle of merchants and canals. Each section of this part of the city is divided into quarters with and inner and outer ring and bridges spanning the river of ooze to connect them. Colorful banners of decaying fabric are draped around the entrances in a mockery of festivity while skulls on signs point the way to the different areas. The inner circle of this region houses merchants and profession trainers among more curious shops. The Undead have though of everything possible to help them in their pursuits.

The northeastern quarter of the city houses the Magic Quarter where Warlocks and Mages can train in their arts. A 'demonstration' of a Warlock pet is ongoing next to the building and can be quite informative. In the inner circle of this quarter robes and implements befitting a mage can be purchased. Moving clockwise takes you to the Rogue Quarter. Trainers wait here to improve the stealthy lives of all Rogues that come to them with greed and murder in their hearts. Within the inner circle, poisons and daggers can be purchased.

In the southwestern region of the city, the Apothecarium and the Royal Quarter are found. The Royal Apothecary Society does many of their experiments with the plague in this area. Their laboratory is something in and of

itself to see with bits and pieces of various creatures strewn about and experiments being carried on in an adjoining room on some unlucky humans. The crackling static of their experiments and the occasional scream will set any visitor's hair on end.

Deep within the Royal Quarter the demon Varimathras stands at the side of the Dark Lady herself. His imposing figure is enough to make any be respectful of her every wish. To the northwest is the War Quarter. Warriors train and strain against target dummies while Priests stand along the building and gaze down at the occurrences. Nearby, the sewers lead out into the grounds of Tirisfal Glades near the Scarlet Crusades southern tower. The bats of Undercity use this as a means to gain access in and out of the city. If there was a pulse among the Forsaken, Undercity would resonate with it. Instead its cold and clammy countenance casts pallor among its visitors in what many would find unwelcoming. The Forsaken that reside here however, seem quite at ease at what their Dark Lady has carved out for them even with the remnants of the Scourge and overzealous Scarlet Crusade breathing down their necks.

World Factions and Reputation

Within the world of Azeroth there are many different groups whose view of you affects how they react to you. This may seem obvious, but many of the groups can come to respect or dislike you through your own actions.

The Horde and Alliance comprise factional teams. All opposing races start at "War" status. Your reputation with factions opposed to you cannot be changed.

Most allied races start with a "Friendly" reputation with other races in the core two groups (Alliance and Horde). The exception is the Forsaken. They start with lower reputation with Trolls, Tauren, and orcs just as Trolls, Tauren, and orcs start with lower reputation with the Forsaken.

While you cannot declare war on your own faction, your lack of actions prompt a lack of esteem from your superiors. Consider your actions and their repercussions carefully.

Reputation Levels

Exalted:	The highest level of reputation a player can achieve with a faction
Revered:	Special reputation level reserved for special heroes
Honored:	10% discount on bought items from vendors
Friendly:	Standard reputation level for factions on the player's team
Neutral:	Starting reputation level for factions not on a player's team that are not KOS (Kill on Sight)
Unfriendly:	Cannot buy, sell, or interact
Hostile:	KOS
Hated:	KOS; all opposing team factions are set permanently to the lowest level here

WORLD FACTIONS

There are many groups in the world for your character to interact with. Only the Horde and Alliance factions are shown originally, but new groups appear as your character meets them for the first time. Included is a list of many of the factions, but many more are discovered during your travels in Azeroth

MONITORING YOUR REPUTATION

Players can check their current reputation with any faction they've had contact with by opening the Reputation tab on their character sheet in game. Using the hotkey, defaulted to "U", can be a faster way of accessing the tab.

Mousing over a faction shows how much reputation you have with them and how much you need to progress to the next level. Accomplishing tasks in game gives you a displayed amount of reputation, so it's fairly easy to calculate how much you need to accomplish to gain the next level.

CHANGING YOUR REPUTATION

There are three basic ways to raise your reputation with a faction. Each is explained below.

QUESTS

Accomplishing quests given by members of the faction is quick and doesn't take you out of your way. These quests often lead to Repeatable Quests or involve Killing. As such, quests are good first steps to raising your reputation.

REPEATABLE QUESTS

Blue question marks show NPCs with repeatable quests. These can be done an infinite number of times, which makes them part of the bread and butter of reputation grinding. Many repeatable quests involve killing so you get a double bang for your buck (you get the money and experience from the monsters while turning in the quest gives you the reputation increase).

KILLING

Everyone has enemies. Killing NPCs who are opposed to a faction can raise you reputation with that faction. The gain is often very little, but you also gain money and experience from the kill. Watch your combat log to see reputation changes as you kill new enemies.

As you gain in standing, the reputation you gain from killing enemies may diminish. The greatest hero of all time killing a lowly skeleton isn't very noteworthy after all.

Faction	How to Raise Reputation
Alliance	
Darnassus	Quests, Repeatable Quests
Gnomeregan Exiles	Quests, Repeatable Quests
Ironforge	Quests, Repeatable Quests
Stormwind	Quests, Repeatable Quests
Horde	
Darkspear Trolls	Quests, Repeatable Quests
Orgrimmar	Quests, Repeatable Quests
Thunder Bluff	Quests, Repeatable Quests
Undercity	Quests, Repeatable Quests

Faction	How to Raise Reputation
PvP Factions (Alliance/Horde)	
Stormpike Guard/Frostwolf Clan	Killing opposing players, Quests, Repeatable Quests, Capturing Objectives
League of Arathor/The Defilers	Gathering 200 Resources, Quests, Repeatable Quests, Capturing Objectives
Silverwing Sentinels/Warsong Outriders	Capturing an enemy flag, Quests, Repeatable Quests, Capturing Objectives
Steamwheedle Cartel	
Booty Bay	Quests, Repeatable Quests, Killing Bloodsail Buccaneers
Everlook	Quests, Repeatable Quests
Gadgetzan	Quests, Repeatable Quests
Ratchet	Quests, Repeatable Quests
Other	
Argent Dawn	Quests, Repeatable Quests, Killing Scourge
Bloodsail Buccaneers	Killing Booty Bay Guards
Cenarion Hold	Quests, Repeatable Quests
Darkmoon Faire	Quests, Repeatable Quests
Gelkis Clan Centaurs	Killing Magram Clan Centaurs
Hydraxian Waterlords	Quests, Killing specific mobs
Magram Clan Centaurs	Killing Gelkis Clan Centaurs
Ravenholdt	Killing Syndicate
Thorium Brotherhood	Quests, Repeatable Quests
Timbermaw Hold	Repeatable Quests, Killing Deadwood/Winterfall Furbolg
Wintersabre Trainers	Quests, Repeatable Quests

THE REWARDS

Raising your reputation can be a long and arduous process. You won't become the symbol of justice in a day, but the rewards make it worthwhile.

CORE FACTIONS

Raising your faction with Alliance, Horde, and Steamwheedle organizations gives the following bonuses:

Exalted:	Ability to learn how to ride another race's mount.
Honored:	10% Discount at all vendors allied with the faction.

PvP FACTIONS

Increasing your reputation with the PvP factions opens goods and services at the vendors near the entrance portals. Many of these items, weapons, and armor are superior to those of equal level found in your travels.

STORMPIKE GUARD

Friendly			
Item	Requirements	Set Name	Cost
Superior Healing Draught (Use: Restores 560 to 720 health)	Level 35, Usable only in Alterac Valley	N/A	5s
Superior Mana Draught (Use: Restores 560 to 720 mana)	Level 35, Usable only in Alterac Valley	N/A	5s
Stormpike Battle Tabard	N/A	N/A	1g
(5)Alterac Heavy Runecloth Bandage (Use: Heals 2000 damage over 8 seconds)	First Aid 225	N/A	80s
(5)Bottle Alterac Spring Water (Use: Restores 4410 mana over 30 seconds, increases Spirit by 10 for 10 minutes)	Level 55, Must remain seated while drinking	N/A	50s

Honored			
Item	Requirements	Set Name	Cost
Major Healing Draught (Use: Restores 980 to 1260 health)	Level 45, Usable only in Alterac Valley	N/A	9s
Major Mana Draught (Use: Restores 980 to 1260 mana)	Level 45, Usable only in Alterac Valley	N/A	9s
Stormpike Soldier's Cloak (Back, 43 Armor, +11 STA, +5 Frost Res., Equip: +24 Attack Power)	Level 55	N/A	6g 79s 50c
Stormpike Sage's Cloak (Back, 43 Armor, +11 STA, +5 Frost Res., Equip: Increases damage and healing done by magical spells and effects by up to 14)	Level 55	N/A	6g 84s 40c
Stormpike Soldier's Pendant (Neck, +15 STA, Equip: +18 Attack Power)	Level 55	N/A	6g 44s 83c
Stormpike Sage's Pendant (Neck, +10 STA, +10 INT, Equip: Restores 4 mana per 5 seconds)	Level 55	N/A	6g 44s 83c
Stormpike Plate Girdle (Plate Waist, 353 Armor, +18 STR, +7 AGI, +8 STA, +5 Frost Res.)	Level 55	N/A	4g 26s 99c
Stormpike Mail Girdle (Mail Waist, 199 Armor, +12 AGI, +12 STA, +12 INT, +5 Frost Res.)	Level 55	N/A	6g 40s 48c
Stormpike Leather Girdle (Leather Waist, 95 Armor, +11 STR, +10 AGI, +15 STA, +5 Frost Res.)	Level 55	N/A	5g 33s 74c
Stormpike Cloth Girdle (Cloth Waist, 48 Armor, +11 STA, +10 INT, +5 Frost Res., Equip: Increases damage and healing done by magical spells and effects by up to 18)	Level 55	N/A	4g 26s 99c
(5)Alterac mana Biscuit (Use: Restores 4410 health and 4410 mana over 30 seconds)	Level 51, Must remain seated while eating	N/A	63s
(200) Ice Threaded Arrow (Adds 16.5 dps)	Level 51	N/A	54s
(200) Ice Threaded Bullet (Adds 16.5 dps)	Level 51	N/A	54s

Revered

Item	Requirements	Set Name	Cost
Stormpike Battle Standard (Use: Place a Battle Standard with 1500 health that increases the damage of all party members that stay within 45 yards of the Battle Standard by 10%)	Lasts 2 minutes. Usable only in Alterac Valley	N/A	4g 50s
Electrified Dagger (One-Hand Dagger, 42.5 dps, +10 AGI, Chance on Hit: Blasts a target for 45 Nature damage)	Level 60	N/A	28g 48s 53c
Crackling Staff (Staff, 55.6 dps, +25 STA, +16 INT, Equip: Increases damage and healing done by magical spells and effects by up to 15)	Level 60	N/A	35g 86s 72c
Stormstrike Hammer (One-Hand Mace, 42.6 dps, +15 STR)	Level 60	N/A	28g 90s 23c
Gnoll Skin Bandolier (16 Slot Ammo Pouch, Equip: Increases ranged attack speed by 15%)	Level 55	N/A	31g 50s
Harpy Hide Quiver (16 Slot Quiver, Equip: Increases ranged attack speed by 15%)	Level 55	N/A	31g 50s

Exalted

Item	Requirements	Set Name	Cost
Stormpike Battle Charger (Use: Summons and dismisses a rideable Stormpike Battle Charger. This is a very fast mount)	Level 60	N/A	720g
Lei of the Lifegiver (Off-Hand, Equip: Increases healing done by spells and effects by up to 53, Restores 3 mana per 5 seconds)	Level 60	N/A	45g
Therazane's Touch (Off-Hand, Equip: Increases damage and healing done by magical spells and effects by up to 33)	Level 60	N/A	45g
Tome of Arcane Domination (Off-Hand, Equip: Increases damage done by Arcane spells and effects by up to 34, Restores 3 mana every 5 seconds)	Level 60	N/A	45g
Tome of Fiery Arcana (Off-Hand, Equip: Increases damage done by Fire spells and effects by up to 40)	Level 60	N/A	45g
Tome of Shadow Force (Off-Hand, +8 STA, Equip: Increases damage done by Shadow spells and effects by up to 34)	Level 60	N/A	45g
Tome of the Ice Lord (Off-Hand, +9 INT, Equip: Increases damage done by Frost spells and effects by up to 34)	Level 60	N/A	45g
The Unstoppable Force (Two-Hand Mace, 61.4 dps, +19 STR, +15 STA, Equip: Improves your chance to get a critical strike by 2%, Chance on hit: Stuns target for 1 second)	Level 60	N/A	140g 84s 10c
The Immovable Object (Shield, 2468 Armor, 44 Block, +15 STA, Equip: Increases the block value of your shield by 27)	Level 60	N/A	71g 57s 67c
Don Julio's Band (Ring, +11 STA, Equip: Improves your chance to get a critical strike by 1%, Improves your chance to hit by 1%, +16 Attack Power)	Level 60	N/A	68g

Exalted

Item	Requirements	Set Name	Cost
The Lobotomizer (One-Hand Dagger, 47.2 dps, Chance on hit: Wounds the target for 200 to 300 damage and lowers INT of target by 25 for 30 seconds)	Level 60	N/A	113g 9s 56c
Don Rodrigo's Band (Ring, +7 STA, Equip: Improves your chance to get a critical strike with spells by 1%, Decreases the magical resistances of your spell targets by 20)	Level 60, Classes: Priest, Mage, Warlock	N/A	68g

FROSTWOLF CLAN

Friendly

Item	Requirements	Set Name	Cost
Superior Healing Draught (Use: Restores 560 to 720 health)	Level 35, Usable only in Alterac Valley	N/A	5s
Superior Mana Draught (Use: Restores 560 to 720 mana)	Level 35, Usable only in Alterac Valley	N/A	5s
Frostwolf Battle Tabard	N/A	N/A	1g
(5)Alterac Heavy Runecloth Bandage (Use: Heals 2000 damage over 8 seconds)	First Aid 225	N/A	80s
(5)Bottle Alterac Spring Water (Use: Restores 4410 mana over 30 seconds, Increases Spirit by 10 for 10 minutes)	Level 55, Must remain seated while drinking	N/A	50s

Honored

Item	Requirements	Set Name	Cost
Major Healing Draught (Use: Restores 980 to 1260 health)	Level 45, Usable only in Alterac Valley	N/A	9s
Major Mana Draught (Use: Restores 980 to 1260 mana)	Level 45, Usable only in Alterac Valley	N/A	9s
Frostwolf Legionnarie's Cloak (Back, 43 Armor, +11 STA, +5 Frost Res., Equip: +24 Attack Power)	Level 55	N/A	6g 79s 50c
Frostwolf Advisor's Cloak (Back, 43 Armor, +11 STA, +5 Frost Res., Equip: Increases damage and healing done by magical spells and effects by up to 14)	Level 55	N/A	6g 84s 40c
Frostwolf Legionnaire's Pendant (Neck, +15 STA, Equip: +18 Attack Power)	Level 55	N/A	6g 44s 83c
Frostwolf Advisor's Pendant (Neck, +10 STA, +10 INT, Equip: Restores 4 mana per 5 seconds)	Level 55	N/A	6g 44s 83c
Frostwolf Plate Belt (Plate Waist, 353 Armor, +18 STR, +7 AGI, +8 STA, +5 Frost Res.)	Level 55	N/A	4g 26s 99c
Frostwolf Belt Girdle (Mail Waist, 199 Armor, +12 AGI, +12 STA, +12 INT, +5 Frost Res.)	Level 55	N/A	6g 40s 48c
Frostwolf Leather Belt (Leather Waist, 95 Armor, +11 STR, +10 AGI, +15 STA, +5 Frost Res.)	Level 55	N/A	5g 33s 74c

Honored

Item	Requirements	Set Name	Cost
Frostwolf Cloth Belt (Cloth Waist, 48 Armor, +11 STA, +10 INT, +5 Frost Res., Equip: Increases damage and healing done by magical spells and effects by up to 18)	Level 55	N/A	4g 26s 99c
(5)Alterac mana Biscuit (Use: Restores 4410 health and 4410 mana over 30 seconds)	Level 51, Must remain seated while eating	N/A	63s
(200) Ice Threaded Arrow (Adds 16.5 dps)	Level 51	N/A	54s
(200) Ice Threaded Bullet (Adds 16.5 dps)	Level 51	N/A	54s

Revered

Item	Requirements	Set Name	Cost
Frostwolf Battle Standard (Use: Place a Battle Standard with 1500 health that increases the damage of all party members that stay within 45 yards of the Battle Standard by 10%)	Lasts 2 minutes. Usable only in Alterac Valley	N/A	4g 50s
Glacial Blade (One-Hand Dagger, 42.5 dps, +10 AGI, Chance on Hit: Blasts a target for 45 Nature damage)	Level 60	N/A	28g 48s 53c
Whiteout Staff (Staff, 55.6 dps, +25 STA, +16 INT, Equip: Increases damage and healing done by magical spells and effects by up to 15)	Level 60	N/A	35g 86s 72c
Frostbite (One-Hand Mace, 42.6 dps, +15 STR)	Level 60	N/A	28g 90s 23c
Gnoll Skin Bandolier (16 Slot Ammo Pouch, Equip: Increases ranged attack speed by 15%)	Level 55	N/A	31g 50s
Harpy Hide Quiver (16 Slot Quiver, Equip: Increases ranged attack speed by 15%)	Level 55	N/A	31g 50s

Exalted

Item	Requirements	Set Name	Cost
Horn of the Frostwolf Howler (Use: Summons and dismisses a rideable Frostwolf Howler. This is a very fast mount)	Level 60	N/A	720g
Lei of the Lifegiver (Off-Hand, Equip: Increases healing done by spells and effects by up to 53, Restores 3 mana per 5 seconds)	Level 60	N/A	45g
Therazane's Touch (Off-Hand, Equip: Increases damage and healing done by magical spells and effects by up to 33)	Level 60	N/A	45g
Tome of Arcane Domination (Off-Hand, Equip: Increases damage done by Arcane spells and effects by up to 34, Restores 3 mana every 5 seconds)	Level 60	N/A	45g
Tome of Fiery Arcana (Off-Hand, Equip: Increases damage done by Fire spells and effects by up to 40)	Level 60	N/A	45g
Tome of Shadow Force (Off-Hand, +8 STA, Equip: Increases damage done by Shadow spells and effects by up to 34)	Level 60	N/A	45g
Tome of the Ice Lord (Off-Hand, +9 INT, Equip: Increases damage done by Frost spells and effects by up to 34)	Level 60	N/A	45g

Exalted

Item	Requirements	Set Name	Cost
The Unstoppable Force (Two-Hand Mace, 61.4 dps, +19 STR, +15 STA, Equip: Improves your chance to get a critical strike by 2%, Chance on hit: Stuns target for 1 second)	Level 60	N/A	140g 84s 10c
The Immovable Object (Shield, 2468 Armor, 44 Block, +15 STA, Equip: Increases the block value of your shield by 27)	Level 60	N/A	71g 57s 67c
Don Julio's Band (Ring, +11 STA, Equip: Improves your chance to get a critical strike by 1%, Improves your chance to hit by 1%, +16 Attack Power)	Level 60	N/A	68g
The Lobotomizer (One-Hand Dagger, 47.2 dps, Chance on hit: Wounds the target for 200 to 300 damage and lowers INT of target by 25 for 30 seconds)	Level 60	N/A	113g 9s 56c
Don Rodrigo's Band (Ring, +7 STA, Equip: Improves your chance to get a critical strike with spells by 1%, Decreases the magical resistances of your spell targets by 20)	Level 60, Classes: Priest, Mage, Warlock	N/A	68g

LEAGUE OF ARATHOR

Friendly

Item	Requirements	Set Name	Cost
Superior Healing Draught (Use: Restores 560 to 720 health)	Level 35, Usable only in Arathi Basin	N/A	5s
Superior Mana Draught (Use: Restores 560 to 720 mana)	Level 35, Usable only in Arathi Basin	N/A	5s
(5)Highlander's Field Ration (Use: Restores 1074 health and 2202 mana over 30 seconds)	Level 25, Must remain seated while eating. Usable only in Arathi Basin	N/A	10s
(5)Highlander's Iron Ration (Use: Restores 1608 health and 3306 mana over 30 seconds)	Level 35, Must remain seated while eating. Usable only in Arathi Basin	N/A	15s
(5)Highlander's Enriched Ration (Use: Restores 2148 health and 4410 mana over 30 seconds)	Level 45, Must remain seated while eating. Usable only in Arathi Basin	N/A	20s
(5)Highlander's Silk Bandage (Use: Heals 640 damage over 8 seconds)	Level 25, First Aid (125), Usable only in Arathi Basin	N/A	10s
(5)Highlander's Mageweave Bandage (Use: Heals 1104 damage over 8 seconds)	Level 35, First Aid (175), Usable only in Arathi Basin	N/A	15s
(5)Highlander's Runecloth Bandage (Use: Heals 2000 damage over 8 seconds)	Level 45, First Aid (225), Usable only in Arathi Basin	N/A	20s
Talisman of Arathor (Use: Absorbs 248 to 302 physical damage)	Level 28, Lasts 15 seconds	N/A	72s 30c

Friendly

Item	Requirements	Set Name	Cost
Talisman of Arathor (Use: Absorbs 310 to 378 physical damage)	Level 38, Lasts 15 seconds	N/A	1g 52s 30c
Talisman of Arathor (Use: Absorbs 392 to 478 physical damage)	Level 48, Lasts 15 seconds	N/A	2g 82s 30c
Talisman of Arathor (Use: Absorbs 495 to 605 physical damage)	Level 58, Lasts 15 seconds	N/A	4g 12s 30c

Honored

Item	Requirements	Set Name	Cost
Highlander's Chain Girdle (Leather Waist, 61 Armor, +5 STA, Passive: +24 Attack Power)	Level 28, Classes: Hunter	N/A	93s 73c
Highlander's Chain Girdle (Mail Waist, 149 Armor, +6 STA, Passive: Improves your chance to get a critical strike by 1%, +8 Attack Power)	Level 40, Classes: Hunter	N/A	2g 60s 40c
Highlander's Chain Girdle (Mail Waist, 178 Armor, +8 STA, Passive: Improves your chance to get a critical strike by 1%, +20 Attack Power)	Level 48, Classes: Hunter	N/A	4g 93s 73c
Highlander's Chain Girdle (Mail Waist, 208 Armor, +10 STA, Passive: Improves your chance to get a critical strike by 1%, +34 Attack Power)	Level 58, Classes: Hunter	The Highlander's Determination	7g 92s 59c
Highlander's Cloth Girdle (Cloth Waist, 88 Armor, +4 STA, +3 INT, Passive: Increases damage and healing done by magical spells and effects by up to 11)	Level 28, Classes: Warlock, Mage, Priest	N/A	72s 7c
Highlander's Cloth Girdle (Cloth Waist, 105 Armor, +4 STA, +4 INT, Passive: Increases damage and healing done by magical spells and effects by up to 14)	Level 38, Classes: Warlock, Mage, Priest	N/A	1g 66s 84c
Highlander's Cloth Girdle (Cloth Waist, 113 Armor, +6 STA, +5 INT, Passive: Improves your chance to get a critical strike with spells by 1%, Increases damage and healing done by magical spells and effects by up to 9)	Level 48, Classes: Warlock, Mage, Priest	N/A	3g 36s 19c
Highlander's Cloth Girdle (Cloth Waist, 150 Armor, +7 STA, +6 INT, Passive: Improves your chance to get a critical strike with spells by 1%, Increases damage and healing done by magical spells and effects by up to 14)	Level 58, Classes: Warlock, Mage, Priest	The Highlander's Intent	5g 36s 1c
Highlander's Lizardhide Girdle (Leather Waist, 91 Armor, +4 STA, +12 INT)	Level 28, Classes: Rogue, Druid	N/A	92s 7c
Highlander's Lizardhide Girdle (Leather Waist, 113 Armor, +4 STA, +15 INT)	Level 38, Classes: Rogue, Druid	N/A	2g 13s 14c
Highlander's Lizardhide Girdle (Leather Waist, 136 Armor, +6 STA, +10 INT, Equip: Improves your chance to get a critical strike with spells by 1%)	Level 48, Classes: Rogue, Druid	N/A	4g 29s 52c
Highlander's Lizardhide Girdle (Leather Waist, 159 Armor, +7 STA, +17 INT, Equip: Improves your chance to get a critical strike with spells by 1%)	Level 58, Classes: Rogue, Druid	The Highlander's Will	6g 67s 62c
Highlander's Leather Girdle (Leather Waist, 91 Armor, +4 STA, +24 Attack Power)	Level 28, Classes: Rogue, Druid	N/A	89s 41c

Honored

Item	Requirements	Set Name	Cost
Highlander's Leather Girdle (Leather Waist, 113 Armor, +4 STA, +30 Attack Power)	Level 38, Classes: Rogue, Druid	N/A	2g 6s 99c
Highlander's Leather Girdle (Leather Waist, 136 Armor, +6 STA, Equip: Improves your chance to get a critical strike by 1%, +20 Attack Power)	Level 48, Classes: Rogue, Druid	N/A	4g 17s 8c
Highlander's Leather Girdle (Leather Waist, 159 Armor, +7 STA, Equip: Improves your chance to get a critical strike by 1%, +34 Attack Power)	Level 58, Classes: Rogue, Druid	The Highlander's Purpose	6g 65s 29c
Highlander's Lamellar Girdle (Mail Waist, 128 Armor, +11 STR, +4 STA, +5 INT)	Level 28, Classes: Paladin	N/A	1g 3s 75c
Highlander's Lamellar Girdle (Plate Waist, 236 Armor, +12 STR, +6 STA, +6 INT)	Level 40, Classes: Paladin	N/A	1g 60s 8c
Highlander's Lamellar Girdle (Plate Waist, 313 Armor, +11 STR, +4 STA, +8 INT, Equip: Improves your chance to get a critical strike by 1%)	Level 48, Classes: Paladin	N/A	3g 47s 32c
Highlander's Lamellar Girdle (Plate Waist, 369 Armor, +15 STR, +6 STA, +10 INT, Equip: Improves your chance to get a critical strike by 1%)	Level 58, Classes: Paladin	The Highlander's Resolve	5g 12s 75c
Highlander's Plate Girdle (Mail Waist, 128 Armor, +12 STR, +5 STA)	Level 28, Classes: Warrior, Paladin	N/A	1g 2s 94c
Highlander's Plate Girdle (Plate Waist, 236 Armor, +15 STR, +6 STA,)	Level 40, Classes: Warrior, Paladin	N/A	1g 58s 83c
Highlander's Plate Girdle (Plate Waist, 313 Armor, +10 STR, +8 STA)	Level 48, Classes: Warrior, Paladin	N/A	3g 53s 76c
Highlander's Plate Girdle (Plate Waist, 369 Armor, +17 STR, +10 STA, Equip: Improves your chance to get a critical strike by 1%)	Level 58, Classes: Warrior, Paladin	The Highlander's Resolution	5g 10s 88c

Revered

Item	Requirements	Set Name	Cost
Highlander's Chain Greaves (Leather Feet, 74 Armor, +8 AGI, +8 STA, Equip: Run speed increased slightly)	Level 28, Classes: Hunter	N/A	1g 32s 17c
Highlander's Chain Greaves (Mail Feet, 183 Armor, +10 AGI, +10 STA, +3 INT, Equip: Run speed increased slightly)	Level 40, Classes: Hunter	N/A	3g 68s 75c
Highlander's Chain Greaves (Mail Feet, 218 Armor, +12 AGI, +13 STA, +6 INT, Equip: Run speed increased slightly)	Level 48, Classes: Hunter	N/A	7g 42s 97c
Highlander's Chain Greaves (Mail Feet, 255 Armor, +15 AGI, +16 STA, +8 INT, Equip: Run speed increased slightly)	Level 58, Classes: Hunter	The Highlander's Determination	12g 24s 28c
Highlander's Cloth Boots (Cloth Feet, 84 Armor, +8 STA, Equip: Run speed increased slightly, Increases damage and healing done by magical spells and effects by up to 7)	Level 28, Classes: Priest, Mage, Warlock	N/A	1g 6s 92c
Highlander's Cloth Boots (Cloth Feet, 103 Armor, +10 STA, +3 INT, Equip: Run speed increased slightly, Increases damage and healing done by magical spells and effects by up to 8)	Level 38, Classes: Priest, Mage, Warlock	N/A	2g 47s 49c

Item	Requirements	Set Name	Cost
Highlander's Cloth Boots (Cloth Feet, 132 Armor, +13 STA, +6 INT, Equip: Run speed increased slightly, Increases damage and healing done by magical spells and effects by up to 9)	Level 48, Classes: Priest, Mage, Warlock	N/A	4g 98s 73c
Highlander's Cloth Boots (Cloth Feet, 161 Armor, +16 STA, +8 INT, Equip: Run speed increased slightly, Increases damage and healing done by magical spells and effects by up to 12)	Level 58, Classes: Priest, Mage, Warlock	The Highlander's Intent	7g 46s 19c
Highlander's Lizardhide Boots (Leather Feet, 104 Armor, +5 AGI, +8 STA, +4 INT, Equip: Run speed increased slightly)	Level 28, Classes: Rogue, Druid	N/A	1g 36s 61c
Highlander's Lizardhide Boots (Leather Feet, 129 Armor, +6 AGI, +10 STA, +5 INT, Equip: Run speed increased slightly, +6 Attack Power)	Level 38, Classes: Rogue, Druid	N/A	3g 16s 28c
Highlander's Lizardhide Boots (Leather Feet, 145 Armor, +8 AGI, +13 STA, +7 INT, Equip: Run speed increased slightly, +12 Attack Power)	Level 48, Classes: Rogue, Druid	N/A	6g 37s 32c
Highlander's Lizardhide Boots (Leather Feet, 181 Armor, +8 AGI, +16 STA, +8 INT, Equip: Run speed increased slightly, +16 Attack Power)	Level 58, Classes: Rogue, Druid	The Highlander's Will	9g 29s 14c
Highlander's Leather Boots (Leather Feet, 104 Armor, +7 AGI, +8 STA, Equip: Run speed increased slighty)	Level 28, Classes: Rogue, Druid	N/A	1g 32s 64c
Highlander's Leather Boots (Leather Feet, 129 Armor, +8 AGI, +10 STA, Equip: Run speed increased slighty, +6 Attack Power)	Level 38, Classes: Rogue, Druid	N/A	3g 7s 5c
Highlander's Leather Boots (Leather Feet, 145 Armor, +11 AGI, +13 STA, Equip: Run speed increased slighty, +12 Attack Power)	Level 48, Classes: Rogue, Druid	N/A	6g 18s 68c
Highlander's Leather Boots (Leather Feet, 181 Armor, +12 AGI, +16 STA, Equip: Run speed increased slighty, +16 Attack Power)	Level 58, Classes: Rogue, Druid	The Highlander's Purpose	9g 25s 64c
Highlander's Lamellar Greaves (Mail Feet, 157 Armor, +6 STR, +6 AGI, +4 STA, +4 INT, Equip: Run speed increased slightly)	Level 28, Classes: Paladin	N/A	1g 58s 10c
Highlander's Lamellar Greaves (Plate Feet, 289 Armor, +8 STR, +8 AGI, +6 STA, +6 INT, Equip: Run speed increased slightly)	Level 40, Classes: Paladin	N/A	2g 42s 87c
Highlander's Lamellar Greaves (Plate Feet, 383 Armor, +11 STR, +10 AGI, +7 STA, +6 INT, Equip: Run speed increased slightly)	Level 48, Classes: Paladin	N/A	4g 89s 38c
Highlander's Lamellar Greaves (Plate Feet, 452 Armor, +14 STR, +12 AGI, +8 STA, +8 INT, Equip: Run speed increased slightly)	Level 58, Classes: Paladin	The Highlander's Resolve	8g 9s 78c
Highlander's Plate Greaves (Mail Feet, 157 Armor, +6 STR, +6 AGI, +6 STA, Equip: Run speed increased slightly)	Level 28, Classes: Warrior, Paladin	N/A	1g 56s 88c
Highlander's Plate Greaves (Plate Feet, 289 Armor, +8 STR, +8 AGI, +8 STA, Equip: Run speed increased slightly)	Level 40, Classes: Warrior, Paladin	N/A	2g 41s 2c
Highlander's Plate Greaves (Plate Feet, 383 Armor, +11 STR, +10 AGI, +10 STA, Equip: Run speed increased slightly)	Level 48, Classes: Warrior, Paladin	N/A	4g 85s 58c

Item	Requirements	Set Name	Cost
Highlander's Plate Greaves (Plate Feet, 452 Armor, +14 STR, +12 STA, +12 STA, Equip: Run speed increased slightly)	Level 58, Classes: Warrior, Paladin	The Highlander's Resolution	8g 6s 90c

Exalted

Item	Requirements	Set Name	Cost
Highlander's Chain Pauldrons (Mail Shoulder, 312 Armor, +20 AGI, +18 STA, +17 INT)	Level 58, Classes: Hunter	The Highlander's Determination	16g 59s 3c
Highlander's Epaulets (Cloth Shoulder, 185 Armor, +18 STA, +17 INT, Equip: Increases damage and healing done by magical spells and effects by up to 12, Restores 4 mana per 5 seconds)	Level 60, Classes: Priest, Mage, Warlock	The Highlander's Intent	11g 56s 54c
Highlander's Lizardhide Shoulders (Leather Shoulder, 258 Armor, +12 AGI, +17 STA, +12 INT, Equip: +30 Attack Power)	Level 60, Classes: Rogue, Druid	The Highlander's Will	14g 40s 55c
Highlander's Leather Spaulders (Leather Shoulder, 258 Armor, +18 AGI, +17 STA, Equip: +30 Attack Power)	Level 60, Classes: Rogue, Druid	The Highlander's Purpose	14g 35s 26c
Highlander's Lamellar Spaulders (Plate Shoulder, 553 Armor, +18 STR, +17 AGI, +15 STA, +10 INT)	Level 60, Classes: Paladin	The Highlander's Resolve	11g 13s 70c
Highlander's Plate Spaulders (Plate Shoulder, 553 Armor, +18 STR, +17 AGI, +20 STA)	Level 60, Classes: Warrior, Paladin	The Highlander's Resolution	11g 9s 46c
Cloak of the Honor Guard (Back, 50 Armor, +5 AGI, +11 STA, Equip: +34 Attack Power)	Level 60	N/A	10g 92s 56c
Ironbark Staff (Staff, 55.8 dps, 100 Armor, +19 STA, +10 INT, Equip: Improves your chance to get a critical strike with spells by 2%, Increases damage and healing done by magical spells and effects by up to 41)	Level 60	N/A	49g 58s 96c
Sageclaw (One-Hand Dagger, 41.7 dps, +8 STA, Equip: Increases damage and healing done by magical spells and effects by up to 30, Improves your chance to get a critical strike with spells by 1%)	Level 60	N/A	39g 81s 26c

THE DEFILERS

Friendly

Item	Requirements	Set Name	Cost
Superior Healing Draught (Use: Restores 560 to 720 health)	Level 35, Usable only in Arathi Basin	N/A	5s
Superior Mana Draught (Use: Restores 560 to 720 mana)	Level 35, Usable only in Arathi Basin	N/A	5s

Item	Requirements	Set Name	Cost
(5)Defiler's Field Ration (Use: Restores 1074 health and 2202 mana over 30 seconds)	Level 25, Must remain seated while eating. Usable only in Arathi Basin	N/A	10s
(5)Defiler's Iron Ration (Use: Restores 1608 health and 3306 mana over 30 seconds)	Level 35, Must remain seated while eating. Usable only in Arathi Basin	N/A	15s
(5)Defiler's Enriched Ration (Use: Restores 2148 health and 4410 mana over 30 seconds)	Level 45, Must remain seated while eating. Usable only in Arathi Basin	N/A	20s
(5)Defiler's Silk Bandage (Use: Heals 640 damage over 8 seconds)	Level 25, First Aid (125), Usable only in Arathi Basin	N/A	10s
(5)Defiler's Mageweave Bandage (Use: Heals 1104 damage over 8 seconds)	Level 35, First Aid (175), Usable only in Arathi Basin	N/A	15s
(5)Defiler's Runecloth Bandage (Use: Heals 2000 damage over 8 seconds)	Level 45, First Aid (225), Usable only in Arathi Basin	N/A	20s
Defiler's Talisman (Use: Absorbs 248 to 302 physical damage)	Level 28, Lasts 15 seconds	N/A	72s 30c
Defiler's Talisman (Use: Absorbs 310 to 378 physical damage)	Level 38, Lasts 15 seconds	N/A	1g 52s 30c
Defiler's Talisman (Use: Absorbs 392 to 478 physical damage)	Level 48, Lasts 15 seconds	N/A	2g 82s 30c
Defiler's Talisman (Use: Absorbs 495 to 605 physical damage)	Level 58, Lasts 15 seconds	N/A	4g 12s 30c

Item	Requirements	Set Name	Cost
Defiler's Chain Girdle (Leather Waist, 61 Armor, +5 STA, Passive: +24 Attack Power)	Level 28, Classes: Hunter, Shaman	N/A	93s 73c
Defiler's Chain Girdle (Mail Waist, 149 Armor, +6 STA, Passive: Improves your chance to get a critical strike by 1%, +8 Attack Power)	Level 40, Classes: Hunter, Shaman	N/A	2g 60s 40c
Defiler's Chain Girdle (Mail Waist, 178 Armor, +8 STA, Passive: Improves your chance to get a critical strike by 1%, +20 Attack Power)	Level 48, Classes: Hunter, Shaman	N/A	4g 93s 73c
Defiler's Chain Girdle (Mail Waist, 208 Armor, +10 STA, Passive: Improves your chance to get a critical strike by 1%, +34 Attack Power)	Level 58, Classes: Hunter, Shaman	The Defiler's Determination	7g 92s 59c
Defiler's Cloth Girdle (Cloth Waist, 88 Armor, +4 STA, +3 INT, Passive: Increases damage and healing done by magical spells and effects by up to 11)	Level 28, Classes: Warlock, Mage, Priest	N/A	72s 7c
Defiler's Cloth Girdle (Cloth Waist, 105 Armor, +4 STA, +4 INT, Passive: Increases damage and healing done by magical spells and effects by up to 14)	Level 38, Classes: Warlock, Mage, Priest	N/A	1g 66s 84c

Item	Requirements	Set Name	Cost
Defiler's Cloth Girdle (Cloth Waist, 113 Armor, +6 STA, +5 INT, Passive: Improves your chance to get a critical strike with spells by 1%, Increases damage and healing done by magical spells and effects by up to 9)	Level 48, Classes: Warlock, Mage, Priest	N/A	3g 36s 19c
Defiler's Cloth Girdle (Cloth Waist, 150 Armor, +7 STA, +6 INT, Passive: Improves your chance to get a critical strike with spells by 1%, Increases damage and healing done by magical spells and effects by up to 14)	Level 58, Classes: Warlock, Mage, Priest	The Defiler's Intent	5g 36s 1c
Defiler's Lizardhide Girdle (Leather Waist, 91 Armor, +4 STA, +12 INT)	Level 28, Classes: Rogue, Druid	N/A	92s 7c
Defiler's Lizardhide Girdle (Leather Waist, 113 Armor, +4 STA, +15 INT)	Level 38, Classes: Rogue, Druid	N/A	2g 13s 14c
Defiler's Lizardhide Girdle (Leather Waist, 136 Armor, +6 STA, +10 INT, Equip: Improves your chance to get a critical strike with spells by 1%)	Level 48, Classes: Rogue, Druid	N/A	4g 29s 52c
Defiler's Lizardhide Girdle (Leather Waist, 159 Armor, +7 STA, +17 INT, Equip: Improves your chance to get a critical strike with spells by 1%)	Level 58, Classes: Rogue, Druid	The Defiler's Will	6g 67s 62c
Defiler's Leather Girdle (Leather Waist, 91 Armor, +4 STA, +24 Attack Power)	Level 28, Classes: Rogue, Druid	N/A	89s 41c
Defiler's Leather Girdle (Leather Waist, 113 Armor, +4 STA, +30 Attack Power)	Level 38, Classes: Rogue, Druid	N/A	2g 6s 99c
Defiler's Leather Girdle (Leather Waist, 136 Armor, +6 STA, Equip: Improves your chance to get a critical strike by 1%, +20 Attack Power)	Level 48, Classes: Rogue, Druid	N/A	4g 17s 8c
Defiler's Leather Girdle (Leather Waist, 159 Armor, +7 STA, Equip: Improves your chance to get a critical strike by 1%, +34 Attack Power)	Level 58, Classes: Rogue, Druid	The Defiler's Purpose	6g 65s 29c
Defiler's Mail Girdle (Leather Waist, 61 Armor, +5 STA, +12 INT)	Level 28, Classes: Hunter, Shaman	N/A	91s 74c
Defiler's Mail Girdle (Mail Waist, 149 Armor, +6 STA, +15 INT)	Level 40, Classes: Hunter, Shaman	N/A	2g 56s 72c
Defiler's Mail Girdle (Mail Waist, 178 Armor, +8 STA, +10 INT, Equip: Improves your chance to get a critical strike with spells by 1%)	Level 48, Classes: Hunter, Shaman	N/A	5g 15s 47c
Defiler's Mail Girdle (Mail Waist, 208 Armor, +10 STA, +17 INT, Equip: Improves your chance to get a critical strike with spells by 1%)	Level 58, Classes: Hunter, Shaman	The Defiler's Fortitude	8g 77s 29c
Defiler's Plate Girdle (Mail Waist, 128 Armor, +12 STR, +5 STA)	Level 28, Classes: Warrior	N/A	1g 2s 94c
Defiler's Plate Girdle (Plate Waist, 236 Armor, +15 STR, +6 STA,)	Level 40, Classes: Warrior	N/A	1g 58s 83c
Defiler's Plate Girdle (Plate Waist, 313 Armor, +10 STR, +8 STA)	Level 48, Classes: Warrior	N/A	3g 53s 76c
Defiler's Plate Girdle (Plate Waist, 369 Armor, +17 STR, +10 STA, Equip: Improves your chance to get a critical strike by 1%)	Level 58, Classes: Warrior	The Defiler's Resolution	5g 10s 88c

Revered

Item	Requirements	Set Name	Cost
Defiler's Chain Greaves (Leather Feet, 74 Armor, +8 AGI, +8 STA, Equip: Run speed increased slightly)	Level 28, Classes: Hunter	N/A	1g 32s 17c
Defiler's Chain Greaves (Mail Feet, 183 Armor, +10 AGI, +10 STA, +3 INT, Equip: Run speed increased slightly)	Level 40, Classes: Hunter	N/A	3g 68s 75c
Defiler's Chain Greaves (Mail Feet, 218 Armor, +12 AGI, +13 STA, +6 INT, Equip: Run speed increased slightly)	Level 48, Classes: Hunter	N/A	7g 42s 97c
Defiler's Chain Greaves (Mail Feet, 255 Armor, +15 AGI, +16 STA, +8 INT, Equip: Run speed increased slightly)	Level 58, Classes: Hunter	The Defiler's Determination	12g 24s 28c
Defiler's Cloth Boots (Cloth Feet, 84 Armor, +8 STA, Equip: Run speed increased slightly, Increases damage and healing done by magical spells and effects by up to 7)	Level 28, Classes: Priest, Mage, Warlock	N/A	1g 6s 92c
Defiler's Cloth Boots (Cloth Feet, 103 Armor, +10 STA, +3 INT, Equip: Run speed increased slightly, Increases damage and healing done by magical spells and effects by up to 8)	Level 38, Classes: Priest, Mage, Warlock	N/A	2g 47s 49c
Defiler's Cloth Boots (Cloth Feet, 132 Armor, +13 STA, +6 INT, Equip: Run speed increased slightly, Increases damage and healing done by magical spells and effects by up to 9)	Level 48, Classes: Priest, Mage, Warlock	N/A	4g 98s 73c
Defiler's Cloth Boots (Cloth Feet, 161 Armor, +16 STA, +8 INT, Equip: Run speed increased slightly, Increases damage and healing done by magical spells and effects by up to 12)	Level 58, Classes: Priest, Mage, Warlock	The Defiler's Intent	7g 46s 19c
Defiler's Lizardhide Boots (Leather Feet, 104 Armor, +5 AGI, +8 STA, +4 INT, Equip: Run speed increased slightly)	Level 28, Classes: Rogue, Druid	N/A	1g 36s 61c
Defiler's Lizardhide Boots (Leather Feet, 129 Armor, +6 AGI, +10 STA, +5 INT, Equip: Run speed increased slightly, +6 Attack Power)	Level 38, Classes: Rogue, Druid	N/A	3g 16s 28c
Defiler's Lizardhide Boots (Leather Feet, 145 Armor, +8 AGI, +13 STA, +7 INT, Equip: Run speed increased slightly, +12 Attack Power)	Level 48, Classes: Rogue, Druid	N/A	6g 37s 32c
Defiler's Lizardhide Boots (Leather Feet, 181 Armor, +8 AGI, +16 STA, +8 INT, Equip: Run speed increased slightly, +16 Attack Power)	Level 58, Classes: Rogue, Druid	The Defiler's Will	9g 29s 14c
Defiler's Leather Boots (Leather Feet, 104 Armor, +7 AGI, +8 STA, Equip: Run speed increased slighty)	Level 28, Classes: Rogue, Druid	N/A	1g 32s 64c
Defiler's Leather Boots (Leather Feet, 129 Armor, +8 AGI, +10 STA, Equip: Run speed increased slighty, +6 Attack Power)	Level 38, Classes: Rogue, Druid	N/A	3g 7s 5c
Defiler's Leather Boots (Leather Feet, 145 Armor, +11 AGI, +13 STA, Equip: Run speed increased slighty, +12 Attack Power)	Level 48, Classes: Rogue, Druid	N/A	6g 18s 68c
Defiler's Leather Boots (Leather Feet, 181 Armor, +12 AGI, +16 STA, Equip: Run speed increased slighty, +16 Attack Power)	Level 58, Classes: Rogue, Druid	The Defiler's Purpose	9g 25s 64c
Defiler's Mail Greaves (Leather Feet, 74 Armor, +8 AGI, +8 STA, Equip: Run speed increased slightly)	Level 28, Classes: Hunter, Shaman	N/A	1g 39s 60c

Revered

Item	Requirements	Set Name	Cost
Defiler's Mail Greaves (Mail Feet, 183 Armor, +10 AGI, +10 STA, +3 INT, Equip: Run speed increased slightly)	Level 40, Classes: Hunter, Shaman	N/A	3g 89s 54c
Defiler's Mail Greaves (Mail Feet, 218 Armor, +12 AGI, +13 STA, +6 INT, Equip: Run speed increased slightly)	Level 48, Classes: Hunter, Shaman	N/A	7g 93s 48c
Defiler's Mail Greaves (Mail Feet, 255 Armor, +15 AGI, +16 STA, +8 INT, Equip: Run speed increased slightly)	Level 58, Classes: Hunter, Shaman	The Defiler's Determination	11g 54s 59c
Defiler's Plate Greaves (Mail Feet, 157 Armor, +6 STR, +6 AGI, +6 STA, Equip: Run speed increased slightly)	Level 28, Classes: Warrior	N/A	1g 56s 88c
Defiler's Plate Greaves (Plate Feet, 289 Armor, +8 STR, +8 AGI, +8 STA, Equip: Run speed increased slightly)	Level 40, Classes: Warrior	N/A	2g 41s 2c
Defiler's Plate Greaves (Plate Feet, 383 Armor, +11 STR, +10 AGI, +10 STA, Equip: Run speed increased slightly)	Level 48, Classes: Warrior	N/A	4g 85s 58c
Defiler's Plate Greaves (Plate Feet, 452 Armor, +14 STR, +12 AGI, +12 STA, Equip: Run speed increased slightly)	Level 58, Classes: Warrior	The Defiler's Resolution	8g 6s 90c

Exalted

Item	Requirements	Set Name	Cost
Defiler's Chain Pauldrons (Mail Shoulder, 312 Armor, +20 AGI, +18 STA, +17 INT)	Level 58, Classes: Hunter	The Defiler's Determination	16g 59s 3c
Defiler's Epaulets (Cloth Shoulder, 185 Armor, +18 STA, +17 INT, Equip: Increases damage and healing done by magical spells and effects by up to 12, Restores 4 mana per 5 seconds)	Level 60, Classes: Priest, Mage, Warlock	The Defiler's Intent	11g 56s 54c
Defiler's Lizardhide Shoulders (Leather Shoulder, 258 Armor, +12 AGI, +17 STA, +12 INT, Equip: +30 Attack Power)	Level 60, Classes: Rogue, Druid	The Defiler's Will	14g 40s 55c
Defiler's Leather Spaulders (Leather Shoulder, 258 Armor, +18 AGI, +17 STA, Equip: +30 Attack Power)	Level 60, Classes: Rogue, Druid	The Defiler's Purpose	14g 35s 26c
Defiler's Mail Pauldrons (Mail Shoulder, 312 Armor, +11 STR, +10 AGI, +18 STA, +17 INT, Equip: Restores 4 mana per 5 seconds)	Level 60, Classes: Hunter, Shaman	The Defiler's Fortitude	17g 99s 35c
Defiler's Plate Spaulders (Plate Shoulder, 553 Armor, +18 STR, +17 AGI, +20 STA)	Level 60, Classes: Warrior, Paladin	The Defiler's Resolution	11g 9s 46c
Deathguard's Cloak (Back, 50 Armor, +5 AGI, +11 STA, Equip: +34 Attack Power)	Level 60	N/A	10g 92s 56c
Ironbark Staff (Staff, 55.8 dps, 100 Armor, +19 STA, +10 INT, Equip: Improves your chance to get a critical strike with spells by 2%, Increases damage and healing done by magical spells and effects by up to 41)	Level 60	N/A	49g 58s 96c
Mindfang (One-Hand Dagger, 41.7 dps, 40 Armor, +8 STA, Equip: Increases damage and healing done by magical spells and effects by up to 30, Improves your chance to get a critical strike with spells by 1%)	Level 60	N/A	39g 81s 26c

SILVERWING SENTINELS

Friendly

Item	Requirements	Set Name	Cost
Rune of Perfection (Trinket, +4 STA, Equip: Decreases the magical resistances of your spell targets by 10)	Level 20, Classes: Priest, Shaman, Mage, Warlock, Druid	N/A	2g
Rune of Perfection (Trinket, +7 STA, Equip: Decreases the magical resistances of your spell targets by 20)	Level 40, Classes: Priest, Shaman, Mage, Warlock, Druid	N/A	4g
Rune of Duty (Trinket, +4 STA, Equip: Restores 3 health every 5 seconds)	Level 20, Classes: Warrior, Paladin, Hunter, Rogue	N/A	4g
Rune of Duty (Trinket, +7 STA, Equip: Restores 4 health every 5 seconds)	Level 40, Classes: Warrior, Paladin, Hunter, Rogue	N/A	4g
Superior Healing Draught (Use: Restores 560 to 720 health)	Level 35, Usable only in Warsong Gulch	N/A	5s
Superior Mana Draught (Use: Restores 560 to 720 mana)	Level 35, Usable only in Warsong Gulch	N/A	5s
(5)Warsong Gulch Field Ration (Use: Restores 1074 health and 2202 mana over 30 seconds)	Level 25, Must remain seated while eating. Usable only in Warsong Gulch	N/A	10s
(5)Warsong Gulch Iron Ration (Use: Restores 1608 health and 3306 mana over 30 seconds)	Level 35, Must remain seated while eating. Usable only in Warsong Gulch	N/A	15s
(5)Warsong Gulch Enriched Ration (Use: Restores 2148 health and 4410 mana over 30 seconds)	Level 45, Must remain seated while eating. Usable only in Warsong Gulch	N/A	20s
(5)Warsong Gulch Silk Bandage (Use: Heals 640 damage over 8 seconds)	Level 25, First Aid (125), Usable only in Warsong Gulch	N/A	10s
(5)Warsong Gulch Mageweave Bandage (Use: Heals 1104 damage over 8 seconds)	Level 35, First Aid (175), Usable only in Warsong Gulch	N/A	15s
(5)Warsong Gulch Runecloth Bandage (Use: Heals 2000 damage over 8 seconds)	Level 45, First Aid (225), Usable only in Warsong Gulch	N/A	20s

Honored

Item	Requirements	Set Name	Cost
Caretaker's Cape (Back, 20 Armor, +4 STA, +2 SPI, Equip: Increases healing done by spells and effects by up to 9)	Level 18	N/A	36s 50c
Caretaker's Cape (Back, 25 Armor, +6 STA, +4 SPI, Equip: Increases healing done by spells and effects by up to 13)	Level 28	N/A	1g 7s 72c
Caretaker's Cape (Back, 31 Armor, +8 STA, +5 SPI, Equip: Increases healing done by spells and effects by up to 18)	Level 38	N/A	2g 49s 34c

Honored

Item	Requirements	Set Name	Cost
Caretaker's Cape (Back, 38 Armor, +9 STA, +6 SPI, Equip: Increases healing done by spells and effects by up to 22)	Level 48	N/A	5g 2s 42c
Caretaker's Cape (Back, 45 Armor, +11 STA, +8 SPI, Equip: Increases healing done by spells and effects by up to 26)	Level 58	N/A	7g 69s 43c
Lorekeeper's Ring (Ring, +2 STA, Equip: Increases damage and healing done by magical spells and effects by up to 5, Restores 2 mana per 5 seconds)	Level 18	N/A	2g
Lorekeeper's Ring (Ring, +4 STA, Equip: Increases damage and healing done by magical spells and effects by up to 7, Restores 2 mana per 5 seconds)	Level 28	N/A	2g 75s
Lorekeeper's Ring (Ring, +5 STA, Equip: Increases damage and healing done by magical spells and effects by up to 9, Restores 3 mana per 5 seconds)	Level 38	N/A	4g 50s
Lorekeeper's Ring (Ring, +6 STA, Equip: Increases damage and healing done by magical spells and effects by up to 12, Restores 4 mana per 5 seconds)	Level 48	N/A	6g
Lorekeeper's Ring (Ring, +8 STA, Equip: Increases damage and healing done by magical spells and effects by up to 14, Restores 4 mana per 5 seconds)	Level 58	N/A	6g 75s
Sentinel's Medallion (Neck, +6 AGI, +2 STA)	Level 18	N/A	2g
Sentinel's Medallion (Neck, +8 AGI, +5 STA)	Level 28	N/A	2g 75s
Sentinel's Medallion (Neck, +11 AGI, +7 STA)	Level 38	N/A	4g 50s
Sentinel's Medallion (Neck, +12 AGI, +8 STA)	Level 48	N/A	6g
Sentinel's Medallion (Neck, +15 AGI, +10 STA)	Level 58	N/A	6g 75s
Protector's Band (Ring, +4 STR, +4 AGI, +2 STA)	Level 18	N/A	2g
Protector's Band (Ring, +6 STR, +6 AGI, +4 STA)	Level 28	N/A	2g 75s
Protector's Band (Ring, +18 STR, +8 AGI, +5 STA)	Level 38	N/A	4g 50s
Protector's Band (Ring, +10 STR, +9 AGI, +6 STA)	Level 48	N/A	6g
Protector's Band (Ring, +12 STR, +11 AGI, +8 STA)	Level 58	N/A	6g 75s
Major Healing Draught (Use: Restores 980 to 1260 health)	Level 45, Only usable in Warsong Gulch	N/A	9s
Major Mana Draught (Use: Restores 980 to 1260 mana)	Level 45, Only usable in Warsong Gulch	N/A	9s

Revered

Item	Requirements	Set Name	Cost
Lorekeeper's Staff (Staff, 19.7 dps, +8 STA, +4 INT, Equip: Restores 3 mana every 5 seconds)	Level 18	N/A	1g 52s 11c
Lorekeeper's Staff (Staff, 27.8 dps, +11 STA, +7 INT, Equip: Restores 4 mana every 5 seconds)	Level 28	N/A	4g 27s 71c

Revered

Item	Requirements	Set Name	Cost
Lorekeeper's Staff (Staff, 38.1 dps, +14 STA, +9 INT, Equip: Restores 6 mana every 5 seconds)	Level 38	N/A	9g 93s 73c
Lorekeeper's Staff (Staff, 45.9 dps, +18 STA, +11 INT, Equip: Restores 7 mana every 5 seconds)	Level 48	N/A	20g 9s 79c
Lorekeeper's Staff (Staff, 54 dps, +21 STA, +13 INT, Equip: Restores 8 mana every 5 seconds)	Level 58	N/A	32g 5s 33c
Outrunner's Bow (Bow, 11.7 dps)	Level 18	N/A	91s 26c
Outrunner's Bow (Bow, 16.7)	Level 28	N/A	2g 56s 63c
Outrunner's Bow (Bow, 22.7 dps, +3 AGI, +6 STA)	Level 38	N/A	5g 96s 24c
Outrunner's Bow (Bow, 27.5 dps, +3 AGI, +8 STA)	Level 48	N/A	12g 5s 87c
Outrunner's Bow (Bow, 32.3 dps, +4 AGI, +10 STA)	Level 58	N/A	18g 53s 62c
Protector's Sword (One-Hand Sword, 15 dps, +4 STR, +2 STA)	Level 18	N/A	1g 21s 69c
Protector's Sword (One-Hand Sword, 21.3 dps, +7 STR, +3 STA)	Level 28	N/A	3g 42s 17c
Protector's Sword (One-Hand Sword, 29.3 dps, +8 STR, +3 STA)	Level 38	N/A	7g 94s 98c
Protector's Sword (One-Hand Sword, 35.2 dps, +11 STR, +5 STA)	Level 48	N/A	16g 7s 83c
Protector's Sword (One-Hand Sword, 41.5 dps, +13 STR, +5 STA)	Level 58	N/A	24g 71s 50c
Sentinel's Blade (One-Hand Dagger, 15.3 dps, +4 AGI, +2 STA)	Level 18	N/A	1g 21s 69c
Sentinel's Blade (One-Hand Dagger, 21.2 dps, +7 AGI, +3 STA)	Level 28	N/A	3g 48s 45c
Sentinel's Blade (One-Hand Dagger, 29.1 dps, +8 AGI, +3 STA)	Level 38	N/A	8g 67s 91c
Sentinel's Blade (One-Hand Dagger, 35 dps, +11 AGI, +5 STA)	Level 48	N/A	17g 49s 10c
Sentinel's Blade (One-Hand Dagger, 41.5 dps, +13 AGI, +5 STA)	Level 58	N/A	25g 26s 44c

Exalted

Item	Requirements	Set Name	Cost
Silverwing Battle Tabard	N/A	N/A	4g 50s c
Berserker Bracers (Plate Wrist, 229 Armor, +14 STR, +6 AGI, +8 STA)	Level 40	N/A	2g 47s 27c
Berserker Bracers (Plate Wrist, 275 Armor, +17 STR, +7 AGI, +9 STA)	Level 50	N/A	4g 81s 75c
Berserker Bracers (Plate Wrist, 323 Armor, +19 STR, +8 AGI, +11 STA)	Level 60	N/A	7g 96s 47c
Dryad's Wrist Bindings (Cloth Wrist, 31 Armor, +6 STA, +6 INT, +5 SPI, Equip: Increases damage and healing done by magical spells and effects by up to 16)	Level 40	N/A	2g 70s 6c

Exalted

Item	Requirements	Set Name	Cost
Dryad's Wrist Bindings (Cloth Wrist, 37 Armor, +7 STA, +6 INT, +6 SPI, Equip: Increases damage and healing done by magical spells and effects by up to 20)	Level 50	N/A	5g 24s 27c
Dryad's Wrist Bindings (Cloth Wrist, 44 Armor, +8 STA, +8 INT, +7 SPI, Equip: Increases damage and healing done by magical spells and effects by up to 22)	Level 60	N/A	7g 87s 94c
Forest Stalker's Bracers (Leather Wrist, 64 Armor, +8 STR, +14 AGI, +6 STA)	Level 40	N/A	3g 9s 9c
Forest Stalker's Bracers (Leather Wrist, 75 Armor, +9 STR, +17 AGI, +7 STA)	Level 50	N/A	6g 2s 18c
Forest Stalker's Bracers (Leather Wrist, 86 Armor, +11 STR, +19 AGI, +8 STA)	Level 60	N/A	9g 8s 27c
Windtalker's Wristguards (Mail Wrist, 130 Armor, +6 STA, +6 INT, +5 SPI, Equip: +28 Attack Power)	Level 40	N/A	3g 70s 90c
Windtalker's Wristguards (Mail Wrist, 156 Armor, +7 STA, +6 INT, +6 SPI, Equip: +34 Attack Power)	Level 50	N/A	7g 22s 62c
Windtalker's Wristguards (Mail Wrist, 182 Armor, +8 STA, +8 INT, +7 SPI, Equip: +38 Attack Power)	Level 60	N/A	10g 89s 93c
Sentinel's Silk Leggings (Cloth Leggings, 188 Armor, +23 STA, +19 INT, +10 SPI, Equip: Increases damage and healing done by magical spells and effects by up to 28)	Level 60	N/A	15g 36s 73c
Sentinel's Lizardhide Pants (Leather Leggings, 263 Armor, +22 STR, +10 AGI, +22 STA, +22 INT, +9 SPI, Equip: Increases damage and healing done by magical spell and effects by up to 11)	Level 60	N/A	19g 6s 82c
Sentinel's Leather Pants (Leather Leggings, 233 Armor, +28 AGI, +27 STA, Equip: Improves your chance to get a critical strike by 1%)	Level 60	N/A	18g 99s 77c
Sentinel's Chain Leggings (Mail Leggings, 364 Armor, +35 AGI, +15 STA, Equip: Improves you chance to get a critical strike by 1% and improves you chance to hit by 1%)	Levl 60	N/A	21g 79s 86c
Sentinel's Lamellar Legguards (Plate Leggings, 646 Armor, +21 STR, +21 STA, Equip: Improves you chance to get a critical strike by 1% and improves you chance to hit by 1% and increases damage and healing done by magical spells and effects by up to 25)	Level 60	N/A	15g 42s 22c
Sentinel's Plate Legguards (Plate Leggings, 646 Armor, +28 STR, +27 STA, Equip: Improves you chance to get a critical strike by 1%)	Level 60	N/A	14g 53s 24c

WARSONG OUTRIDERS

Friendly

Item	Requirements	Set Name	Cost
Rune of Perfection (Trinket, +4 STA, Equip: Decreases the magical resistances of your spell targets by 10)	Level 20, Classes: Priest, Shaman, Mage, Warlock, Druid	N/A	2g
Rune of Perfection (Trinket, +7 STA, Equip: Decreases the magical resistances of your spell targets by 20)	Level 40, Classes: Priest, Shaman, Mage, Warlock, Druid	N/A	4g
Rune of Duty (Trinket, +4 STA, Equip: Restores 3 health every 5 seconds)	Level 20, Classes: Warrior, Paladin, Hunter, Rogue	N/A	4g
Rune of Duty (Trinket, +7 STA, Equip: Restores 4 health every 5 seconds)	Level 40, Classes: Warrior, Paladin, Hunter, Rogue	N/A	4g
Superior Healing Draught (Use: Restores 560 to 720 health)	Level 35, Usable only in Warsong Gulch	N/A	5s
Superior Mana Draught (Use: Restores 560 to 720 mana)	Level 35, Usable only in Warsong Gulch	N/A	5s
(5)Warsong Gulch Field Ration (Use: Restores 1074 health and 2202 mana over 30 seconds)	Level 25, Must remain seated while eating. Usable only in Warsong Gulch	N/A	10s
(5)Warsong Gulch Iron Ration (Use: Restores 1608 health and 3306 mana over 30 seconds)	Level 35, Must remain seated while eating. Usable only in Warsong Gulch	N/A	15s
(5)Warsong Gulch Enriched Ration (Use: Restores 2148 health and 4410 mana over 30 seconds)	Level 45, Must remain seated while eating. Usable only in Warsong Gulch	N/A	20s
(5)Warsong Gulch Silk Bandage (Use: Heals 640 damage over 8 seconds)	Level 25, First Aid (125), Usable only in Warsong Gulch	N/A	10s
(5)Warsong Gulch Mageweave Bandage (Use: Heals 1104 damage over 8 seconds)	Level 35, First Aid (175), Usable only in Warsong Gulch	N/A	15s
(5)Warsong Gulch Runecloth Bandage (Use: Heals 2000 damage over 8 seconds)	Level 45, First Aid (225), Usable only in Warsong Gulch	N/A	20s

Honored

Item	Requirements	Set Name	Cost
Battle Healer's Cloak (Back, 20 Armor, +4 STA, +2 SPI, Equip: Increases healing done by spells and effects by up to 9)	Level 18	N/A	36s 50c
Battle Healer's Cloak (Back, 25 Armor, +6 STA, +4 SPI, Equip: Increases healing done by spells and effects by up to 13)	Level 28	N/A	1g 7s 72c
Battle Healer's Cloak (Back, 31 Armor, +8 STA, +5 SPI, Equip: Increases healing done by spells and effects by up to 18)	Level 38	N/A	2g 49s 34c

Honored

Item	Requirements	Set Name	Cost
Battle Healer's Cloak (Back, 38 Armor, +9 STA, +6 SPI, Equip: Increases healing done by spells and effects by up to 22)	Level 48	N/A	5g 2s 42c
Battle Healer's Cloak (Back, 45 Armor, +11 STA, +8 SPI, Equip: Increases healing done by spells and effects by up to 26)	Level 58	N/A	7g 69s 43c
Advisor's Ring (Ring, +2 STA, Equip: Increases damage and healing done by magical spells and effects by up to 5, Restores 2 mana per 5 seconds)	Level 18	N/A	2g
Advisor's Ring (Ring, +4 STA, Equip: Increases damage and healing done by magical spells and effects by up to 7, Restores 2 mana per 5 seconds)	Level 28	N/A	2g 75s
Advisor's Ring (Ring, +5 STA, Equip: Increases damage and healing done by magical spells and effects by up to 9, Restores 3 mana per 5 seconds)	Level 38	N/A	4g 50s
Advisor's Ring (Ring, +6 STA, Equip: Increases damage and healing done by magical spells and effects by up to 12, Restores 4 mana per 5 seconds)	Level 48	N/A	6g
Advisor's Ring (Ring, +8 STA, Equip: Increases damage and healing done by magical spells and effects by up to 14, Restores 4 mana per 5 seconds)	Level 58	N/A	6g 75s
Scout's Medallion (Neck, +6 AGI, +2 STA)	Level 18	N/A	2g s
Scout's Medallion (Neck, +8 AGI, +5 STA)	Level 28	N/A	2g 75s
Scout's Medallion (Neck, +11 AGI, +7 STA)	Level 38	N/A	4g 50s
Scout's Medallion (Neck, +12 AGI, +8 STA)	Level 48	N/A	6g
Scout's Medallion (Neck, +15 AGI, +10 STA)	Level 58	N/A	6g 75s
Legionnaire's Band (Ring, +4 STR, +4 AGI, +2 STA)	Level 18	N/A	2g
Legionnaire's Band (Ring, +6 STR, +6 AGI, +4 STA)	Level 28	N/A	2g 75s
Legionnaire's Band (Ring, +18 STR, +8 AGI, +5 STA)	Level 38	N/A	4g 50s
Legionnaire's Band (Ring, +10 STR, +9 AGI, +6 STA)	Level 48	N/A	6g
Legionnaire's Band (Ring, +12 STR, +11 AGI, +8 STA)	Level 58	N/A	6g 75s
Major Healing Draught (Use: Restores 980 to 1260 health)	Level 45, Only usable in Warsong Gulch	N/A	9s
Major Mana Draught (Use: Restores 980 to 1260 mana)	Level 45, Only usable in Warsong Gulch	N/A	9s

Revered

Item	Requirements	Set Name	Cost
Advisor's Gnarled Staff (Staff, 19.7 dps, +8 STA, +4 INT, Equip: Restores 3 mana every 5 seconds)	Level 18	N/A	1g 52s 11c

Revered

Item	Requirements	Set Name	Cost
Advisor's Gnarled Staff (Staff, 27.8 dps, +11 STA, +7 INT, Equip: Restores 4 mana every 5 seconds)	Level 28	N/A	4g 27s 71c
Advisor's Gnarled Staff (Staff, 38.1 dps, +14 STA, +9 INT, Equip: Restores 6 mana every 5 seconds)	Level 38	N/A	9g 93s 73c
Advisor's Gnarled Staff (Staff, 45.9 dps, +18 STA, +11 INT, Equip: Restores 7 mana every 5 seconds)	Level 48	N/A	20g 9s 79c
Advisor's Gnarled Staff (Staff, 54 dps, +21 STA, +13 INT, Equip: Restores 8 mana every 5 seconds)	Level 58	N/A	32g 5s 33c
Outrider's Bow (Bow, 11.7 dps)	Level 18	N/A	91s 26c
Outrider's Bow (Bow, 16.7)	Level 28	N/A	2g 56s 63c
Outrider's Bow (Bow, 22.7 dps, +3 AGI, +6 STA)	Level 38	N/A	5g 96s 24c
Outrider's Bow (Bow, 27.5 dps, +3 AGI, +8 STA)	Level 48	N/A	12g 5s 87c
Outrider's Bow (Bow, 32.3 dps, +4 AGI, +10 STA)	Level 58	N/A	18g 53s 62c
Legionnaire's Sword (One-Hand Sword, 15 dps, +4 STR, +2 STA)	Level 18	N/A	1g 21s 69c
Legionnaire's Sword (One-Hand Sword, 21.3 dps, +7 STR, +3 STA)	Level 28	N/A	3g 42s 17c
Legionnaire's Sword (One-Hand Sword, 29.3 dps, +8 STR, +3 STA)	Level 38	N/A	7g 94s 98c
Legionnaire's Sword (One-Hand Sword, 35.2 dps, +11 STR, +5 STA)	Level 48	N/A	16g 7s 83c
Legionnaire's Sword (One-Hand Sword, 41.5 dps, +13 STR, +5 STA)	Level 58	N/A	24g 71s 50c
Scout's Blade (One-Hand Dagger, 15.3 dps, +4 AGI, +2 STA)	Level 18	N/A	1g 21s 69c
Scout's Blade (One-Hand Dagger, 21.2 dps, +7 AGI, +3 STA)	Level 28	N/A	3g 48s 45c
Scout's Blade (One-Hand Dagger, 29.1 dps, +8 AGI, +3 STA)	Level 38	N/A	8g 67s 91c
Scout's Blade (One-Hand Dagger, 35 dps, +11 AGI, +5 STA)	Level 48	N/A	17g 49s 10c
Scout's Blade (One-Hand Dagger, 41.5 dps, +13 AGI, +5 STA)	Level 58	N/A	25g 26s 44c

Exalted

Item	Requirements	Set Name	Cost
Warsong Battle Tabard	N/A	N/A	4g 50s
Berserker Bracers (Plate Wrist, 229 Armor, +14 STR, +6 AGI, +8 STA)	Level 40	N/A	2g 47s 27c
Berserker Bracers (Plate Wrist, 275 Armor, +17 STR, +7 AGI, +9 STA)	Level 50	N/A	4g 81s 75c
Berserker Bracers (Plate Wrist, 323 Armor, +19 STR, +8 AGI, +11 STA)	Level 60	N/A	7g 96s 47c

Exalted

Item	Requirements	Set Name	Cost
Dryad's Wrist Bindings (Cloth Wrist, 31 Armor, +6 STA, +6 INT, +5 SPI, Equip: Increases damage and healing done by magical spells and effects by up to 16)	Level 40	N/A	2g 70s 6c
Dryad's Wrist Bindings (Cloth Wrist, 37 Armor, +7 STA, +6 INT, +6 SPI, Equip: Increases damage and healing done by magical spells and effects by up to 20)	Level 50	N/A	5g 24s 27c
Dryad's Wrist Bindings (Cloth Wrist, 44 Armor, +8 STA, +8 INT, +7 SPI, Equip: Increases damage and healing done by magical spells and effects by up to 22)	Level 60	N/A	7g 87s 94c
Forest Stalker's Bracers (Leather Wrist, 64 Armor, +8 STR, +14 AGI, +6 STA)	Level 40	N/A	3g 9s 9c
Forest Stalker's Bracers (Leather Wrist, 75 Armor, +9 STR, +17 AGI, +7 STA)	Level 50	N/A	6g 2s 18c
Forest Stalker's Bracers (Leather Wrist, 86 Armor, +11 STR, +19 AGI, +8 STA)	Level 60	N/A	9g 8s 27c
Windtalker's Wristguards (Mail Wrist, 130 Armor, +6 STA, +6 INT, +5 SPI, Equip: +28 Attack Power)	Level 40	N/A	3g 70s 90c
Windtalker's Wristguards (Mail Wrist, 156 Armor, +7 STA, +6 INT, +6 SPI, Equip: +34 Attack Power)	Level 50	N/A	7g 22s 62c
Windtalker's Wristguards (Mail Wrist, 182 Armor, +8 STA, +8 INT, +7 SPI, Equip: +38 Attack Power)	Level 60	N/A	10g 89s 93c
Outrider's Silk Leggings (Cloth Leggings, 188 Armor, +23 STA, +19 INT, +10 SPI, Equip: Increases damage and healing done by magical spells and effects by up to 28)	Level 60	N/A	15g 8s 70c
Outrider's Lizardhide Pants (Leather Leggings, 263 Armor, +22 STR, +10 AGI, +22 STA, +22 INT, +9 SPI, Equip: Increases damage and healing done by magical spell and effects by up to 11)	Level 60	N/A	19g 84s 15c
Outrider's Leather Pants (Leather Leggings, 233 Armor, +28 AGI, +27 STA, Equip: Improves your chance to get a critical strike by 1%)	Level 60	N/A	19g 77s 10c
Outrider's Chain Leggings (Mail Leggings, 364 Armor, +35 AGI, +15 STA, Equip: Improves you chance to get a critical strike by 1% and improves you chance to hit by 1%)	Levl 60	N/A	22g 54s 14c
Outrider's Mail Leggings (Mail Leggings, 364 Armor, +14 STR, +22 STA, +22 INT, Equip: Improves you chance to get a critical strike by 1% and improves you chance to get a critical strike with spells by 1% and restores 6 mana per 5 sec)	Level 60	N/A	22g 79s 28c
Outrider's Plate Legguards (Plate Leggings, 646 Armor, +28 STR, +27 STA, Equip: Improves you chance to get a critical strike by 1% and improves you chance to hit by 1%)	Level 60	N/A	14g 91s 63c

OTHER FACTIONS

ARGENT DAWN

Friendly

Item	Requirements	Set Name	Cost
(5)Enriched Mana Biscuit (Use: Restores 2148 health and 4410 mana over 30 seconds)	Level 45, Must remain seated while eating	N/A	60s

Honored

Item	Requirements	Set Name	Cost
Recipe: Transmute Air to Fire (Use: Teaches you how to transmute Essence of Air into Essence of Fire)	Alchemy (275)	N/A	1g 50s
Plans: Girdle of the Dawn (Plate Waist, 341 Armor, +21 STR, +9 STA)	Blacksmithing (290)	N/A	2g 20s
Pattern: Dawn Treaders (Leather Feet, 114 Armor, +18 STA, Equip: Increases your chance to dodge an attack by 1%)	Leatherworking (290)	N/A	2g 20s
Pattern: Argent Boots (Cloth Feet, 57 Armor, +21 STA, +7 SPI, +4 Shadow Res.)	Tailoring (290)	N/A	2g 20s
Formula: Powerful Anti-Venom (Use: Target is cured of poisons up to level 60)	First Aid (300)	N/A	10g
Formula: Enchant Bracer - mana (Use: Teaches you to permanently enchant a bracer to restore 4 mana every 5 seconds)	Enchanting (290)	N/A	3g

Revered

Item	Requirements	Set Name	Cost
Plans: Gloves of the Dawn (Plate Hands, 417 Armor, +23 STR, +10 STA)	Blacksmithing (300)	N/A	4g
Pattern: Golden Mantle of the Dawn (Leather Shoulder, 134 Armor, +22 STA, Equip: Increases your chance to dodge an attack by 1%)	Leatherworking (300), Dragonscale Leatherworking	N/A	4g
Pattern: Argent Shoulders (Cloth Shoulder, 68 Armor, +23 STA, +8 SPI, +5 Shadow Res.)	Tailoring (300)	N/A	4g
(5)Blessed Sunfruit (Use: Restores 1933 health over 27 seconds. Increases STR by 10 for 10 minutes)	Level 45, Must remain seated while eating	N/A	60s
(5)Blessed Sunfruit Juice (Use: Restores 4410 mana over 30 seconds. Increases your SPI by 10 for 10 minutes)	Level 45, Must remain seated while drinking	N/A	60s
Formula: Enchant Bracer - Healing (Use: Teaches you to permanently enchant a bracer to increase the effects of healing spells by 24)	Enchanting (300)	N/A	6g
Arcane Mantle of the Dawn (Use: Permanently adds 5 arcane resistance to a shoulder slot item)	N/A	N/A	9g
Flame Mantle of the Dawn (Use: Permanently adds 5 fire resistance to a shoulder slot item)	N/A	N/A	9g
Frost Mantle of the Dawn (Use: Permanently adds 5 frost resistance to a shoulder slot item)	N/A	N/A	9g

Revered

Item	Requirements	Set Name	Cost
Nature Mantle of the Dawn (Use: Permanently adds 5 nature resistance to a shoulder slot item)	N/A	N/A	9g
Shadow Mantle of the Dawn (Use: Permanently adds 5 shadow resistance to a shoulder slot item)	N/A	N/A	9g

Exalted

Item	Requirements	Set Name	Cost
Chromatic Mantle of the Dawn (Use: Permanently adds 5 resistance to all magic schools to a shoulder slot item)	N/A	N/A	36g

CENARION CIRCLE

Friendly

Item	Requirements	Set Name	Cost
Pattern: Spitfire Bracers (Mail Wrist, 160 Armor, +9 AGI, +9 INT, Equip: Restores 4 mana every 5 seconds, Increases damage and healing done by magical spells and effects by up to 8)	Leatherworking (300)	N/A	4g
Pattern: Sandstalker Bracers (Mail Wrist, 220 Armor, +7 STA, +15 Nature Res.)	Leatherworking (300)	N/A	4g
Plans: Heavy Obsidian Belt (Plate Waist, 397 Armor, +25 STR, Equip: +5 all resistances)	Blacksmithing (300)	N/A	5g
Plans: Ironvine Belt (Plate Waist, 408 Armor, +12 STA, +15 Nature Res., Equip: Increased Defense +3)	Blacksmithing (300)	N/A	5g
Pattern: Sylvan Shoulders (Cloth Shoulder, 74 Armor, +18 STA, +20 Nature Res., Equip: Increases damage and healing done by magical spells and effects by up to 7)	Tailoring (300)	N/A	5g
Pattern: Cenarion Herb Bag (20 Slot Herb Bag)	Tailoring (300)	N/A	2g
Formula: Enchant Cloak - Greater Fire Resistance (Use: Teaches you how to permanently enchant a cloak to increase Fire Resistance by 15)	Enchanting (300)	N/A	10g

Honored

Item	Requirements	Set Name	Cost
Pattern: Spitfire Gauntlets (Mail Hands, 228 Armor, +12 AGI, +12 INT, Equip: Restores 5 mana every 5 seconds, Increases damage and healing done by magical spells and effects by up to 11)	Leatherworking (300)	N/A	4g
Pattern: Sandstalker Gauntlets (Mail Hands, 308 Armor, +9 STA, +20 Nature Res.)	Leatherworking (300)	N/A	4g
Plans: Light Obsidian Belt (Mail Waist, 224 Armor, Equip: +24 Attack Power, Improves your chance to get a critical strike by 1%, +5 all resistances)	Blacksmithing (300)	N/A	5g

Honored

Item	Requirements	Set Name	Cost
Plans: Ironvine Gloves (Plate Hands, 454 Armor, +10 STA, +20 Nature Res., Equip: Increased Defense +10)	Blacksmithing (300)	N/A	5g
Pattern: Sylvan Crown (Cloth Head, 80 Armor, +10 STA, +30 Nature Res., Equip: Increases damage and healing done by magical spells and effects by up to 18)	Tailoring (300)	N/A	5g
Formula: Enchant Cloak - Greater Fire Resistance (Use: Teaches you how to permanently enchant a cloak to increase Fire Resistance by 15)	Enchanting (300)	N/A	10g

Revered

Item	Requirements	Set Name	Cost
Pattern: Spitfire Breastplate (Mail Chest, 365 Armor, +16 AGI, +16 INT, Equip: Restores 6 mana per 5 seconds, Increases damage and healing done by magical spells and effects by up to 15)	Leatherworking (300)	N/A	4g
Pattern: Sandstalker Breastplate (Mail Chest, 485 Armor, +13 STA, +25 Nature Res.)	Leatherworking (300)	N/A	4g
Plans: Ironvine Breastplate (Plate Chest, 726 Armor, +15 STA, +30 Nature Res., Equip: Increased Defense +7)	Blacksmithing (300)	N/A	5g
Pattern: Sylvan Vest (Cloth Chest, 98 Armor, +15 STA, +30 Nature Res., Equip: Increases damage and healing done by magical spells and effects by up to 12)	Tailoring (300)	N/A	5g
Pattern: Gaea's Embrace (Back, 49 Armor, +6 STA, +20 Nature Res.)	Tailoring (300)	N/A	9g
Pattern: Satchel of Cenarius (24 Slot Herb Bag)	Tailoring (300)	N/A	5g

Exalted

Item	Requirements	Set Name	Cost
Pattern: Dreamscale Breastplate (Mail Chest, 434 Armor, +15 AGI, +15 STA, +14 INT, +30 Nature Resis., Equip: Restores 4 mana per 5 seconds)	Leatherworking (300), Dragonscale Leatherworking	N/A	6g

THORIUM BROTHERHOOD

Friendly

Item	Requirements	Set Name	Cost
Formula: Enchant Weapon - Strength (Use: Teaches you how to permanently enchant a weapon to increase your strength by 15)	Enchanting (290)	N/A	3g
Plans: Dark Iron Bracers (Plate Wrist, 394 Armor, +7 STA, +18 Fire Res.)	Blacksmithing (295), Armorsmith	N/A	7g

Friendly

Item	Requirements	Set Name	Cost
Pattern: Corehound Boots (Leather Feet, 126 Armor, +13 AGI, +10 STA, +24 Fire Res.)	Leatherworking (295), Tribal Leatherworking	N/A	15g
Pattern: Molten Helm (Leather Head, 150 Armor, +16 STA, +29 Fire Res., Equip: Increases your chance to dodge an attack by 1%)	Leatherworking (300), Elemental Leatherworking	N/A	16g
Pattern: Flarecore Gloves (Cloth Hands, 60 Armor, +10 STA, +14 INT, +25 Fire Res.)	Tailoring (300)	N/A	8g
Recipe: Transmute Elemental Fire (Use: Teaches you how to transmute a Heart of Fire into three Elemental Fires)	Alchemy (300)	N/A	12g

Honored

Item	Requirements	Set Name	Cost
Pattern: Flarecore Mantle (Cloth Shoulder, 71 Armor, +9 STA, +10 INT, +10 SPI, +24 Fire Res.)	Tailoring (300)	N/A	18g
Pattern: Flarecore Robe (Cloth Chest, 102 Armor, +35 STA, +15 Fire Res., Equip: Increases damage and healing done by magical spells and effects by up to 23)	Tailoring (300)	N/A	6g
Pattern: Black Dragonscale Boots (Mail Feet, 270 Armor, +10 STA, +24 Fire Resl, Equip: +24 Attack Power)	Leatherworking (300), Dragonscale Leatherworking	Black DragonMail	16g
Pattern: Lava Belt (Leather Waist, 223 Armor, +15 STA, +26 Fire Res.)	Leatherworking (300)	N/A	6g
Plans: Fiery Chain Girdle (Mail Waist, 214 Armor, +10 STA, +9 INT, +8 SPI, +24 Fire Res.)	Blacksmithing (295), Armorsmith	N/A	9g
Plans: Dark Iron Helm (Plate Head, 758 Armor, +20 STA, + 35 Fire Res.)	Blacksmithing (300), Armorsmith	N/A	6g
Plans: Dark Iron Reaver (Main-Hand Sword, 42.7 dps, +10 STA, +6 Fire Res.)	Blacksmithing (300), Master Swordsmith	N/A	21g
Plans: Dark Iron Destroyer (Main-Hand Axe, 42.7 dps, +10 STR, +6 Fire Res.)	Blacksmithing (300), Master Axesmith	N/A	21g
Formula: Enchant Weapon - Mighty Spirit (Use: Teaches you how to permanently enchant a weapon to increase your spirit by 20)	Enchanting (300)	N/A	8g

Revered

Item	Requirements	Set Name	Cost
Pattern: Flarecore Leggings (Cloth Legs, 94 Armor, +21 STA, +16 Fire Res., Equip: Increases damage and healing done by magical spells and effects by up to 43)	Tailoring (300)	N/A	9g
Pattern: Molten Belt (Leather Waist, 118 Armor, +28 AGI, +16 STA, +12 Fire Res.)	Leatherworking (300), Elemental Leatherworking	N/A	9g

Revered

Item	Requirements	Set Name	Cost
Pattern: Corehound Belt (Leather Waist, 118 Armor, +16 INT, +12 Fire Res., Equip: Increases healing done by spells and effects by up to 62)	Leatherworking (300), Tribal Leatherworking	N/A	9g
Pattern: Chromatic Gauntlets (Mail Hands, 279 Armor, +5 Fire, Nature, Frost, Shadow Res., Equip: +44 Attack Power, Improves your chance to get a critical strike by 1%, Improves your chance to get a critical strike with spells by 1%)	Leatherworking (300), Dragonscale Leatherworking	N/A	9g
Plans: Fiery Chain Shoulders (Mail Shoulder, 299 Armor, +10 STA, +14 INT, +25 Fire Res.)	Blacksmithing (300), Armorsmith	N/A	20g
Plans: Dark Iron Leggings (Plate Legs, 778 Armor, +14 STA, +30 Fire Res.)	Blacksmithing (300), Armorsmith	N/A	18g
Plans: Dark Iron Gauntlets (Plate Hands, 495 Armor, +12 AGI, +16 STA, +28 Fire Res.)	Blacksmithing (300), Armorsmith	N/A	8g
Plans: Amnesty (One-Hand Dagger, 47.8 dps, Chance on Hit: Reduce your threat to the current target making them less likely to attack you)	Blacksmithing (300), Master Weaponsmith	N/A	7g
Plans: Blackfury (Polearm, 62.6 dps, +35 STR, +15 STA, +10 Fire Res., Equip: Improves your chance to get a critical strike by 1%)	Blacksmithing (300), Weaponsmith	N/A	7g
Formula: Enchant Weapon - Mighty Intellect (Use: Teaches you how to permanently enchant a weapon to increase your intellect by 22)	Enchanting (300)	N/A	10g

Exalted

Item	Requirements	Set Name	Cost
Plans: Blackguard (One-Hand Sword, 51.7 dps, +9 STA, Equip: Increases your chance to parry an attack by 1%)	Blacksmithing (300), Master Swordsmith	N/A	12g
Plans: Nightfall (Two-Hand Axe, 67.0 dps, Chance of Hit: Reduces enemy's spell resistances by 60 for 5 seconds)	Blacksmithing (300), Master Axesmith	N/A	12g
Plans: Ebon Hand (One-Hand Mace, 51.5 dps, +9 STA, +7 Fire Res., Chance on Hit: Sends a shadowy bolt at the enemy causing 125 to 275 Shadow damage)	Blacksmithing (300), Master Hammersmith	N/A	12g
Plans: Dark Iron Boots (Plate Feet, 664 Armor, +28 Fire Res.)	Blacksmithing (300), Armorsmith	N/A	8g

TIMBERMAW HOLD

Friendly

Item	Requirements	Set Name	Cost
Pattern: Warbear Harness (Leather Chest, 158 Armor, +11 STR, +27 STA)	Leatherworking (275), Tribal Leatherworking	N/A	1g 44s
Pattern: Warbear Woolies (Leather Legs, 142 Armor, +28 STR, +12 STA)	Leatherworking (285), Tribal Leatherworking	N/A	1g 98s
Recipe: Transmute Earth to Water (Use: Teaches you how to transmute Essence of Earth into Essence of Water)	Alchemy (275)	N/A	1g 35s

Honored

Item	Requirements	Set Name	Cost
Furbolg Medicine Pouch (Off-Hand, +10 STA, Use: Restores 100 health every 1 second for 10 seconds, 20 minute cooldown)	N/A	N/A	13g 50s
Furbolg Medicine Totem (Main-Hand Mace, 31 dps, +6 STA, +6 SPI)	N/A	N/A	11g 98s
Plans: Heavy Timbermaw Belt (Mail Waist, 193 Armor, +9 STA, Equip: +42 Attack Power)	Blacksmithing (290)	N/A	1g 80s
Plans: Might of the Timbermaw (Leather Waist, 93 Armor, +21 STR, +9 STA)	Leatherworking (290)	N/A	1g 98s
Pattern: Wisdom of the Timbermaw (Cloth Waist, 46 Armor, +21 INT, Equip: Restores 4 mana every 5 seconds)	Tailoring (290)	N/A	1g 98s
Formula: Enchant Weapon - Agility (Use: Teaches you how to permanently enchant a weapon to increase your agility by 15)	Enchanting (290)	N/A	2g 70s

Revered

Item	Requirements	Set Name	Cost
Plans: Heavy Timbermaw Boots (Mail Feet, +23 STA, Equip: +20 Attack Power)	Blacksmithing (300)	N/A	3g 60s
Pattern: Timbermaw Brawlers (Leather Hands, 112 Armor, +23 STR, +10 STA)	Leatherworking (300)	N/A	3g 60s
Pattern: Mantle of the Timbermaw (Cloth Shoulder, 68 Armor, +21 INT, Equip: Restores 6 mana every 5 seconds)	Tailoring (300)	N/A	3g 60s

Exalted

Item	Requirements	Set Name	Cost
Defender of the Timbermaw (Use: Call forth a Timbermaw Ancestor to fight at your side and heal you, 10 minute cooldown)	Quest	N/A	

ZANDALAR TRIBE

Friendly

Item	Requirements	Set Name	Cost
Pattern: Bloodvine Boots (Cloth Feet, 63 Armor, +16 INT, Equip: Improves your chance to hit with spells by 1%, Increases damage and healing done by magical spells and effects by up to 19)	Tailoring (300)	Bloodvine Garb	5g
Pattern: Primal Batskin Bracers (Leather Wrist, 79 Armor, +14 AGI, +7 STA, Equip: Improves your chance to hit by 1%)	Leatherworking (300)	Primal Batskin	5g
Plans: Bloodsoul Gauntlets (Mail Hands, 238 Armor, +10 AGI, +17 STA, Equip: Improves your chance to get a critical strike by 1%)	Blacksmithing (300)	Bloodsoul Embrace	5g

Friendly

Item	Requirements	Set Name	Cost
Plans: Darksoul Shoulders (Plate Shoulders, 507 Armor, +24 STA, Equip: Improves your chance to hit by 1%)	Blacksmithing (300)	The Darksoul	5g
Schematic: Bloodvine Lens (Leather Head, 147 Armor, +12 STA, Equip: Improves your chance to get a critical strike by 2%, Slightly increases your stealth detection)	Engineering (300)	N/A	5g
Recipe: Greater Dreamless Sleep (Use: Puts the imbiber in a dreamless sleep for 12 seconds. During that time the imbiber heals 2100 health and 2100 mana)	Alchemy (275)	N/A	5g
Formula: Brilliant mana Oil (Use:While applied to a target weapon, it restores 12 mana to the caster every 5 seconds and increases the effect of healing spells by up to 25. Lasts 30 minutes)	Enchanting (300)	N/A	4g

Honored

Item	Requirements	Set Name	Cost
Pattern: Bloodvine Leggings (Cloth Legs, 80 Armor, +6 INT, Equip: Improves your chance to hit with spells by 1%, Increases damage and healing done by magical spells and effects by up to 37)	Tailoring (300)	Bloodvine Garb	5g
Pattern: Primal Batskin Gloves (Leather Hands, 113 Armor, +10 AGI, +9 STA, Equip: Improves your chance to hit by 2%)	Leatherworking (300)	Primal Batskin	5g
Pattern: Blood Tiger Shoulders (Leather Shoulders, 136 Armor, +13 STR, +13 STA, +12 INT, +10 SPI)	Leatherworking (300)	Blood Tiger Harness	5g
Plans: Bloodsoul Shoulders (Mail Shoulders, 286 Armor, +24 AGI, +10 STA)	Blacksmithing (300)	Bloodsoul Embrace	5g
Plans: Darksoul Leggings (Plate Legs, 722 Armor, +22 STA, Equip: Improves your chance to hit by 2%)	Blacksmithing (300)	The Darksoul	5g
Schematic: Bloodvine Goggles (Cloth Head, 75 Armor, Equip: Improves your chance to hit with spells by 2%, Improves your chance to get a critical strike with spells by 1%, Restores 9 mana every 5 seconds)	Engineering (300)	N/A	5g
Recipe: Major Troll's Blood Potion (Use: Regenerate 20 health every 5 seconds for 1 hour)	Alchemy (290)	N/A	5g
Formula: Brilliant Wizard Oil (Use: While applied to target weapon, it increases spell damage by up to 36 and increases Spell Critical chance by 1%. Lasts 30 minutes)	Enchanting (300)	N/A	4g
(10)Essence Mango (Use: Restores 2550 health and 4410 mana over 30 seconds)	1 Zandalar Honor Token, Must remain seated while eating	N/A	

Revered

Item	Requirements	Set Name	Cost
Pattern: Bloodvine Vest (Cloth Chest, 92 Armor, +13 INT, Equip: Improves your chance to hit with spells by 2%)	Tailoring (300)	Bloodvine Garb	5g
Pattern: Primal Batskin Jerkin (Leather Chest, 181 Armor, +32 AGI, +6 STA, Equip: Improves your chance to hit by 1%)	Leatherworking (300)	Primal Batskin	5g
Plans: Bloodsoul Breastplate (Mail Chest, 381 Armor, +9 AGI, +13 STA, Equip: Improves your chance to get a critical strike by 2%)	Blacksmithing (300)	Bloodsoul Embrace	5g
Plans: Darksoul Breastplate (Plate Chest, 736 Armor, +32 STA, Equip: Improves your chance to hit by 1%)	Blacksmithing (300)	The Darksoul	5g
Pattern: Blood Tiger Breastplate (Leather Chest, 181 Armor, +17 STR, +17 STA, +16 INT, +13 SPI)	Leatherworking (300)	Blood Tiger Harness	5g
Recipe: Mageblood Potion (Use: Regenerate 12 mana every 5 seconds for 1 hour)	Alchemy (275)	N/A	5g
Sheen of Zanza (Use: Increases the chance that the player will reflect hostile spells cast on them by 3% and grants a 100% chance to reflect the first spell cast on the user)	1 Zandalar Honor Tokens. Lasts 2 hours. Only one type of Zanza potion may be active at any given time.	N/A	
Spirit of Zanza (Use: Increases the players SPI by 50 and STA by 50)	3 Zandalar Honor Tokens. Lasts 2 hours. Only one type of Zanza potion may be active at any given time.	N/A	
Swiftness of Zanza (Use: Increases the player's run speed by 20%)	3 Zandalar Honor Tokens. Lasts 2 hours. Only one type of Zanza potion may be active at any given time.	N/A	

Exalted

Item	Requirements	Set Name	Cost
Recipe: Living Action Potion (Use: Makes you immune to stun and movement impairing effects for the next 5 seconds. Also removes existing stun and movement impairing effects)	Alchemy (285)	N/A	5g
Zandalar Signet of Might (Use: Permanently adds 30 attack power to a shoulder slot item)	15 Zandalar Honor Tokens	N/A	
Zandalar Signet of Mojo (Use: Permanently adds to a shoulder slot item increased damage and healing done by magical spells and effects by up to 18)	15 Zandalar Honor Tokens	N/A	
Zandalar Signet of Serenity (Use: Permanently adds to a shoulder slot item increases healing done by spells and effects up to 33)	15 Zandalar Honor Tokens	N/A	

The Races of Azeroth

World of Warcraft is a world built on war and conflict. The races of Azeroth have found themselves choosing sides and allying in order to stay safe from their many enemies and the creatures that roam it. Two factions have come of this; the Horde and the Alliance. Choosing a faction means choosing a side in a war, so consider carefully.

Alliance

| Dwarf | Gnome | Human | Night Elf |

Horde

| Orc | Tauren | Troll | Forsaken |

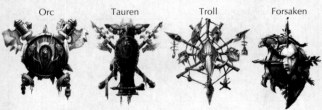

Dwarves

Starting Statistics

Class	Strength	Agility	Stamina	Intellect	Spirit
Warrior	25	16	25	19	19
Paladin	24	16	25	19	20
Hunter	22	19	24	19	20
Rogue	23	19	24	19	19
Priest	22	16	23	21	22

Much like the stone and metal the dwarves shape so adeptly, the dwarves themselves are sturdy and durable. This gives them more physical staying power than some of the other races. While neither stupid nor clumsy, the dwarves are often the last to leave a battlefield.

Racial Traits

STONEFORM

Dwarves can gain certain aspects of stone for short periods of time. Activating Stoneform gives you immunity to poisons, disease, and bleed effects as well as increasing your Armor by 10% for 8 seconds. This ability has a 3 minute cooldown.

This is most useful when under heavy attack. The ability to purge existing poison, disease, and bleed effects can keep your health from dropping as quickly. Combined with the added Armor and you're more likely to survive long enough to finish the enemy or get healing.

TREASURE FINDING

The dwarves have been searching for treasures hidden in the very rock for longer than anyone can remember. It hasn't been until recently that the dwarves realized that concentrating allows them to find treasures above the ground as well. Activating this ability shows treasure chests on the mini map as yellow dots. This ability lasts until cancelled.

Using Treasure Finding can help you decide whether to venture down a side passage in a tunnel or check up a set of stairs. As a number of useful items are contained in chests, this has both survival and monetary uses. As only one type of tracking can be active at a time, characters with other tracking skills (Hunters, Herbalists, Miners) will get used to which tracking to have on at a given time.

FROST RESISTANCE

Life on the wintry peaks of Dun Morogh has left the dwarves resistance to icy wind. All dwarves have +10 to Cold Resistance. This is a passive ability and does not need to be activated in any way.

The upside of increased Cold Resistance, aside from lower heating bills, is lower damage from Cold-based attacks. As resistance increases both your chance to resist part of an attack's damage and your chance to fully resist the damage, Frost Resistance is quite useful. A full resist also keeps you from being affected by Cold-based Root and Snare effects.

GUN SPECIALIZATION

Friendly shooting competitions are commonplace at many dwarven holidays. As such, dwarves are more proficient with firearms and receive +5 to their maximum Gun Skill. As a passive trait Gun Specialization need not be activated.

The increased maximum Gun Skill offers several advantages if you're willing to put in the training time. As your Gun skill will be higher than normal for your level, you'll have a higher chance to hit your target and a higher chance for a critical strike when using your gun. Take the time to train your Gun skill to maximum.

LANGUAGES

While Dwarvish is still taught to all dwarven children, it isn't used as often as Common. Common is the native tongue of the humans and because they were many of the first tradesman to make connections outside their own race, Common became the tongue of tradesman. As people visited more of the foreign markets, Common spread more until it became the universal language that all Alliance races can speak. This has made a number of cooperative projects, both military and civilian, easier.

BRIEF HISTORY

The stoic dwarves of Ironforge spent countless generations mining treasures from deep within the earth. There, the dwarves unearthed a series of ruins that held secrets to their ancient heritage. Driven to discover the truth about his people's fabled origins, the great King Magni Bronzebeard ordered that the dwarves shift their industry from mining to archaeology. As part of the Grand Alliance, the stalwart dwarven armies have been called away to battle the merciless Horde in far away lands. In these perilous times, the defense of the mountain kingdom falls to brave dwarves like you. The spirits of the ancient kings watch over you and the very mountains are your strength. The future of your people is in your hands.

Some speculate that the dwarves are descended from the mysterious race known as the "Earthen". As the children of the Titans, they were to shape and guard the earth from deep within. With the implosion of the Well of Eternity, the Earthen sealed themselves away until some unknown event mysteriously woke them from their slumber. In time, they made their way to the surface and found homes within the mountains, founding their home of Ironforge.

Three clans rose among them, and they lived in relative peace among one another until High King Anvilmar passed away, leaving no heir. War broke out among the three factions until Madoran Bronzebeard at last managed to gain leverage and cast out the other clans. The Bronzebeards rule the Ironforge dwarves to this day.

ROLEPLAYING TIPS

Playing a dwarf can be quite enjoyable. They are a very passionate people. They work hard and they play hard. Dwarves will rarely stop before a task is complete. Whether this be to take an enemy keep, fully excavate a set of ruins, forge a unique sword, or relax after a day of work, dwarves give their full attention to whatever they are doing at the time. Each task has its own time and you should concentrate on the task at hand.

FORSAKEN

STARTING STATISTICS

Class	Strength	Agility	Stamina	Intellect	Spirit
Warrior	22	18	23	18	25
Rogue	20	21	22	18	25
Priest	19	18	21	20	28
Mage	19	18	21	21	27
Warlock	19	18	22	20	27

The Forsaken have been freed from the chains of mortal bodies.
They only continue to exist because of their dominant Spirit. While
a higher Spirit benefits all classes with increased health and mana
regeneration, the mystic classes make more use of it

RACIAL TRAITS

WILL OF THE FORSAKEN

The Forsaken have not been defeated by either death or the Lich King.
When activated, the Will of the Forsaken makes them immune to Fear,
Sleep, and Charm effects for five seconds. This can also be used to break
free from already existing Fear, Sleep, and Charm effects and has a two
minute cooldown.

With the most common forms of combat control being Fear, Sleep, and
Charm, the benefit of being able to break these without outside assistance
is amazing. In both PvP and PvE, you will be much more difficult to
nullify quickly. All classes benefit from this trait.

CANNIBALIZE

Transcending death has given the Forsaken more than
just the ability to move around as rotting flesh. They
can repair their rotting flesh by consuming the flesh
of the recently deceased. When activated, Cannibalize
restores 7% of your total health every two seconds for a maximum of ten
seconds. Only humanoid or undead corpses near the Forsaken can be used
and any movement or damage taken will interrupt Cannibalize. It has a
two minute cooldown.

While useful to all classes, this is most useful to melee classes as they have
only their health to restore after combat. This can be used in both PvE and
PvP to regenerate health quickly between battles.

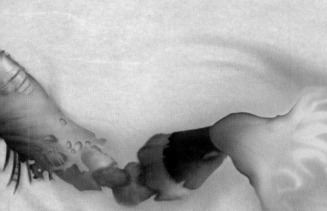

LANGUAGES

The Forsaken are allied with the orcs but only use orcish when communicating with the other races of the Horde. They intentionally use Gutterspeak when conversing with each other as only Forsaken are taught it. The Forsaken have decided to keep their language from the other races so they can converse and plan without being overheard.

BRIEF HISTORY

Bound to the iron will of the tyrant Lich King, the vast Undead armies of the Scourge seek to eradicate all life on Azeroth. However, a group of renegades, led by the Banshee Sylvanus Windrunner, has broken away from the Scourge and freed themselves of the Lich King's domination. Known as the Forsaken, this group fights a constant battle not only to retain its freedom from the Scourge but also to slaughter those who would hunt them as monsters.

With Sylvanus as their Banshee Queen, the Forsaken have built a dark stronghold beneath the ruins of Lordaeron's former capital. This hidden Undercity forms a sprawling labyrinth that sprawls beneath the haunted woods of Tirisfal Glades. Though the very land is cursed, the Scarlet Crusade still cling to their scattered holdings and obsess with the destruction of all undead. Convinced that the primitive races of the Horde can help them achieve victory over their enemies, the Forsaken have entered into an alliance of convience. Harboring no true loyalty for their new allies, they go to any lengths to ensure their dark plans come to fruition. As one of the Forsaken, you must massacre any who pose a threat to the new order; human, Undead, or otherwise.

With Undeath comes new capabilities and immunities no other race is afforded. Just as the Forsaken do not need to draw breath, they have no mortal desires apart from survival. They are free to devote themselves to an unlife of working for their own revenge and power. Their dark lands are plagued by the remnants of the Scourge and the vile Scarlet Crusade, but they remain vigilant in their pursuit to rid themselves of both menaces and establish themselves as a dominant force on Azeroth.

UNDERWATER BREATHING

While the Forsaken have no need for breathing, extended time underwater causes their body to deteriorate and fall apart. This is not pleasant to see or experience. All Forsaken have a passive ability to remain underwater 300% more than living races.

While this trait doesn't seem like much at first, it's very useful to explorers and those who think out of the box. While others fear fighting or searching beneath the water, you can do so with little worry. In PvP, running into the water will force your enemy to engage you on your terms or allow you to escape.

SHADOW RESISTANCE

Undeath holds very few secrets for the Forsaken. Possibly powered by Shadow magic itself, they gain +10 to their Shadow Resistance. This trait is passive and does not need to be activated.

The upside of increased Shadow resistance is lower damage from Shadow-based attacks. Shadow resistance increases your chance to resist partial damage from a Shadow attack or effect as well as your chance to fully resist the effects. These effects include combat control abilities. Higher resistances are always useful.

ROLEPLAYING TIPS

The Forsaken are as varied as the humans they once were. Most died in very horrible and painful ways and feel nothing but hatred and the need for revenge. There are others who are able to see further and make much more long reaching plans…such as to kill all living things.

GNOMES

STARTING STATISTICS

Class	Strength	Agility	Stamina	Intellect	Spirit
Warrior	18	23	21	24	20
Rogue	16	26	20	24	20
Mage	15	23	19	27	22
Warlock	15	23	20	26	22

At first look, gnomes appear much like children. Don't underestimate them, though. Those large eyes staring serenely at you hide a very active and articulate mind. They also keep your attention from the gnome's hands as he ties your bootlaces together.

RACIAL TRAITS

ESCAPE ARTIST

Very few races are as small as gnomes and most nets weren't made for them. Activating Escape Artist breaks all existing root and snare effects on you. It requires one and a half seconds to cast and one minute to cool down.

If a gnome puts their mind and fingers to it, nothing can hold them for long. Enemies that root or snare you to provide themselves with an escape route or to stop your escape are in for a rude surprise. The casting time can be slowed by taking damage, but the ability to escape some of the more common types of combat control is wonderful.

EXPANSIVE MIND

While very small, gnomes have curiosity and imagination that surpasses most people twice their height. All gnomes gain a 5% increase in their Intellect beyond other races. This is a passive trait and is always active.

The increased Intellect does a number of things. Higher Intellect makes weapon training faster as well as giving you more Mana to cast spells with. It also affects your chance to get a critical strike with spells. While faster weapon training helps the more physical classes in a modest way, the bonuses for casters are immense.

ARCANE RESISTANCE

The curiosity of gnomes knows no bounds. They have dabbled with so many things, both arcane and mundane, and had them blow up in their face, that they've become slightly resistant. +10 Arcane Resistance is a passive trait and does not need to be activated.

The upside of increased Arcane Resistance is lower damage from Arcane-based attacks. Arcane Resistance increases your chance to resist partial damage from an Arcane attack as well as your chance to fully resist the effects. These effects include combat control abilities. Higher resistances are always useful.

TECHNOLOGIST

Not everything gnomes do explodes. Many of their inventions work quite well, and they have pushed Engineering past the barriers of all other races except for the Goblins. All gnomes have +15 to their maximum Engineering Skill.

This allows them to learn more for each level of crafting. While a slim lead, it gives them the ability to understand certain schematics that Engineers of the same level would be unable to comprehend.

LANGUAGES

Listening to an excited gnome talk in your own language can sometimes be trying. Hearing them talk in their native gnomish will help you realize why no one takes the time to learn it aside from gnomes. As such, gnomes now teach Common to their children to make communication with other races more productive.

BRIEF HISTORY

The eccentric, often-brilliant gnomes are held as one of the most peculiar races of the world. With their obsession for developing radical new technologies and constructing marvels of mind-bending engineering, it's a wonder that any gnomes have survived to proliferate. Over the years, gnomes have contributed ingenious weapons to aid the Grand Alliance in its fierce battles against the Horde. Thriving within the wondrous city of Gnomeregan, the gnomes shared the resources of the forest of Dun Morogh peaks with their dwarven cousins. Yet recently, a barbaric menace rose up from the bowels of the earth and invaded Gnomeregan. The gnomes fought a valiant battle to save their beloved city. Nevertheless, Gnomeregan was irrevocably lost. The surviving gnomes fled to the safety of the dwarven stronghold of Ironforge. There they remain, devising strategies to retake their city.

As a gnome of proud standing, it falls to you to answer the challenge and lead your curious people to a brighter future.

The gnomes work hard to this day within the well fortified halls of Ironforge to create bigger and better inventions. No problem is safe from gnomes. They will prevail and answers to every problem will be found.

It is their passion, and it can be seen in their choice of environs when visiting their small section of the city. With the energy they exhibit and their affinity for inventions, you begin to wonder if you should see a wind-up key in their backs.

ROLEPLAYING TIPS

Gnomes are insatiably curious and active. Very little slows them down and they are seldom idle for long. For this reason, few gnomes are curious about mundane things for terribly long. Most of them spend their days, and nights, trying to understand the two most powerful forces in the world: technology and magic.

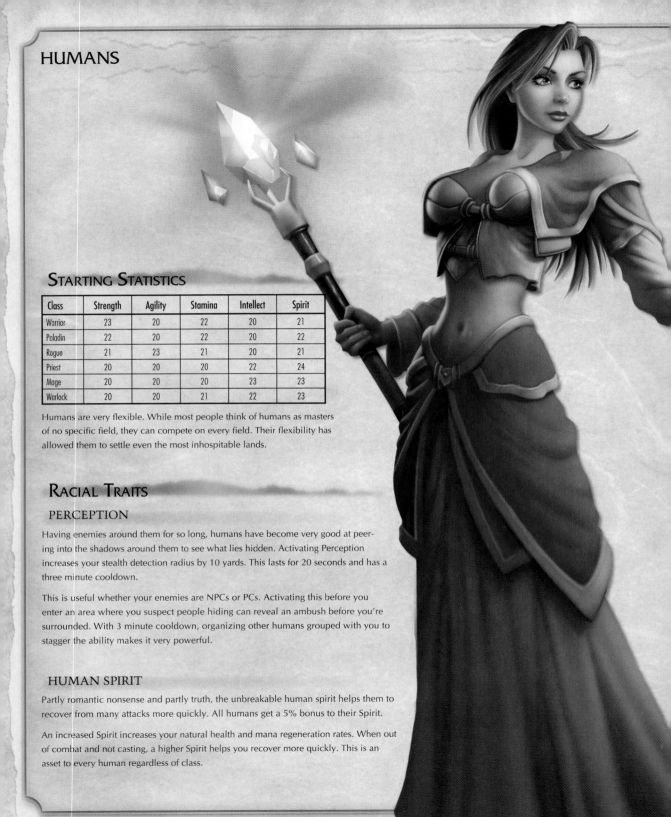

HUMANS

STARTING STATISTICS

Class	Strength	Agility	Stamina	Intellect	Spirit
Warrior	23	20	22	20	21
Paladin	22	20	22	20	22
Rogue	21	23	21	20	21
Priest	20	20	20	22	24
Mage	20	20	20	23	23
Warlock	20	20	21	22	23

Humans are very flexible. While most people think of humans as masters of no specific field, they can compete on every field. Their flexibility has allowed them to settle even the most inhospitable lands.

RACIAL TRAITS

PERCEPTION

Having enemies around them for so long, humans have become very good at peering into the shadows around them to see what lies hidden. Activating Perception increases your stealth detection radius by 10 yards. This lasts for 20 seconds and has a three minute cooldown.

This is useful whether your enemies are NPCs or PCs. Activating this before you enter an area where you suspect people hiding can reveal an ambush before you're surrounded. With 3 minute cooldown, organizing other humans grouped with you to stagger the ability makes it very powerful.

HUMAN SPIRIT

Partly romantic nonsense and partly truth, the unbreakable human spirit helps them to recover from many attacks more quickly. All humans get a 5% bonus to their Spirit.

An increased Spirit increases your natural health and mana regeneration rates. When out of combat and not casting, a higher Spirit helps you recover more quickly. This is an asset to every human regardless of class.

DIPLOMACY

While not the first race to interact with others, humans have a gift for establishing long friendships and trade agreements. Faction reputation gain is increased by 10% for humans.

This ability is extremely powerful for those that make use of it. A faster reputation gain enables you to attain reputation levels much more quickly and access crafting recipes and items with less work than people from other races. Crafters will find this ability immensely useful as will characters who participate in PvP (many PvP rewards are based on reputation).

SWORD AND MACE SPECIALIZATION

With so many devoted to martial pursuits, humans hold many competitions where combatants can test their skill without risking their life. The result is that all humans gain +5 to their maximum skill for Swords, Two-Handed Swords, Maces, and Two-Handed Maces.

The increased maximum for combat skills offers several advantages if you're willing to put in the training time. As your melee skill will be higher than standardly appropriate for your level, you'll have a higher chance to hit your target and a higher chance for a critical strike when using your sword or mace. Keep your combat skills at their maximum to take full advantage of this.

LANGUAGES

Humans have touched so many others they have created a legacy of cooperation and communication for the coming generations to enjoy. As one of the first races to work toward bring other races together in harmony, the native language of humans, Common, has been adopted as a global language for communication between races. While children of other races spend the time to master a second language, human children spend time learning about gnomish engineering, dwarven crafting, and night elf magic.

BRIEF HISTORY

The noble humans of Stormwind are a proud, tenacious race. Though the recent invasion of the Undead Scourge and demonic Burning Legion decimated their sister kingdom of Lordaeron, the defenders of Stormwind have stood vigilant against any who would threaten the sanctity of their lands. Nestled in the foothills of Elwynn Forest, Stormwind city is one of the last bastions of human power in the world. Ruled by the child-king Anduin Wrynn, the people of Stormwind remain steadfast in their commitment to the Grand Alliance. Backed by their stalwart allies, the armies of Stormwind have been called away to fight the savage Horde on distant battlefields. With the armies gone, the defense of Stormwind now falls to its proud citizens. You must defend the kingdom against the foul mongrels that encroach upon it and hunt down the subversive traitors who seek to destroy it from within. Now is the time for heroes; now Humanity's greatest chapter can be written.

Humans once lived a nomadic life in tribes wandering from place to place as the seasons changed or the hunting became lean. It wasn't until the rise of the Arathi that they began to form within one nation. They founded the fortified city of Strom and, as they grew, so did they gain the attention of the High Elves who, like them, were suffering brutal attacks from the Trolls. As allies, they beat back the Trolls, and the High Elves began to teach their newfound friends the ways of magic. With time, the humans also came into contact with the dwarves, and, while the dwarves were initially unsure of these strange new people, they developed a strong bond of friendship.

Over the years, the region of Lordaeron grew so large that it fractured into smaller kingdoms, each with its own beliefs, government, and lifestyle. The humans began to outstrip their teachers in the use of magic, which alarmed their High elf friends. The same corruption that had filled the world before was becoming evident. To combat this problem, the Council of Silvermoon joined with the Magocrat Lords of Arathor in a pact. They formed a secret order called the Guardians of Tirisfal. The Guardians sought to protect the world from the onslaught of the demons of the Burning Legion should they return. This legacy came to its end when the Guardian made a terrible misjudgement in her power and slew an avatar of the Demon Lord Sargeras a bit too easily. She then took his body and secreted it away where none could find it. However, Sargeras was too clever and instead hid his spirit inside her, later implanting his essence into her unborn child who would one day be the inheritor of her powers.

ROLEPLAYING TIPS

Partly because of their ability to live anywhere, humans are as varied as the world itself. While many are loyal citizens and defenders of Stormwind, there are those who care only for themselves. If there is one thing that links humans together, it would be their goal to be something better.

NIGHT ELVES

STARTING STATISTICS

Class	Strength	Agility	Stamina	Intellect	Spirit
Warrior	20	25	21	20	20
Hunter	17	28	20	20	21
Rogue	18	28	20	20	20
Priest	17	25	19	22	23
Druid	18	25	19	22	22

Night elves are as agile as they are long lived. While casters find the extra chance to dodge appealing, melee classes love the added chance for a critical strike provided by the increased Agility.

RACIAL TRAITS

SHADOWMELD

Spending much of their time beneath the canopy of the forest, night elves have become adept at vanishing into the shadows. When out of combat and immobile, night elves can enter stealth mode by activating Shadowmeld. It lasts until canceled and has a ten second cooldown. Any action taken is considered movement and will cancel Shadowmeld.

The ability to hide from your enemies is of tremendous power. Hiding from NPCs can give you the time you need to recover from the last fight while hiding from other players also guarantees you get to start the fight on your terms.

QUICKNESS

Night elves are beyond agile. They move with the grace of a reed in the wind…always moving. Night elves gain a passive bonus of 1% to dodge.

Any time you are the focus of a melee attack, this trait might save you. For either casters trying to survive long enough for friends to come to their aid or melee attackers trying to survive long enough to kill their enemy, the added dodge can come in handy several times in every fight.

WISP SPIRIT

While most people must travel the world as ghosts after their death, the strong attunement to the world allows night elves to travel as wisps. This gives a 50% speed bonus, whereas others gain only a 25% speed bonus as ghosts.

In group settings this ability isn't as powerful unless your entire party is comprised of night elves. As a solo hero, this allows you to return to your body faster and thus continue your fight against evil more quickly.

NATURE RESISTANCE

You don't tend every beast of the woods without becoming more resistant to their poisons and fangs. Thus, night elves have a passive +10 Nature Resistance.

The upside of increased Nature Resistance is lower damage from Nature-based attacks. Nature Resistance increases your chance to resist partial damage from a Nature attack or effect as well as your chance to fully resist the effects. These effects include combat control abilities. Higher resistances are always useful.

LANGUAGES

Early in the friendship between the night elves and humans, it became apparent that much of the human population had neither the time nor patience to learn full Darnassian.

As communication is a cornerstone of friendship, the night elves decided to teach their population Common in addition to their own language. After several years every night elf was trained and can now communicate effortlessly in Common.

BRIEF HISTORY

For 10,000 years, the immortal night elves cultivated a druidic society within the shadowed recesses of Ashenvale forest. Yet recently, the catastrophic invasion of the Burning Legion shattered the tranquility of their ancient civilization. Led by the Arch Druid Malfurion Stormrage and the High Priestess Tyrande Whisperwind, the mightly night elves rose to challenge the demonic onslaught. Though victorious, the night elves were forced to sacrifice their cherished immortality and watch their beloved forests burn. Seeking to regain their immortality, a number of wayward Druids conspired to plant a special tree that would link their spirits to the eternal world. Despite Malfurion's warnings that nature would never bless such a selfish act, the Druids planted the great tree Teldrassil off the stormy coasts of northern Kalimdor. Within the twilight boughs of the colossal tree, the wondrous city of Darnassus took root. However, the great tree was not consecrated with nature's blessing and soon fell prey to the corruption of the Burning Legion. Now the wildlife and even the limbs of the great tree itself are tainted by a growing darkness. As one of the few night elves left in the world, it is your sworn duty to defend Darnassus and the wild children of nature against the Legion's encroaching corruption.

Night elves were once known as the Kaldorei and have lived on Kalimdor for thousands upon thousands of years. It was their delving into the magic of the Well of Eternity that caught the attention of Sargeras and the Burning Legion, and it was because of the night elves' misuse and addiction to magical power that caused the Great Maelstrom and creation of the evil Naga. Even Malfurion Stormrage's own brother Illidan played a major role in the destruction that followed. And yet, night elves have also brought beauty and triumphs to the world. Without their aid and sacrifices, the other races would have certainly been doomed. Their devotion to nature and healing the land is also well known. Even the betrayer Illidan contributed through the creation of the Moonwells. Thus many of the major events that have shaped Azeroth, both positively and negatively, can be traced back to the night elves. Perhaps it is a sense of responsibility that drives the night elves to this day to continue their vigil to safeguard and restore the natural world to what it once was.

ROLEPLAYING TIPS

As one of the longest living races in Azeroth, night elves tend to be slow to change. Slow to anger and slow to cool off, the night elves experience emotions as deeply, or perhaps more so, then the younger races. While generally slow to respond emotionally, their minds have seen much and tend to have a honed wit and sense of humor.

ORCS

STARTING STATISTICS

Class	Strength	Agility	Stamina	Intellect	Spirit
Warrior	26	17	24	17	23
Hunter	23	20	23	17	24
Rogue	24	20	23	17	23
Shaman	24	17	23	18	25
Warlock	23	17	23	19	25

Centuries of demonic influence and war have honed orcs to be strong and lasting. With higher Strength and Stamina, orcs are adept at melee combat and a high Spirit gives them an edge as casters.

RACIAL TRAITS

BLOOD FURY

Screaming through the veins of orcs runs a fury that is monstrous when called upon and dangerous to be on the wrong side of. Activating Blood Fury increases your base melee Attack Power by 25% while decreasing all healing spells and effects on you by 50%. This state lasts for 15 seconds and has a two minute cooldown.

When the battle is desperate and your healer is out of mana, Blood Fury can pull you to victory. The primary downside to Blood Fury is the reduced effect of healing. If you are alone or your healer is out of mana, this isn't an issue since you won't be getting healing anyway. This ability is far better for melee classes as an increase to melee Attack Power doesn't really do anything if you're a caster staying at range.

HARDINESS

Surviving the wars against the human kingdoms and the land of Durotar have left the orcs more resistant to certain attacks. Thus orcs have a passive 25% chance to resist stun effects.

There are no downsides to having a resistance to stun effects. Melee classes are able to keep moving and attacking, and, while casters will have their casting delayed by the attacks, they won't be interrupted by the stun. This ability is equally useful in PvP and PvE.

COMMAND

Having been at the command of others before, orcs have firsthand knowledge of what works and what doesn't. Pets of orc Warlocks and Hunters deal 5% more damage. This ability is passive and does not need to be activated.

While this ability doesn't do much for Warriors, Rogues, or Shamans, it's a blessing to Warlocks and Hunters. Having a pet that deals more damage without having to pay for the increase means faster kills and better aggro management.

AXE SPECIALIZATION

The tree cutting hasn't been for naught. Orcs have become very adept in the use of axes and gain +5 to their maximum skill with both Axes and Two-Hand Axes. As a passive trait, Axe Specialization has no activation or cooldown.

The increased maximum for combat skills offers several advantages if you're willing to put in the training time. As your melee skill will be higher than standardly appropriate for your level, you'll have a higher chance to hit your target and a higher chance for a critical strike when using your axe. Keep your combat skills at their maximum to take full advantage of this.

LANGUAGES

From a young age, orcs are trained to keep themselves and those they care about safe. Many learn to walk the same time they hold their first weapon. With such a martial upbringing and so little time between wars, orcs have had little time to learn any languages beyond their own. It is fortunate that the rest of the Horde are so accommodating that orcish has become the common language between the races of the Horde.

Brief History

Long ago, the orcish Horde was corrupted by the Burning Legion and lured to the world of Azeroth. For 10 years, the orcs made war upon the human kingdoms of Stormwind and Lordaeron. Though the Horde was ultimately defeated and subjugated by the humans, a visionary young war chief named Thrall rose to lead his people in their darkest hour. Under Thrall's rule, the orcs freed themselves from the chains of demonic corruption and embrace their Shamanistic heritage. After breaking free of the human slave camps and wandering for years, the orcs have finally founded their own kingdom in the harsh wastelands of Durotar. Based in the warrior city of Orgrimmar, they stand ready to destroy all who would challenge their supremacy. As a proud defender of Durotar, it is your duty to crush your enemies both seen and unseen, for the nefarious agents of the Burning Legion still wander the land.

It was Sargeras' second-in-command, Kil'jaeden, who discovered Draenor and the races that lived there. Finding the orcs to be a race worth molding into a driving force of bloodlust, he began to corrupt them, turning them from their Shamanistic ways toward the powers of the Warlocks. The powerful Shaman Ner'zhul was seduced by the power of Kil'jaeden and all the demon offered, and it was not long before he led his people against the peaceful Draenei destroying many of them.

Despite the power Kil'jaeden had over Ner'zhul, he couldn't quite convince him to give the orcs completely over to the power of the Burning Legion. He instead recruited a new, more corruptible, young orc named Gul'dan. Gul'dan became an avid student and a powerful Warlock among his people.

In time, Gul'dan, under the manipulation of Kil'jaeden, maneuvered all of the orc clans into partaking in a ritual that would make them indebted slaves to the Burning Legion and give them a blood lust they could not quench. He then opened a portal into Azeroth, where the will of the Burning Legion was once more loosed upon the denizens of the land.

Roleplaying Tips

The orcs of Durotar have been through quite a lot. They have been corrupted by demons and forced into war after war.

Now free, orcs are quick to join in combat since that is what they know best. Some are loyal followers of Thrall and his ideals and wish to see their people free from the taint of the Burning Legion. There are others who still feel the fire burning inside of them and follow their Warchief Thrall into glorious battles.

TAUREN

STARTING STATISTICS

Class	Strength	Agility	Stamina	Intellect	Spirit
Warrior	28	15	24	15	22
Hunter	25	18	23	15	23
Druid	26	15	22	17	24
Shaman	26	15	23	16	24

The Tauren are massive. Their Strength surpasses even that of the orcs and dwarves. Combine this with their high Stamina and Spirit, and the Tauren are practically made to fit melee classes; in fact, the more Intellectual caster classes aren't even available to them.

RACIAL TRAITS

WAR STOMP

No one can argue with a Tauren for long. When he or she puts her hoof down, everyone knows. War Stomp stuns up to five opponents within eight yards for two seconds when activated. It has a two minute cooldown and a one second casting time.

The ability to stop an enemy in their tracks is tremendous. Using War Stomp can stop a caster from finishing his spell, slow the escape of an enemy, or give you the moment you need to escape. While War Stomp won't win fights for you, its many uses and short cooldown ensure that it will be useful whenever you need it.

ENDURANCE

Tauren have been hunters and gatherers for generations. Whether in times of war or times of peace, they are constantly pushing and testing themselves. This never-ending training affords them a 5% increase in maximum health.

You can't go wrong with more hit points. While the classes that tend to be in the face of the enemy, such as Warriors benefit the most from this, the additional health can keep the softer classes alive long enough to finish the fight or for the Warrior to pull the enemies back. In a PvP setting, where longevity is never a guarantee, the addition health will help you contribute longer.

CULTIVATION

Understanding the delicate balance between the land and the Tauren has let them live more effectively with nature. They have learned how to gather in such a way as to avoid unnecessary damage to the plant and encourage its regrowth. All Tauren gain a passive +15 to their maximum Herbalism.

With an increase in your maximum Herbalism, you are able to harvest plants normally beyond your level. Keep this skill trained to maximum and the bonus will also reduce your failure rate.

NATURE RESISTANCE

You don't tend every beast of the woods without becoming more resistant to their poisons and fangs. Thus Tauren have a passive +10 Nature Resistance.

The upside of increased Nature Resistance is lower damage from Nature-based attacks. Nature Resistance increases your chance to resist partial damage from a Nature attack or effect as well as your chance to fully resist the effects. These effects include combat control abilities. Higher resistances are always useful.

LANGUAGES

The Tauren have adopted orcish as a trade language. While keeping their language, customs, and beliefs intact, the Tauren have found the value of conversing with the other races.

BRIEF HISTORY

Once a nomadic people, the Tauren roamed the endless plains of the Barrens hunting the mighty Kodo. Scattered across the land, the wandering tribes were only united by their common hatred for the marauding Centaur. Seeking aid against the Centaur, the chieftain Cairne Bloodhoof befriended the orcs, who had recently journeyed to Kalimdor. With the orcs' assistance, Cairne and his tribe were able to drive back the Centaur and claim the grasslands of Mulgore for their own. Upon the windswept mesa of Thunder Bluff, Bloodhoof built a refuge for his people. Over time, the scattered tribes united under a single banner. Though the noble Tauren are peaceful in nature, the rights of the great hunt are venerated as the heart of their spiritual culture. As a tribesman of Mulgore, you must test your skills in the wild and prove yourself in the great hunt.

The Tauren found mutual benefits in befriending the orcs and Trolls. While the orcs and Trolls helped the Tauren to drive back the Centaur and keep their lands safe, the Tauren have aided (and continue to aid) them on the spiritual path as a Shamanistic society.

ROLEPLAYING TIPS

While some view the Tauren as nothing more than brutes and hunters, they are much more. They have found a way to live with the land rather than off it. Though their size is immense, the Tauren are a patient and peaceful people on the whole.

TROLLS

STARTING STATISTICS

Class	Strength	Agility	Stamina	Intellect	Spirit
Warrior	24	22	23	16	21
Hunter	21	25	22	16	22
Rogue	22	25	22	16	21
Priest	21	22	21	18	24
Shaman	22	22	22	17	23
Mage	21	22	21	19	23

Only one thing is similar among all Trolls. They are very adaptable to their profession. Trolls of any class can compete with those of other races. While their lower Intellect can be seen as a weakness, it isn't a great one and negligible at later levels.

RACIAL TRAITS

BERSERKING

Their adaptability manifests itself most when a Troll is backed into a corner. They can increase their body's functions to such a level that they enter a Berserk state. When activated, Berserking increases casting and attack speed by a base of 10%, increasing as the Troll's health lowers, and a maximum of 30%. The effects only last 10 seconds with a 3 minute cooldown.

The ability to increase your casting and attack speed, and thus your damage output, as you become weaker is incredible. Its cooldown is short enough that unless you are reckless, it will always be there when you need it.

REGENERATION

Everyone knows the stories of Trolls regrowing limbs in minutes. While these are exaggerations, Trolls have a 10% increased heath regeneration rate. Even more potent is that 10% of their total health regeneration remains active during combat. This is a passive ability and is always active.

While the increased health regeneration is great for recovering between battles, the real gem is the health regeneration during combat. Other races may have more hit points than you, but you recover yours during combat without the use of spells or potions. This can be of great value to any class.

BEAST SLAYING

When it comes to killing, the Trolls have been doing it for a long time. They've studied killing long enough that they receive a 5% damage bonus when attacking Beasts. This affects all Beasts, and only Beasts, and does not need to be activated.

This trait is valuable for any class as the target determines the bonus. Quests and dungeons with Beasts in them will be faster for you than other races as you can kill them more quickly. Choosing your targets with this in mind will help you take full advantage of this trait.

BOW AND THROWING WEAPON SPECIALIZATION

The Trolls are not strangers to ranged combat. They have been honing their skills for long enough to give them a +5 to their maximum Bow Skill and Throwing Weapon Skill. This is always active and has no cooldown.

The increased maximum skill offers several advantages if you're willing to put in the training time. As your Bow or Throwing Weapon skill will be higher than standardly appropriate for your level, you'll have a higher chance to hit your target and a higher chance for a critical strike when using these weapons. Take the time to train your Bow or Throwing Weapon skill to maximum.

LANGUAGES

The Darkspear tribe has allied itself closely with the orcs of Durotar, but they have not forgotten their own ways. Troll is still taught to the young, with orcish being taught in addition. Few dare to learn Troll as the Darkspear tribe tend to be very aggressive when asked about it.

BRIEF HISTORY

The vicious Trolls that populate the numerous jungle islands of the South Seas are renowned for the cruelty and dark mysticism. Barbarous and superstitious, they carry a seething hatred for all other races. Long since exiled from its ancestral homeland in Stranglethorn Vale, the Darkspear Tribe was nearly destroyed by rampaging Murlocs. Rescued by the young Warchief Thrall and his orcish warriors, the Darkspear tribe swore allegiance to the Horde. Led by the cunning Shadow Hunter, Vol'jin, the Darkspears now make their home in Durotar along with their orcish allies. As one of the only surviving Darkspears, it falls to you to regain the glory of your tribe.

The Trolls have a long history of war with the humans. Even before the Burning Legion came into the land, they had waged war against the humans and Elves with hit-and-run raiding parties. They hate the humans above all other races. After nearly being completely wiped from the face of Azeroth, however, they now relish in protecting their new home in Durotar and look for any reason to convince the remaining Horde of the complete treachery of humans. It was Grand Admiral Proudmoore's attack on the Horde that enraged them even more, and now the fires of hate burn even hotter within the breasts of the Trolls. For now, they cooperate with the remaining members of the Horde to maintain their homes and retain the alliances that let their people continue to rebuild.

ROLEPLAYING TIPS

The Trolls have learned to harness the power of hate. After using it for generations, they have become adept at its cultivation. Their hatred for the humans is well known, and few Trolls are without the burning need for spilt human blood.

Classes of Azeroth

This section offers a glimpse of the role that each class plays in Azeroth. All of the classes have played a part in the history of the world, and this shapes how they are viewed today. Choosing a class is an opportunity to immerse yourself in the past events and make a place for yourself in the future of the land.

Druid

The keepers of nature, the Druids care for the natural world, its creatures, and the balance of existence. Many of them have watched over the world through the Emerald Dream, and ethereal realm that exists separate from Azeroth but intimately interwoven with it. This spirit world allows the regulation of the ebb and flow of nature and the evolutionary path of the world itself. It is the realm of one of the great Dragon Aspects; Ysera the Dreamer.

To help guide the course of the natural world, the Druids entered into the Emerald Dream, agreeing to exist apart from their friends and loved ones in an extended state of hibernation. However, because of the threat posed by Archimonde and the Burning Legion, the Druids awoke and used their power to fight to protect the world. Currently, some of the Druids have reentered the Emerald Dream, while others have stayed in Azeroth, working to repair the great damage that has been done to the natural order.

The Druids exist apart from the political boundaries empires and clans. What does it matter if one is Horde or Alliance in the great expanse of nature? The night elves and Tauren, united in their love of the land, have set aside their differences to work together, safeguarding Azeroth and helping to mend areas contaminated by pain and war. Therefore, the Druids offer hope of what all Azeroth could accomplish if all the races worked for the betterment of the world together.

Hunter

The lands of Azeroth are home to a great many beasts, everything from wolves and cats to bears and large birds, to name but a few. These species care nothing for the war between Horde and Alliance; their lives are filled with their own struggle to find food and live from day to day. By the same token, there have always been those individuals who exist outside the boundaries of civilized society. These free spirits have found a connection to nature and a way of living with it. These wilderness people have taken the chance to explore the various lands of Azeroth and formed bonds linking themselves with the beasts of the world.

A Hunter is never without their weapon and their partner, the beast that they have formed a relationship with. The two of the work together and learn from each other. This allows the Hunter to embrace the natural world and their pets to be free from some of the more pressing aspects of their existence, such as finding prey and having a safe place to rest.

Some of the races have taken easily to this way of life. The Tauren and night elves have a great respect for nature as a whole, and working as partners with it is an extension of that. The Trolls, as well, have never moved far away from the rhythms of the natural world. For these people, becoming a Hunter allows them the chance to bond with nature and the beasts within it.

For others, it appeals to their independent spirit. The dwarves and orcs are strong individuals, and some of them have grown tired of the political bickering of the cities and accepted the wilderness as their homes. These are Hunters who seek to find their own ways in the world.

Mage

The call of magic is a powerful one. Some have decided to dedicate their lives to it, studying it, practicing it, and spreading it throughout the world. In the history of Azeroth, no other kingdom fully embraced the force of magic as strongly as that of Dalaran, where the entire culture was guided by mages. As a political

entity, Dalaran was a source of great knowledge not jaded by certain moral concerns, seeking only to understand the nature of magical power.

The kingdom of Dalaran is being rebuilt. Destroyed by the Burning Legion, its remnants have fled throughout the lands of Azeroth, and the practitioners of magic have taken new apprentices and students. This has led to knowledge of magic being spread throughout all of Azeroth.

In the Alliance lands, it is the humans and gnomes who look into the mystery of magic. The Trolls of Durotar have always been accused, rightly so, for dark mysticism while many of the Forsaken are from Dalaran itself and continue the pursuit of power.

PALADIN

The Paladins are the champions of Light and the defenders of the Alliance. Dedicated fighters, Paladins safeguard the populace and act as a symbol all can look up to. These men and women uphold honor and bravery, protect the people, honor the will of the nation, and bring light against the darkness.

Lordaeron was once the center for Paladins, a bright shining city that was a bastion of civilization. The defending Paladins were a great force of order and respect for their nation. However, there were dark forces at work, and a great sickness took hold of the land, spreading the curse of the undead throughout the country. Lordaeron was destroyed and some of its Paladins fell to corruption leaving the rest of the knightly order to fight against the undead and their former comrades.

The loyalty and brotherhood of the dwarves and humans make up the ranks of Paladins. These people are stout defenders and work within the boundaries of their political organizations. Beyond all else though, the Paladins are dedicated to ideals of honor and bravery. Light guides them.

The pursuit of Holy magic is the love of life and healing, replenishing and protecting the caster and those for whom they care. Shadow is the opposite, a force of raw destructive power that damages the target and wounds the spirit. Both forces are powerful and require skill to use.

Those dedicated to healing of the mind and soul often become Priests, because of the appeal of Holy magic to salve the wounded. However, because of the strength that Shadow promises, darker individuals move to the profession as well. Of the races on Azeroth only humans, dwarves, night elves, Forsaken, and Trolls have all the pieces of the puzzle to unlock its teachings.

ROGUE

There have always been, and always will be, Rogues. These individuals use stealth and cunning to accomplish what a broadsword and shield can't. While the darker folk following this path are dangerous assassins, thieves, and brigands, there are those who train for the betterment of their own people. Spies put themselves at great risk and are perhaps the greatest rogues as they hide in front of an enemy instead of behind.

As times grew more dangerous, Rogues have learned to defend themselves. They have learned fighting styles that allow someone with the thinnest armor and two small blades to stand up to someone in chain wielding a hammer and shield. With the prominence of magic-wielders on battlefields and their ability to destroy standard troops, Rogues have been given an important duty. They must safeguard their friends by eliminating the enemy casters first.

PRIEST

Holy and Shadow are forces, separate from those of the world itself. There are those individuals that seek to use them within the world, dedicating themselves to these unseen forces. For these people, the use of these powers, requiring great study and great reverence.

Of all the races of Azeroth, only one will not accept training as a Rogue. The Tauren are not suited for the concept either physically or mentally. They believe the deception dishonorable. The ends justify the means for the other races.

SHAMAN

The Shaman are the spiritual leaders of their clans and tribes, guiding the peoples of the Horde to their destinies. Gifted with great insight, the Shaman seek to provide the best lives for their people within Azeroth. This common structure has formed a network among several disparate races.

The races of the Horde have always had strong beliefs and a willingness to defend them. In addition, most have a clan or tribal political structure with loyalty to their tribe being strongly valued. The Shaman help to meld these tribal forces together, so that all the various tribes and peoples can accomplish a unified goal that benefits all of them.

It was the Shaman of the orcs that lead them into Kalimdor and the Shaman of the Tauren and Trolls who helped them relearn their Shamanistic heritage. Of the Horde, only the

Forsaken are without Shaman. This is a source of disquiet among the races as the Tauren, orcs, and Trolls have a common set of goals and the Forsaken may not share these.

WARLOCK

For some mages, the lure of dark power and knowledge proved too great for mere study. They found a new wellspring of chaotic magic, allowing them to reach into the strength of the demons. Gifted with the ability to manipulate these demonic forces, the Warlocks are powerful sorcerers, and the pacts that they form with demons are a sight of their devotion to the dark arts.

Demons are never far from a Warlock's call and the Warlock is a master at controlling them. These sinister creatures follow the Warlock's orders, attacking enemies and protecting their master. A Warlock's servant fights for them, and often the Warlock thinks nothing of sacrificing their demonic pet if the situation calls for it; a new summoning spell is all that it takes to drag the demon back to the world of Azeroth.

Because of their devotion to dark arts, Warlocks are feared and distrusted by most of the races. Within the lands of the Alliance, Warlocks are shunned and their places of teaching are outside major cities. Only humans and gnomes are curious enough to dabble with these forces. The orcs also have a great deal of suspicion toward Warlocks; most want nothing to do with demons every again, and orc history is replete with pain and anguish caused by demonic involvement. Only the Forsaken fully accept Warlocks as part of their civilization, giving them freedom and respect. However, despite the mistrust engendered by these practices, there will always be people who pursue dark and powerful knowledge.

WARRIOR

There have always been the Warriors who both defend their families and attack their enemies. While some spend their time training in hallowed halls to become powerful mystics, not everyone has that chance. The people living out on the frontier, away from large cities and the training there, have nothing to defend themselves with but a sword. They spend their days becoming stronger and faster. More than just their lives depend on their abilities…their family and friends live or die on their abilities.

Not everyone takes up arms to help others. There will always be those who are excited by the adrenaline rush of heated combat or simply enjoy watching life drain from an opponent's eyes. Whatever their reason for fighting, these men and women are the undisputed masters of melee combat. They train day and night mastering several stances of combat to be able to defeat any opponent that stands in front of them.

Any race that can forge weapons can train Warriors. humans, night elves, dwarves, and gnomes train Warriors and pit them against the mightiest of foes. Of the Horde, Tauren, Trolls, orcs, and Forsaken sharpen their blades and prepare for the coming war.

BEYOND THE BASICS

Before getting involved with specific class abilities, data tables, templates, and so forth, it's important to evaluate play strategies that are used by all characters in World of Warcraft. This chapter explains various methods to improve your ability to gather money, rise in level, move around Azeroth, engage in combat, and find special areas.

COMMON TACTICS

It takes considerable time to teach someone about World of Warcraft. This game has enough complexity to keep players on their tops for many days, even while learning the basics. This section is organized as well as possible to give you the tips and ideas to cut down on lost opportunities during that learning phase. There is always money and experience to be made, and there is no harm in starting from the beginning!

GAINING EXPERIENCE

Experience points get you closer to your next level. Characters progress from Levels 1 to 60 in WoW (and beyond toward level 70 later in 2006 when the expansion comes), and each advancement brings better attributes, higher health/mana, and the potential for greater deeds. Whether you focus on pulling in experience is one thing, but everyone gains levels if they enjoy the game and keep heading out into the wild.

WHAT MAKES AN EQUIVALENT MOB

Monsters are worth experience if they are close to your character's level. There is allowed to be a 20% difference in levels between your character and the monster OR a difference of five levels (whichever is greater will be used).

Anything beneath this threshold gives zero experience when slain because the challenge is so trivial. However, such creatures still drop treasure.

Quick Equivalence Chart	
Character Level	**Allowed Levels of Difference**
Until Level 25	5
30	6
40	8
50	10
60	12

SOLOING MONSTERS

The most basic way to gain experience is to walk into an area with monsters and start fighting them. Every victory against a monster of equivalent level gets you experience. These points add up nicely if you try to kill monsters as quickly as possible. Trying to gain levels solely through monster killing is called "grinding" by many players. Some people find this method dull because it offers less variety of action compared to questing, going exploring, and so forth. Others feel relaxed by bringing down a stable flow of money, experience, and nasty monsters. There is nothing wrong with this method either way if it's what you like.

Grinding itself can be a very fast method for leveling. Or, it can be slower than other available techniques; this entirely depends on the current level of your character, you equipment, local quest options, and more subtle aspects of play. Indeed, some grinders are able to gain levels with impressive speed by choosing a class build that is keen for soloing and finding areas where tandem fighting (going after one mob, then another right afterward, then another, etc.) is easy to do.

- Many Monsters Available
- Enough Space Between Monsters That They Can be Fought Individually
- Creatures in Area Lack Powerful Special Abilities that Harm Your Class/Race (If you can't cure poison or disease, these are brutal on soloers, as are curses and many other debuffs)
- Monster Levels are Just Low Enough to Keep the Kills Fast and Downtime Short (a couple levels under your character for characters with modest gear, or monsters of equal level for those with better equipment)
- Few Players Compete for Kills in the Area
- A Vendor is Somewhat Accessible (for making repairs and dropping off loot items)
- Enemies Drop Cloth (if you bandage frequently)
- Preferably, a Graveyard is Close Enough to Shorten Downtime if an Accident Happens; This Isn't as Important as the Other Factors

INSTANCE GRINDING

Instance grinding is very different from grinding on monsters out in the field. Getting into a group of four or five characters and repeatedly taking on instances near your level is a wonderful way to get your character into better gear. It is not, however, a fast way to gain levels. Looking at pure experience per hour, instances are only better for the absolute worst grinding characters (e.g. people who specialize only on surviving, healing, and other non-damaging abilities).

This does not mean that you lose out in the long run by leveling in this way. Slow leveling often has a few perks. The longer you take at each level, the more money your character has throughout the game and the more your gear stays up-to-date.

QUESTING FOR EXPERIENCE

During the lower levels (certainly through Levels 1 to 40), characters gain quite a bit of experience through questing. It isn't hard to gather multiple quests from towns in this period, and completing several at a time is both easy and exciting. The awards for turning in these quests catapult characters through their levels. And, when played correctly, the best elements of grinding and questing can be combined once players understand the locations they are visiting.

First off, it's useful to grind while approaching quest sites and while leaving them! If you have a quest in the northwest of The Barrens, asking you to kill Harpies, it is helpful to kill Centaur, Raptors, and other enemies on the way. Walking to the edge of a zone may take five or six minutes (more in a number of cases). That time is somewhat wasted if you simply travel because your characters are full on health and mana. Use those resources to blow through enemies quickly; be inefficient with mana, if you have it, because you are going to regenerate it as you go anyway.

Blast through the odd target here and there and you will find that experience gained per hour improves by a fair margin. This also makes traveling a lot more fun!

PICK AND CHOOSE

A subset of questing is to avoid getting all quests in a region while doing only those that fit your character's needs. This becomes quite common at the later levels, when people prefer to fight in certain regions, and dungeons.

To pick and choose with quests means to look through all available choices and decide which ones have rewards that you need OR which ones have targets that you want to kill anyway. This is a solid, mercenary approach. If your character likes to grind against Trolls in the Hinterlands, there is no reason on Azeroth not to help the local Dwarves (who have a few problems with said Trolls). Grinding is all well and good, but dropping off a quest each time you head back to sell loot nets practically free experience when you play in this manner.

Even at the lower levels, you may want to skip delivery quests or anything that you know takes a long time without keeping you hip-deep in slaughter. If experience is your goal, collecting ground spawns in areas without many enemies is a bad thing.

UNDERSTANDING ATTRIBUTES

At the most basic level of play, higher attributes equal a better character. However, you are often forced to decide which attributes are the most important to your style of play. This means that it's crucial to understand what the attributes do, how they affects your class, and which systems can be influenced by your choices.

Attributes and What They Do

Attribute	Purpose
Strength	Improve Melee Damage (DPS), Raise Amount of Damage Absorbed by Shield Blocks
Agility	Higher % Chance to Dodge, Higher Critical Rate, Increases Damage for Some Characters (e.g. Hunters, Rogues)
Spirit	Improves Rate of Health/Mana Regeneration While Out of Combat
Stamina	Raises Health (One Points of Stamina Adds Ten Points of Health)
Intellect	Raises Mana (One Point of Intellect Adds Fifteen Points of Mana); Also Raises Critical Rates for Spellcasters

Strength improves your character's DPS and helps to block more damage from incoming attacks. Warriors always need a fair bit of strength, but all melee characters are interested in getting more when they can. Rogues need more Agility, but Strength isn't bad for them at all, and Hunters who do a bit more melee work (especially some Survival Hunters) take some Strength as well.

Agility affects Dodge and Critical percentages for all characters. This makes Agility a secondary damage attribute for tanks (Warriors, Paladins, etc.) and a primary damage attribute for Rogues and Hunters. The reason for this is that ranged damage is influenced by Agility. Also, Rogues receive half of their melee damage bonuses from Strength and half from Agility!

Spirit determines how much health/mana you regain with each tick of the game's clock. Health does not regenerate during normal combat, without items or abilities to grant such restoration. Mana regeneration, however, is only interrupted by casting spells (whether in battle or not). Your character's class makes a huge difference in what is regenerated. Warriors and Rogues, for instance, have no mana; their Spirit is used only for health regeneration. Hybrid classes (Druids, Hunters, Paladins, Shaman) are split between a moderate gain of health by their Spirit and a fair increase in mana as well. Then the heavier casters (Priests, Mages, and Warlocks) gain very little health from their Spirit but receive potentially large chunks of mana each tick.

Spirit is one of the more complex attributes because it's either worthless, if you fight creatures out in the field or go against easier instances, or very important, if you are a caster taking on late-game raid monsters.

Stamina gives characters ten points of health for every point of Stamina they gain. This is a flat sum. Stamina can easily account for half (or more) of your character's health, even before the later stages of the game. Though having more health does nothing to increase a character's combat output, Stamina is still crucial. Classes that hold aggro to protect a group **need** to have high health. This gives healers a great deal more leeway in saving lives! Even hybrid classes and full casters need health though, especially if tougher dungeons are being run, if you solo, or if you plan to hit the Battlegrounds. In World of Warcraft, everyone gets beaten on, and even glass cannons want to survive a few hits before going down.

Intellect is similar to Stamina, though it gives mana to characters instead of health. Intellect also increases casters' rate for Critical spell effects; that is something that both healers and damage dealers are interested in getting. For non-casters, Intellect is almost a worthless Attribute. Rogues and Warriors are able to master Defense and Weapon Skills faster if they have a high Intellect, but this difference is not worth the loss of Stamina, Agility, etc. Also, getting an Arcane Intellect buff from Mages is more than enough to boost melee characters while learning new weaponry.

STAYING ON PAR

For each level of your character, there is a hidden par value for your attributes. This value is meant to reflect the improvements that are available to your character during advancement. If you stay at par, your percentages won't change in a major way; Critical rates, Dodging, and such are meant to be fluid yet stay within certain bounds.

If your character falls below par by having low-level equipment, not spending Talent points, or otherwise focusing on different elements, your percentage chance to achieve various effects may drop! Look at your character now and compare the numbers for Criticals and Dodge to what you had five levels ago; there is no guarantee of improvement in these things. You MUST increase your Agility to stay on par with melee/ranged Criticals and Dodge. You need to keep raising Intellect to maintain frequent spell Criticals.

By the same token, getting +20 to Stamina in your teen levels doesn't sound bad at all. A couple hundred more points of health. Great! But at level 58, you want to have at least a couple thousand more health for tanking enemies or PvPing.

To see your chance to Dodge and Critical opponents, open your Abilities Menu ("P" Key) and highlight these given aspects. They should be listed on the first page.

For even more interesting data, remove various pieces of equipment and notice the immediate and profound changes to said percentages. Equipment choices DO matter!

But How Do I Raise Attributes?

So if leveling raises your attributes and the par for said attributes, how do you actually keep up or even pull ahead with your true performance?

The key is to find equipment that focuses on the stats you need. As long as your character pushes to find Rare/Blue gear, starting around level 20, you can stay well ahead of par. Even if you stick to Uncommon/Green gear, you can stay close to or above par for your character.

Don't just take every weapon upgrade with higher DPS and every armor piece that raises your Damage Mitigation. This is **not** wise for the long run. Instead, look at the attributes given by each equipment piece you find. Choose two or three attributes that you are looking for, and make sure to get the most points possible for those.

First, avoid equipment pieces that only give one attribute bonus unless the piece is extremely good. You receive more total attribute points by choosing pieces with two or three attributes. When these are the two or three attributes you want already, this makes everything work out wonderfully.

Also, look for a consistent Enchanter in your guild or circle of friends. Have them help you increase your attributes. At all levels, Enchanters are able to add a fair number of points to your equipment pieces. Though pricey, this is a superb way to stay ahead of men and beasts that are competing against you.

Example: Warriors should avoid equipment that gives bonuses to Intellect and possibly Spirit as well, unless you greatly need the extra armor or your old equipment isn't giving you what you want either. Instead, search for appropriate Mail (or later Plate) that has Strength, Stamina, and Agility. If you tank a great deal, lean on Strength and Stamina. If you are more of a DPS Warrior, take all three and try to balance your needs.

SPECIALIZING A CHARACTER

Nobody in WoW is meant to be exactly the same. There are many ways to configure your character for different forms of combat, and this goes well beyond a person's class. Use of Talents, style, equipment, and professions all make a difference in the end result.

The big question for each player is what do I want to accomplish in battle. Are you a healer, a damage dealer, or a support character? Do you want to be good for short bursts or for sustained effort? Is disruption of enemy forces more important to you than getting kills and glory?

Before jumping into the "how" end of things, we'll investigate the question of "why?"

Perks of Character Specialization

Customizing your character is an enjoyable experience because you are making an avatar into your own reflection of a class. You are leaving the simple distinction of Warrior/Rogue/Mage, etc. behind; what appears in its place is your representation of that class. Making a name for yourself, exploring new ideas and style choices, and seeking new modes of victory are all waiting down this path. The rewards are considerable.

If you stay along a general line, your character ends up with few weaknesses (only those given by your race/class). However, you are rarely able to play to your strengths unless you develop them. Specializing your character makes it much easier to win in battles where you are able to use your advantages.

Does this mean that you lose more often when you cannot play to your strengths if you heavily customize? Yes, it does. In a well-balanced game, there have to be penalties to your choices as well as perks, and WoW makes great efforts to balance your options.

The reason this isn't as much of a problem as it sounds is that a skilled player can often play to their strengths. Against many mobs and even some players, the ability to drive forward with your best abilities precludes the dangers of your weaknesses. That is why playing to your strengths and customizing is useful, doable, and a great deal of fun.

Using Your Talent Points

- Talents are gained from levels 10-60 (for 51 total Talent points)
- It is often powerful to specialize in two Talent trees, taking one until the mid 40s, then switching to a secondary Talent tree
- You can Respec Talents at your character's trainer for a scaling fee (this fee increases from one Gold, to five, and then to ten and beyond for additional Respecs)
- Talents greatly define what style of your class you wish to play

General Ability Tradeoffs		
Ability Type	Powerful For	Weakest In
Burst Damage/Healing	PvP	Group Settings
Efficient Damage/Healing	Soloing	PvP
Increased Potential Damage/Healing	Grouping/Instances	Soloing
Higher Damage Mitigation	Grouping/Tanks	Soloing
Disable Enemies	PvP	Efficient Experience Grinding

The most obvious form of customization is provided directly by the class system. At level ten, you start gaining Talents. The abilities gained from this system are very powerful, especially when people devote their characters into specific lines; the deeper stages of specific Talent lines are quite impressive and rewarding.

Before spending these points, take a *long* look at the lines available to your character. Because of the extended hours involved in reaching the higher levels, it's nice to know what you are getting into. Instead of taking any Talent that looks nice for now, try to come up with a path that nets as many permanent, useful Talents as possible.

On the whole, there are several varieties of Talent specializations. These are not identified directly, but an astute player can see where specific Talents are the most useful. Anything that reduces downtime and raises efficiency in battle is good for extended fighting against weaker targets; this is a style more for soloers than group members. On the other hand, abilities that are expensive but raise burst damage and effectiveness are critical in Instances and PvP fighting.

PvP builds are often about doing the greatest amount of activity in a short period. Instant abilities, helpful passive Talents, and other reactive perks are the focus here. Player vs. Player combat is often much shorter in duration than fighting against monsters in the field or in Instances. Thus, efficiency has less value compared to immediate power and survival. Specialize in burst healing or damage to be able to respond to the unpredictability of facing live, intelligent players in PvP combat.

Soloers need to be independent; they don't have backup healing, easy damage, or safety. This necessitates a build where the character is fully functional in multiple aspects of play. Efficiency is stressed because there are no allies to fall back on, and long downtime is a very bad thing if you don't have anyone to talk to or to keep the experience rolling. If you are a soloist, seek Talents that make your favorite actions more effective, then use those abilities to their fullest.

Group-friendly builds are some of the most specialized characters of all. These builds are intended to extend the weaker areas of many classes while honing specific strengths that are useful to allies. Seek increased potential in areas that are hailed by groups (better Damage Mitigation for a tank, more potent and dependable heals for a healer, and safe/constant damage from DPS classes). The group is present to negate the weaknesses of each member while extending the strengths of each member's build.

Remember that a soloist can group, a PvPer can and will farm Instances, and so forth. Everyone should be capable of filling a variety of roles, but it's going to be harder going against your element. Choose the line that makes your favorite role more enjoyable, because that is what you spend the most time doing.

This has given you an idea about how to think about Talents for your characters. This discussion has still occurred in a vacuum. Shortly, in the next chapter, you will learn about specific Talents choices and the tradeoffs involved with specializing each character class. These choices are too numerous and complex to evaluate here.

Decide what variety of character you are interested in playing. There is always the chance that your needs and interests will change, but many people know somewhat what they enjoy doing from the very beginning. Try to create a Talent path that advances the areas of the game you enjoy.

Honing Equipment

Talents are by no means the end of character customization. Equipment choices account for a great deal of a person's effectiveness. This doesn't boil down to a simple numbers game (i.e. Go for higher level gear all the time and don't stop). Rather, a focus on the type of equipment that completes your build is needed.

The most basic example is for casters who are rising in level. These characters need both Spirit and Intellect (Spirit for regaining mana and Intellect for having a large pool of Mana to draw from). A Soloist wants to have quite a high Spirit to maintain their mana and minimize downtime, since they are the ones casting in each battle. PvPers, at the other end, need to survive their current encounter no matter what the mana cost; they use Intellect for having the highest possible DPS for a given encounter. Even if recovery is slow as nails, they are free to drink water and cheer their victory.

Attribute Preference Examples		
Class/Style	Primary Attribute	Secondary Attribute
Defensive Tank	Agility and Stamina	Strength
Offensive Melee	Agility and Strength	Stamina
Rogue	Agility and Stamina	Strength
Melee Hybrid	Strength and Stamina	Intellect
Healing/Caster Hybrid	Stamina and Intellect	Spirit
PvP Caster	Stamina	Intellect
Group Caster	Intellect and Spirit	Stamina

These examples are neither exhaustive or absolute. There are major exceptions created when people see a niche that needs to be filled. Imagine a PvP Mage who enjoys going into large-scale battles that last for several minutes of direct fighting. Such a character might shun the pure Intellect model and grab more Spirit and +Damage gear for their favorite spell lines. The goal is not to memorize a specific table to select what you need. Instead, view the process that others use to create their customized equipment sets and see how it relates to your character.

WEAPON SPEED

Fast Weapons

- Enhanced by Direct Plusses to Damage
- Better Against Casters
- Feel More Responsive

Slower Weapons

- Deal Damage in Bursts, Very Good for PvP
- Do More Damage with "Instant Cast" Melee Attacks

Weapon speed has a number of complex aspects, and the system for it has changed several times during the evolution of WoW. Faster melee weapons were the ideal choices for Alpha and early Beta use, then things grew interesting. During early retail and for some time afterward, slow weapons grew to prominence because instant-use abilities would do so much damage with them. Rogues often tried to get the slowest available weaponry for their attacks, and Arms Warriors were no different.

In modern WoW, there have been changes to normalize the amount of damage instant melee and ranged weapon attacks deal. This makes a much wider variety of weaponry useful to characters, and in many ways is quite a positive change. All characters now have good reasons to go with each fast or slow weaponry. Faster ones are better for getting consistent DPS, poison use (for Rogues), or other +Damage On Hit abilities/items to work. General proc effects, however, are fine with any speed. And, if you want to have higher burst damage, the slower weapons are still superior for that.

Ask yourself where your character will do the most damage, in burst situations or extended fighting? For PvP, especially with physical classes, burst damage is very important. The moment you start dealing damage, someone is going to come after you. Crowd control abilities are soon to follow, and your DPS is going to shut down for a bit. That is why it's good to slap a character with a 3.8 second weapon shot! If they end up controlling or avoiding you for a few seconds afterward, you haven't lost much of anything. If you had been using a 1.2 second weapon, you would have missed at least a couple hits.

High-speed weapons are often better for PvE because of their consistency. You won't have sudden bursts that rip aggro off of things when you aren't ready for it, and neither will you have entire seconds of waiting for an attack when you just need to do a few points more.

REFINING YOUR PLAYSTYLE

Once you have the Talents, equipment, and knowledge to support your interests, victory comes from refining the techniques you use in battle. Which attacks aren't as useful in light of your new Talents; which moves are now essential, and need to be used earlier in the fight? Try to work on pounding your techniques into a trim and effective weapon of their own. If you want to get really scientific about it, time your battles against monsters of the same type and level and see if you can reduce the period it takes to defeat them. The same method can be used to reduce damage taken (kill-time and limiting damage taken are often linked to some extent anyway).

Look at the abilities you use in battle. Which of these make the most difference over the course of the battle? If you have status buffs and debuffs, see if there are better times to cast them. Some of these can be done before battle is engaged, so work on mastering a lead in to fights that frees your character to use direct combat abilities as soon as possible.

Perhaps a change of quickbar is in order at this stage. One thing that slows players down a great deal is the inefficient use of the game's interface. Many players who take the time to reorganize their quickbars are impressed at the difference in their character's performance. Keep abilities that aren't used often on entirely different bars and streamline the buttons that are used in each and every combat. Try to use an ascending order that fits the progression of battle, such that your fingers know where to go without you losing time looking down at the keyboard.

Don't rely on the mouse to click abilities! Sure, you can put up extra quickbars from the Interface Menu and click on things that aren't needed in the heat of the moment (e.g. Hearthstones). For in-combat abilities, hotkeys are king!

Even these issues are part of customization. If something doesn't feel right, work hard to change it. Look through the key bindings and make sure everything is where you need it to be; Stance/Form shifting can be bound to keys as well. You may want to put those beneath your most active fingers to

smooth the transitions. Warriors and Druids must be able to move from one stance/form to the next without any delay or problem; this is essential to their proper dominance in both PvE and PvP.

MAKING MONEY AND FINDING GEAR

Being an adept player is great, but money still makes the world go around. Buying from vendors and players is only one sink for money in WoW, and you are going to need plenty of cash just for those folks! Trainers take their fair share as well, and by the end of the day very few people have more gold than they need. So, how do you plan to stay in the black?

UNDERSTAND LOOT TABLES

Being out in the wild is interesting when looking for treasure. Unlike the rewards for quests or defeating specific, named enemies, there are many random pieces of treasure that drop from normal creatures. This is entirely random within the bounds of loot tables.

Your characters receive the majority of simple Uncommon/Green items and trade items while out in the wild. While fighting easier creatures, you are likely to find high quantities of gear that is slightly beneath the monsters' level. Rare and Epic gear is extremely unlikely to drop from these easier fights, and when it does there is a fair chance that the item won't be one for you specifically.

Outdoor fighting is great for leveling, fine for getting trade materials, but is too unpredictable for gearing up characters beyond a certain point.

The drop-rate for Rare gear tremendously improves when you fight large groups of Elite monsters in dungeons. These Instanced areas also have set bosses with loot tables that are specific in what they drop (giving you the ability to know what is likely to fall each time they die, within a modest margin). Thus, gearing up is very much about hitting dungeons with your allies. Go into such fighting with a group of mixed character classes to reduce competition for high-end drops.

To find out what is available from a given encounter, look up a creature's loot table. This guide and a number of other Brady products, reveal where to get quite a few of the best items in the game. There are also online resources that allow you to search by monster name or item name/type to find out where equipment is gained. Asking other players where they found specific gear is yet another source of information.

Selling to Vendors

Just as the most simple way to gather experience comes from grinding against monsters, you can gather a great deal of money from selling loot to vendors. Almost all of the creatures in the wild have something worth selling (whether they are living, dead, beast, or construct). Fight against creatures at a fast rate and harvest their goodies for future sale to players and vendors.

Sell anything that cons grey to your character, then take a look into the uses for the various crafting items and other goodies that fall. If there is a market for the remainder of your inventory, hold onto that until you can make an Auction House run.

It's a very big mistake to be picky about the items you snag from monsters. Sure, some creatures are terrible about dropping good stuff (Slimes take forever before they started dropping fun stuff), but even these enemies occasionally have a rare gem or magical item. Beyond that, if you have tons of space in your bags, there is no reason not to grab everything in sight! It takes almost no time to sell items, and every single piece of gold adds up. Indeed, it sounds foolish not to loot a corpse with a mere silver piece on it. Why then, would anyone stop collecting vendor trash that could add up to many gold pieces in the long run?

For faster looting, hold down shift while right-clicking on bodies; this loots everything at once and is slightly faster for getting you on your way again. BoP items won't bind to you by doing this; a query bar rises instead, and you have the choice to take the item or leave it on the body.

A very wise investment early in your character's career is to buy bags from the Auction House. The vendor prices for bags are **never good for you**. Indeed, there are always crafters making bags for alts and newcomers, and you

make a great deal of money in the long run by having larger packs to stash goodies. You never want to run out of space in a dungeon and have to pass up loot that could pay for one or two of your packs just by itself!

Gathering Materials

Profession	Means of Income
Skinning	Selling Leather on the Auction House (Much More Lucrative in the Later Levels)
Mining	Selling Metal and Stones on the Auction House (Iron is When This Becomes Highly Profitable)
Herbalism	Selling Herbs on the Auction House (Everything after the First Few Herbs are Worth Gold)
Enchanting	Break Uncommon and Rare Items And Auction The Materials

There are plenty of craftsfolk out there who need a constant supply of leather, cloth, metal, herbs, and magical powders. If you aren't interested in creating items, try out the gathering professions. In any event, selling the ingredients for crafted items to their creators is profitable throughout the levels. Use the Auction House to accomplish this unless you have friends or guild sources that need first crack at these items.

Knowing where to gather your items can make the difference between slim pickings and a lucrative trade. People don't usually go to Teldrassil for making it rich as a Miner, eh. Indeed, talk to other people and learn where some of the best spots are for getting the items you seek. Open fields have more beasts for leather, humanoid caves often have both metal deposits and cloth or leather to harvest, and herbs are specifically located because of their inability to grow in inhospitable regions.

Don't let your inventory control you either. You may harvest enough material to fill your bank vault and your packs, but understand what your merchandise is worth. Stay current on the going rates for your items and only slide a bit under that quantity when selling. A few silvers can attract a buyer almost as quickly as entire gold pieces worth of discounts. It's similar to running away from a bear when you have a gnome in your party; you don't have to outrun the bear (you just have to outrun the gnome). When competing against other sellers, there is no need to cut the market.

Farming for Loot

There may be specific places that bring in money at a fast pace for your character. Perhaps you have a group that brings down clusters of enemies quickly with AoEs. Or, you may have a favorite cave where there is metal, cloth, and vendor loot that sells half-decently. In any event, farming for money is a tradition with a long and glorious past.

Much like grinding for experience, you can grind with loot in mind. Find an area with as many of the target monsters as possible and hop to it. Though this is often a good solo practice, groups sometimes form with different needs. Perhaps you are trying to get an Uncommon or Rare Elemental drop (Breath of Wind or some equivalent item), and another character wishes to hunt for experience in the same area. Joining together can help both individuals; agree to divide loot in a way that lets you farm for your items while the grinder gets what they need as well.

Small teams with different Professions work nicely in this field as well. Having a person to skin, another to mine, a cloth gatherer, and so forth keeps the peace perfectly. Everyone can get what they want while journeying around the world without having to roll for items.

HUNTING FOR RARES

Bind-on-Equip Rare items are extremely valuable. These blue pieces fetch a massive sum on the Auction House because people who are funding their alts are interested in getting the best gear without always putting in the work to hunt through dungeons or wait for drops that are never a given. Thus, you can strike it rich very easily by going through dungeons and waiting for the right pieces to drop.

A prime example of this comes from Shadowfang Keep. This Instance dungeon drops a Rare BoE piece every few runs (this is random, but making a few fast runs gives you a high chance of getting what you want). Because such pieces are going to be a few levels below the enemies that drop them, you can expect to find many items in the high teens from that dungeon. This makes Shadowfang Keep **ideal** for grabbing "twink" equipment to sell on the Auction House. Alts with a huge amount of money who want to camp at level 19 in the Battlegrounds sometimes pay 20-100 gold pieces for even these low-level items. One lucky drop that doesn't take more than a few hours of farming to find can fund your character for quite some time.

By the time you are in your 30s and 40s, your character can blow through Shadowfang Keep without any help, delays, or frustrations. Money, money, money.

BECOME ONE WITH THE AUCTION HOUSE

- You Pay a Deposit Every Time You Post an Item on the Auction House (Based Off a Percentage of that Item's Value Multiplied by the Duration of the Auction)
- A Percentage of the Sell Price Is Also Taken by the Auction House as a Fee (This Percentage is High for Neutral Auction Houses)
- You Won't See the Exact Duration of an Existing Auction; Instead, the System Lists a General Time (Short, Medium, Long, Very Long)
- The Upper Price for an Item is the Amount of the Current Bid on it; The Lower Value is the Amount Needed to Immediately Buy Out the Item
- Be Very Careful When Typing in Sale Values and Bid Quantities (A Slip Here can Cost You Dearly)
- Purchased Items and Money for Sales Appear in Characters' Mailboxes

The Auction House is a blessing in every way. Having a major center of trade opens the window for players to cooperate with everyone in their faction (and beyond, in the case of the neutral Auction Houses in the Goblin towns). Setting your Hearthstone to a capital city with an Auction House is rarely a bad choice, considering how often people return here to talk, trade, and find new items.

Sell useful items through the Auction House instead of vendoring them. Players who do this make far more money in the long run. There is a deposit every time you put items into the AH, and this increases proportionally as you set the timer for an auction for a longer duration. There is also a tax on final sales in the AH, and this is higher for the neutral Ahs.

The best bet for keeping your money flowing freely is to sell only your higher quality items (the ones that move quickly through the AH). People are rarely interested in equipment of low quality, so the profits for such items are higher through vendoring in a number of cases. Watch the AH by the searching for the very items you wish to sell and see what prices they are going for (and if people are really bidding on them). If the products aren't moving well, try a lower buyout than the other sellers.

If moving inventory is more important to you than the raw price, try very low starting bids. This really encourages impulse buying for anything useful; as long as the price is still low, players may push back and forth trying to keep their bid on the item. This sometimes leads to prices above what the players would have paid originally, but they become somewhat attached to the auction itself. You can't count on this, but it does happen.

Goods and Services

Profession/Ability	Service Provided
Alchemy	Selling Potions, Transmutes for Higher Metals and Elements (On Timers)
Blacksmith	Occasional Weapon or Mount Enhancements (Not Highly Valuable)
Enchanting	Wide Variety of Equipment Enhancements
Engineering	Make Scopes for Ranged Weapons, Make Ammo, Some Explosives Are Usable By Non-Engineers Also
Leatherworker	Cure Rugged Hides (On a Timer)
Tailor	Make Bags, Make Mooncloth (On a Timer)

- Orgrimmar and Undercity Are Major Trade Centers for the Horde
- Ironforge and Stormwind Are Major Trade Centers for the Alliance

Your characters can also make money by selling services to other players. Because everyone can master two professions (at most), it is common for players to need the services of other people from time to time. Blacksmiths attach Shield Spikes, Riding Spurs (for mounts), and other such goodies for weapons and armor. Enchanters prepare special concoctions to boost the power of items. Rogues can learn Lockpicking and open lockboxes for a tip or for goodwill.

When advertising your own skills, use the Trade Chat channel and prepare a text macro that quickly states your available skills and associated costs (if any). Try to keep this to one or two lines to prevent your message from filling up everyone's message windows. Use your macro periodically, but not more often than every few minutes. While doing this, participate in the channel and help others; it's useful to have a clientele that already knows who you are and respects your attitude.

To receive services, ask in Trade Chat if anyone has the skill level you seek in a profession. Be up front about what you want and they often are just as forthcoming about the price they require for their time. Don't by shy about saying "How much do you want?" if they don't list a specific sum. Under the friendly conditions, the other character may not answer firmly. Be sure to tip such people if you can afford to; it keeps the goodwill flowing and won't hurt you on any return visits.

Spending Your Wealth

There are more ways to spend money than to make it; that is the usual truth of things. Carefully choosing when and where to spend your hard-earned cash is very important, especially at low levels (where it's harder to make substantial amounts).

Learn Class Abilities First

Before looking for new items or having fun with your money, make sure that your character's abilities are current. Every even level, talk to your class trainers and see which new abilities are available. If you use said abilities or would like to, buy these before any purchases of equipment, services, or whatever else you enjoy. Having abilities trained to their fullest is extremely important, and the cost is minimal if you are willing to do some hunting on the side from time to time.

To avoid taking a more substantial hit to the wallet every two levels, it is possible to ignore some abilities (for some classes). If you are a Warrior who never uses Berserk Stance, don't train in Slam or Cleave. A sword-wielding Rogue could forego Backstab and Ambush for quite some time too. Almost all classes have abilities that they may not use, depending on playstyle. Save money in the short term by holding off on their purchase. It's always possible to return later and train these skills when the cost is lower (compared to your total earnings).

RESTORE IMPORTANT ITEMS

Whether you are finding, creating, or purchasing items that are used while adventuring, be certain to resupply from time to time. Bandages, food (for you or any pets), ammunition, repairs, potions, explosives, and other treats all cost time or money. If you enjoy using these goodies or at least fall in love with what they can do for you, put the money down and make sure your characters stays prepared.

KEEP EQUIPMENT UP TO DATE

Many, many gold pieces go toward keeping your character's equipment up to date. At first, quests and general loot are able to keep characters up-to-speed. Decent items drop somewhat easily over the first 20 levels, and there are substantial numbers of quests with useful rewards.

In the mid-and-later levels, however, characters start to need better equipment. This necessitates going into dungeons more often and buying at least Uncommon items from the Auction House, with an occasional purchase of Rare gear. When doing this on a budget, look for the items you need over several days and only jump at bids that are priced below the norm. This saves you considerable money (at the cost of your time and patience). If you instead need an item as soon as possible, pay the premium and start buying out everything that looks nice; the sellers will love you.

Without a heavy investment in farming for money, you won't likely be able to purchase every Rare piece of equipment you like from the Auction House. The best middle road, for those of us who never have quite enough cash, is to plan your equipment ahead of time for every ten levels or so. Look at the Rare gear in each bracket and decide what your dream pieces are. Find out which of these can be sough directly and which are instead world drops (in other words, which ones are quite random).

Once you have done that, hunt for the pieces that drop in specific locations and only seek the Auction House for item slots that don't have any farmable choices for the next six to ten levels. By doing this, you only have to purchase a slot of gear from the Auction House every now and then.

THE BANK

Using the bank saves characters from losing bag space. It's unfortunate to lose vendorable items because you have your bags loaded with ammunition, food, potions, skins, and whatever else has crept in there. Anything that isn't needed for a specific outing should be left in the bank vault and taken out at your convenience (especially trade goods).

For a one-time investment of cash, you can purchase extra bag slots in your bank vault. Notice how quickly the prices rise for additional slots; it is far more effective to use high-end bags than to purchase many bank slots. Each new tier of space costs more than the previous slot, so people need a heavy sum to unlock the later ones.

Though bags are a bit costly early on, crafters can save you tremendous time and frustration by creating some of the larger bags at a decent price. Ask your guild or friends if they know a good Tailor, then see if those folks are able to set you up with four larger bags at a fair cost. It's only worth buying bags from stores when you are entirely wealthy and only need a spare 6-Slot for an alt; otherwise, crafters are able to make bags at immensely lower prices.

Bags can drop from monsters as well. Though these aren't found with high frequency, you are going to find a few during your rise through the levels. These are best used to supplement your bank (rather than hoping to find four of the highest sized ones in any short period).

Bag Size by Loot Tables	
Monster Level	**Possible Bag Drop**
1 to 10	6-Slot Bag (Linen Equivalent)
11-19	8-Slot Bag (Wool Equivalent)
20-29	10-Slot Bag (Silk Equivalent)
30-39	12-Slot Bag (Mageweave Equivalent)
40-49	Journeyman's Backpack (Runecloth Equivalent)
50-60	Traveler's Backpack (Mooncloth Equivalent)

SPEND WISELY

The simple way to decide what to spend money on is to look at future earning potential. What items/skills are going to help you make money faster? Is it going to help you more to master a ranged weapon or get a new chest piece? Look at what your character does well and what they do poorly; spend money at both ends of that spectrum first, then deal with the in-between later. Mages deal tons of damage but die quickly (spend money on doing even more damage or on saving your rump). Don't fret over raising less important attributes, peripheral abilities, and other such concerns until you know that your best equipment is on par and your central abilities are fully trained.

Do a bit of research to avoid spending money at the wrong time. If there are important class quests coming up, you often have some nice items in your future; it's better to buy equipment for slots that aren't going to receive quest upgrades anytime soon. By the same token, don't waste serious gold enchanting an item that you are going to ditch in a level or two.

EXPLORING

Moving around the world and seeing the impressive variety of locations is a source of lasting joy. The zones in WoW are well differentiated, so it's a shame not to fully explore Kalimdor and the Eastern Kingdoms. This is a task that has subtle but worthwhile benefits for future play, as you also learn more about camp locations, monster variety, and other such matters while exploring.

FILLING IN YOUR MAPS

Region maps start off without many locations uncovered. It is your responsibility to fill out the map over time by visiting the major points of interest. Each location you discover opens a new section of the map and awards you an exploration bonus (a slight gift of experience). Though this process isn't profitable by itself, given that hunting earns far more experience than wandering, it feels very good to have your maps uncovered for all major regions.

Instead of racing off to fully explore each map when you enter a new region, take the time to explore naturally, using the direction of quests and hunting to guide you. This way, you are never just exploring. You are finishing quests, making money, gaining experience from multiple sources, and having a good time too. If you choose to grind your way through an entire zone, fighting everything you see, the map uncovers just as nicely as if you spent all the time looking about and avoiding those fun skirmishes.

If you have trouble getting a specific section to come clear, try to walk closer to the major buildings, caves, and general landmarks inside that area. Just because a new text name appears in your map header doesn't mean that the area is uncovered (that doesn't happen until you receive the "You Have Discovered XXX" message and get the experience bonus. Walk deeper into each new area to find such bonuses.

GOING INTO SMALLER DUNGEONS

Dungeons are a useful point of interest because they often have heavy fighting, some metal or herb deposits, and quests to complete. Try to find where all of the dungeons are located when you are exploring even if you don't have quests for them at the time; it's common for quests to send people all around the world for various goals, and knowing where you are going can cut down on lost time.

Microdungeons are found in most regions. These areas are part of the normal terrain (in other words, you face no loading screen and can freely walk into the dungeons and back out without delay). There are often many monsters in microdungeons, but they won't usually be much tougher than the beasts and enemies walking out in the fields nearby. Unlike Instances, microdungeons aren't based on elite monsters, large pulls, and having a group to protect you.

Microdungeons are some of the best places to camp for metal in WoW. Though you can get more metal by running around entire areas, taking everything you see (once you know the spawn points for the deposits), there are several benefits to camping a cave. For one, the creatures there are worth plenty of experience if you are at the right level for fighting in the dungeon (which is often the case if you stay current on your Mining). Getting metal, experience, and loot at the same time is a major boon. Beyond that, the flow of metal out of a dungeon is reliable compared to searching external sources that people can mine casually.

For the best of both worlds, find all of the dungeons in a given region. Look on the maps once they are filled out to find caves and other places to explore, then go to each place at least one time. Record the items you need from each place (metal here, herbs there, cloth-dropping foes at this location, etc.), then create a loop. Visit one site, kill everything, take all of the items there, then move on to the second site. Moving around a zone in this fashion is amazing for raising gathering Professions, collecting materials to sell, and for gaining a moderate amount of experience.

TAKING ON WORLD DUNGEONS

World dungeons are very different from microdungeons. As you might guess, these dungeons are much larger than their cousins. However, this is one of the superficial differences between the two. In fact, there are far more daunting challenges in world dungeons.

If you have missed the term Instance before, it means that an area is not part of the shared world. If twenty groups go there, twenty versions (e.g. Instances) of the dungeon are created. So, only your group is going to head into the fire; expect no surprise assistance or enemy intervention.

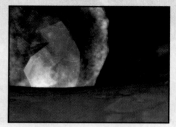

Always discuss loot rules and any pertinent etiquette **before** entering the actual Instance. In fact, get everything straightened out with other players before people head all the way out to the appropriate region for the dungeon crawl. If you think you need a dedicated healer, don't assume that a Shaman is specced for it. Ask them, "Are you comfortable being our primary healer?" If they say no, don't put them in your group to heal. If you only have that one slot left, apologize, then explain that you need to find a healer and thank them for their time.

TRAITS OF WORLD DUNGEONS

- These Dungeons are Instanced (Every Group Goes into Their Own Version of the Dungeon)
- There is a Loading Screen to Mark the Separation Between the Shared Game World and the Instance
- Many Creatures in World Dungeons are Elite
- Battles Inside World Dungeons are Often Harder, Involve Scripted Bosses (in Some Cases), and Have Greater Rewards
- Horde and Alliance Members can do All World Dungeons (Even Those in Enemy Territory)

At the suggested levels, parties without five people and very impressive gear may have trouble. Unlike fighting out in the field, world dungeons are meant to challenge, frustrate, and even defeat parties that aren't experienced enough to survive the complex battles within. This is not a measure of a party's worth, as the vast majority of groups have to contend with full wipeouts and other such setbacks the first few times they try to overcome new world dungeons.

To make your attempts safer, be sure to mold the group before it heads into a world dungeon. Find people who you know and trust to play their characters with high skill. Beyond that, make sure everyone is willing to dedicate several hours to completing the task (most of the world dungeons are somewhat long, and having people leave in the middle can be disastrous for the group). Practice techniques against many of the creatures early in the dungeon and get a feel for the style of the place. In general, a group that has trouble early on needs a couple more levels or some better gear before they can complete that Instance.

Choose a very good leader for every Instance run. It is so important to have skilled and trusted leadership that a well-run group can function better than one with members of higher level, carrying better equipment. If you want to be a leader, run the Instance multiple times, look for key ways to avoid extra aggro, reduce fight times, and finish the boss battles without losing people left and right. Exchange strategies with other leaders and test out new methods frequently to keep your groups trim. With a good leader, Instances can be run sooner and without resorting to specific class combinations.

What World Dungeons Should I Seek (And When)		
Dungeon Name	**Expected Levels**	**Region**
Ragefire Chasm	13 to 18	Orgrimmar
Wailing Caverns	17 to 24	The Barrens
Deadmines	17 to 26	Westfall
Shadowfang Keep	22 to 30	Silverpine Forest
Blackfathom Deeps	24 to 32	Darkshore
The Stockades	24 to 32	Stormwind
Razorfen Kraul	25 to 35	The Barrens
Gnomeregan	29 to 38	Dun Morogh
Razorfen Downs	33 to 40	The Barrens
The Scarlet Monastery	34 to 45	Tirisfal Glades
Uldaman	35 to 47	The Badlands
Zul'Farrak	44 to 54	Tanaris Desert
Maraudon	46 to 55	Southwestern Desolace
The Sunken Temple	47 to 55	Swamp of Sorrows
Blackrock Depths	52+	Burning Steppes
Dire Maul	55+	Central Feralas
Scholomance	57+	Between Western and Eastern Plaguelands
Blackrock Spire	58+	Burning Steppes
Strathome	58+	Eastern Plaguelands

Be especially careful not to be impulsive or greedy during dungeon runs. It takes a great deal of time and work to get a good group together and push through a challenging dungeon for an hour (or two, or three). Because of that, it's even more important than ever to watch what you are doing.

Click Carefully: Many of the groups that don't run with a Master Looter are going to be using Group Loot or Need Before Greed. Either way, you are going to see many loot items appear. Listen carefully when group rules are explained, make any objections at that time, and do not break your contract with the group once everything is settled. Only roll the way you stated you would from the very beginning. There should be no changing the system, no calling dibs suddenly, and no sudden surprises.

Loot When You Are Safe: Do not run off to open chests, mine, harvest herbs, or do other activities during battle. By the same token, don't waste time looting corpses while a battle is still in progress. This is certain to get your group annoyed, and it risks people's safety.

Stay With the Group: Unless you are the one pulling monsters back to the group, stay with everyone else and don't wander. Failing to heed this is a sure way to pull an extra patroller back onto the group at just the wrong time.

Disagreements: Everyone thinks that they know how to do things the best way (well, it seems like everyone feels that way). It may be true that your ideas are better than the existing group leader. Regardless, do not call them out in the group chat at first. Message them privately with your clever ideas. They might very well use them! If the leader is outright rude, poor, or acts like a genuine nutter, consider telling the group your ideas then and see what they think. It's not likely to make things better, but it's a good second course to take.

If that fails, leave. Don't yell, don't whine, don't argue. Apologize and leave. This is the best way to keep your dignity without busting your head against the wall for hours on end.

Mind Those Pets: Note that pets can get entire groups into major trouble. If you send your pet into the wrong enemy group, everyone might die. If your pet paths oddly, everyone might die. If you leave your pet on aggressive, everyone in the group will strangle you (not quite, but don't do it). Use your pet carefully at all times. If you are about to drop to a lower area, put the pet away.

On the flipside, healers should look out for pets too. Hunters especially don't like losing their beloved allies, and it sure helps to have a free tank in the group. When you can spare the mana, keep those pets hale and hearty. Remember that you can target pets quickly using the same function key of that group member (e.g. if the third group member is a Hunter, hitting F3 would target the Hunter normally; tap the key a second time to target the pet instead)

Warlocks Are Not Your Toy: Warlocks can summon characters under certain circumstances. This requires the Warlock to use one of their items, get two other group members to help them, and takes their time and energy to put together. It is not their obligation to do this for you. If you are on the other side of the world as a group is forming, you should ask any Warlocks in the group if they are willing to summon you. Offer sincere thanks if they say yes. Offer a tip too (many of the Warlocks will say no). If the Warlock wants a tip, pay them a portion of what it would take you to get there anyway. Remember that you lose time and money to get places. If a Warlock wants 50 silver pieces for a sum-

mon, pay them and kill a few creatures while the group gets together. You can make the money in the time that Warlock just saved you!

Mage Food/Water: Mage Food and Water is a gift for dungeons. It saves people a massive amount of money. Again, offer to tip Mages when you ask for these favors, and certainly thank them for their time.

Warriors Pay the Price: Warriors don't have a major service to sell, and their repair bills are higher than anyone else's. It's sometimes tough to be a Warrior. For other classes, remember that. Help out your Warriors by giving them a bit of leeway on the items they roll Need for. Remember that most tanks need a two-handed weapon, a one-hander, a shield, perhaps a second one-hander, and a full list of tanking gear (perhaps a PvP set as well). Quite a few guilds help to gear up their Warriors for this reason. Love your Warrior. Support your Warrior. The good ones ensure that you don't eat dirt for a living.

"Heal Me Now:" Don't yell at your healers. Either they stink or they don't. If a healer is poor, they won't heal well no matter what you say. Don't invite those healers back into your groups, but don't ruin their night by calling them names either. You don't know if it's a nine-year-old behind that screen; they really might be doing their best already. You aren't obligated to play with people who are poor at their class (and you shouldn't), but don't get nasty just because you died. It happens. Healers get more blame than just about anyone. Think about that, empathize, and play a healer to level 60 yourself before getting too judgmental. Beyond that, you might have been doing something you shouldn't if you are getting a lot of aggro. If you aren't the main tank, maybe the healer shouldn't be healing you that much.

One Puller Only: Make sure one person is assigned for pulling monsters to a group. If that person messes up, let them die on their own and Resurrect them when the monsters are gone. If you aren't that person, don't start any fight unless you have no choice (e.g. a patroller is aggroing on the back of the group and is about to attack the Priest, so you attack it first).

Rely on the Main Assist: Make a macro to /assist "character who is main assist" and use that for your targeting. This is ideal for keeping the group's fire on one target.

Don't Run: Most of the time running gets you killed in Instances anyway. Unless your group leader orders everyone to ditch, hold your ground. If you are going to die, then die with honor.

GROUP ROLES

Group Roles take the general knowledge and tactics of this chapter and expands on that to cover group functionality. Being able to control your character, rise in level and power, and find the right items is enough to bring you up in the ranks. However, a group with five soloers is not as effective as a group with five players who are skilled at grouping! There are tricks that work quite well when you have others on your side that would be worthless when tried solo. Learning these creates a synergy within well-played groups; that edge is what leads to victory in world dungeons, raids, and mass PvP combat.

ROLES: IN SHORT

Going past the terminology, players benefit from understanding what the true components of a group are capable of providing. Look at the following list and consider the way battles are won in a mathematical sense. By reducing incoming damage, shortening encounters, and extending survival time, characters of different roles are able to assist the greater needs of a group in separate ways. When facing various and unknown opponents, it is essential to have multiple answers to each problem.

Group Roles and Functions

Role	Importance in Battle
Mitigation/Tanking	Reduces Damage Directed at Group
Damage	Kills Enemies
Healer	Maintains Group

Various classes exist between these three niches, so the distinction we make here is one of action rather than an innate role. A Warrior, for example, can be both a damage dealer and a tank! Amusingly, Mages are quite the same; they deal damage to enemies while mitigating damage through crowd control.

The key to a successful group is to figure out what ratio of mitigation/damage/healing is needed for a given challenge, then to assemble a group that creates such a ratio.

MITIGATION

Tanks and crowd controllers are intended to stop incoming damage in one way or another. Tanks gather enemies around themselves and force the aggro to stay put; this reduces incoming damage by keeping it centered on characters with high armor and survival rates. Crowd controls perform the same function by stopping enemy attacks, preventing their movement toward desirable targets, and so forth.

Warriors, Paladins, and Druids in Bear Form are able to survive hits far better than many of the other classes. These three tanks use abilities to get aggro then disable enemies as best as possible (e.g. Warriors use Demoralizing Shout and Thunder Clap to reduce incoming damage beyond what their plate armor already accomplishes).

Crowd controllers, like Mages, Warlocks, Rogues, and sometimes Priests try to take a specific enemy's damage entirely out of the battle for a time. Polymorph, Banish, Sap, Mind Control, and Shackle Undead are all abilities with the potential to stop enemies from being productive.

Obviously, characters can mitigate damage while still contributing to party health or DPS. A Warrior who is immensely survivable but can't hold aggro isn't of very much use. The key is to understand when to mitigate damage and when to switch toward other aspects of battle. See the following table for a better understanding of this.

Mitigation Abilities and When to Use Them

Class	Ability	When to Use
Druid	High Armor in Bear Form	During Battle: To Give Other Tanks Time to Regain Aggro or to Delay PvP Forces
Hunter	Traps	Before Combat: Traps Are Used to Slow Groups or Immobilize Individuals
Mage	Polymorph, Many Frost Spells	During Combat: Mages Take Enemies Out of Combat With Polymorph or Greatly Slow Groups With Ice Snare/Root Effects
Paladin	High Armor, Stuns	During Battle: Paladin Stuns Stop Enemies Fully for a Short Time, Paladin Armor Allows Them to Survive Aggro Gained from Healing
Priest	Shackle Undead, Psychic Scream, Mind Control	Various: Their Specific Uses Are Quite Powerful (Discussed in Character Chapter)
Rogue	Sap, Many Stuns, Blind	Before Combat: Rogue Saps Cause Very Long Incapacitation Time to Humanoids; In-Combat Stuns Are Also Useful Against PvP Enemies and Lesser Targets
Shaman	Frost Shock, Earthbind Totem	During Combat: Shamans Slow or Stop Enemy Forces Even on the Run
Warlock	Banish, Seduce, Fear	During Combat: Warlocks Are Able to Produce Very Long In-Combat Crowd Control
Warrior	High Armor, Immense Damage Mitigation, AOE Fear	During Combat: Warriors Get Aggro and Shut Down Incoming Enemy Damage

Whatever class you choose, understand the time and place for your mitigation. During light combat, mitigation is of less importance than healing or damage. When there are many incoming enemies (such as you see during many dungeons), mitigation becomes the most important aspect of group survivability. Without proper mitigation, healers won't be able to keep up.

Mitigation is also not a practice for any single member of the group. This is an ongoing and multi-faceted affair. The Warrior mitigates by engaging a full group of enemies, pulling them onto herself, and using abilities to reduce their damage. Then, a Mage in the same group uses Polymorph against a caster off in the distance to mitigate that enemy. The Shaman of the group drops totems to decrease the damage coming at the Warrior, and also uses Frost Shock to slow anything that breaks away from the Warrior and tries to get to her healers. Don't let enemies do what they want! Reduce their damage, reduce their movement, reduce their options. This is the key. The character chapter, Rising in the Ranks, goes into great length on this matter.

The person chosen to be Main Assist should be a player who understands the given raid/dungeon area extremely well. For there, it helps if that person is a melee class (so that they are actually there in the action). Everyone else who is on damage duty needs to have an /assist macro for the Main Assist so that damage is properly focused.

DAMAGE DEALERS

Almost every class can deal damage when configured properly. This person's duty is to knock down enemies quickly. Every foe that falls is unable to deal damage for the rest of the fight, meaning that DPS characters are able to protect the party by negating enemy activity in a permanent sense.

The most effective way for DPS characters to operate is to deal targeted damage to enemies who are most likely to die quickly (or to target the enemies who deal the most damage). To wound all enemies is not good enough for most situations; slaying targets is the true benefit of damage dealing! Thus, damage done by DPS characters needs to be concentrated so that each target dies as quickly as possible. A leader should be chosen among the damage dealers, and this person picks each target with a mind for kill rate vs. threat of target (this person is called the Main Assist). The faster the kill, the better the target. The more dangerous the target, the more important the kill. Quickly rate all of the enemies in a battle along these lines to decide what needs to be destroyed, then start opening the metaphoric can of beatdowns on your list.

Factors in Creating Your Own Hate List

To decide which targets come first, look at how past battles have gone. Which enemies deal the most damage to your party? Casters, creatures with major debuffs/combat control, and other such aggressive foes are usually high risk. Luckily, they are also softer kills. This ranks highly for both criteria you use.

Take down high damage or crowd control targets as soon as possible, then move on to foes with less opportunity. Often, the most enduring targets are the weakest, so they can be dispatched at the end of combat. Bosses are the big exception to this; removing any substantial allies a boss has may not be possible because of a boss' immense DPS (in other words, you may have to ignore fast kills to make a mad scramble against a superior target). Each boss fight has its own strategy and tactics, so that isn't something to worry about here.

Dealing Damage

Class	DPS Methods
Druid	Wield Weapons With High Stat Bonuses (Avoid Procs), Use Cat Form, Spec for Feral Combat
Hunter	Sustainable DPS is the Best in Game, Multishot + Pet + Rapid Fire + Stings Alone Add Up (Volley Against Large Groups)
Mage	Spec in Fire and Arcane, Use Many AoEs Against Groups of 3+ Enemies, Many Instants When Mana Efficiency Doesn't Matter
Paladin	Spec for Retribution, Rely on High-End Weaponry (Not Easy to Deal High DPS as a Paladin)
Priest	Not Often a DPS Class, Though Holy AoEs in Massed PvP, Shadow Spec for Ruining Single Targets
Rogue	High End Weapons, Backstab and Assassination for PvP Damage, Combat Spec for PvE
Shaman	Great Single-Target DPS Through Elemental or Enhancement Spec, Windfury Totem for Lucky Bursts; Poor for AoE DPS
Warlock	Spec with Affliction and Destruction, DOT Everyone, AoEs, Break Out the Dangerous Pets (e.g. Infernals)
Warrior	Spec for Arms or Fury (or Both), Heavy Gear Dependence, AoEs Assist Greatly (Sweeping Strikes/Whirlwind), 2H Weapon or Dual Wield

HEALER

Healers extend the length of time a group can survive in a battle; they also decrease downtime between battles to raise experience and money-gaining efficiency. This is done by using Mana to negate damage done against a group. With careful casting and high Spirit, these characters can dramatically lengthen the survival time of a group.

Also, there is a targeted advantage to the boost Healers provide. Though Tanks are able to reduce damage coming in against a party, they have only a few chances to turn the tide of battle if aggro is cemented and they fall close to death. If the Tank goes down because of this, all of the potential that protector brought to the group disappears in an instant. Healers smooth out damage so that individual members of the group do not die before their time. Proper healing ensures that Tanks last as long as possible, use all of their abilities and items, then only start to die off when the group has nothing left to give. Preventing premature deaths is as much a part of a Healer's service as ensuring total group survivability.

In tougher dungeons and end-game raids, healing is the only way to survive. Full DPS groups, even with crowd control, simply cannot make their way through the later portions of the game. In PvP, raiding, and even the harder five-man Instances, healers are a requirement. Priests are the acknowledged powerhouses of this, just as Warriors are the leaders of standard tanking. That said, Druids, Shamans, and Paladins that are willing to heal carefully are immensely powerful as well. Anyone who specializes in healing can fill the role nicely, and even characters without a Talent focus in healing can save lives!

These backup healers (such as Paladins or Druids/Shamans who haven't focused on healing) lack some of the healing efficiency and potential of a solid and true Healer. The best place for these backup healers is to be in a group with a full-time healer. Just as a backup tank is often ready to rip aggro off of group members when the main tank cannot, a backup healer exists to save the life of the primary healer or other characters when the worst luck happens.

During more frantic combat, it's hard to maintain composure. When multiple characters are taking damage and monsters are flying back and forth, it's essential that the healers focus on saving lives. Keep trickling the spells to the entire group while the Tanks hold all the aggro they can. Only unleash the massive, aggro-drawing flurry of heals when it's make or break time. Once that happens, hope that you can do enough to allow a secondary rezzer to survive and bring you back, because considerable aggro is coming your way.

Save the Tank!

There are times when healers have to make the hardest choice of all (to let some characters die while saving others). In dire fights, there won't always be mana to keep the entire group/raid alive. Even before end-game content, there are a number of encounters that greatly challenge any group that isn't higher in level or equipment. For these, a healer may have to acknowledge openly or in their own plans that some characters are expendable.

In general, the way to decide on healing priorities is to figure out what each person adds to the group. The main tank is the savior of a party because they control the aggro, protect the healers, and lower incoming damage in general. Keeping them alive is usually the top priority. After that, healers are the most important ones to save because they accomplish the same function (e.g. keep the group from wiping during an intense fight). Finally, the damage dealers are sorted. Within the damage dealers, the sorting is usually done by intelligence level of the player. Let players who foolishly deal too much damage and rip aggro off of the tanks often die. It's for the best; heals on those damage dealers risk the group!

An important exception to this list exists when a healer or damage dealer is out of mana. They are almost useless to the group then, and should only be saved if they are a rezzer.

Restoring Health	
Class	**Healing/Restoration**
Druid	Heal Over Times, Direct Heals, Battle Rez
Hunter	Can Heal Their Pets
Mage	Offers Free Food/Water to Groups; Otherwise None
Paladin	Survivable Heals (They Want the Aggro), Powerful Lay on Hands (Once Per Hour), Rez
Priest	Best Heals in the Game, Efficient Healing, Increase Health Totals Through Buffs, Rez
Rogue	None
Shaman	Less Efficient Healing, Totems for Modest Healing Over Time, Totems for Mana Regeneration, Rez
Warlock	Can Heal Themselves, Soul Stone Rezzers to Rez Them in Case of Wipe
Warrior	Healers: These Guys/Girls Are Your Customers

HYBRID

As stated, most classes have elements in each of the three primary aspects. The devoted classes lean heavily toward one of the three roles (e.g. Priests are mostly healers), while the hybrid and support classes divide their skillsets somewhat evenly between the groups. Specialization within a class pushes characters closer toward one extreme or into a more versatile role.

Thus, no matter what character you choose to play, there are ways to become a bit of everything or ways to accentuate the strengths already found in the class. Characters that are specialized offer the greatest potential within their portion of the group roles, but end up requiring other characters to function normally. In other words, a Warrior who becomes a full tank loses so much DPS that they don't kill quickly on their own anymore. Priests with a full specialization on the Holy line are able to fight better than they used to, but still perform far better with a group there to help them survive.

For the players who want to fill the gaps in a group or be able to solo under a variety of conditions, the hybrid classes and specializations are preferable. Take a look at Druids (the epitome of a hybrid class). Druids can heal, deal ranged damage, fight in melee, stealth, and even get a combat rez. What can't Druids do? Nothing, quite honestly. Druids and other hybrid classes are never left without the ability to contribute; their only problem is in defining themselves while in the shadow of specialized classes/roles.

During the first fifty levels of the game, hybrids have a great deal of power. Druids can heal for a group of five and keep them going in an Instance, or they can switch to Bear Form and tank if there isn't a Warrior, or they can stay in Cat Form and deal damage. Restoration Shamans are easily heal for a group, just as Enhancement Shamans are fine tanks until the end-game challenges appear.

In late-game battles, the hybrid characters find their own niches. Backup healing, spare DPS, and other secondary roles never go out of fashion in raids. With a group of 40, there are many needs. When you play a hybrid class, be especially on the lookout in the long- and short-term for the needs of a guild, group, raid. If people need more healing, try to use more healing gear, respec your Talents if needed, and so forth. Become what is needed and there will always be a place for you.

Hybrid Class Potential

Class	Directions
Druid	Melee DPS/Tanking with Feral Combat (Cat and Bear Form), Ranged Damage with Balance (Caster Form), and Healing Through Restoration (Caster Form)
Paladin	Healing With Holy Talents, DPS With Retribution and 2H Weapons, Tanking With Protection (Though This is Difficult)
Shaman	Magical Damage With the Elemental Line, Tanking and Melee Damage with Enhancement, and Healing Through the Restoration Line

PROFESSIONS

There is an entire section devoted to professions and other trades later in the guide, yet several aspects of the crafting system are worth developing here for incoming players. This section uncovers the basics of choosing your professions, the terminology of the system, and how to know what you are looking for in-game.

WHAT ARE PROFESSIONS?

Professions cover the resource gathering and item creation systems in World of Warcraft. Each character is allowed to learn and maintain two professions, and doing so can be used for profit, improved equipment and usable items, or simply for the enjoyment of supporting friends/your guild.

List of Professions

Profession	Purpose	Benefits
Alchemy	Create Potions/Transmute Metals	Temporary Attribute Enhancement, Create High-End Metals, Elemental Transmutes
Blacksmithing	Forge Weapons, Chain/Plate Armor, and Peripheral Equipment	Increase Weapon Damage and Speed (for 2H), Improve Shields, Increase Mount Speed
Enchanting	Improve Equipment, Used to Create Goods used by Others	Sell Enchantments for Profit, Raise Attributes on Gear (Very Expensive Until High-Tier, Then Profits Are Immense)
Engineering	Construct Bombs, Rifles, and Accessories	Battle Pets, AoE Explosives, Ammunition, Scopes for Ranged Weapons
Herbalism	Gather Herbs	Ingredients for Alchemy, Sell for High Profit
Leatherworking	Make Leather Armor, Ammo Quivers/Pouches, and Armor Patches	Add Bonuses to Ranged Combat, Increase Armor Rating
Mining	Mine Metal	Ingredients for Blacksmithing and Engineering, Sell for High Profit
Skinning	Skin Beast Corpses for Leather	Ingredients for Leatherworking, Sell for Profit
Tailoring	Sew Cloth Armor and Items, Make Bags	Sell Bags to Other Characters

Professions have trainers (just like classes) that are found in small towns and large cities alike. There are higher concentrations of trainers in the capitals, and so much trade happens there that people often seek those specific trainers to do most of their work.

Trainers are needed to initially grab a profession, but they are also needed to gain new tiers of skill, and to pick up extra recipes for various items. All of these projects cost money, so it is often a question of much how time and money you wish to invest in a profession. In the later stages, some professions are worth sizable fortunes (especially the ones that gather resources for other professions). As long as you are willing to throw the extra energy into these skills, they are quite lucrative in the long run.

Learning how to create various items does not stop at the trainer. Hidden recipes can be found on monsters and special vendors around the world.

 Talk to other crafters to find out more about the locations of these items (and read the tables in our Crafting and Professions Chapter for more info as well).

WHAT ARE SECONDARY SKILLS?

List of Secondary Skills

Skill	Purpose	Benefits
Cooking	Create Food/Fires	Reduce Downtime w/ Food and Spirit Buffs
First Aid	Stitch Bandages	Allow for Fast Healing of Moderate Damage
Fishing	Collect Items from Water	Ingredients for Cooking, Spare Equipment, Find Recipes for Other Trades

Secondary Skills aren't limited by anything except time and money. Each character can take these skills whether they are interested in professions or not. In fact, many soloers take all three skills to reduce downtime and increase their self-sufficiency without losing constant money on store-bought food and such.

TRANSPORTATION

World of Warcraft takes place in Azeroth, a land that cannot be crossed quickly. There is much to see and do out there, and it sure helps to know how to get around! This section explains what the various means of transportation are, what their cost is, and what you can do to save the most time at the best prices.

POUNDING THE DIRT

> Cost: None
> Making it Cheaper: No Need
> Making it Better: Boot Enchantment (Run Speed Increase)

The most basic form of transportation is to walk anywhere that you need to go. Though this is a very slow method, it certainly isn't costly. From level 1 forward, your character is going to do quite a bit of this. Even at the higher levels, when you have mounts at your disposal, walking is the primary means of travel within Instances and in areas where the monsters are plentiful (no need to waste time mounting when you can simple engage another target).

There are a few ways to enhance your basic walking speed. There are boot enchantments to add several percent to this (though modest, such enchantments certainly add up over longer distances or for PvP, when any bonus can be critical). Certain boots even come with a movement speed enchancement!

FLIGHT PATHS

> Cost: Modest Copper or Silver
> Making it Cheaper: Rep/PvP Rank Reduce Cost 10%
> Making it Better: Not Possible

One of the most common forms of fast transport is to take the flight paths around Azeroth. Both factions have flight masters in just about every major city and town. The first time that you see a new flight master there is a green mark above their head to let you know that there is a new route to discover! Right click on the NPC to learn the route; after that point you can fly to and from that point without any problems (so long as you know at least one path that connects to the one in question).

Each character starts with the flight location from the nearby capital city. Most paths, however, you need to find by exploring the world. The first flight paths you are likely to actually discover are in The Barrens, Silverpine, Westfall, Loch Modan, or Darkshore.

After learning your flight paths, right click again on these NPCs to display a map of the continent you are currently on. From there, you get a view of all the points that connect to your current location. Highlight any of these to see the total cost for flying there, then left-click to select your target. These flights take several minutes, usually, but the trip is still a great deal faster than walking. Beyond that, you are free to go /afk and take care of looking up information, taking bio breaks, and so forth.

BOATS AND ZEPPELINS

Cost:	None
Making it Cheaper:	None
Making it Better:	None

Boats and Zeppelins are provided as free forms of intercontinental travel. These are slower, in that you often have to wait for a modest period before the craft arrives, but characters without access to an appropriate Mage or Warlock have little choice in the matter.

Once a sea vessel or airship arrives, step onto the craft and wait for it to leave. There is a brief time for everyone to board, then the craft leaves the area. There is a loading period, and before long everyone should arrive safely at their destination. Note that jumping off of the zeppelins from very high altitudes can and will kill your character. Do not follow people off unless you are sure that you will be okay (this is most often an issue with the Tirisfal Glades tower, where people sometimes leap off early after Rogues or Mages who have means to reduce their falling damage).

In very odd cases where lag is high, a vessel might dump you. If that happens, try to reach land or safe water before your character dies from fatigue. In the case of falling off of a zeppelin from lag, simply retrieve your body and move on. When dumped too far out in the water, Rez at the Spirit Healer and move on. This happens so rarely that with a few thousand hours logged into WoW with the writing team, most have never seen this happen.

Zeppelins

Location	Access To
East of Orgrimmar	Grom'gol (Stranglethorn Vale) and Undercity (Tirisfal Glades)
Grom'gol Basecamp	Orgrimmar (Durotar) and Undercity (Tirisfal Glades)
North of Undercity	Grom'gol (Stranglethorn Vale) and Orgrimmar (Durotar)

Boats

Location	Access To
Auberdine	Rut'theran Village (Teldrassil), Menethil Harbor (Wetlands), Theramore (Dustwallow Marsh)
Booty Bay	Ratchet (The Barrens)
Menethil Harbor	Auberdine (Darkshore), Theramore (Dustwallow Marsh)
Ratchet	Booty Bay (Stranglethorn Vale)
Rut'theran Village	Auberdine (Darkshore)
Theramore	Auberdine (Darkshore), Menethil Harbor (Wetlands)
Western Feralas	Short Trip to Feathermoon

AZEROTH

THE DEEPRUN TRAM

The Deeprun Tram runs between Stormwind and Ironforge. Look in the north-east side of Stormwind, in the Dwarven Quarter, for one entrance to this free transport. Or, in Ironforge, seek Tinker Town.

Step onto the Tram when it arrives and wait for the journey to commence. This is a very short trip and even saves time over flying in a number of cases. You must stay alert on the Tram though, otherwise you miss your destination and end up on the return trip!

TRAVEL FORMS AND ABILITIES

HUNTERS: ASPECT OF THE CHEETAH/PACK

Hunters learn Aspect of the Cheetah at level 20; this Aspect lets them move at 130% run speed, making it very useful to reach locations quickly. Switching between Aspects is instant, and this is another great boon. Hunters can immediately shift to a higher speed when there aren't any enemies nearby, then switch back as danger approaches.

At level 40, Aspect of the Pack is learned. This Aspect grants the same power of Aspect of the Cheetah to all group members within range. Getting through cleared areas of Instances has never been easier than with a Hunter using AotP!

The danger of these Aspects, and the reason they aren't used during battle, is that anyone under the influence of either Aspect is immediately dazed if they are damaged. Daze slows your character down greatly, and negates any of the benefits you were receiving from having the buff in the first place. Thus, take Aspect of the Cheetah off as soon as there is anything nasty approaching. In PvP especially, **beware Aspect of the Pack**. Everyone in your group getting dazed because of your mistake is going to cause a few sharp comments.

SHAMAN: GHOST WOLF

Shamans learn how to shift into their Ghost Wolf form at level 20. This form increases movement to 140% run speed. Only usable outdoors, this form is of great benefit for running around in the Battlegrounds, getting to quest locations, or for making herbing/mining runs. Through the use of Talents, Shamans can make their Ghost Wolf form faster to cast (in the heat of the Battlegrounds, this is a huge benefit). Certain class items and Talents together make Ghost Wolf even better by increasing run speed to a level that rivals that of a standard mount.

SHAMAN: ASTRAL RECALL

Astral Recall allows Shamans to essentially Hearth back to their bind point more often than normal characters. You can still use your Hearthstone normally, and when it is down, casting Astral Recall gets you home just as easily.

DRUID: TRAVEL FORM

Though not learned until level 30, Druid Travel Form is very fast and useful. Moving at 140% of normal run speed, this form also adds the advantage of ditching movement debuffs during the Shapeshift and also protects the caster from Polymorph spells. Druids make wonderful runners in the Battlegrounds because of this, so long as their team is able to stop intercepting characters. In the 30-39 bracket, before mounts are introduced, Druids are the supreme flag runners of Warsong Gulch.

ROGUE: SPRINT

Rogue Sprint is a sudden burst of movement speed that lasts for 15 seconds (there is a five minute cooldown between uses). There are three ranks of Sprint, so the buff to movement increases as your character levels. This is a great ability for getting out of trouble, running flags in the Battlegrounds, moving at impressive speeds even while Stealthed, and so forth.

WARRIOR: CHARGE AND INTERCEPT

Warriors don't have a lot of abilities for getting around, but a clever Warrior learns to make their own path. While trying to run through groups of grey or green monsters in the levels before you own a mount, use Charge and later Intercept as well to leap forward. If you don't want to fight the monsters, Hamstring them and move on. Over time, this method truly does get you where you are going faster (and it's darn funny to watch).

MOUNTS

The first tier of mounts are available after reaching character level 40. These cost 100 gold pieces before any discounts are given; a portion of the money goes toward learning how to actually ride such a creature, and the remaining money is for the purchase of the actual mount (20 gold pieces to learn riding, 80 gold pieces to get the mount itself).

Note that you can only learn how to ride a mount in your faction's capital from someone of the same race. Unless, that is, you reach Exalted reputation with other race (e.g. orcs can learn to ride Tauren Kodos **if** they reached Exalted status with Thunder Bluff).

Once you learn how to ride a mount, you can buy multiple mounts if you wish (though there is seldom a good reason to buy another mount until you reach level 60). At that time, epic mounts become available. Though extremely expensive, costing 1000 gold pieces before discounts, epic mounts travel faster than normal mounts and look better as well.

Once you own a mount, equip it to bind the mount to you, then place the icon on one of your quickbars for easy access. Mounting takes several seconds, so it is only useful for trips that take longer than six or so seconds. In other words, don't mount to move 50 yards and attack another creature. Dismounting is done by using the mount a second time **or** right-clicking on the buff icon that appears while you are riding.

There are several things that automatically dismount your character. Going indoors does this, as you cannot stay mounted in most indoor locations. Walking through water dismounts everyone too, so jump as far as you can when entering water. Certain types of crowd control also force a dismount (e.g. Polymorph).

WARLOCKS AND PALADINS GET FREE MOUNTS

At level 40, Warlocks and Paladins receive quests to find their own mounts. These mounts have a specific appearance, cost nothing, and are fully functional in every way. This is quite a nice financial boon to these classes!

SUMMONING AND PORTALS

As has been discussed in this guide, Mages and Warlocks have travel powers that help people to move immediately over immense distances. Mages past level 40 can portal entire teams from their current location to some of the major cities for their faction. Warlocks past level 20, on the other hand, use the souls of downed enemies to call group members to themselves.

MAGE TELEPORTS AND PORTALS

At levels 20 and 30, Mages master the ability to teleport themselves to the various capital cities of their faction. This requires a special reagent (Rune of Teleportation, found on Reagent Vendors). Because of this power, Mages should set their Hearthstones in the areas where they quest for experience and use teleportation to head back to capital cities. That way, the Mages almost never need to use slower forms of transportation except when moving into new areas entirely.

At levels 40 and 50, Mages can use these spells in a portal form, allowing other characters to instantly teleport as well. This requires a different reagent (a Rune of Portals). People who request such a service from Mages are likely to tip them for the immense time saved! These gateways last for a short period, and even people not in the Mage's group will be able to use the portals. Thus, folks who are on one continent are often able to save a huge amount of travel time by tipping a Mage 20 or more silver to open a portal to the other continent.

Warlock Summoning

- The Ritual of Summoning Requires a Level 20 or Higher Warlock, Two Group Members already with the Warlock, and the Desired Teleportee to be in Group as Well
- Warlocks Need to Use Soul Shards to Summon; This Also Takes Time, So Love/Tip Your Warlocks
- You Cannot Summon Someone Outside an Instance Into an Instance (They Must Zone Into the Instance Before Being Summoned)

After level 20, Warlocks can use their Ritual of Summoning to bring a person in their group to their current locations. The Warlock needs everyone involved to be in their group already. At least two people must already be with the Warlock to assist in creating the summoning portal, and the Warlock has to have Soul Shards on hand already. Soul Shards are gained by killing creatures while using Drain Soul on them. The Warlock casts the spell and remains in a channeling state while the two characters with the Warlock right click on the appearing portal.

To prevent a certain number of casual exploits with dungeon content, it was made impossible to summon characters outside of an Instance into that Instance. Thus, if a Warlock is already inside of a dungeon or similar place, the desired character must enter the Instance portal before summoning is usable on them, unless the Warlock and Assistants leave the instance.

The box in the lower-left is for any item that you wish to send. Though soul-bound items cannot be sent through the mail, just about anything else can be. Also, type in any numbers for the gold, silver, and copper slots nearby to either send money to the person as well **or** to create a sell price for the item you are sending. The default is to send money, but the buttons in the lower right can be used to change this to COD if you like (Cash on Delivery). By doing so, the other person must pay the amount you type in to receive the item you are sending. COD can be held up to 30 days before purchase, so use wisely.

Scammers

You won't likely run into this during your World of Warcraft experience, but there are a few people who try to scam people out of money by sending items COD. If you get a gift-wrapped package of some sort from a person that you don't know, don't accept the charges. It's probably just a fish or something equally worthless.

The Mail System

The World of Warcraft mail system is extremely useful, easy to use, and costs very little. For just coppers a day, you can contact other members of your faction and send them letters, money, goods, or even sell items (through the Cash on Delivery system). This is a wonderful function of the game, and everyone should know about it.

What Can I Do?

- Mail Costs 30 Copper Pieces to Send
- Letters, Money, and Auction Items/ Receipts Arrive Almost Instantly
- Items Take One Hour to Deliver
- You Can Send Your Alts Items/Money Directly Through the Mail (No Worrying About Middlemen!)

While standing near a mailbox, right click on the object. This brings up the mail screen. You are shown a list of pending messages, if there are any for your character. This Inbox screen is the default. Look at the tab on the bottom of the box and click on "Send Mail" to switch modes. From there, you can type in a character to send the mail to, a subject header, and any text for the body of your email.

WHERE CAN I DO IT?

- Mailboxes Look Slightly Different Between Regions, But Are Often Found by Inns or Banks (Highlight Them With Your Mouse to be Sure)

You can use these functions at any mailbox in either continent. The visual appearance of mailboxes is determined by region, but the general look of them remains similar. Also, you can find mailboxes in the same type of places throughout the world (near Inns and Banks most commonly). Mailboxes are placed in both major cities and minor towns, so it's very rare that you need to Hearth back just to take care of some mail.

HOW CAN I SEND GIFTS?

There are shops in the major cities where you can buy gift-wrapping paper. Right click on the paper, once purchased from a general vendor, then select the item you wish to wrap. Afterward, send the desired package in the mail to a friend!

Auction Houses: Gateway to Wealth

Auction Houses offer far more to the game than players might first suspect. These places are great meeting grounds for trade, and the wealth that pours from their vaults each day is legion. Use this section to learn about the tricks of the trade in WoW's Auction Houses.

Icon	Picture of the item; Highlight this specifically to see the stats of the piece in question
Name of Item	Just the name
Minimum Level to Use/Equip Item	Useful for looking ahead and getting equipment to grow into
Time Left in Auction	Gives you an idea for the duration until the auction expires
Seller	Knowing the name might allow you to whisper and person and ask about where they found such a recipe, if they can make more of an item, etc.
Current Bid and Buyout Price	The top number on the right side is the current bid (you must bid a higher number to have a chance at the time); the lower number is the buyout price

THE BASICS

The first point of order is to learn how the Auction House is used. When you have items to sell or want to search for goodies to buy, travel to one of the capital cities in your faction (Orgrimmar, Thunder Bluff, or Undercity for Horde; Stormwind, Ironforge, or Darnassus for Alliance). Or, if you are reaching the higher levels, consider the neutral AHs (in Gadgetzan, Everlook, and Booty Bay). It is less expensive to use your faction's AHs, as the neutral ones charge a higher fee.

Once you find the NPCs who are listed as Auctioneers, right-click on them to open the Auction House. From here, you can browse for items to buy, check on current bids, and place your treasure up for auction.

BUYING

From the initial screen you can browse and purchase items. At the top are systems to help you search for specific items. These filters allow you to search by:

Name	Type in a portion of an item's name or a type of stat modifier (such as Power, Falcon, etc.)
Level Range	Choose a minimum or maximum level for the item
Rarity	Choose the minimum quality level of the items (Rare would display blue items and onward)
Usable Items (Yes/No)	Will constrain results to items that you character can currently equip or use

Remember that equipment, usable items (potions, ammo, bandages, etc.), trade goods, and all manner of random drops can be found in the Auction House. Search through the entire AH at least once to get an idea for the scope of these auctions.

When you actually find an item you want, look at the display that appears on the main portion of the Auction House window; highlight the item you are interested in and read the information on that line. From left to right, there is the following type of data:

Bidding on an item starts the war to see if you can wait out any other buyers. Auctions can be placed for as long as 24 hours, so only auctions listed at short (under 30 minutes), or medium (30 minutes to 2 hours) are going to close soon without a buyout. Once your bid is down, the game notifies you if another bidder comes forward on the item (and your existing bid money will return to your mailbox). If you really want a specific item but it has no buyout or one that you cannot afford, stay close to the Auction House when the Time Left reaches short and stay on top of the bidding.

A buyout immediately takes the full price for the listed item from you supplies, ends the auction, and mails the item to your mailbox. This is often rather costly for major pieces, but trade goods and lower-level items are usually bought out without the process being too painful.

SELLING

Click on the third tab of the Auction House window (Auctions) to switch into selling mode. From here, drag and drop an item that you wish to post into the Auction Item box on the left. The default Starting Price that appears below is quite minimal, but it is enough to cover your costs. This default is useful for items of lower value that don't require a major investment of time to sell carefully.

Below that is the Auction Duration selection. Choose either a 2-hour run, an 8-hour auction (the default), or post the item for 24-hours. The deposit you pay to the Auction House will not be refunded if the item does not sell, and the price of said deposit increases proportionally with the duration of your auction. Still, many items are worth posting for 24-hours if you want to put them up at all. Give people the time to notice your goods, especially if you are posting items during off-hours.

If is entirely optional whether you want to post a buyout price for your items. Most of the time, it is very much in your interest to do this; many players aren't interested in start a buying war, especially for minor purchases. Trade goods, usable items, and even equipment are treats that people don't want to monitor, wait for, and potentially lose. Post a buyout price to allow the less patient buyers to grab what they want instantly. Your price can be a single copper higher than the starting price, or it can be immensely higher. There are reasons to go in either direction, and these are discussed shortly.

If you post an auction and suddenly find that you have changed your mind, select that item in the auctions tab and look at the bottom of your window. There is an option to close auctions; though you lose your deposit forever, this is **extremely** useful if you accidentally post something far below its value. Get it back soon! A few sharp buyers are watching the Auction Houses almost every hour of every day.

BEYOND THE BASICS

Most people learn quickly how to use the Auction House. It's so useful that you can hardly live without it sometimes. But there are many players who never actually stop and consider how much money there is to be made here. A level 15 character that has scrounged together a single gold piece can start an empire of wealth by wheeling and dealing on the AH.

BUY LOW, SELL HIGH

The old adage is both trite and truthful. The trick is to learn how low is for a given type of item and to figure out what high price the market will bear when selling. If you really want to master the Auction House on your server, keep a logbook for common item prices near your computer.

For items that are sold frequently (e.g. cloth, leather, potions), you can find the current prices quickly by searching as a buyer. See what other sellers are trying to get for their goods. You can post your auctions at a mere 5 silver discount and get some easy sales if everyone is clumping around the same price. As long as you aren't putting up much material, you aren't likely to start a seller's war.

One of the best ways to sell high is to sell when there aren't a lot of items being posted of the given type. If you check as a buyer and see a full page of Briarthorn, today might not be a good day to sell your stack (put it in the bank and wait). When you search late the next evening and see one or two other stacks, it is a very good time to sell. Even if sellers post low prices when there aren't many items for sale, try for a higher price anyway. Remember that those great deals are likely to buyout early. After that, your goods are the ones setting the price trend.

For goods that are always in demand for crafters and such, the middle of the week is a solid selling time; you won't have nearly as much competition. For equipment pieces, the weekends are better (because there are more buyers online, but sellers may not have the equipment pieces to compete with you). Trade goods are a more consistent market; the scarcity of good equipment pieces makes it possible to gouge people tremendously when there are more folks on.

HIGH IN A BRACKET

Selling to PvPers in a great way to make money. Rare items that are levels x6-x9 in a given bracket are often worth a huge sum (e.g. level 16-19, 26-29). When selling these goods, be sure to start high. Losing a deposit, even a couple times, is not that big a deal compared to the long-term potential for a huge sale. Thus, don't undercut others who are selling similar items that don't drop as often. Wait, post your item a few times, and wait for that magical buyer to appear.

Rogue and Hunter twink gear is the best of all. There are always players creating PvP characters for the lower brackets. Thus, you can charge even more for powerful goods at the low levels when the items are for those classes. Level 16-19 Rogue gear can and does fetch hundreds of gold. Hunt through Shadowfang Keep looking for a lucky Bind-on-Equip drop, and you might just fund your character all the way into the 40s.

Don't feel guilty for gouging twink PvPers. The majority of those players have high-level characters already, more gold than they can handle, and are overgearing their characters in an attempt to dominate a given bracket. Almost nobody on the other side of the field is going to love the twinks, and even a number of people on their own side find this practice "weak" or "cheesy." So, gouge away! They can afford it.

NICHE MARKETS

With work and some investment, you can corner a specific market, at least for a time. To do this, you must take the risk and buyout everything below a price threshold that you decide on. Afterward, you repost those items at your price and maintain an alert watch on the AH to keep the process going until other people naturally post their goods at the new price.

By maintaining a niche, you stand to make a fair sum, even while other sellers benefit from your work. If a specific group of sellers band together to undercut you and post at times when you aren't guarding the AH, the process must be started again.

GUILD CREATION AND UPKEEP

So you've decided that you want to start a guild. Guilds are an integral part of the game, allowing like-minded players to join together to achieve goals, not to mention getting to wear a really cool tabard. In explaining guilds, we'll cover the formation of a guild and its upkeep.

FORMING THE GUILD

A charter is the first item required on your path to having a guild. Charters may be purchased from Guild Masters located in each of the major cities. Local guards are quite eager to point the way, so it shouldn't be too hard to the necessary NPCs.

Alliance Charters	
City	NPC
Darnassus	Lysheana
Ironforge	Jondor Steelbrow
Stormwind City	Aldwin Laughlin

Horde Charters	
City	NPC
Orgrimmar	Urtrun Clanbringer
Thunder Bluff	Krumn
Undercity	Christopher Drakul

Crowning Another

There is a safeguard in place that prevents the guild from disbanding if a guild leader chooses to quit in the heat of the moment. A guild leader may not quit without designating another leader for the guild. This is not the case however if the guild leader chooses the /gdisband option.

When you purchase your charter you are asked to supply a name for your guild. Be sure to choose an appropriate (non-offensive) name. Give the name some thought and allow it to express your guild and what it stands for. In the wee hours of the morning after you've been smashing Murlocs for hours on end, the name "Crazy Murloc Deathbringers" might sound completely appropriate. However, shorter names that roll off the tongue with ease are quite successful. Your guild tag will catch the attention of players, so be sure it's the kind of attention you're seeking.

Here's a suggestion that alleviates frustration when purchasing the charter; be sure to have two or three alternate versions of your guild name that you're comfortable with. Many times a name will be disallowed by Blizzard if it has been taken by another group.

Charters cost ten silver pieces and require 9 additional "signatures" for completion. This is easy if you have 9 friends running around waiting to come to your aid. However, many guilds are started by soliciting the aid of low-level characters in the starter zones. There is also a guild recruiting channel available in large cities where you can broadcast your new guild and need for signatures. Each signature must come from a separate account. In other words you can't have your buddy log onto his account and sign nine times with all of his characters. People who are already in guilds are also unable to sign your charter.

Once you have all of your signatures, return to the Guild Master and submit the charter.

Congratulations! Your guild has been formed. Each of the players who signed your charter receive a system message informing them that they are a founding member of your guild. These players automatically receive a default rank of "Member." The person who purchased the charter becomes the initial "Leader" of the guild.

Guild Commands	
COMMAND	ACTION PERFORMED
/ginfo	Basic information about your guild
/g <message>	Sends chat text to all members of the guild
/o <message>	Sends chat text to all officers and leaders of the guild
/ginvite <player>	Invites player to join your guild
/gremove <player>	Removes player from guild
/gpromote <player>	Promotes player one rank
/gdemote <player>	Demotes player one rank
/gmotd <message>	Guild message seen by all members upon login to game
/gquit	Removes you from a guild
/groster	Provides a complete roster for guild (accessible to officers and leaders only)
/gleader <player>	Changes guild leader to chosen player. (guild leader command only)
/gdisband	Permanently disbands guild

You may also perform many guild commands through the guild screen. This screen can be opened by hitting the "O" key. Click on the "Guild" tab at the bottom of the screen to view information about your guild.

THE GUILD SCREEN

The guild screen shows members who are currently online. At the top of the screen you'll see "Show Offline Members." By clicking the box you'll be able to view a complete guild roster.

Name	The character's name
Zone	Location of the character
Level	That character's level
Class	The class of that guild member

GUILD COMMANDS

There are basic commands that guild leaders and officers use to perform certain actions while running a guild. The table below includes all of the current text commands for guild actions.

At the bottom of this list you'll see "Show Player Status." Click on the arrow icon to display additional guild status information.

You may sort each section by clicking on the title. For example if you click on "Level" the roster will be sorted by character level from lowest to highest or vice versa if you click one more time.

By highlighting a member name and clicking on it you bring up an additional box that displays information for that particular player. Members who have been designated may demote, promote, or remove at this screen. Regular members may invite the selected character to a group by clicking "Group Invite" at the bottom right of the box.

RANK

The player's position in the guild as determined by the officers of the guild or by those members who are designated to alter ranks.

NOTE

This section is for public notes regarding the character. Only designated members may enter information here. It can be used to list Professions, let people know if this is an alt, or for inside jokes.

LAST ONLINE

Shows the last time the player was online. This is a useful tool for officers when tracking player activity.

GUILD FUNCTIONALITY

Guilds are created with 5 default ranks:

- Initiate
- Member
- Veteran
- Officer
- Leader

Only the guild leader may rename, add or remove ranks. A guild must have a minimum of five ranks and may create up to the maximum of ten ranks. When creating new ranks the system automatically makes the newest rank entered the entry level rank. Take care to enter your ranks from highest to lowest when creating new ones for your guild.

To add new ranks click on the "Guild Control" tab at the bottom right hand corner of the guild screen. Enter the rank name into the "Rank Label." Set the permissions for each rank by checking off the boxes that are appropriate.

Permissions

Command	Function
Speech	The member is allowed to enter text into the guild channel
Officerchat Listen	Allow designated members to read conversations in the officer chat channel
Officerchat Speak	Designated members can type messages in the officer chat channel
Promote	Members can promote other members of the guild
Demote	Members can demote other members of the guild
Invite Member	Members are permitted to invite players to the guild
Remove Player	Members can remove members from the guild
Set Motd	Member has the ability to set the guild message of the day
Edit Public Note	Member is able to edit public notes
View Officer Note	Member is able to view notes written by officers for players
Edit Officer Note	Member is able to change hidden officer notes for each player on the roster

RUNNING YOUR GUILD

Beyond the command, tabard, and charter, there is a great deal of social management that goes into a guild. A huge number of guilds run into problems with their player base at some time or another (bored, anxiety about end-game matters, ego conflicts, drama, and so forth). A skilled guild leader needs to be far more than a good player; these leaders need to be listeners, enforcers, and diplomats. It's not always easy, or sometimes even possible, to fill all of these roles at once! Sound a little intimidating? It should. Don't get involved with guild leadership unless you truly are ready and willing to devote some time and energy into herding cats!

Rules

Creating a good foundation for a guild ensures a long, productive existence for it. This also promotes players who are happy to be members of that guild. If you haven't already done so, create a set of rules for guild members. Keep the rules simple. No one wants to read 43 pages of rules and regulations just to become a member of a guild. Games are meant to be fun and guilds are meant to enhance that experience. You can always adjust the rules as the need arises during the course of your adventures in Azeroth.

COMMON GUILD ISSUES

- Loot Distribution
- Proper PvE and PvP Conduct
- Language Restrictions
- Required Play, Grouping, Etc.
- Roleplaying Matters

Most disputes within guilds arise from arguments over items. When creating your set of guild rules pay close attention to "Loot Rules." Once again, keep them simple. Members need to be aware of rules pertaining to item drops prior to venturing into Instances. Go over rules pertaining to item drops at the start of every group run. Yes, you've said them 100 times before, but stating the rules at the beginning of run through a dungeon alleviates arguments later (usually).

Make sure that members have easy access to these rules at all times.

LOOT DISTRIBUTION

Usually loot issues are easier to handle for the sub-60 levels. Many guilds are going to go with some form of Need Before Greed and stick to it. With the later levels, however, this is a big push to come up with a system for "fairly" distributing Epic loot (and beyond). DKPs, or Dragon Kill Points are used heavily by a number of WoW guilds to try and ensure that people who invest the most time in guild raids get the gear that they want. Other guilds may try to encourage Need Before Greed and rolling even in the raid instances, though this is not as common.

CONDUCT

Some guilds have standards of conduct even with people outside of the guild (or with the opposing faction). You may have things so that guild members must always accept duels, never run from PvP fights in the world, avoid Graveyard Camping for any reason, don't spit, or whatever else. These rules are highly subjective, based on the guild's interests, and should be adhered to by guild members. Anyone who signs on and understands the rules is free to walk away if they disagree.

If a guild member consistently breaks the rules of conduct, use a system of warnings and eventually remove the person from the guild if they are causing internal drama or strife. Be sure that the warning system is in writing, is fair, and is applied evenly whenever possible.

LANGUAGE RESTRICTIONS

If some words are taboo in your guild, be clear about it, correct people when they slip, and be very consistent. There isn't much to say about this matter, save that quite a few guild members have sore points about one word or another. Be sensible and treat guild chat as a large table in the middle of a restaurant; everyone can hear you, even strangers might catch an odd bit of conversation, and feelings can easily be hurt.

REQUIRED PLAY

Larger guilds may require a certain level of playtime per week/month for a person to stay in the guild. This may even be restricted to specific activities (members must participate in one MC/BWL Raid per week, members must put in ten hours of BG time per week). Be very clear with all new members about these requirements.

The trickiest time of all is when your guild considers placing new requirements on members. This is the type of scenario that splits guilds (sometimes taking even the members that wanted the change in the first place). Be very careful of placing demands on your player base.

ROLEPLAYING

Roleplaying guilds may have extra rules to demand that guild chat be IC (in character). For guilds of this sort, there is often a chat channel used on the side for speech outside of your character.

Forums

No one expects you to rush out and purchase a hosting plan or have someone design an elaborate Flash site for the guild. There are many free forum hosting sites available on the web.

On this site, place your guild rules in plain view for members and potential members.

Forums are great for posting information on dungeon crawls, roleplaying events, and guild communication. Be sure to setup a forum for Officers so that issues can be posted for all members in leadership positions.

THE TABARD VIEWER

Guild tabard designs are purchased from the Guild Master in major cities. Speak to the Guild Master and select "I'd like to create a Guild Crest." A guild tabard design may only be purchased by the guild leader but members may view the selections available.

Tabard Creation

Icon	The image that appears on the front and back of the member tabard. Click the directional arrows to browse the available icons
Icon Color	Selects the icon color
Border	Selects the style of border for the tabard
Border Color	Select the border color
Background	Select the overall color for the tabard

CHOOSING OFFICERS

A common drive when choosing officers is to hand out ranks to close friends, but this might not be the best choice for the guild. When you choose officers, be sure to select those players who have proven leadership skills and the ability to arbitrate disputes between members. Everyone handles things differently and it's a good idea to have a diversified group of people as officers.

Use promotions as rewards for dedication to the guild. Players want to upgrade their characters and there are many players who enjoy earning rank within the guild structure.

As a leader, remember to trust your officers and support their decisions. You've taken the time to select them and put them in charge; don't hover over them.

RECRUITING

There are many ways to recruit members for your guild. There is no right or wrong way. Recruiting processes should be determined by your vision for the guild.

Do you want a guild with hundreds of members? Perhaps you want a small guild that will focus on exploring all of the content that the game provides. Guilds come in all sizes as well as types. Some guilds massively recruit members by issuing random invites in starter zones. A lot of role playing guilds use an interview process.

Do what's best for you and your guild.

THE TABARD

Admit it. We all love those tabards. They show the community that we're all together in everything we do. Tabard selection can be a process that the guild leader handles or it can be a guild decision. Many guilds have members contribute what they can toward the purchase of the guild design. Tabard designs cost ten gold pieces. Individual tabards cost one gold piece (and are influenced by faction and PvP discounts).

Once you've made a choice for each selection click "Accept." The tabard design will appear on your equipped tabard. If members have trouble viewing the design on their tabards this is remedied with a quick logout and login.

GUILD EVENTS

Even the most hardcore "lone wolf" player enjoys a planned guild event. Be sure to post the event several days in advance so that members can arrange to be present. The typical event is completing quests in an "Instance." These events bring experience and item upgrades for members.

REWARDS AND DISCIPLINE

Reward good behavior and punish bad behavior. No guild leader is perfect and sometimes members step over the line in regard to rules. Your members look to you and your officers to maintain the guild environment they expected when they joined. Offensive conversation in the guild channel, bad conduct on a guild raid, or constant belligerence can undermine a guild quickly if not dealt with just as quickly.

Reward members who show dedication to the guild. You don't have to empty your coin purse to do so. Acknowledging the generosity of a player's time, skills, and knowledge is just as good. You can create special ranks to show praise, have a forum for "Guild Mate of the Month," or an event to honor the player(s). A little praise goes a long way!

The secret to being a great guild leader or having a great guild is respect for the players who bear the tabard. The friendships that can develop from guild membership can be some of the most rewarding out there.

DUNGEONS AND RAIDS

What is the Difference Between a Dungeon and a Raid?

At the core, there is only one difference between a dungeon group and a raid. Dungeon groups have a maximum of 5 characters while Raids have anywhere from 6 to 40. This very simple distinction makes the two very different however. As the size of a group increases, specialization in each character is fundamentally necessary.

Dungeons

Instance Dungeons in World of Warcraft should be done in groups of five. Instances often allow as many as ten, but quests are not able to be completed.

ROLES IN A DUNGEON

Role Table		
Role	Responsibility	Classes
Tank	Gather, Maintain, and Survive Aggro	Warrior, Druid, Paladin, Shaman
Secondary Tank (Off-tank)	Pull Aggro from non-tank members	Warrior, Druid, Paladin, Shaman, Warlock, Hunter
Healer	Keep Party Members Alive	Priest, Druid, Shaman, Paladin
Crowd Control (CC)	Neutralize Enemies	Mage, Rogue, Hunter, Priest, Warlock
Damage (DPS)	Kill Enemies	Rogue, Mage, Warlock, Hunter, Druid
Area of Effect Damage (AoE)	Damage multiple enemies at once	Mage, Warlock, Hunter, Warrior, Druid, Priest
Resurrection (Rez)	Revive Fallen Members	Priest, Shaman, Paladin, Druid
Wipe Recovery	Resurrect or Survive a Total Party Wipe	Paladin, Warlock, Shaman, Engineer

That's More Than Five Roles!

While you are limited to five members in your party, there are many jobs to do. Many characters can fill multiple roles. A Priest can be Healer, Crowd Control, and Resurrection while a Hunter can be Secondary Tank, Damage, and Crowd Control.

Some roles take more attention than others. No one should ever be both Tank and Healer. It's too much responsibility and doesn't work.

Tank

As one of the most important roles, a good tank can make a party while a bad tank can break one. The party tank should start the fights to get early aggro, and use abilities to maintain the aggro. Often this is done after all forms of CC are in effect.

WARRIOR

Warriors make the best tanks. They have the heaviest armor (mail until level 40 when they learn to wear plate), can use a shield, have abilities to hold single enemies, and abilities to hold multiple enemies. Taunt and Mocking Blow are useful to pull an enemy's attention off another party member while Sunder Armor and Heroic Strike cause higher threat and are useful for keeping an enemy on you. When all goes wrong, Challenging Shout pulls all enemies in range onto you. Combine these abilities with Defensive Stance, Demoralizing Shout, Shield Block, and Shield Wall and you've seen the very basic abilities a Warrior can bring to the table as a tank.

DRUID

At first, Druids seem like a poor choice as a tank. Their leather armor doesn't stand up to much. Only Druids using Bear Form or Dire Bear Form should be considered for the role of tank. Speccing in the Feral talent tree makes you even more effective. As a bear (or dire bear), the Druid's armor is increased greatly and they gain access to a number of abilities that help them substitute nicely. Feral Charge and Maul work well to keep a single target's attention, while Swipe and Demoralizing Roar affect multiple enemies. With a Druid as your tank, your group needs to be careful about focusing fire as the Druid doesn't have as many ways to quickly peel aggro off other members.

PALADIN

Like Warriors, Paladins have access to the heaviest armor in the game (mail until level 40 when they learn to wear plate) and can equip a shield. This combined with their ability to heal themselves, can make the Paladin extremely durable as a tank. They aren't quite as effective with holding aggro as a Warrior, but they have a number of abilities to aid them. Blessing of Salvation keeps other party members from drawing as much threat. Blessing of Sanctuary reduces all damage, while Seal of Justice and Hammer of Justice can stun an enemy to further reduce the damage they deal. Righteous Fury multiplies the threat generated by the Paladin's holy spells. Used in conjunction with Holy Shield and Consecrate, this creates a decent amount of threat. Paladins are very good at reducing the damage enemies can deal to a party, but not as talented at maintaining the attention of several enemies. Keep your parties fire focused when using a Paladin as tank.

SHAMAN

Of all the classes that can perform the role of tank, Shaman are the most dangerous. They have several tools to hold aggro, but they can only wear leather (and mail after level 40). While a Shaman can be a passable tank for instance groups until level 50 or so, the instances after that are much more difficult for the Shaman to survive in. While Stoneskin Totem reduces melee damage dealt to the party and Shaman can equip shields, it's their ability to hold aggro that qualifies them to fill the role of tank. Rockbiter Weapon and Earth Shock generate great amounts of threat, while Windfury Weapon can dramatically increase the Shaman's damage output for a short time. Shaman make better secondary tanks, but can be used as tanks if absolutely needed.

SECONDARY TANK

If party members aren't focusing fire well enough or an enemy resists CC or you just plain get unlucky, enemies jump from the tank to your healers or dps. Rather than having the tank run around trying to regain aggro, it's better to have an off-tank grab the aggro and pull it back to the main tank before returning to the primary target or simply tie it up.

WARRIOR

As having all the tools to be primary tank, Warriors are fully qualified as secondary tanks. Using Taunt or Mocking Blow (to pull aggro off another party member) in conjunction with Sunder Armor or Heroic Strike (to build aggro quickly) allows the Warrior to perform this role with flying colors. Warriors acting as secondary tanks should consider switching to a two-handed weapon or using Berserk Stance to increase their damage to the primary tank's target when they aren't acting as off-tank.

DRUID

As secondary tanks aren't always needed, the Druid is free to use whatever form he or she chooses when not performing this role. When a party member pulls aggro off the main tank, a Druid can shift to Bear or Dire Bear Form and keep the enemy tied up until the main tank can pull it off. Another option is to tear aggro off the other party member and move to the front lines so the main tank can pull it off you. Once the job of secondary tank is accomplished, the Druid is free to return to the role they were fulfilling prior.

PALADIN

Paladins have a few more tools as secondary tank than they do as primary tank. Without many opponents to interfere with their casting, Paladins can use heals as well as their damage to pull aggro off party members. Holy Shock can be used as instant damage against the enemy or to instantly heal a friend and give you enough time to pull the enemy off. Stun the target with Hammer of Justice, then use Judgement of Command because the threat is multiplied by Righteous Fury. As with Warriors, Paladins fulfilling this role should consider using a two-handed weapon to increase their damage as their heavy armor is enough to keep them alive against a single enemy.

SHAMAN

The aggro grabbing tools of the Shaman make them a great choice for this role. A quick Earthshock combine with a Lesser Healing Wave can quickly pull aggro off a party member. As you'll likely only have a single enemy on you, the survivability problems of the Shaman aren't an issue. Your armor is enough to keep you alive until the party is ready to deal with your target. Using a two-handed weapon increases a Shaman's damage output, but have a shield bridges the gap between their armor and the heavier types. Consider using a one-handed weapon and a shield until your enemy is dead or looking at the main tank before pulling out your two-handed weapon.

WARLOCK

Clad in cloth, the Warlock doesn't seem a wise choice for a secondary tank. Indeed, they are very poor choices for this role. However, their pets are great choices for it. A Voidwalker has an impressive amount of health and is fairly durable. The best part about it is the Warlock's ability to simply summon another one outside of combat, if their pet dies. This allows you to sic your Voidwalker on an enemy, have it use Torment to grab and maintain aggro, and forget about it as you go back to the primary target. If a Warlock is to fulfill this role, let them know ahead of time as it takes a good while to summon a Voidwalker and their other pets are generally poor choices for secondary tanks.

HUNTER

Both a Hunter and their pet can fulfill this role. Putting a pet on an enemy and Growling keeps that enemy tied up until the pet is dead or Cowers it off. Hunters speccing in the Beast Mastery talent tree have pets that can nearly rival Warriors for their durability and ability to maintain the attention of an enemy.

The Hunter can also fulfill this role. Distracting Shot followed by Arcane Shot is often enough to pull an enemy off a softer party member. With leather armor (mail after level 40), the Hunter isn't nearly as killable as other party members. Once the tank is ready to pull aggro off the Hunter, using Disengage or Feign Death makes this much easier. The ability to quickly pull and drop aggro combined with a pet, make Hunters an almost optimal choice for this role.

HEALER

This role is fairly self explanatory, but there are a few subtleties to it. Healing someone is pretty straight forward. Using the right heal at the right time is a bit more difficult. A Healer's first priority is to keep the tank alive. The second priority being to keep themselves alive (who will heal after you are dead?) and healing others comes third. A Healer's mana should be watched by the entire party as once it runs out, things get more serious.

PRIEST

The Priest is the first obvious choice as healer. With heals of several sizes, the Priest can avoid overhealing and drawing aggro. The other assets of the Priest are their buffs. Power Word: Fortitude is a long duration buff that increases the party member's Stamina, and thus their health. Power Word: Shield is a very short term buff that absorbs damage. This draws more aggro, but can give the party the time it needs to pull an enemy off before a member dies. Shielding the tank before battle begins avoids the aggro issue and gives the tank several moments to generate threat before taking damage. Drawing aggro isn't the worst problem of the Priest, as using Fade reduces your threat level considerably.

DRUID

While in caster form, the Druid has a great many tools for the role of healer. They have the standard heals of varying size to keep from overhealing and drawing aggro, but their true strength lies elsewhere. Mark of the Wild is a long term buff that increases all stats and armor of a party member. This increases health while decreasing incoming damage. Regrowth and Rejuvenation are both heal over time spells. This allows the Druid to heal while spreading out the threat they draw. Using these before a battle begins ensures that damage is being healed without the attention of the Druid or drawing aggro.

SHAMAN

Shaman have a number of tools to buff and heal party members. In addition to the standard heals of differing size to keep from overhealing and drawing aggro, their totems can heal and buff party members. Healing Stream Totem and Mana Spring Totem restore health and mana to all party members in range. While not having any way to reduce the amount of threat they are drawing, Shaman wear heavier armor and can survive unwanted aggro longer.

PALADIN

Paladins have fewer tools for this role, but can be used as a backup or when none of the other classes are available. Blessing of Protection can keep a party member safe from physical attacks for a short duration. This gives the Paladin enough time to heal the party member or the party to kill the enemy. The greatest tools the Paladin has for this role are the wide array of blessings. Blessing of Light coupled with Flash of Light (rank 3) can be cast repeatedly with very high mana efficiency. As blessings have short durations, the Paladin will be very busying keeping them active. A Paladin's Lay on Hands can turn a disastrous situation into a livable one. As it uses all the Paladin's mana, it's a last ditch effort to safe a party and once it's used, the party is without further healing.

CROWD CONTROL

It's always easier to survive three enemies attacking you than four. CC keeps enemies tied up for lengthy periods without lowering your damage or increasing your risk. CC is often broken any time the affected enemy takes damage. There are two distinct types of CC; in-combat and out-of-combat.

Out-of-Combat CC tends to last longer, but can only be used when you or the enemy is out of combat. Groups using any of these abilities should use them before the fight begins.

MAGE

Mages are useful crowd control in a variety of circumstances. Should there be a single enemy the party can't deal with at the time, a Polymorph neutralizes them for a good long time; as long as the enemy is a humanoid, beast, or critter. When the Polymorph breaks, it can be recast with only a duration penalty. Frost Bolt and Cone of Cold can snare single enemies, while Mages have other tools to hamper the movement of enemy groups. Frost Nova roots for several seconds, while Fire and Ice specced Mages can make use of Blast Wave and Improved Blizzard. Counterspell is also a powerful means of controlling a caster

ROGUE

Both in-combat and out-of-combat, CC is what the Rogue brings to a group. Sap can only be used on humanoids and before combat begins. It can only be used on one enemy and the Rogue is detected immediately by other enemies unless he or she has the Improved Sap talent. Blind lasts for several seconds and takes a reagent. Gouge is a nearly free CC, but doesn't last long and can only be used if the enemy is facing the Rogue. Only lasting a few seconds, Gouge can barely be called CC, but it can be useful in emergency situations. Kidney Shot also works if things start ot get chaotic.

HUNTER

Most Hunter abilities are out-of-combat crowd control. Traps can only be used if the Hunter is out of combat. This can be accomplished before the battle begins or by using Feign Death (provided your pet isn't engaged). Freezing Trap creates an area that slows all enemies who enter, while Frost Trap can encase a single enemy in a block of ice for an extended period of time. If the Hunter is specced in the Survival talent tree, Wyvern Sting can also be used to put an enemy to sleep before combat begins. Marksmanship Hunters have a short in-combat CC in Scatter Shot. This is only useful in emergencies when a few seconds makes the difference.

PRIEST

Priests have three forms of CC. Psychic Scream sends nearby enemies running in fear for several seconds. This gets them off your party, but may send them into more enemies and make the situation much worse. Use this ability with extreme caution in the confined spaces of instances. Shackle Undead can only affect undead enemies, but very few classes have any ability to CC undead, so it's still fairly powerful. It neutralizes the enemy for several seconds and can be recast if broken with only a duration penalty. The third is Mind Control. It is dangerous to use in pick-up groups, but for a seasoned group this is a powerful way to start a fight.

WARLOCK

Enemies can be CCed several ways by a Warlock. Demons and elementals can be Banished for a long time. Banish can be recast and cannot be broken until the duration passes. During the time it is banished, the demon or elemental is immune to damage. Fear causes a single enemy to flee, while Howl of Terror causes several enemies to flee. This gets them off the party, but can make the situation worse if the fleeing enemies find friends to bring back. Deathcoil is a short duration fear, but is really only useful in emergencies. The final form of CC the Warlock possesses, is actually a pet ability. The Succubus can use Seduction to CC a humanoid target for extended durations.

DAMAGE

Doing damage is easy. Doing a lot of damage is a little harder. Doing a lot of damage and living to tell about it is even more difficult. Focusing all the damage so things die quickly and aggro is maintained…that is the penultimate.

Start slow with the damage and increase it as the enemy's health drops. This helps your tank maintain aggro until you're ready to finish it.

ROGUE

With so many tools to deal damage and avoid aggro, the Rogue is a great selection for this role. Deadly Poison and Instant Poison can proc extra damage on every swing the Rogue makes. Using damage over time abilities (Garrote, Deadly Poison, and Rupture) against harder targets keep the Rogue from getting aggro as quickly while using fast damage abilities (Ambush, Backstab, Sinister Strike, Instant Poison, and Eviscerate) can kill weaker targets very quickly. Slice and Dice is a good finisher for those pesky bosses. Feint can keep a Rogue from generating too much threat and Vanish can be used in emergencies to dump threat quickly.

MAGE

Mages are all about damage. Once aggro is established, Mages should feel free to blast away, but don't start with Pyroblast or any other large spells. Keep these for your second or third volley against a target. Instead start with Arcane Missles, Fireball, or Frost Bolt. These don't do quite as much damage, but Mages should start small and finish big. As the fight progresses and the enemy's health drops, start throwing everything you have at it. Pyroblast, if you're specced in the Fire talent tree, Scorch, and Fire Blast throws a good bit of damage in a short period of time. Being able to create their own water, Mages shouldn't be worried about mana efficiency against weaker enemies as they can recover between fights.

WARLOCK

Many of the Warlock's spells don't do much up front damage. Against weaker opponents, the Warlock isn't ideal. Against very tough enemies, however, the Warlock's DoTs really start to shine. Any of the pets the Warlock can choose from aid in doing damage with the Succubus being most damaging. Throwing Corruption, Curse of Agony, and Immolate on an enemy doesn't do much damage at first, but as the seconds pass, the enemy's health continuously drops. Being able to Drain Mana or Drain Health, also make the Warlock great for longer fights as they can maintain consistent damage. If you are Destruction specialized, Shadowbolts with an occasional Conflagrate deals awesome damage.

HUNTER

Constantly firing arrows or bullets at an enemy makes the Hunter a valid choice for a damage slot. To increase the damage they are putting out, Hunters can use Serpent Sting, Aimed Shot (if they are specced in the Marksmanship talent tree), and Arcane Shot. If the party is fighting a single enemy, using Multi-Shot adds further damage. In fights where fast damage is important, Rapid Fire and Beastial Wrath (if you are specced in the Beast Mastery talent tree) increases the damage of the Hunter and the pet for a short duration and have a fairly short cooldown.

DRUID

When in Cat Form, Druids function a great deal like Rogues. The reduced survivability of this form is offset by the increased damage potential. As such, a Cat Form Druid makes a perfectly acceptable damage slot occupant. For quick fights against weaker enemies, starting with Ravage, using Shred or Claw to build combo points, and finishing with Ferocious Bite does a great deal of damage in a very short time. Using the DoT abilities of Cat Form is more ideal for longer fights against tougher opponents. Begin with Pounce, use Rake and Shred to build combo points, and finish with Rip. While this does just as much damage, it spreads it out over time and makes it easier for the tank to maintain aggro.

AREA OF EFFECT DAMAGE

There are times in dungeons where it takes far too long to kill the enemies one at a time and trying to do so can result in the entire group dying. For these fights, (often against a dozen or more non-elite enemies) being able to damage many at once is the wisest course of action. This must be done quickly as only very skilled tanks can hold aggro against multiple enemies in these situations.

MAGE

One of the kings of AoE damage is the Mage. Arcane Explosion allows the Mage to continue doing AoE damage even while being attacked because of its instant cast time and limited targeting time (it is cast with you as the center of the effect). Blizzard and Flame Strike can be cast at range, but have differing effects. Flame Strike does damage immediately and continues damaging any enemies in the area over time. Blizzard is a channeled spell and does damage over the duration of the cast, but can slow the enemy's approach if you have the Improved Blizzard talent. Often a good line up is to start with Blizzard or Flame Strike and switch to Arcane Explosion as the enemy advances on you.

HUNTER

Hunters are a good second place when it comes to the AoE slot. They can do almost as much damage to almost as many targets as a Mage. Setting an Explosive Trap before the fight and using Multi-Shot then Volley throws a lot of damage out very quickly and generates a great deal of threat. Feign Death to allow the tank to grab aggro, before putting another Explosive Trap and backing off to Multi-Shot and Volley again. Keeping you pet on Passive and not attacking allows you to set another trap.

WARLOCK

Warlocks have a number of tools that qualify them for an AoE slot. Warlocks have a ranged AoE (Rain of Fire) and a point blank AoE (Hellfire). If the Warlock is the only AoE party member, they should start the fight with their Voidwalker. Cast Rain of Fire until the enemies closes with you and begins attacking. Sacrifice your Voidwalker to protect you from casting interruptions and use Hellfire to finish the enemies. While not having as many tools as the Mage, the Warlock is still quite impressive in this position.

WARRIOR

Few people think of a Warrior in the damage slot, let alone the AoE damage slot. Warriors have a few abilities that can be used in each fight, and a few tricks that can be used in very difficult fights. Switching to a two-hand weapon and using Whirlwind and Cleave allows the Warrior to hit multiple enemies for reasonable damage. Warriors speccing in the Arms talent tree can use Sweeping Strikes to hit extra targets for a short duration and a moderate cooldown (30 seconds). In very tough fights, Warriors can use Challenging Shout (10 minute cooldown) to force all enemies to attack them, then use Retaliation (30 minute cooldown) to counter-attack each enemy. This tactic results in devastating damage, but can only be used every 30 minutes and is often saved for particularly dangerous fights.

DRUID

Druids only have one spell to add to an AoE engagement. They don't have the versatility to be a primary or only AoE party member, but they can support another. Hurricane is a channeled spell and should be done very early in the fight. This draws aggro onto the Druid. Shift into Bear Form or Dire Bear Form to survive the enemy damage, while the primary AoE member (free from interruption for the next few seconds) finishes the enemies.

PRIEST

A Priest's contribution, like the Druid's isn't as impressive, but can certainly supplement. Holy Nova doesn't do as much damage, but doesn't draw any aggro. While only available to Priests that spec in the Holy talent tree, Holy Nova can add enough damage to finish enemies before they finish your primary AoE member.

RESURRECTION

No matter how careful you are, there is always the chance that something will go wrong and someone in the party dies. Having someone who can resurrect a fallen member (rezzer) can save the time of running back to your body, or save the entire run if enemies have respawned behind you.

PRIEST

Resurrection can be cast any time outside of combat and doesn't have a cooldown. The fallen party member must be within line of sight. If the party member has already released their spirit, cast the spell, then click on the body to target the person's corpse.

SHAMAN

Shaman have very similar restrictions as Priests. Ancestral Spirit cannot be used during combat and has no cooldown. Line of sight and range are still concerns and players who have released can be rezzed in a similar fashion by casting the spell before clicking on their corpse.

PALADIN

Paladins can ask Redemption for dead party members. Constricted by line of sight, range, and combat just as Priests are, Paladins are not often the primary rezzers, but they are just as qualified for the position.

DRUID

The Druid has the most restrictions on their ability to rez others, but make up for it by having one of the common restrictions removed. Rebirth is the only rez spell that can be cast during combat. It costs a reagent each time it is used (the reagent varies depending on level) and has a 30 minute cooldown. Line of sight and range are still issues, but Druids are generally secondary or emergency rezzers.

WIPE RECOVERY

Total party wipes happen sooner or later and can be a crushing blow to morale, but having a fast way to recover from them can save time and your entire run as enemies may have respawned between the instance entrance and where your party died.

WARLOCK

By far, the Warlock is the easiest and most versatile class to use as wipe recovery. For the cost of a Soul Shard, the Warlock can use Create Soul Stone for a party member. This allows the 'stoned' person to instantly resurrect himself instead of releasing their spirit. The soul stone buff lasts one hour, has a 30 minute cooldown, and needs to be renewed. Instanly rezzing yourself uses the stone, so choose when to resurrect yourself carefully. Classes that can resurrect others are almost always the ones chosen to have their soul stored.

PALADIN

Paladin wipe recovery is a little trickier to use and is more like wipe prevention. By using a Symbol of Divinity and sacrificing themselves, Paladins can call upon Divine Intervention and remove a party member from combat and all danger for 3 minutes. At the end of the duration, the party member can be attacked as normal, so it should be cast on someone who can resurrect others and is outside of the enemy's aggro detection. Couple this with the restriction of having to cast Divine Intervention before the person dies makes proper use of this spell nearly an art form.

SHAMAN

Shaman are the only class that can resurrect themselves (and only themselves) without any form of setup (aside from buying the Ankhs before they came). Reincarnation has a one hour cooldown (unless you have taken the Improved Reincarnation talent), and consumes an Ankh each time it is used. Also possessing the ability to resurrect others, Reincarnation makes Shaman quite ideal at recovering from wipes. As Shaman can resurrect themselves, they are often a poor choice for Soul Stones, unless they have used their Ankh recently.

ENGINEERS

Hunters or Rogues with Engineer skill can remove themselves from combat (FD or Vanish), then use Goblin Jumper Cables to restore a priest. Remember, Goblin Jumper Cables are unreliable.

DUNGEON LISTING

Dungeon Quick Table

Level Range	Dungeon	Zone
13-18	Ragefire Chasm	Orgrimmar
17-24	Wailing Caverns	Barrens
17-24	Deadmines	Westfall
22-26	Shadowfang Keep	Silverpine Forest
24-28	Blackfathom Deeps	Ashenvale
24-28	The Stockades	Stormwind
25-30	Razorfen Kraul	Barrens
29-38	Gnomeregan	Dun Morogh
33-40	Razorfen Downs	Barrens
34-45	The Scarlet Monastery	Tirisfal Glades
35-47	Uldaman	Badlands
44-50	Zul'Farrak	Tanaris
47-55	The Sunken Temple	Swamp of Sorrows
45-50	Maraudon	Desolace
52+	Blackrock Depths	Searing Gorge/Burning Steppes
55+	Dire Maul	Feralas
58+	Stratholme	Eastern Plaguelands
57+	Scholomance	Western Plaguelands
58+	Blackrock Spire	Searing Gorge/Burning Steppes

RAGEFIRE CHASM

Zone: Orgrimmar	
Level Range: 13-18	
Primary Enemies: Humanoid	
Special Items: None	
Entrance Requirements: None	

Ragefire Chasm is only accessible to Horde parties as it lies deep within the heart of orc and Troll territory. It's a good training ground for groups as many of the things you will encounter in later instances are present here.

It's fairly important to have a good variety in classes as there is little overlap with abilities at this level. Having a tank is always important. A Warrior is the best choice, but a Shaman or Druid in bear form can be used also. Druids, Priests, and Shaman all have the ability to act as a healer, but don't ask a Druid or Shaman to be both healer and tank. Mages are very useful for their Polymorph spell's ability to control combat.

After the more difficult jobs are filled, it's time to add some damage to your group. Every class can add damage. Extra Warriors can serve as backup for the main tank while they cut through the enemies. Additional Priests can serve as backup healers while they blast the enemies with the power of shadows.

What makes this particular Instance troublesome is that most classes have yet to acquire many of their class-defining skills so CC can be a major issue.

WAILING CAVERNS

Zone: Barrens	
Level Range: 17-24	
Primary Enemies: Humanoid, Beast	
Special Items: Embrace of the Viper armor set	
Entrance Requirements: None	

The primary enemies are humanoids and beasts. This means both Rogues and Druids can be used to control pulls in addition to Mages. A number of the enemies cast their own crowd control spells and having someone to wake sleeping members or interrupt enemy attacks is vital. Warriors, Rogues, and Shaman all have interrupts and should watch for casters. Green glowing effects usually warn of healing spells, while white glowing effects warn of sleeping spells. Priests can Dispel Magic and Shaman can use Tremor Totems to wake party members.

The last few enemies really puts your tank and healer to the test. Having a highly skilled tank and healer make these fights seem easy while having less skilled members will make these fights nightmares.

For the collectors in us all, the Embrace of the Viper leather armor set drops from enemies in Wailing Caverns. While ideally for a Druid, the pieces of this set are quite good for their level and can be used by a number of classes.

DEADMINES

Zone: Westfall	
Level Range: 17-24	
Primary Enemies: Humanoid	
Special Items: Defias Leather armor set	
Entrance Requirements: None	

With almost an entire instance of humanoids, Mages and Rogues are primary choices for crowd control. Enemies are fairly close together but run for help, so killing them quickly is fairly important as is having a tank that can take the attacks of multiple enemies.

In the Deadmines, but not quite in the instance you will find undead. While the undead portion is fairly small, Priests can take up the CC duties while you're there. Deeper in the dungeon are casters. Once you begin meeting the casters, have an interrupt order ready as their spells (primarily fire based) can be quite damaging and are cast at range. Consider Polymorphing casters if running to them to interrupt casting risks pulling more enemies.

The Defias Leather armor set is quite nice. Rogues, Hunters, and Shaman are certain to enjoy the armor, while Warriors and Paladins may even find the bonuses to their liking.

SHADOWFANG KEEP

Zone: Silverpine Forest	
Level Range: 22-26	
Primary Enemies: Undead	
Special Items: None	
Entrance Requirements: None	

Shadowfang Keep has few humanoid targets but an abundance of undead. Many of the enemies are immune to shadow magic, so Warlocks should switch to their fire spells while Priests should make use of their holy spells. Have a Priest to CC the undead while a Mage can CC the few living enemies, makes pulls more manageable.

The enemies also use a variety of abilities to debuff your party. Magic, Disease, and Curse debuffs will surely be cast on your party, and having someone who can remove them makes your run much faster and safer.

Priests can Dispel Magic debuffs. Shaman and Priests can remove disease effects. Mages and Druids can remove curses. These abilities take little mana or attention so can be done in addition to the member's standard role.

BLACKFATHOM DEEPS

Zone: Ashenvale	
Level Range: 24-28	
Primary Enemies: Humanoid	
Special Items: None	
Entrance Requirements: None	

Be certain to have a group with crowd control, many interrupts, and some good armor. There are some very large fights in the Deeps, and you often are faced with multiple casters.

While the instance has a number of enemy types, the larger fights are against humanoid targets or against too many targets to effectively CC. Mages and Rogues make good choices for controlling pulls. Bring someone in for some AoE work as there are a couple fights at the end that can be very dangerous and confusing.

THE STOCKADE

Zone: Stormwind	
Level Range: 24-28	
Primary Enemies: Humanoid	
Special Items: None	
Entrance Requirements: None	

Just as Ragefire Chasm is only accessible to Horde parties, The Stockade is only accessible to Alliance groups. Standing in the very center of Stormwind (the very heart of the Alliance), only fools would attempt to enter the Stockade as Horde parties.

The Stockade is a short dungeon populated nearly exclusively by humanoids. Having a Mage or Rogue to help control the pulls and an off-tank to keep the enemies from jumping on casters is ideal, but not fully required. Though the pulls are larger than much you have dealt with so far, do not attempt to use AoEs to kill the targets more quickly as they are all elites and can kill your AoE members very quickly.

RAZORFEN KRAUL

Zone: Barrens	
Level Range: 25-30	
Primary Enemies: Humanoid, Beast	
Special Items: None	
Entrance Requirements: None	

Because of the multitude of Quilboars using magic and ranged attacks, having a party member who is familiar with the dungeon can make the assault easier. If the entire party is new to Razorfen Kraul, take it slow and have someone who is familiar with pulling casters and ranged attackers lead. Using terrain to pull enemies into melee range keeps the Quilboar from feasting on your corpses. Hit the enemies from range and duck around a corner or run past your party to force the enemy to come closer.

Characters with ranged interrupts make this easier. Mages with Counterspell and Shaman with Earth Shock can force enemy casters to come to you. Several of the fights within are against enemies that do tremendous damage. Using anything but a Warrior or Paladin for your tank is doable but risky.

GNOMEREGAN

Zone: Dun Morogh	
Level Range: 29-38	
Primary Enemies: Humanoid	
Special Items: None	
Entrance Requirements: Horde parties need to complete Chief Engineer Scooty to use the teleporter in Booty Bay	

Many of the fights within Gnomeregan are against enemies that are highly resistant or immune to most forms of CC. Having an off-tank watching for enemies that escape the attention of the tank is important. As enemy groups are close together, having a character with a ranged attack pull the enemies back to the party is preferable.

There are many things that can go wrong in Gnomeregan. Druids have a hard time keeping up as rezzers, so a Priest, Paladin, or Shaman is preferable. Warlocks, Shaman, and Paladins gain their wipe recovery abilities at level 30 and you should have one in the party as one unlucky pull can doom your group.

RAZORFEN DOWNS

Zone: Barrens	
Level Range: 33-40	
Primary Enemies: Undead, Humanoid	
Special Items: None	
Entrance Requirements: None	

While forming your party, consider bringing someone who can cure diseases. The Quilboar have forged an alliance with the Scourge. You'll be afflicted with many diseases as you travel through Razorfen Downs and having the ability to cure them makes this assault easier, even possible to some groups.

A number of fights have several enemies. Having strong AoE potential in the party can make these fights much easier. Mages and Warlocks are ideal for this with Hunters being a reasonable backup.

With so many undead in the area, most forms of CC are useless. Having a Priest to shackle can make quite a difference.

THE SCARLET MONASTERY

Zone: Tirisfal Glades	
Level Range: 34-45	
Primary Enemies: Humanoid	
Special Items: Chain of the Scarlet Crusade armor set	
Entrance Requirements: The Scarlet Key is required to enter the Cathedral or Armory.	

This dungeon is split into four parts with four separate portals. The Library and Graveyard can be accessed at any time, but the Armor and Cathedral are behind closed doors (the key can be obtained in either of the unlocked portions). Rogues who are highly skilled at picking locks can open the doors (this is also a wonderful place to train lockpicking). For this reason many parties only do one portion of the instance at a time.

The Scarlet Crusade allows very little deviation in their order. This instance is almost entirely humanoid (making Mages, Warlocks, and Rogues very useful for controlling pulls), but undead run rampant in the graveyard portion (making Priests the only viable CC).

There are very few non-elite enemies in the dungeon, but having at least one person with an AoE ability makes the final fight in the Armory much more fun. The humans are very social and run for help. Kill them quickly and have someone ready to snare enemies to prevent late additions to a fight (crippling poison is your friend).

Those visiting the Scarlet Monastery for loot should keep an eye out for the Chain of the Scarlet Crusade. This mail armor set has some wonderful stats but is very near an armor change level. Warriors and Paladins switch to plate armor soon after level 40, and Hunters and Shaman can't use any of the pieces until level 40.

ULDAMAN

Zone: Badlands	
Level Range: 35-47	
Primary Enemies: Humanoid, Golem	
Special Items: None	
Entrance Requirements: None	

The dwarves and Troggs early in the dungeon can be CCed like any other humanoids, but as you progress deeper the enemies become more difficult to CC. Take an off-tank to keep extra enemies from getting to your softer members.

Having a party member with high armor and high HP is crucial for surviving this dungeon. Chain-wearing classes can handle the Shadowforge dwarves and the Troggs, but when you reach the Golems, you need someone in plate. The Golems hit extremely hard and have very high health. Another necessity for Uldaman is including classes that have snare or root abilities. Many enemies flee when at low health and there are always more enemies close by.

ZUL'FARRAK

Zone:	Tanaris
Level Range:	44-50
Primary Enemies:	Humanoid, Beast
Special Items:	None
Entrance Requirements:	The Mallet of Zul'Farrak is required to spawn Gaz'rilla.

Most of the fights in the troll city involve several humanoid enemies. Rogues, Warlocks, and Mages make your fights more manageable. The hardest fights are against swarms of enemies, so having a strong AoE member (Mage or Warlock) and a support AoE member (Druid, Warrior, Hunter, or Priest) is important.

Focus fire well and your enemies drop quickly. Fracturing damage will be the end of your party as many of the enemies possess high health and run when wounded. One party member is unlikely to be able to kill a runner before it finds friends so stay on the same target and be ready to root or snare fleeing enemies.

THE SUNKEN TEMPLE

Zone:	Swamp of Sorrows
Level Range:	47-55
Primary Enemies:	Humanoid, Undead, Wyrmkin
Special Items:	None
Entrance Requirements:	The Ancient Egg is required to spawn the Avatar of Hakkar.

The population of enemies is as varied as this dungeon is complex. Though only one portal allows access to the temple, there is a major split between the upper and lower floors of the dungeon. Check with your party to make sure everyone has the same goal before entering as there are quests for both levels.

Your party will be bloated if you try to bring someone for each type of CC in the dungeon. Instead, use whatever CC you have when you can and make the best with the other fights. Priests can shackle the undead trolls while Rogues, Warlocks, and Mages can CC the living trolls and only Druids can sleep the Wyrmkin.

The final fight of the instance is against the Shade of Eranikus which can cast sleep on party members. Have an off-tank ready to pickup the duties if the tank is put to sleep as it cannot be dispelled.

MARAUDON

Zone:	Desolace
Level Range:	45-50
Primary Enemies:	Demon, Elemental, Beast
Special Items:	The Sceptre of Celebras allows teleporting to the center of the instance.
Entrance Requirements:	None

There is very little that can be CCed in Maraudon. The satyrs and elementals can be banished by Warlocks, but that's about it. Instead stack your group with damage so enemies can be killed quickly and healing to keep your tank alive.

Having an off-tank proves invaluable when you fight small groups of tough opponents (Warlock and Hunter pets work best) and having multiple ranged damage classes make some of the earlier fights against the slimes easier (the slimes do AoE damage).

Running the purple side and orange side of Maraudon completely gives you the opportunity to create the Sceptre of Celebras. This allows you to portal past much of the instance and straight to the final portion. Groups often do 'Princess runs', meaning they intend to port in. Specify early which entrance you are taking.

BLACKROCK DEPTHS

Zone:	Searing Gorge/Burning Steppes
Level Range:	52+
Primary Enemies:	Humanoid, Elemental, Beast
Special Items:	None
Entrance Requirements:	The Shadowforge Key unlocks the deeper portion of the instances

Having a party with combat control is essential as many fights involve a large number of enemies. Sap, Polymorph, Mind Control, and Banish are all extremely useful in the chambers under the mountain.

The largest fights are against humanoids, but the most difficult fights will be against elementals. As Warlocks can CC both types (Seduce and Banish), they are extremely useful.

Large enemy groups often include healers. These should be interrupted until they can be killed. Having several members with spell interrupts is very important.

DIRE MAUL

Zone:	Feralas
Level Range:	55+
Primary Enemies:	Elemental, Humanoid, Demon
Special Items:	Ogre Tannin (required to make the Ogre Suit) is acquired in the northern wing.
Entrance Requirements:	The Crescent Key is required to enter the northern or western wings.

Dire Maul is another dungeon with several wings. The eastern wing is the only unlocked wing and is where you acquire the key for the other two wings (north and west). Very few groups do all of Dire Maul in a single sitting (it's just too long), so specify which side you intend to do when recruiting party members. Rogues who are highly skilled at picking locks can open all the doors.

The enemies and fights vary greatly among the wings. With the proliferation of satyrs in the east wing, Warlocks make a good choice for CC. The ghosts and elementals in the west wing make Priests and Warlocks good choices. The north wing is mostly ogres. This makes Rogues, Mages, Warlocks, and Priests all valid choices for CC.

There are fights in all the wings where several weaker enemies attack you. One AoE member makes these fights faster, but is not a requirement to defeat them.

STRATHOLME

Zone:	Eastern Plaguelands
Level Range:	58+
Primary Enemies:	Undead
Special Items:	The Key to the City allows entrance through the back door. Parts of the Beaststalker, Devout, Dreadmist, Elements, Lightforge, Magister, Shadowcraft, Valor, Wildheart armor sets drop.
Entrance Requirements:	None

The ruins of Stratholme are home to both the living and unliving survivors of the plague. Most groups only do one wing of the dungeon at a time, but some do both. Knowing your goals ahead of time makes your choices easier.

West side (also known as live side or scarlet side) has many undead in the beginning, but the harder fights are against fewer and tougher humanoid targets so Rogues, Warlocks, and Mages are useful for CC purposes.

East side (also known as undead side or Baron side) is populated by the undead. Many of the fights are against large groups of elite and non-elite undead. Priests can CC an elite each fight while the party kills the non-elites first. This can be done with AoEs, but is dangerous and should be discussed first. Without at least one strong AoE class, however, some of the later fights are very difficult.

Stratholme is the first of the three dungeons that contribute to your first dungeon armor set. While several enemies can drop various pieces of different sets, Baron Rivendare is the only enemy in the game who drops the leggings for all the sets.

SCHOLOMANCE

Zone: Western Plaguelands	
Level Range: 57+	
Primary Enemies: Undead, Humanoid	
Special Items: The Blood of Innocents is required to spawn Kirtonos the Herald. Parts of the Beaststalker, Devout, Dreadmist, Elements, Lightforge, Magister, Shadowcraft, Valor, Wildheart armor sets drop. The Cadaver, Bloodmail, Necropile, and Deathbone armor sets can be found.	
Entrance Requirements: The Skeleton Key is required to enter Scholomance.	

Scholomance is locked. The key can only be obtained by completing a quest chain that begins at Chillwind Point and the Bulwark for Alliance and Horde individuals. A Rogue with a high lockpicking skill can open the door as well.

The dungeon is almost entirely populated with undead and some humanoids. Priests, Mages, and Warlocks are prime choices for CC. Rogues with Improved Sap can also fill the slot, but Rogues without it shouldn't attempt to Sap (they can still fill a damage slot).

Several of the fights are against multiple enemies. Some are against very tough opponents making an off-tank very useful, while others are against many weaker enemies making AoE members useful.

Scholomance also has parts of the first dungeon armor set. Many of the enemies within drop various parts of the sets, but Darkmaster Gandling is the only enemy in the game who possess the head piece for the sets.

LOWER BLACKROCK SPIRE

Zone: Searing Gorge/Burning Steppes	
Level Range: 58+	
Primary Enemies: Humanoid	
Special Items: Parts of the Beaststalker, Devout, Dreadmist, Elements, Lightforge, Magister, Shadowcraft, Valor, Wildheart armor sets drop. The Spider's Kiss weapon set drops.	
Entrance Requirements: None	

Blackrock Spire is a single instance, but is separated between a non-raid portion (lower) and a raid portion (upper). The door to upper can only be opened by obtaining the key through a quest chain that begins inside lower Blackrock Spire. Rogues cannot pick this door as it is magically shut and only the key can open it.

The enemies in the spire are predominantly humanoid. This makes Improved Sap Rogues, Warlocks, and Mages very good choices for their ability to control the pulls. Hunters make an excellent addition with their traps as the enemies hit very hard but don't often attack in large groups.

CC is good, but a well equipped and skilled tank is better. As most of the fights aren't as large as in Scholomance or Stratholme, Paladins and Druids can make successful tanks.

Many of the enemies in lower Blackrock Spire drop parts of the dungeon armor sets. General Drakkisath drops the chest piece for all the dungeon sets.

RAIDS

There are many tasks that are simply too large for a single group of five to handle. Some of these only require a second group while others require nearly an entire army.

HOW TO FORM A RAID

Forming a raid is slightly different to forming a group. Invite people into your group as normal. When you have the first five people, open your social window (defaulted to 'o') and select the Raid tab. Push Convert to Raid and continue inviting.

There are two things that make the inviting process easier and faster.

Promoting others: With the raid window open, right click on a members name and promote them. This makes them an assistant and allows them to aid with inviting others.	
Long names: Some people have very long or difficult to type names. If the person has spoken recently, right click on their name in the chat box and invite them.	

ROLES IN A RAID

Role Table		
Role	**Responsibility**	**Classes**
Main Tank	Gather, Maintain, and Survive Aggro	Warrior, Druid
Backup Tank	Gather, Maintain, and Survive Aggro on Boss adds	Warrior, Druid,, Paladin
Secondary Tank (Off-tank)	Pull Aggro from non-tank members	Warrior, Druid, Paladin
Healer	Keep Party Members Alive	Priest, Druid, Shaman, Paladin
Debuff Removal	Remove Damaging and Debilitating Debuffs	Priest, Paladin, Druid, Shaman, Mage
Crowd Control (CC)	Neutralize Enemies	Mage, Rogue, Hunter, Priest, Warlock
Mitigation	Reduces Damage Dealt by Enemies	Rogue, Warlock, Priest, Shaman, Druid, Hunter, Warrior, Paladin
Burst Damage (DPS)	Kill Enemies Quickly	Mage, Rogue, Druid
Sustained Damage (DPS)	Maintain High Damage Level Over Time	Hunter, Rogue, Warlock, Warriors
Area of Effect Damage (AoE)	Damage multiple enemies at once	Mage, Warlock, Hunter, Warrior, Druid, Priest
Resurrection (Rez)	Revive Fallen Members	Priest, Shaman, Paladin, Druid
Wipe Recovery	Ressurect or Survive a Total Party Wipe	Paladin, Warlock, Shaman, Engineer

Depending on which raid you are attending, not all of these roles need to be filled. Crowd Control is very important in Upper Blackrock Spire, while Decursers and Dispellers are necessary to take on Lord Kazzak.

MAIN TANK

As one of the most important roles, a good tank can make a party while a bad tank can break one. The main tank should start the fights to get early aggro, and use abilities to maintain the aggro. Against the most vicious of the raid enemies, main tanks often need very high resists in addition to high armor, defense, and health. Some fights involve several enemies that are immune to CC, so there may be several main tanks in your raid.

WARRIOR

Warriors make the best tanks. They have the heaviest armor (plate), can use a shield, have abilities to hold single enemies, and abilities to hold multiple enemies.

DRUID

Only Druids using Dire Bear Form and specced in the Feral talent tree should be considered for this role. As a dire bear, the Druid's armor is increased greatly and they gain access to a number of abilities that help them fill this role.

BACKUP TANK

This person is generally bored until boss fights. This role becomes the raid's only hope when there are adds in boss encounters.

WARRIOR

As with main tanks, Warriors make the greatest backup tanks. They have the armor and shield to survive against a tough opponent and have several abilities to turn the fight around at a moments notice. Charge brings you into battle with rage to burn. If you were already engaged and have little rage, use Blood Rage. Taunt, Mocking Blow, and Challenging Shout will pull the enemy's attention very quickly. Follow with a few Sunder Armors to lock aggro onto you.

DRUID

Only Druids using Dire Bear Form and specced in the Feral talent tree should be considered for this role. The Druid only has a few abilities to pick up aggro quickly. Cooperation from the rest of the raid is essential for a Druid to fill this role. Challenging Roar is your only tool to gathering aggro quickly. With its ten minute cooldown, it's only useful in emergency situations, but that's what this is. Frenzied Regeneration can keep you alive longer without taxing your healers as much, but drains your rage, so be careful about using it.

PALADIN

Like Warriors, Paladins have access to the heaviest armor in the game (plate) and can equip a shield. This combined with their ability to heal themselves, can make the Paladin extremely durable as a tank.

SECONDARY TANK

If party members aren't focusing fire well enough or an enemy resists CC or you just plain get unlucky, enemies will jump from the tank to your healers or dps. Rather than having the tank run around trying to regain aggro, it's better to have an off-tank grab the aggro and pull it back to the main tank before returning to the primary target or simply tie it up.

WARRIOR

As having all the tools to be primary tank, Warriors are fully qualified as secondary tanks.

DRUID

As secondary tanks aren't always needed, the Druid is free to use whatever form he or she chooses when not performing this role. When a party member pulls aggro off the main tank, a Druid can shift to Bear or Dire Bear Form and keep the enemy tied up until the main tank can pull it off. Once the job of secondary tank is accomplished, the Druid is free to return to the role they were fulfilling prior.

PALADIN

Paladins have a few more tools as secondary tank than they do as primary tank. Without many opponents to interfere with their casting, Paladins can use their heals as well as their damage to pull aggro off party members.

HEALER

In raids, there are often multiple healers. This is necessary as the enemies are either more numerous (meaning more tanks to heal) or more devastating. Determining who heals who and when is important and avoids wasting mana. There are several ways to divvy the duties of healing:

One Healer Per Group: Putting one healer in each group and making each only responsible for their group spreads the healing out a good bit, but some healers will be lax while others (the healer with the main tank) over-taxed.

One Healer at a Time: Having a single healer casting all the heals until they are out of mana can allow your raid to last longer against certain opponents as the healers not actively healing are regenerating mana. The major downside is when damage comes it too quickly for a single healer to deal with and people start dying or the healer pulls aggro.

Only Use Small Heals: Using smaller heals splits aggro more effectively, but depletes your healer's mana more quickly (as smaller heals are less mana efficient). It gives all the healers a chance to interrupt their casting if their target gains health from another caster.

PRIEST

The Priest is the first obvious choice as healer. With heals of several sizes, the Priest can avoid overhealing and drawing aggro.

DRUID

While in caster form, the Druid has a great many tools for the role of healer. Regrowth and Rejuvenation are both heal over time spells. This allows the Druid to heal while spreading out the threat they draw. Using these before a battle begins ensures that damage is being healed without the attention of the Druid or drawing aggro.

SHAMAN

Shaman have a number of tools to buff and heal party members. In addition to the standard heals of differing size to keep from overhealing and drawing aggro, their totems can heal and buff party members.

PALADIN

Paladins have fewer tools for this role, but can be used as a backup.

DEBUFF REMOVAL

Debuffs can be crippling to a raid. Many of these abilities hamper you, while some do damage, and some even force you character to fight for the wrong side. Recognizing and dispelling these effects make fights much less difficult.

Most fights, the character will have another role and remove debuffs as needed. There are four types of removable debuffs; magic, poison, curse, and disease. Only a couple classes can remove each type.

Debuff Removal	
Debuff	Class (Ability)
Magic	Priest (Dispel Magic), Paladin (Cleanse)
Poison	Druid (Abolish Poison), Shaman (Cure Poison, Poison Cleansing Totem), Paladin (Cleanse)
Curse	Druid (Remove Curse), Mage (Remove Lesser Curse)
Disease	Shaman (Cure Disease, Disease Cleansing Totem), Paladin (Cleanse), Priest (Cure Disease, Abolish Disease)

CROWD CONTROL

CC keeps enemies tied up for lengthy periods without lowering your damage or increasing your risk. Many forms of CC are broken any time the affected enemy takes damage. There are two distinct types of CC; in-combat and out-of-combat.

Out-of-Combat CC tends to last longer, but can only be used when you or the enemy is out of combat. Groups using any of these abilities should use them before the fight begins.

MAGE

Mages are useful crowd control in a variety of circumstances. Should there be a single enemy the party can't deal with at the time, a Polymorph neutralizes them for a good long time; as long as the enemy is a humanoid, beast, or critter. When the Polymorph breaks, it can be recast with only a duration penalty.

ROGUE

Both in-combat and out-of-combat CC is what the Rogue brings to a group. Sap can only be used on humanoids and before combat begins. Blind lasts for several seconds and takes a reagent.

HUNTER

Most Hunter abilities are out-of-combat crowd control. Traps can only be used if the Hunter is out of combat. This can be accomplished before the battle begins or by using Feign Death (provided your pet isn't engaged). Freezing Trap creates an area that slows all enemies who enter, while Frost Trap can encase a single enemy in a block of ice for an extended period of time.

PRIEST

Priests have two forms of CC. Psychic Scream sends nearby enemies running in fear for several seconds (rarely is this used in Raids). Shackle Undead can only affect undead enemies, but very few classes have any ability to CC undead, so it's still fairly powerful.

WARLOCK

Enemies can be CCed several ways by a Warlock. Demons and elementals can be Banished for a long time. Banish can be recast and cannot be broken until the duration passes. The Warlock's Succubus can use Seduction to CC a humanoid target for extended durations.

MITIGATION

Many of the enemies you may fight deal to much damage to survive alone. Even with a healer helping, your tank will likely die if some of the damage is not mitigated. Nearly every class has the ability to reduce the damage dealt to your main tank. With people working on concert, even the most damaging enemies become

manageable. Note, most bosses are immune to stuns, disarms, etc.

ROGUE

Against any opponent not immune to stun, Rogues are one of the greatest mitigation classes. Opening a fight with Cheap Shot leaves the enemy stunned for several seconds. Use Sinister Strike or Backstab to build combo points before finishing with Kidney Shot to leave the enemy stunned once again. Multiple Rogues staggering their stuns can keep an enemy stunned from the start of the fight until the end. Against stun immune targets, a well-timed Kick still interrupts casting.

WARLOCK

Just as enemy curses make your party weaker, Warlock curses make enemies weaker. Curse of Tongues increases the casting time on enemy spells and is quite useful against casters. Lengthening the cast time gives the rest of the raid more time to interrupt the spell. Against melee enemies, Curse of Weakness can drastically reduce the amount of damage they are dealing. By debuffing the enemy, Warlocks are able to mitigate a reasonable amount of damage.

PRIEST

Priests have a number of abilities that can be used to reduce the damage a raid takes. Mana Burn can destroy an enemy caster's mana pool and render them unable to cast spells, while Shadow Protection raises the resistance of members to shadow damage. Power Word: Shield surrounds a raid member, protecting them from damage, until the shield is destroyed. As an instant spell, it's very useful for emergency mitigation, but used before a fight begins reduces the amount of damage your tank takes from an enemy groups first volley.

SHAMAN

Shaman are able to reduce magical and physical damage taken by party members. Stoneskin Totem reduces damage on all melee attacks to party members while Windwall Totem reduces all physical ranged attacks. Grounding Totem can absorb non-AoE spells cast at the party. Well-timed Earthshocks interrupt enemy casting and the Nature, Fire, and Frost Resistance Totems reduce the damage from the appropriate types of spells to party members.

Why Isn't Everyone Getting the Totem Buffs?

Totems only affect raid members who are in the same party as the Shaman who dropped them. For this reason, it's not a great idea to have all the Shaman in the same party.

DRUID

Druids have a couple abilities that can mitigate damage. Mark of the Wild increases the armor of raid members (in addition to increases their stats). If the Druid is using bear or dire bear form, they also have Demoralizing Roar (which decreases enemy attack power) and Bash (which stuns for a short while). Druids aren't terribly adept at damage mitigation, but they can do it if needed.

HUNTER

Like Druids, Hunters only have a couple abilities that mitigate damage raid members take. Aspect of the Wild increases the nature resistance of all party members and, by doing so, reduces the damage from nature effects. Scorpid Sting reduces the enemy's strength and agility. While not terribly useful against caster enemies, it can have a noticeable effect against melee targets. Marksmanship Hunters have a change to stun an enemy when using Concussive Shot.

WARRIOR

Warriors not fulfilling a tanking role can assist the tank greatly with a number of abilities. Disarm can reduce the damage a humanoid melee enemy can deal by quite a bit, while Protection Warriors can even stun the enemy for several seconds with Concussion Blow. Thunderclap and Demoralizing Shout reduce enemy attack speed and attack power, rendering their physical attacks much less damaging. If the enemy is a caster, Pummel and Shield Bash can interrupt a spell when timed well.

PALADIN

Much like a Rogue, a Paladin's primary ability to mitigate damage to others is through stuns. Hammer of Justice and Seal of Justice can keep an enemy from doing much at all. When timed with a Rogue or another Paladin, enemies can be stunned for quite some time. Paladins have other tricks however. Paladins can surround themselves and their party members in Shadow, Fire, or Frost Resistance Auras. This reduces the damage of shadow, fire, or frost effects by increasing resistances. Greater Blessing of Sanctuary reduces all incoming damage to raid members and Devotion Aura can raise group members' armor. As one of the best ways for a Paladin to mitigate damage, Blessing of Sacrifice transfers some of the damage taken by a target to the Paladin.

BURST DAMAGE

Burst damage is useful when getting to a boss. The weaker enemies around the boss or in the dungeon can often be killed before they can significantly damage your party. Burst damage characters often have lower survivability, but if the fight is finished quickly it doesn't matter. Even with downtime afterward, it's often a better plan to use burst DPS on weaker enemies.

ROGUE

Many Rogues can dish out a great deal of damage very quickly. Without worrying about avoiding aggro, they can push their damage even higher. Ambush is a good way to start a fight. Garrote and Cheap Shot are options for non-dagger Rogues. Use Backstab or Sinister Strike to build combo points quickly. If the enemy isn't going down fast enough, consider using Thistle Tea to restore your energy when it depletes. Finish the fight with a several combo-point Eviscerate. Having Instant Poison on your weapons further adds quick damage.

MAGE

Mages are wonderful with burst damage. They have several tools that can quickly turn their sizable mana pool into damage. Start the fight with Combustion and Pyroblast if you're specced in the Fire talent tree or Arcane Power if you chose the Arcane tree. If you're clearing several groups, use your abilities with cooldowns more sparingly, but remember that you'll be drinking between battles anyway. Follow up with Cone of Cold and Fireblast. Both of these are instants. Cast Arcane Missles while you wait for Cone of Cold and Fireblast to cool down. Continue throwing your mana at the enemy until they are dead.

DRUID

When in Cat Form, Druids function a great deal like Rogues. The reduced survivability of this form is offset by the increased damage potential. As such, a Cat Form Druid makes a perfectly acceptable burst damage slot occupant. Start with Ravage, using Shred or Claw to build combo points, and finishing with Ferocious Bite. This does a good bit of damage in a very short time and is exactly why you're here.

level low. When you've built up combo points, use Slice and Dice for sustained DPS. Coating your weapons with Deadly Poison adds more damage but spreads it out just like the abilities mentioned. Keep the DPS moving and have Vanish ready if the enemy turns to you.

WARLOCK

Many of the Warlock's spells don't do much up front damage which makes them ideal for longer fights. Any of the pets Warlocks can choose from aid in doing damage with the Succubus causing the most damage herself, but the Imp allows the Warlock to caster longer. Throwing Corruption, Curse of Agony, and Immolate on an enemy doesn't do much damage at first, but as the seconds pass, the enemy's health continues to drop. Being able to Drain Mana or Drain Health as needed keeps the Warlock doing damage consistently. Should you run out of mana, use Dark Pact (if you're an Affliction Warlock) to steal some from your pet. Another option when you run out of mana is to use Life Tap to trade your health for mana.

HUNTER

Constantly firing arrows or bullets at an enemy makes the Hunter a valid choice for this role. Auto Fire keeps the Hunter doing damage, provided you are able to stay at range, while the pet can chew on the enemy. To increase the damage they are putting out, Hunters can use Serpent Sting (though it takes up a debuff slot), Aimed Shot (if they are specced in the Marksmanship talent tree), and Arcane Shot. Use your special abilities until you are low on mana then stop casting. Auto Fire keeps the damage going while allowing you to regenerate mana. In the larger fights, use Feign Death often to keep your threat level low.

SUSTAINED DAMAGE

Many enemies are too tough to blown down with burst DPS. In these cases, it's more important to be able to sustain a high level of damage for a prolonged time. The damage is often lower than burst DPS, but spreading the damage out (making it easier for the tank to hold aggro) is very important.

ROGUE

Rogues have a number of tools that make them a good choice for this role. Starting a fight with Garrote guarantees you'll do nearly as much damage as an Ambush (if you're specced for it)…just over several seconds. Use Backstab or Sinister Strike to build combo points. Mix a Feint in to keep your threat

AREA OF EFFECT DAMAGE

There are times in dungeons where it takes far too long to kill the enemies one at a time and trying to do so can result in the entire group dying. For these fights, often against a dozen or more non-elite enemies, being able to damage many at once is the wisest course of action.

MAGE

Arcane Explosion allows the Mage to continue doing AoE damage even while being attacked because of its instant cast time and limited targeting time (it is cast with you as the center of the effect). Blizzard and Flame Strike can be cast at range, but have differing effects. Often a good line up is to start with Blizzard or Flame Strike and switch to Arcane Explosion as the enemy advances on you.

HUNTER

Hunters are a good second place when it comes to the AoE slot. Setting an Explosive Trap before the fight and using Multi-Shot then Volley throws a lot of damage out very quickly and generates a great deal of threat. Feign Death to allow the tank to grab aggro. Keep your pet on Passive.

WARLOCK

Warlocks have a number of tools that qualify them for an AoE slot. Warlocks have a ranged AoE (Rain of Fire) and a point blank AoE (Hellfire).

RESURRECTION

Having someone who can resurrect a fallen member can save the time of running back to your body, or save the entire run if enemies have respawned behind you.

PRIEST

Resurrection can be cast any time outside of combat and doesn't have a cooldown.

SHAMAN

Ancestral Spirit cannot be used during combat and has no cooldown.

PALADIN

Paladins can ask Redemption for dead party members.

DRUID

Rebirth is the only rez spell that can be cast during combat. It costs a reagent each time it is used (the reagent varies depending on level) and has a 30 minute cooldown.

WIPE RECOVERY

Total party wipes happen, especially in Raids. Having good wipe recovery is the only thing that keeps the Raid going.

WARLOCK

For the cost of a Soul Shard, the Warlock can use Create Soul Stone for a party member. This allows the 'stoned' person to instantly resurrect himself instead of releasing their spirit. The soul stone buff lasts one hour, has a one hour cooldown, and needs to be renewed. Classes that can resurrect should be given stones.

PALADIN

By using a Symbol of Divinity and sacrificing themselves, Paladins can call upon Divine Intervention and remove a party member from combat and all danger for 3 minutes. At the end of the duration, the party member can be attacked as normal, so it should be cast on someone who can resurrect others and is outside of the enemy's aggro detection.

SHAMAN

Reincarnation has a one hour cooldown (unless you have taken the Improved Reincarnation talent), and consumes an Ankh each time it is used.

ORGANIZING A RAID

Once you have everyone in a raid, it's important to move people into group configurations that are beneficial to your goal. In the raid window, the raid leader can simply click and drag people from one group to another.

The most obvious way to organize people is as several small groups; each with their own healer, tank, dps, etc. This is a very balanced way to do it and is often a good start. As you become more comfortable with organizing raids and knowing the abilities of all the classes, forming specialized groups becomes quite powerful.

The following are merely examples of specialized groups. Knowing your raid-mates, their abilities, and their play style will be the ultimate factors in group placement.

Main tank

Class	Role
Warrior	Main Tank
Paladin/Shaman	Healer/Mitigation
Warlock w/Imp	Damage
Priest	Healer/Mitigation
Druid	Healer

This group would be quite durable. It would have all the healing the Main Tank would need and have the Backup Tank ready to take over should something go wrong. With the mitigation and healing provided by the Paladin or Shaman, the Warrior would become even more durable

Ranged Damage

Class	Role
Shaman	Heal/Buff
Hunter w/Wolf	Damage/Buff
Hunter w/Wolf	Damage/Buff
Hunter w/Wolf	Damage/Buff
Hunter w/Wolf	Damage/Buff

This group is a bit stale, but it's still effective. The Shaman using Grace of Air Totem increases the agility of all the Hunters in the group. The Hunters should keep their wolves near (rather than sending them to attack) and use their Furious Howl manually. If the Hunters time it well, always have the Furious Howl buff and each attack has its damage raised significantly. The Shaman is fairly superfluous and can be replaced by a Feral Druid or a Paladin using Blessing of Might.

AoE Damage

Class	Role
Ice Mage	AoE Damage
Fire Mage	AoE Damage
Warlock	AoE Damage
Warrior	Tank/AoE Damage
Priest	Healer/Mitigation/AoE Damage

Starting the fight with dual Blizzards and a Rain of Fire might scare most people, but there is a method to this madness. When the enemies approach the casters, the Priest uses Power Word: Shield and the Warrior Charges and uses Challenging Shout. Once all aggro is on the Warrior, pull back so all enemies are in front of you and use Retaliation (30 minute cooldown and not fully necessary if you're saving the ability for Shield Wall). The enemies won't be pulling off the Warrior for some time so use Arcane Explosion, Holy Nova (if you're Holy specced), Hellfire, and Whirlwind to finish the enemies quickly.

Melee DPS

Class	Role
Fury Warrior	Damage/Buff
Rogue	Damage
Shaman	Damage/Buff
Feral Druid	Damage/Buff
Hunter w/Wolf	Damage/Buff

Any of these classes can deal damage on their own, but together they can buff each other and further raise their damage. The Warrior raises everyone's attack power with Battle Shout. The Shaman raises everyone's strength with Strength of Earth Totem and increases melee attacks with Windfury Totem or raises agility with Grace of Air Totem. The Feral Druid increases everyone's critical chance with Leader of the Pack. The Hunter has their pet use focus only on Furious Growl which raises the damage of each person's next attack. Combine all of these together and this group puts out the damage.

Sustained Magic Damage

Class	Role
Warlock	Sustained Damage
Warlock	Sustained Damage
Warlock	Sustained Damage
Shadow Priest	Damage
Paladin	Healer

One Warlock uses Curse of Shadows while another uses Curse of Elements to keep the targets shadow and fire resistance low while the other uses Curse of Agony. After that, everyone starts throwing shadow damage and DoTs. Corruption, Immolate, and Shadow Word: Pain all stack and will keep doing damage as you switch to Firebolt, Shadowbolt, Mind Flay, and Mind Blast. The Priest should use Fade often to keep his or her threat lower. The Paladin brings a good bit to the party with emergency healing and his Blessing of Wisdom which regenerates mana for each party member. A Shaman using Mana Spring Totem can be substituted or a Balance Druid in Moonkin form to increase spell critical chance. This is a highly specialized group, it is almost always better to assign a Warlock to a tank.

WHAT IS THE DIFFERENCE BETWEEN A RAID INSTANCE AND AN OUTDOOR RAID?

Raid Instances take place inside an instanced dungeon. This means you cannot have any outside assistance, but it also means you won't have any outside interference (especially on PvP servers). Raid Instances are often long dungeons with many smaller enemies leading to the larger threat.

Outdoor Raids occur in the world. People from outside your raid can help or hinder your attempt at these targets. You may also be competing with others as these enemies often take several days to respawn. Outdoor Raids are often in areas where your raid will have to fight past small groups of enemies to get to the boss, but not nearly as many as a dungeon raid.

RAID LISTING

Raid Quick Table

Name	Zone	Player Limit
Upper Blackrock Spire	Searing Gorge/Burning Steppes	10
Ruins of Ahn'Qiraj	Silithus	20
Zul'Gurub	Stranglethorn Vale	20
Blackwing Lair	Blackrock Spire	40
Molten Core	Blackrock Depths	40
Naxxramas	Western Plaguelands	40
Onyxia's Lair	Dustwallow Marsh	40
Temple of Ahn'Qiraj	Silithus	40

UPPER BLACKROCK SPIRE

Zone: Searing Gorge/Burning Steppes	
Level Range: 58-60	
Player Limit: 10	
Primary Enemies: Humanoid, Wyrmkin	
Special Items: Parts of the Beaststalker, Devout, Dreadmist, Elements, Lightforge, Magister, Shadowcraft, Valor, Wildheart armor sets drop. Dal'Rend's Sacred Charge weapon set drops.	
Entrance Requirements: A completed Seal of Ascension is required to enter the upper floors of Blackrock Spire	

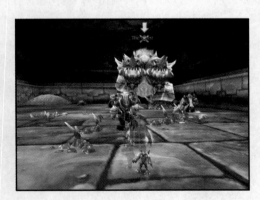

After completing the Seal of Ascension, make a left in the first room to the sealed door. The braziers light and the door opens. The path is filled with the humanoids and Wyrmkin loyal to the Black Dragonflight.

Having Mages and Druids for CC is quite important as is having a heavily armored tank and watchful healer. The enemies at the end of the instance hit very hard. Have your wipe recovery stay well back from a fight so that if a wipe occurs they can rez safely without re-aggroing the enemies.

ZUL'GURUB

Zone: Stranglethorn Vale	
Level Range: 60+	
Player Limit: 20	
Primary Enemies: Humanoid	
Special Items: Many armor and weapon pieces including class specific armor sets.	
Entrance Requirements: None	

While the outcasts of the ancient Gurubashi Empire fled to the Swamp of Sorrows to continue their worship of the blood god Hakkar, they soon found that only in the capital of the shattered empire could Hakkar be fully summoned. The capital has been taken by the Atal'ai and the preparations to summon Hakkar have been completed.

The other troll tribes have sent their greatest High Priests, but to no avail. Rather than defeating Hakkar and his followers, these mighty spiritual warriors have been taken by Hakkar and are now counted among his allies.

The quests for Zul'Gurub are obtained on a small island off the northwest coast of Stranglethorn Vale. The entrance to Zul'Gurub, in northeastern Stranglethorn Vale, is guarded by a few trolls but you can easily run past them and zone into the area.

MOLTEN CORE

Zone: Blackrock Depths	
Level Range: 60+	
Player Limit: 40	
Primary Enemies: Elemental, Demon	
Special Items: Class-specific epic armor sets as well as many epic weapons. The starter for the Priest and Hunter epic quests drops here.	
Entrance Requirements: Attunement to the Core	

While there is no key to Molten Core, you can't take all 40 people through Blackrock Depths each time. There is a Blood Elf who offers a quest that allows you to be 'attuned' to Molten Core. Once the quest is complete, you can enter Molten Core from the Blood Elf rather than going all the way through Blackrock Depths.

Molten Core is a cave of molten rock and creatures that flourish in the impressive heat. With many targets being opposed to the Hydraxian Waterlords, this is a good place to increase your reputation as you will need it to summon some of the more powerful monsters in Molten Core.

Bring your fire resistance gear and couple good secondary tanks. Many of the enemies throw off any CC you put on them and have to be tanked individually. Focus your fire and kill the enemies one at a time.

ONYXIA'S LAIR

Zone: Dustwallow Marsh	
Level Range: 60+	
Player Limit: 40	
Primary Enemies: Wyrmkin	
Special Items: A plethora of rare and epic items can be found in the horde of the dragon.	
Entrance Requirements: Completing the Marshal Windsor or Warlord's Command quest chain is required for Alliance and Horde raids to enter Onyxia's Lair. Blackhand's Command	

While a very short instance, it is very challenging. The multiple whelps can cause a great deal of trouble and Onyxia herself is no pushover. Be ready with your fire resistance gear.

BLACKWING LAIR

Zone: Upper Blackrock Spire	
Level Range: 60+	
Player Limit: 40	
Primary Enemies: Humanoid, Wyrmkin	
Special Items: Many armor and weapon pieces including class specific armor sets.	
Entrance Requirements: None	

Lord Nefarion commands his agents from high atop Blackrock Spire. Like Molten Core, the entrance to Blackwing Lair is within another instance (Upper Blackrock Spire). To become attuned, kill the Quartermaster outside Blackrock Spire and read his orders. Once the quest is begun, proceed into Upper Blackrock Spire and kill Drakkisath. With him dead, use the orb behind him to complete your attunement. In the future, you are able to enter Blackwing Lair by using the orb where you found the Quartermaster.

The fights within Blackwing Lair are quite varied and exciting. Each fight is extremely different from the previous and it will take several attempts before your raid will progress through this raid instance. Be prepared for the wipes and be ready to think about new strategies that will lead you to victory.

RUINS OF AHN'QIRAJ

Zone: Silithus	
Level Range: 60+	
Player Limit: 20	
Primary Enemies: Constructs, Silithid	
Special Items: Many armor and weapon pieces including class specific armor sets.	
Entrance Requirements: The Gates of Ahn'Qiraj world event must be completed before the Ruins of Ahn'Qiraj can be entered.	

Following the War of the Shifting Sands, the Qiraji were left in a devastated city cut off from the world. Though not defeated, they were sealed within. Many generations have passed, but the Qiraji have not been idle. The Ruins of Ahn'Qiraj are teeming with an army anxious to strike against Azeroth.

As the primary enemies are constructs and silithids, there are few ways to CC them. Instead concentrate on using tanks to hold them while your raid blows them down.

TEMPLE OF AHN'QIRAJ

Zone: Silithus	
Level Range: 60+	
Player Limit: 40	
Primary Enemies: Silithid	
Special Items: Many armor and weapon pieces including class specific armor sets.	
Entrance Requirements: The Gates of Ahn'Qiraj world event must be completed before the Temple of Ahn'Qiraj can be entered.	

The War of the Shifting Sands never reached the center of the city. Even as the outskirts were laid to waste, the Temple of Ahn'Qiraj was never taken. The breeding grounds were never destroyed and the leadership was never attacked.

After so many generations have passed, the armies are ready. The monument to unspeakable gods is not one to be taken lightly. Many of the enemies will have unique abilities and will take several attempts before they can be defeated. Repair your armor before you enter as you'll need all the durability you have and be prepared for many deaths.

Honored	Revered	Exalted
5x Arcane Crystal	2x Arcane Crystal	Free
2x Nexus Crystal	1x Nexus Crystal	
60g	30g	
1x Righteous Orb		

Both the living and unliving servants of the Lich King aid Kel'Thuzad in Naxxramas. The Necropolis has everything that is needed to wage war against Azeroth. Defeating this unbelievable evil will mean far more than victory…it will mean survival.

Druids, Priests, and Mages make excellent choices for CC classes, but be ready to encounter enemies that are immune to CC entirely. Have several off-tanks and healers ready for fights against large groups of enemies.

Shaped like a giant wheel, there are four wings in the Necropolis, determine which wing you intend to enter before the raid forms. This will save hurt feelings and time.

NAXXRAMAS

Zone: Eastern Plaguelands	
Level Range: 60+	
Player Limit: 40	
Primary Enemies: Undead, Beasts	
Special Items: Many armor and weapon pieces including class specific armor sets.	
Entrance Requirements: Gaining reputation with Argent Dawn at Light's Hope Chapel allows you to enter Naxxramas cheaper.	

Floating above the greenish haze of Eastern Plaguelands, Naxxramas is the ultimate destination for those helping the Argent Dawn.

EXISTING OUTDOOR RAIDS

Outdoor Table	
Name	**Zone**
Ysondre	Ashenvale, Feralas, Duskwood, The Hinterlands
Taerar	Ashenvale, Feralas, Duskwood, The Hinterlands
Lethon	Ashenvale, Feralas, Duskwood, The Hinterlands
Emeriss	Ashenvale, Feralas, Duskwood, The Hinterlands
Azurgos	Azshara
Lord Kazzak	The Blasted Lands

DRAGONS OF NIGHTMARE

Something has happened within the Emerald Dream. Ysera's four most trusted lieutenants have emerged from the dream, but they are tainted. They attack anyone who comes near and some of them have visible signs of the taint.

There are several things that all four dragons have in common.

1. Generate floating green clouds that cause Sleep.
2. Green Dragon Breath which slows ability cooldowns.
3. Attack members behind with Tail Swipe.
4. Use specific abilities at 75%, 50%, and 25% health.
5. Are guarded by groups of green dragonkin and drakes.

YSONDRE

Zone:	Ashenvale, Feralas, Duskwood, The Hinterlands
Level Range:	60+
Primary Damage Type:	Nature
Special Items:	Many items of epic and rare quality.

As one of the Dragons of Nightmare, Ysondre shares the sleep, breath, and tail swipe abilities of her brethren. Have your raid prepared to avoid the green clouds and your main tank ready to keep Ysondre facing away from the largest portion of the raid.

As her health drops, Ysondre summons several druids who attack members of your raid. Ysondre also has a Lightning Wave attack that she uses against the main tank. This does considerable nature damage and can leap from one person to the next. Avoid keeping people too close to the main tank to reduce the overall damage done by this ability. The more people you bring to this fight, the more damage you do, but the more chaotic things become.

TAERAR

Zone:	Ashenvale, Feralas, Duskwood, The Hinterlands
Level Range:	60+
Primary Damage Type:	Nature
Special Items:	Many items of epic and rare quality.

Taerar also shares the tail swipe, green dragon breath, and sleep attacks. Have your raid prepared to avoid the green clouds and stay away from the front of Taerar.

As his health drops, Taerar will become a full shadow and summon three Shades of Taerar. These look identical to Taerar and have many of his abilities. They have fewer hitpoints and must be killed before Taerar engages your raid again. Only the true Taerar has the ability to fear large portions of your raid. Fear immunity and dispelling effects greatly aids your success. The more people you bring to this fight, the more damage you do, but the more chaotic things become.

LETHON

Zone:	Ashenvale, Feralas, Duskwood, The Hinterlands
Level Range:	60+
Primary Damage Type:	Nature, Shadow
Special Items:	Many items of epic and rare quality.

Tail swipe, green dragon breath, and sleep are all abilities Lethon shares with the other Dragons of Nightmare. Keep your raid away from the floating green clouds and to the sides of Lethon to reduce the effectiveness of his attacks.

As the battle with Lethon continues, he often casts Shadowbolt Whirl that hits everyone in the raid. This makes life on healers more difficult so be ready. With his health falling, Lethon stuns your entire raid for a few seconds and summon wraiths from your bodies. These travel toward Lethon slowly and heal him when contact is made. Be ready to AoE these to death or face a reinvigorated dragon.

The more people you bring to this fight, the more damage you do, but the more chaotic things become and the more people possibly healing him.

EMERISS

Zone: Ashenvale, Feralas, Duskwood, The Hinterlands	
Level Range: 60+	
Primary Damage Type: Nature	
Special Items: Many items of epic and rare quality.	

As one of the Dragons of Nightmare, Emeriss also possesses the sleep, breath, and tail swipe abilities. Avoid standing in front of her (unless you're the main tank), behind her, or in the floating green clouds.

Throughout the fight, Emeriss casts infections on your raid members. These cause the targeted member to inflict massive damage to all nearby members over several seconds. Should you get hit with this, run away from others until it can be dispelled. Emeriss, when her health drops, will release a DoT that deals 100% of your health over 10 seconds. A single heal keeps you from dying, but won't leave you with much health. Be ready to dispel and heal quickly after she does this.

The ancient blue dragon has many tricks to use against your raid. Keep everyone close enough to get teleported with him, but far enough away to avoid his AoEs. Don't attempt to resurrect after he's killed you as he will freeze you every time he uses a cold attack until the fifteen minute debuff wears off.

LORD KAZZAK

Safe within the Tainted Scar, Lord Kazzak prepares for his attack on the world. Move your raid into position as one group as the patrolling demons in the scar are very dangerous and will kill any small groups wandering through.

Lord Kazzak has several shadow attacks and curses that make him rather difficult to defeat. Keep all curses and magic debuffs dispelled and be ready for a quick fight. Should the fight take too long and Kazzak become bored, he begins casting shadowbolt volleys every couple seconds until your raid is dead. Do not bring more than 40 people against Kazzak. Any larger force (pets included) cause Kazzak to cast shadowbolt volleys every couple seconds until your raid is dead.

Zone: The Blasted Lands	
Level Range: 60+	
Primary Damage Type: Shadow	
Special Items: Many items of epic and rare quality.	

AZUREGOS

Zone: Azshara	
Level Range: 60+	
Primary Damage Type: Cold	
Special Items: Many items of epic and rare quality.	

Azuregos guards the magical secrets of Azshara. He does not attack you until provoked. This makes assembling a raid easier as he patrols around. Clear any of the mobs in the area before engaging Azuregos.

TO THE BATTLE

When World of Warcraft released, there wasn't nearly as much to say about player versus player combat. Everything was handled in duels, or out in the open fields, and these contests were for personal distinction alone. With the introduction of the Battlegrounds, the Honor System, and some substantial balances for the character classes, things have changes immensely. This chapter does all that it can to explain the rules, concepts, and purpose of PvP combat in World of Warcraft. It also goes into specifics about the various locations for such conflict, and how to come out on top in your many engagements.

PvP 101

Though there are many specifics in PvP combat, there are also a number of universal traits. The Honor System, gaining Ranks, rules of conduct, and many strategies are shared between the various Battlegrounds and in the open field. Before trying to master Warsong Gulch, Arathi Basin, or the legendary Alterac Valley, a person must try to understand how PvP works, at its core.

HONOR AND REPUTATION

One of the first questions that new players wonder is what you can get through PvP. You don't get experience from killing other characters, and even victory in the Battlegrounds awards such a modest level of experience that it won't be a major focus for anyone there. Instead, PvP offers Honor, Reputation (Battlegrounds Only), fun, and a number of equipment rewards.

There are two major paths of equipment upgrades that are earned from the Battlegrounds. Honor is gained from just about any PvP action (winning a Battleground, sometimes losing a Battleground, slaying a target that is not grey to your character, taking part in a raid against an enemy faction's leader, etc.). This Honor is gathered for a full week, then is calculated during server maintenance to see how your character has performed compared to other characters of the same faction. You are then given a Standing (from first, which would be the most honor gained on the server for your faction, to all of the Standing values for those who PvPed at all). The higher your Standing, the more your character's Rank will progress. There are 14 PvP Ranks, though characters start without any Rank at all. After each maintenance, your character has the chance to gain or lose Rank; this is a dynamic system that pushes characters to PvP constantly if they want to achieve or even maintain the higher Ranks in the game.

The Long and Short of Honor System Terms

- **Honor:** Gained for Kills and Battleground Activity; Used at the End of the Week, then Are Reset
- **Standing:** Calculated After Server Maintenance for Each Week, Used to Determine Whether Your Character Gains or Loses Rating Points
- **Rank:** Your Current PvP Title; This Determines What Rewards You Can Access from Your Faction; Rank/Title is Based Off of Your Character's Current Rating Points
- **Rating:** The Actual Measure of Your Character's Honor System Progress; This is More Accurate Than Rank, But Cannot Be Seen In-Game

At first this might seem complex, and some aspects of it genuinely are. Many people participate in the Honor System without fully understanding how it works. That is fine; they only need to get out there and fight if they want a few Ranks. But to conquer the system and get the most out of it, people need to sit down and really see what is going on behind the scenes.

UNDERSTANDING HONOR, STANDING, RATINGS, AND RANK

A Quick Look at the Ranks

Rank	Rating Points	Required Level	Alliance Title	Horde Title	Reward
1	Score 25 Kills in a Week	N/A	Private	Scout	Tabard
2	2,000	N/A	Corporal	Grunt	Trinket (Removes Certain Status Effects)
3	5,000	N/A	Sergeant	Sergeant	Rare Cloak; 10% Discount on Items/Requires From Faction Merchants
4	10,000	33	Master Sergeant	Senior Sergeant	Rare Necklace
5	15,000	38	Sergeant Major	First Sergeant	Rare Bracers
6	20,000	41	Knight	Stone Guard	Entry to Officer's Brackets in Racial Capital, Officer's Tabard, Inexpensive Potions
7	25,000	44	Knight-Lieutenant	Blood Guard	Rare Boots and Gloves (PvP Set)
8	30,000	46	Knight-Captain	Legionnaire	Rare Chest and Leggings (PvP Set)
9	35,000	48	Knight-Champion	Centurion	Battle Standard (Enhances Health to Allies, Reusable)
10	40,000	51	Lieutenant Commander	Champion	Rare Helm and Shoulders (PvP Set Complete)
11	45,000	53	Commander	Lieutenant General	Inexpensive Epic Mount (Unique Appearance), Ability to Chat in Defense Channels
12	50,000	55	Marshal	General	Epic Gloves, Leggings, and Boots (Upgraded PvP Set)
13	55,000	57	Field Marshal	Warlord	Epic Helm, Shoulders, and Chest (Upgraded PvP Set Complete)
14	60,000	60	Grand Marshal	High Warlord	Epic Weapons/Shield

Rules of Rank Advancement

- Rating Advances By Having a High Standing (End the Week With More Honor Than Others)
- Rating Decays Every Week; You Are In a Fight to Earn More Than You Lose
- Because Lower Level Battlegrounds and Characters Are Worth Fewer Honor Points, Competition for High Standing Isn't Possible Before the Higher Brackets
- Rating/Rank is Capped at Various Levels; Only a Character at Level 60 Can Reach Rank 14 (All Brackets Have a Cap of Some Sort Before Then)
- Dishonorable Kills (Taking Out Civilians) Immediately Reduces Your Rating, Effectively Lowering Your Rank Progress

If Standing gets you the Rating/Ranks you need, and a high Standing is based on getting more Honor than other characters in your faction, the obvious question is how to get the most Honor.

Duels get you nothing of any sort. Open field PvP is almost worthless, contributing only a small amount of Honor over time. In reality, the higher Ranks are not accessible without entering the Battlegrounds. In these battles, your character gains a high sum of Honor for victories while still getting supplemental Honor for the kills that naturally take place during the contest. Because Battlegrounds have Reputations (and rewards) of their own, the vast majority of focused PvP takes place within them.

Knowing that the Battlegrounds are the place to go for Honor, your next step is to find a solid team to play with. Sure, PUGing the BGs (going into the Battlegrounds by queueing on your own) is okay here and there. But to get a ton of Honor, start forming groups ahead of time. Join a good PvP guild, or just find a number of friends who are skilled in PvP and enjoy playing with you. This helps teamwork immensely, and leads to victory after victory in many engagements.

If Honor and victories are even more important, make sure that your guild has a voice chat server of some sort so that they can always be on a voice chat program while in the Battlegrounds. It's much faster to hit a key and say "Incoming Ramp" than to type it. In fact, speaking even allows you to quickly convey "Three incoming ramp, a Paladin, a Druid, and a Priest." Get as many people as possible on voice chat and get the folks to speak out about important actions in the Battlegrounds.

With these systems in place, practice and play often. Investing more hours into the PvP system is always a way to increase the Honor you are getting each week. A couple of hours here and there are easily enough to pull your character up through the first few Ranks. As the climb continues, you need to put in more time. Competition starts at Rank 4, but it is trivial. You only need to be placing somewhere in the top few hundred to make consistent progress. It isn't until Rank 8 or 9 that casual players in the PvP system start to really push themselves for progress.

By Rank 11, even those people in a good guild that PvPs often start to see real challenges. To advance at that stage, your character has to be placing in the very high Standings every week. And to reach Rank 14, you need to be able to steal that top slot on your faction for a couple of weeks in a row.

It's possible to hit Rank 14 by getting in the top three Standing Slots, but you can't afford to see far below the leader in Honor, whatever the case.

Moving through the PvP Ranks takes a few months, even if you devote all of your WoW time to PvPing. And, depending on the level of PvP on your server, hitting Ranks 12 and beyond may demand ten or more hours of PvP per day. Anyone can get through the lower Ranks (and enjoy their rewards). Anyone can eventually get enough Reputation to enjoy the Battleground-specific rewards! And most players can even hit the middle-Officer Ranks without too much trouble. Just be aware that going to Rank 11 and beyond requires major work and dedication to PvP and the game itself. Skill can only take you so far; time, time, and more time are needed in the end.

For the highest Ranks in the system, many players start to organize themselves even between the guilds. Quite a few servers have formed a queue for advancing to the highest Ranks. This way, the high-end players enter into an agreement to allow specific people to get the highest totals. By avoiding competition between each other in this fashion, they dramatically reduce the level of tension in the process and allow themselves more free time to do other WoW activities or even logoff (it does happen). Use the PvP Rankings from the worldofwarcraft.com site to find out who you are competing with at the highest tiers. Talk to them and see what can be worked out; it's always worth a try!

DIMINISHING RETURNS AND WASTED EFFORT

- A person's honor decreases by 10% each time you kill them in a Battleground
- Honor From Kills Does Not Mean Very Much in the Long Run
- Your Sum Total of Honorable Kills Does Nothing, Means Nothing, is Worth Nothing

Further information about Honor is useful for your progress. Many players who are new to the system don't believe that the Bonus Honor from the Battlegrounds is the key to success in achieving a higher Rating. Instead, these players try to farm Honor from repeatedly killing their enemies. Not only does this make for a less interesting and longer match, but it doesn't pay off! Observe the following table.

Diminishing Returns for Repeatedly Killing the Same Person	
Times Killed	Percentage of Full Honor Value
1	100%
2	90%
3	80%
4	70%
5+	60%, 50%, 40%, etc.

This table shows what happens when you and your groups kill the same person repeatedly. The first time a specific enemy character is slain, they yield their full Honor value to you (up to several hundred points). The second kill is reduced to 75% of the total value, and so on from there.

Honor gained from kills is purely supplemental for this reason. You can't farm targets; you can't gain major Rating from mass slaughter, and so forth. This is even more reason not to camp graveyards, not to farm kills in the Battlegrounds, and to push for your objectives!

Every 24 hours, the diminishing returns system resets, and those who you killed yesterday go back to being worth a full value (until you trash them again). This system is the main reason why places like Alterac Valley and open field PvP sites are not ultimate honorfests.

RATING DECAY

- ⮡ Your Character Loses 20% of Their Accrued Rating Every Week
- ⮡ In the Higher Ranks, 20% of Your Rating Leads to Slower and Slower Progress Because This Value Becomes Greatly Higher
- ⮡ There is a Safety Net That Prevents You From Losing More than 2,500 Rating Per Week if You Go Into the Negatives (This is usually Half a Rank)

Every week, after maintenance, your character has their Rating for the completed week compared to their old Rating. If you didn't PvP much at all, it is likely to you will lose points from your overall Rating. This can cause you to fall up to half a Rank per week.

If you look at the required Rating values for the Ranks, you can see why the 20% Rating penalty per week becomes so fierce. At the lowest part of Rank 13, this means that your character needs to get at least 11,000 Rating Points per week just to break even. That means getting a substantial percentage of the number one character's Honor total. The person with the highest Standing only gets 13,000, so we're not talking about a very high margin for slipups.

There isn't a set total for Rating Given to anyone below first Standing. While the number one person gets that lovely 13,000, everyone else receives an amount weighted by their percentage of the leader's Honor. So, if you got the number two slots and only missed by a hair, don't fret! Your character is still going to get a sum in the high 12,000s (12,920 for example).

THERE CAN BE ONLY ONE

Despite all of the rules for progression that we just mentioned, there are some exceptions. The system is set up to prevent too many characters from being in the higher Ranks at the same time. When passing into the really high Ranks (11 and up), this number dwindles to a paltry sum.

This is yet another reason why many players work together and form queues for getting into the higher Ranks. Once a person has gotten to their desired goal, it is important for them to fall back and make room for other players in their faction. Someone who was crazy enough to camp Rank 14 would be keeping the rest of their faction from reaching it. Though rare, more than one Rank 14 player can exist at one time on a server.

Thus, get your gear and get out! You can certainly still BG and will be happily welcomed into your old groups. But try not to BG so much that you threaten to get into the top 20 Standing positions. That way, the people who need the high Ranks can push you out of the way.

A FEW MORE TIPS

If you are trying for those highest Ranks, remember these final words of advice. First, learn to love Warsong. Stomping PUGs in Warsong Gulch offers the best Honor/hour in the game. Arathi Basin matches **can** be even better if you are able to seize a 5-0 victory in five or six minutes, but there are some problems with that. It's not easy against any team worth a darn. It's also extremely unlikely that such teams will queue constantly and let your guild/PvP group obliterate them.

Thus, Warsong is the most consistent source for defeatable PUGs. Be nice and respectful to the enemies (to keep them queueing and to be a good person). Beyond that, remember to bring your appropriate PvP gear and trinkets, keep the Stamina high, buy Healing Potions and possibly Free Action Potions as well if you like to run the flag.

If Ranks are that important, choose Talents specifically for the Battleground that you plan to camp. Don't worry about PvE Talents and survivability if all that you do and plan on doing for several months will involve Battleground work. Keep an eye out for anything that will improve your burst damage or

limit enemy capabilities. Stuns are great, instant attacks are wonderful too. Mana efficiency is less important, considering that you won't often live for too long once you start casting heavily.

RULES, EVEN IN WAR

Another general theme of PvP is the sense of proper conduct that runs through its most respected players. There are many people who are going to break into an "us vs. them" mentality, and those are the types that often a lot more difficult to work with. If you want to play on consistent, mature, and skilled teams, it usually means learning the rules of conduct and sticking to them at all times.

You might wonder what is fair and what is unfair on the field of war. By the terms of the game, almost everything is kosher in the Battlegrounds; using /spit and /rude, slaughtering people two seconds after they Rez, and being a general jerk to friend and enemy alike is not going to get you kicked off the server (unless you use language that violates the ToS, obviously).

What those actions may do, however, is get you blacklisted from the best PvP groups available. That is a very bad thing, because the rate of Honor for PUGs isn't even close to what a skilled group can rake in. And for the higher Ranks, even a single group hitting more Honor than you is going to prevent you from moving forward well.

Thus, whether you believe in being nasty to the enemies or not, it's very much to your advantage to learn how to behave in the way that your server deems appropriate. The specifics of that may vary a fair bit, but we'll still discuss some of the usual problems that come up here; that way, you at least know the sides before you have to choose which one to take.

Graveyard Camping

Graveyard Camp is considered a normal tactic on PvP servers. Though frowned upon, don't be surprised to see it more since the cross-server Battleground merger of 1.12

In Arathi Basin, never approach the file graveyard for the other side; these are located at the northwestern hill for the Alliance and the southeastern hill for the Horde. Don't climb the hill, don't let enemies kite you up there, and just stay away. If the other side is outnumbered and being 5-0ed there, just let them stay back if they don't want to fight. Keep it painless, take your free victory, and be happy it isn't happening to you. Never rub it in.

In Warsong Gulch, there on time when you want to attack the graveyard. Yup, you guessed it; when their flag runner stands in the middle of the graveyard. This is done by turtling teams to give them the best chance to keep constant healing on their carrier. With enough healers, it can be very hard to defeat without a good group of crowd controllers (and you just might not have said crowd controllers in your raid). When that is the case, hop on

every healer that Rezzes and kill em outright until the flag runner is dead and the flag is returned. That is the **only** exception to the rule when in Warsong.

In Alterac Valley, graveyard camping is built into the system somewhat. Because the teams are forced to capture graveyards, there are times you simply have to clear out recent rezzers to ensure that it is safe to capture and hold the area. Don't laugh, spit, or be a jerk about it. Just kill the targets, get it done, and move on. As long as your side isn't mean about the process, the enemies are likely to understand that it's just something that had to happen.

Spitting and Other Emotes

This problem comes up all the time. Some people really like to /spit on their foes. You will see it, and you might see it a lot (depending on your server). Even on some RP servers, there is a sense that /spit is an insult to the player and not the character. That isn't universal, but it is a commonly-held view. Unless you truly wish to insult an enemy and are willing to risk offending even your own team, avoid using the Spit Emote.

For roleplaying or just having fun, try /shake, /grin, and /roar instead. There are many cool emotes out there that don't have the same weight as /spit. Also, remember that /say and non-standard emotes /em "Other Test" are not viewable by the other side. Don't use these to try and convey a message, because they won't get across.

Laughing at other players is another emote that might be taken personally. This won't evoke the same response at spitting, and sometimes it just makes sense (e.g. That Paladin just bubbled with the flag, omg /lol). If you do this a lot though, and do care about being nice to the other side, try a /hug or a /comfort to go along with it. Let people know that you aren't ripping into them, but laughing at the situation.

Because the system Blizzard uses to garble text between the factions is consistent, people have figured out how to state something that is gibberish to their own team and understandable by the other side. Please don't use this to insult the other team; it's not funny or amusing to many people, and it gets old pretty quickly.

Text Spamming

Spamming /say or /yell in the BGs can also get to be a major pain. Don't create macros to tap and fill people's textbars. This annoys folks on both sides of the fight, and it isn't going to win you terribly many friends. If you have specific messages for your team, keep it in /raid or /party chat.

If you are roleplaying and have a battlecry or something similar, use it sparingly. There is nothing wrong with doing this; try to keep the message short, and only use it from time to time. There is a big difference between spamming something to be a pain and doing some roleplaying (most characters on both sides will recognize this).

ITEM USE

This is an issue that is brought up from time-to-time; people complain about the use or over-use of items in the Battlegrounds. People with more money are going to drink a great number of potions, including Healing/Mana Potions, attribute-enhancing ones, and even Flasks in truly extreme cases. Free Action and Swiftness Potions are used commonly, and quite a few Engineering pieces too.

There is nothing wrong with this; the rules of the game and even the rules of decency say nothing about avoiding money use for the BGs. You can choose not to use these items, and that is fine too, but there is no way that both sides are going to enter into an agreement to abstain from all of their toys. Indeed, some players get the most joy out of using Mind Control Caps, Rocket Boots, and a way array of Trinkets.

Get used to Purging/Dispelling when you see heavy item users on the field; for a slight use of mana, you get to rip effects right off of these characters, wasting money and cooldowns in the process!

BRACKET CAMPING/TWINKING

Each bracket starts at x0 and goes up to x9 (except for the capped bracket, for players of the highest level). Thus, the first bracket is 10-19, then 20-29, and so forth. For brackets like the 10-19 and 50-59, it is extremely common to find bracket campers; those who are staying at the highest level of the BGs and avoiding experience. These are folks who are trying to get either

more honor in a somewhat easier bracket, or they are specifically Twinking to get an edge over others in PvP (this is most often the case with level 19 characters).

The issue itself becomes rather complex. There is nothing in the game rules that says a person has to level up, and twinking is not an avoidable thing either. Blizzard is likely to limit some of the potential for twinkers in the future; it has been stated that high-tier Enchantments are going to be limited to higher-level characters at some point in the future. This will relieve some of the pressure on the earlier brackets.

Okay, so what does twinking look like? Expect a certain type of level 19 player to have almost all Rare equipment (AH purchased), be wielding high DPS weaponry, and be using Enchantments that are very expensive. Life Stealing is one of the most brutal Enchantments for this tier of Battlegrounds. Rogues are one of the most common twink classes because their DPS is already quite capable in the high teens, while Warriors don't have enough of their abilities, and casters can only do so much to twink their characters.

Twinking does have a vague wrongness. There isn't anything against the rules here, but non-twinks in the lower brackets have no chance against you. A level 10-15 character can be one-shotted by a twink. Even level 19 characters are doomed against a dual-Lifesteal Rogue. Play how you want, and have a good time, but realize that people don't like to be splattered without even a fighting chance. Not everyone has a level 60 character already for easy funds, and not everyone is willing to play the Auction House for hours trying to make smooth deals. Thus, not everyone can twink their characters. It's not a fair fight.

A bracket camper, on the other hand, has no specific gear. They may be wonderfully equipped or poorly equipped. These characters are simply put in the Battlegrounds to reach a certain objective before moving on. Some bracket campers are really cool folks who just have PvP goals to reach. Others are trying to keep an edge in PvP as long as possible. On some servers there is antagonism between capped players and those one level below them. You can reach Rank 13 at level 59, meaning that most of the PvP journey can be spent without leveling to 60. It's easier to find and roll PUGs in the 50s (where equipment is lower, the levels are obviously varied, and more fresh blood moves through).

There is no clear cut right and wrong here. The best way to avoid drama and difficulty is to keep a good attitude, play with friends, and avoid the folks on both sides of the issue if they start to get nasty. Whether you bracket camp or not, keep a clean smile, fight a fair fight, and most PvPers will like you. Those who don't can take a kind leap off the side of the Lumber Mill.

STRATEGY AND TACTICS

Time to get new players started with a few general tips. We'll get into BG-specific tips farther down, but the ideas here are useful almost anywhere.

COMMUNICATION IS ESSENTIAL

This can't be stressed enough. The only way to way consistently against good teams is to have effective communication with the rest of your allies. The Battlegrounds aren't about killing; they are focused on goals: running a flag, capturing resource locations, and pushing up the field toward the enemy's base. These are not done well without a plan.

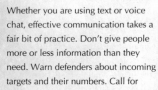

Whether you are using text or voice chat, effective communication takes a fair bit of practice. Don't give people more or less information than they need. Warn defenders about incoming targets and their numbers. Call for attackers to form at a specific site, and let them know when to hit.

If you aren't the leader of a raid, listen closely to what is being said, then contribute information that would be valuable to the leader. State when you see defenders moving about, notify is sites are light on defense or heavy, and so forth.

Learn to get this information across efficiently. Instead of saying/typing "There are five people coming toward out ramp," try "inc ramp 5." Lingo is used heavily in all of the BGs. Expect everything possible to be abbreviated when text is used, and even over voice some of this sticks.

Examples of Communication

Poor Form	Good Form	Meaning
ZERG!!!!111	6+ Inc Farm	Six or more people are rushing toward the Farm
Flag Lost	Ramp	The flag was taken, and the runner is going out to our ramp
Healers NOW	Kill Kith, Then Chay	Take down Kith the Priest, as she is healing their people; Take Out Chay After Kith is dead
Get their flag	Push Ramp now	Push forward into the enemy base using their ramp
Hold midfield	Rez, form on me, and stay with me	After your characters Rez, group together on my location

The more specific your information, the more powerful it becomes. Do everything possible to learn the lingo of your server and master it. Then, practice conveying information during downtime or even minor breaks within combat. If you get Stunned for four seconds, then type "FC Balcony" (enemy flag carrier is on the balcony). If you get Sapped by a defensive point, type "LM!" hit enter, then "Sapped, flag in trouble!" (the first line means Lumber Mill, then they get the next line, I'm crowd controlled and the flag is being captured).

Don't leave Caps Lock on, don't curse, and never yell at your teammates. This is asking for a loss. The last thing that you want to do is sow discord within the ranks of your buddies. If a game is already going poorly, any drama is going to make things a lot worse. Winning teams are much better able to roll with the punches than those teams that have already gotten beaten up a few times. Try to keep an upbeat attitude about it all, and spread that to others when you can. Ignore the naysayers and fools who are fast to decry every player and pitfall that appears.

NOT A SOLOERS PARADISE

Solo players are the bane of the Battlegrounds, even when they are effective killers. Cooperation allows for a synergistic increase to a raid's firepower. Thus, soloers are taking away from the group's potential even if they play their classes well.

Picture a scenario where one team has six people crossing the field in Warsong Gulch; they are grouped tightly together, their healers are ready to heal, their DPSers are set to target with a main assist on their leader, and so forth. The other side is crossing the field with seven characters, but they are strung out across the landscape. The first group hits them in pockets, facing two or three each time. When that happens, their crowd controllers keep all but the prime target Stunned or otherwise out of commission and the rest of the group obliterates the primary foe. This takes almost no time or mana, and the healers quickly restore the health of anyone who gets hurt.

The first group is very likely to reach the other side of the field without a single casualty, even though they were outnumbered at the beginning of the run. This is because the other group didn't focus fire, didn't stay together, didn't have a chance to heal, and so forth.

This event isn't theoretical. It happens, and it happens a lot. Stay grouped, stay together on offense and defense, and support your buddies. Attack the targets that they are already attacking, and do all that you can to heal and protect those allies who are being beaten upon. Attacking everything at once doesn't work in PvE, so why should it fare any better here?

Don't make solo runs for flags/goals unless you see a massive lapse in the enemy's defense. Even then, let people know what you are doing and why you are doing it. "They just ditched the Stables entirely, I'm NJing it."

Use your minimap to coordinate groupwork. Hit Shift + M to bring up the extra map and move toward your buddies if you are separated from them. There is no excuse for not knowing where people are!

DEFENSE, DEFENSE, DEFENSE!

Too many players underestimate the value of light but solid defense. Having too many players near a flag is a waste of resources that can spell for a long game or even a loss. Indeed, you need to have a trim but effective defense at all times.

Arathi Basin is the best example of a Battleground where this is true at all times; there are five points to defend (if you are lucky), and only up to 15 players on each side. There **must** be a single person at all owned sites at all times. Even if you think that a site is completely safe, it's amazingly important to have a set of eye there,

watching for stealthers and people who might be hidden in the terrain. Enemies are always hoping to find an undefended site; never give it to them!

During fierce contests you are going to need more than a single defender. A lone person won't slow anyone down. If they are immediately CCed through Sap or Polymorph there is plenty of time to capture the flag. If the enemies are being smart, a pair of defenders is well more than twice as powerful. It's much harder for the enemies to crowd control two people at once without making an obvious move toward the site. Beyond that, a direct attack requires that both characters die before the flag is captured. This leaves a window for the first character to Rez and return to the fight! If you are really lucky, the second person will die and do the same, allowing a duo to sometimes face four or five people and win in the long run.

All of that said, avoid the turtle in most circumstances. If you place six or seven people at a single point, there enemies are going to figure out a way to beat you. Turtling on defense slows games, hurts everyone's Honor, and leads to way too many defeats. Turtling is only useful for buying time (so it's a nice way to stall after a few people /afk or leave the BG because another one popped). Turtle to wait for reinforcements, then start the offense again.

To defeat a turtle, use crowd control. Psychic Scream, Howl of Terror, Frost Nova, Frost Traps, and other such abilities make it very hard for a larger force to bring its DPS to bear. This makes it quite possible to jump in, steal a flag, and head out again. This is most prominent in Warsong Gulch. For the other BGs, where there are more targets, the enemies are likely to just avoid your turtle and take everything else on the field.

Burst Damage

PvP kills are most easily gained by burst damage. Take a look at Fury and Arms Warriors to see a great example of this; the Fury Warriors deal more damage over time, so they should be awesome at PvP, right? It's true that they are still good, but Arms Warriors are able to frontload a ton of their damage. Charge, hit, Hamstring, hit, Mortal Strike, and watch the opponent's squirm as they try to respond. They just took a boatload of damage; even if they get some distance, they have a lot of health to make up, and that Arms Warrior is happily enjoying his cooldowns for another big swing. Fury Warriors, who

often use faster attacks, are forced to stick to enemies to maximize their DPS, and that just isn't possible in PvP.

The reason bursts are easier to maintain is that PvP combat is filled with Stuns, Snares, Roots, fast movement by opponents, some lag, and many other problems to get in the way of fast attacks. This encourages big hits rather than many hits.

Even better is that big hits scare people. When they lose a third of their health in a moment or two, it's harder for the victim to concentrate on doing damage in return. It's also harder for their healers

to respond; laying heavy damage on one target makes it possible to kill the person even when they have a whole team ready to try and save them. Two or three burst damage types working in concert can kill a flag carrier before a single heal lands!

Good burst abilities/equipment includes Mortal Strike, Aimed Shot, two-handed weapons, Pyroblast, Soul Fire, and Ambush. Anything with high cost or high charge times is likely to be fun in PvP. These lend themselves toward sudden strikes from behind, Stealth, out of sight, and so forth. Even classes without any ability to hide can surprise foes in PvP. A Warrior hiding inside of a bush might not be seen as an enemy rushes toward the Farm in Arathi Basin. This allows the Warrior to start with a Charge, from behind, getting them quite a bit of Rage and some damage before the victim even responds.

Using and Knowing the Terrain

The map is not the terrain! Get your character into a wide range of PvP activities, and you will soon start to see opportunities that were not initially available. There are many ways to get into various locations, and finding places to hide for surprise attacks is amazingly easy. Though some classes can Track and figure out where you are, only Hunters are especially good at doing this under a variety of circumstances. For almost every other target, the terrain is your friend!

Look for bushes, small buildings, tiny corners to hide in, and balconies to jump down from. These positions are all over the place, in world PvP and in the Battlegrounds. Don't fight foolishly when you have a choice; start from range, observe your enemies, stay hidden and wait for your team to arrive, and only get close to foes when you are a melee class.

A few classes have ways to observe the battlefield even while tucked away in safe locations (e.g. Warlocks, Hunters, Priests, Shaman). Use your class' abilities to look around an area when you are out of sight. If enemies come close, surprise them after informing your team where they are and how many there are. If you can scout at really long range, report on enemy force activity when there isn't direct fighting in your area; this allows defenders to accomplish several goals at the same time!

HEALERS

Healers are the blessing and bane of PvP, depending on whether they are on your side or the enemy's. Be prepared for healing classes to save important targets time and time again. This is why your team has to murder healers first, always.

It's not nice, but slaughtering healers is a face of PvP. Druids and Priests are first on the chopping block; they are squishy and concerted assault. Allow the ones that are in animal or Shadow Form to live while other healers die, but switch back as soon as they revert to Caster Form or non-Shadow Form. Then, take down the Shamans/Paladins on the other team.

These targets take longer, but they can't heal as well either, especially once the aggro turns their way.

One trick for defeating good healers (the ones that are healing frequently and seem to be very effective at it) is to crowd control them over long periods. Let your team know that this is the plan so that others don't break the control early. For example, say there is a high-level Priest that is always buffing and healing their team. Instead of killing her, which would only delay the character for a portion of a minute, dedicate a Mage to Polymorph her for as long as possible. Poly, cast a few spells on other people, Poly her again when she breaks, repeat. Not only does this keep the person out of combat for as long as possible, it frustrates them to no end. It's not fun to be chain crowd controlled. And though it's mean to say this, you don't want the best healers on the other team to have too much fun.

If you are one of the aforementioned healers, remember to stay out of sight as often as possible. Use terrain, obstacles that don't break line of sight for your spells, buildings, and other characters to hide yourself. Don't charge in with the main group; let other players engage and get the attention of foes before you enter casting range. If the other team isn't highly skilled, they aren't as likely to look past the Warriors, Hunters, and other obvious attackers that are jumping onto them. If they do not notice you, use disruptive abilities to delay the enemies while your DPSers beat on them (Psychic Scream, Earthbind Totem, Entangling Roots, and such).

CROWD CONTROL AND DISRUPTION

Crowd control is about as important as healing for the Battlegrounds (and sometimes it's even more valuable to a team). Use your class' crowd control abilities as often as possible. Your goal out in the field isn't to kill as many foes as possible, except in very odd cases. Indeed, you are there to capture a flag, hold terrain, etc. Killing isn't needed for that, but disruption is.

Crowd Control and Disruption Abilities

Class	Abilities to Use Heavily
Druid	Entangling Roots (godly against melee targets and flag carriers), Hibernate (Hunter Pets, Feral Druids, Ghost Wolf Shamans)
Hunter	Freezing and Frost Traps (on choke points), Wing Clip and Concussive Shot (flag carriers, melee targets), Wyvern Sting (anyone), Scare Beast (Pets, Feral Druids, Ghost Wolf Shamans)
Mage	Polymorph (anyone), Frost Nova/Cone of Cold/Blizzard (groups of foes supporting their team)
Paladin	Hammer of Justice (best against casters), Repentance
Priest	Psychic Scream (pockets of enemies), Mind Control (especially when cliffs are nearby), Mind Flay
Rogue	Sap (healers, as usual), Many Stuns, Crippling Poison
Shaman	Earthbind Totem (slows group or singles wonderfully), Frost Shock
Warlock	All Fear Abilities (these destroy team coordination), Seduce (with Succubus), Curse of Exhaustion
Warrior	Hamstring (use this on everyone), Piercing Howl (wonderful to keep reinforcements from getting to their flag carriers), Intimidating Shout (breaking turtle defenses), Protection Warrior Stuns

POWER-UPS IN THE BATTLEGROUNDS

Be on the lookout for areas where special power-ups spawn in the Battlegrounds. These items are fairly useful, and their proper use certainly helps to win games for the side that dominates them.

In Arathi Basin, all of these power-ups spawn near the resource nodes. Look in the mine cart about the Gold Mines, inside the house at the farm, in the center of the mill at the Lumber Mill, and just inside the Stables. These power-ups rotate between all three types of effects. The respawn rate for the Gold Mine power-ups seems to be faster than the others.

In Warsong Gulch there are also several power-up locations. Inside the main tunnel for each base is a cubby area where a Speed power-up spawns. Use this for getting out of the base when capturing a flag; if you are a defender of the base, make sure to get this whenever possible to prevent attackers from snagging it.

There are also outdoor buildings in Warsong Gulch, in the southwestern part of the field and in the northeast there are Berserking power-ups; these are especially useful for taking out the early rush of people who are crossing the field toward your base. Then, smaller buildings on the southeast and northwest have Restoration power-ups.

Battleground Power-Ups

Name	Effect	Duration	Found in
Berserking	30% Increased Damage, 10% More Damage Taken	One Minute	Arathi Basin (Near Resource Points), Warsong Gulch (Outdoor Buildings)
Restoration	Restores 10% Health/Mana/Pet Happiness per Second	Ten Seconds	Arathi Basin (Near Resource Points), Warsong Gulch (Outdoor Buildings)
Speed	Doubles Movement Speed	Ten Seconds	Arathi Basin (Near Resource Points), Warsong Gulch (Base Tunnels)

THE STEALTHER CONUNDRUM

It's never easy to stay on defense when you know that stealthers could be lining up their best attacks against you. There are quite a few abilities that deal with this problem, and many people don't know about at first. The Hunter ability, Flare, is obviously intended to reveal Stealthers. But, anything that deals damage in an area-of-effect is useful as well. When stealther activity is suspected, use the abilities to keep Stealthers at bay or to actively break them out of Stealth Mode.

Detecting or Breaking Stealth

Class	Abilities to Use Heavily
Druid	Switch to Cat Form and Stealth Yourself
Hunter	Flare, All Traps, Leave Pets on Aggressive (If They Spot the Stealthers, They'll Attack Very Quickly)
Mage	Arcane Explosion
Paladin	Consecration (If Learned)
Priest	Shield If You Expect Stealthers Inc
Rogue	Stealth Yourself
Shaman	Magma Totem, Drop to Ghost Wolf for Sap Immunity
Warlock	Use Felhunter to Detect Stealthers; Warlocks Destroy Stealthers
Warrior	Use Bloodrage and Get Battleshout up (Bloodrage Puts Warriors In Combat, Making Them Immune to Sap for a Time)

I THOUGHT THAT ABILITY WAS USELESS

Abilities function so different in PvP than they do in PvE. Some of the things that are very useful normally become worthless (e.g. anything relating to Threat). On the flipside, a number of abilities that are rarely bothered with become quite potent, such as the scouting abilities like Eagle Eye.

Play around with all of your class' abilities in PvP to see how they function. You might be surprised what combinations become available.

LOCATIONS FOR PvP

There are different locations for PvP, with varying rewards and strategies. Though it would take a full book of its own to go into the massive level of detail for higher-level Warcraft PvP, this offers a brief overview of what can be done.

DUELING

🦂 Standard Rewards: Nothing Tangible

🦂 Honor: None

🦂 Goal: Practice PvP Techniques

🦂 Requirements: None

Dueling can be engaged with members of either faction, though it will flag your character for combat if you duel a person of the opposing faction when they are flagged (or if they flag during the fight).

This form of battle does not cause the death of either character, no Honor is awarded, but otherwise this fight occurs like a normal 1-on-1. Nobody can interfere with the encounter, and if either side runs too far from the duel flag that appears the battle will end (resulting in a loss for the fleeing person).

Losses and victories are not recorded in any way, so these have no effect on your character at all. Duels are done to pass the time, have fun, and test out techniques. Note that these have very little bearing on true PvP because the Battlegrounds are for group-on-group fighting. The best duelist in the world still needs solid communication skills to accomplish anything worthwhile in BG PvP.

Remember to establish "rules" before going into a duel. If you get deeply upset when other people blow timers, use potions, etc., then let that be known well before the fight starts. Otherwise, everything goes.

To maximize your successes in duels, come up with a plan ahead of time. Use burst damage, kiting, or outright attrition, and stick with your theme. If you are going for burst damage, don't waste anything on drawing the fight out. If you are kiting, learn how far you can run, keep your enemy Snared/Rooted, and so forth. For attrition combat, slap down the DOTs and keep your foe controlled or at range as much as possible.

WORLD PVP

- Standard Rewards: Just Honor
- Honor: Very Low
- Goal: Kill Enemy Faction Leaders, Sow Anarchy, Just Fight
- Requirements: None

World PvP consists mostly of rolling PvP encounters (small fights on PvP servers) and raids on towns or cities. The smaller encounters behave somewhat like duels, but often start with one side at a great disadvantage. Instead of having people face off against each other, one side is usually taken by surprise due to Stealth, terrain, already being engaged, etc.

To reduce the problem of being rolled in world PvP, watch your back while fighting various monsters, stay in a group for questing, and don't let your health stay low for very long, even if it means using bandages more often. Treat every minute as if it could be your last, and assume that there is always a Stealther nearby. Even when there isn't, it's always possible that a few people could come over the hill at any moment.

Going after towns and cities is more direct, and it requires quite a few more people. Get a group, or preferably a raid, together. If you only have five to ten people, head to a smaller place, like Astranaar or Hammerfall. The distant locales of these places prevent massive numbers of people from arriving quickly to counter you; instead, a moderate assortment of levels and classes should be there or soon arrive. This makes for a somewhat fair fight.

If your raid has 30 or more people, try for a major location, and keep trying to rally more and more people from your side to join in. Take on one of the major cities from the other faction, and keep the pressure going. During primetime hours, it's nearly impossible to kill an enemy faction's leaders (the leader of each city). But during off-hours, it is possible to kill these tough targets if your raid uses skill and speed to clear their way through the city.

When defending against these attacks, remember that time is on your side. It is easier to get reinforcements for your forces than it is for their group, and Rezzing is also easier for the defenders, who often have many places and people to hide and protect them. Because of this, it is easier to make the enemy forces pay dearly for every inch, even if it means that your character is doomed. Use AoE death runs to soften large groups of attackers. Be sure to spam Snare abilities when enemies try to rush through an area; don't let them bypass guards, NPCs, and other hindrances! Snare, Fear, Daze, and do whatever you can to keep the NPCs beating on your targets for as long as possible.

Because of diminishing returns, you can't get a lot of Honor from world PvP even if you kill a fair number of people per day. This is a very fun form of combat, and it is purely based on the fighting (instead of on capturing terrain or flags). But, you won't reach the higher PvP ranks by doing things this way.

BATTLE GROUNDS

WARSONG GULCH

- Standard Rewards: A Trinket, Rare Equipment (Rings, Bow, Staff, Sword, Dagger, Necklace), Epic Bracer, Epic Leggings
- Honor: Very High
- Goal: Capture the Enemy's Flag Three Times
- Requirements: Five People per Team Minimum

Warsong Gulch is the first Battleground that most young PvPers will encounter. From level ten forward, this BG is available, and it only takes five people queued from each side to open the Gulch.

There are two bases, the Alliance one in the north, and a Horde one in the south. Between them is an open field that is wide enough to allow for groups to pass each other without spotting the movement of their foes.

The goal is to reach the enemy base, right click on their flag to capture it, then return and place their flag on top of yours (by walking over it). If the enemies take your flag in the meanwhile, you won't be able to score. Flag carriers drop the flags if they are made immune to damage, mount, or right click on the flag icon, on the upper-right side of their screen.

The key is to figure out exactly how many people you need on defense, how many should stay in midfield to thwart enemy actions, and how many should go after the flag. Normally, you want your smallest group to be on pure defense. Then, use most of the raid for attack if the enemy is turtling or split your forces between flag running and midfield if the enemy is being more aggressive.

The only graveyards in Warsong Gulch are just to the right as a defender walks out of their base. These are up on hills to prevent enemies from easily getting to them for ganking, but foes can come into the bases by the main tunnels and leave up top to enter the graveyards (or they can take the ramps on the left side of the base and move over to the graveyards from there).

Flag carriers receive massive attention and often need at least one dedicated healer; sometimes three won't be enough. Keep shields and healing spells coming while other characters slow the attackers to keep them away from the carrier. It is essential that one escorting person stays near the carrier at all times, to pick up the flag if the carrier is slain. Doing this, your side can pass off the enemy's flag multiple times on the way home, with Rezzers returning to help with the run as quickly as possible.

For defenders, the goal is to right click on a flag when it drops. Once you see that a carrier is going to collapse, position the cursor above their heads and start to right-click rapidly. This raises the chance that your character will return the flag if it falls.

Remember that everyone except the flag carrier can still use mounts in the 40+ brackets. Thus, people on both sides can move rapidly into position. For these more intense brackets, tougher carriers are sometimes required. During earlier brackets, when speed is a greater factor, softer classes have an edge (Mages can Blink, Druids with Travel Form destroy the 30s bracket, Shamans with Ghost Wolf are always nice, etc.).

Don't try to defend from the flag room most of the time. Though it's nice to have one person who stays very close to the flag (primarily to call out the direction of enemy flag runners as they flee), it's best to hit enemy forces **before** they reach the flag room. Think about this; hitting an enemy force ahead of time means that some of your slain defenders get to respawn and hit the force again before they reach the flag. Attackers have to travel across the entire field, to this attrition favors the defending team! If you hole up in the flag room, the other team has a chance of being all the way outside the base by the time your fallen members respawn. There is no advantage to that!

When attacking, stay as tightly grouped as possible. New players have a strong tendency to fragment and string their way into the enemy base. Defenders aren't going to be like that (most of the time); they are going to be sticking together. That gives them the opportunity to bum rush your lone attackers, eat them alive, and be at full health for the new loner. Don't let three, grouped defenders beat six, soloing attackers by falling for this.

Warsong Gulch Legend

| 1 | Horde Base | 3 | Tunnels | 5 | Graveyards | 7 | Battleground Exit Portals | 9 | Alliance Base |
| 2 | Flag Rooms | 4 | Ramps | 6 | Powerup Buildings | 8 | Midfield | | |

Mastering the Gulch

For a confident team, a very aggressive front is quite lucrative for fast matches and high honor. Nobody is going to get the most out of these events by having both sides turtles, so it is important to get a strong offense going. To do that, form the groups so that only one or two people are planning to stay behind in the base. As a risky gambit, you can even have these people come out to midfield to assist in the fighting.

Remember that defending your flag **is not** about keeping the enemies from touching it; it is about preventing enemies from getting back to their base with your flag. Thus, it's very useful to dominate midfield and destroy enemy flag carriers as they come out of the base. Non-stealthers have a hard time making it in at all when people do this, and stealthers are not at their best when carrying flags across a heavy midfield.

Be ready to stop carriers who are using maximum speed! That is the best counter to this heavy offense/midfield technique. A single Rogue or Druid can easily get your flag, and they might have the ability to go across the field at very high speed. This demands a midfield team that cooperates well, communicates immediately, and knows have to stop/slow flag runners.

Also expect to deal with Sprint Potions, Free Action Potions, and other toys. Dedicated runners blow these all the time, especially on older servers. For those targets, be certain to come at them with many types of delaying techniques. If the roots/snares won't work, try to polymorph and wait out the potion/buff that is helping the runner. This also gives you midfield team more time to get other there (you always want to have a few people beating on runners).

An entirely different technique is to wear enemies down emotionally with a heavy turtle. This is not the way to win outright! Rather, it is a method that diminishes a powerful enemy team's ability to work together. It is often considered dishonorable, but is very effective and needs to be discussed.

You realize that you are facing an enemy team that is extremely good. They might be as good as your people; they might even be a good better. However, you still have folks who are willing to work together. So, to buy time and frustrate your foes, you order everyone except a lone stealther onto defense. You them proceed to trash wave after wave of foes until the enemies lose their cohesion. At that time you shift your force into a more aggressive stance and push to the other side of the field.

Arathi Basin Legend

1	Horde Base	4	Lumber Mill Flag	7	Blacksmith Graveyard	10	Stables Flag	13	Powerup Location (Random
2	Farm Flag	5	Lumber Mill Graveyard	8	Gold Mine Flag	11	Stables Graveyard		Powerup)
3	Farm Graveyard	6	Blacksmith Flag	9	Gold Mine Graveyard	12	Alliance Base		

During this, your stealther keeps the other team honest. If they try to rush with all or almost all of their people, the stealther should grab the enemy flag and try to carefully move home. Avoid the center of midfield in this case, and choose a side to stay along. Scoring under these circumstances can happen! The best timing is to start a flag run just as a big fight is approaching at the home base. That way, your stealther can get the flag and be on the way home before a number of the enemies respawn.

Turtling should not be a choice that people take under normal circumstances. It's slower than a more aggressive stance, and that means fewer points of honor. This is a last resort, and should be reserved for tougher fights.

ARATHI BASIN

 Standard Rewards: A Trinket, Rare Equipment (Boots, Leggings), Epic Equipment (Dagger, Cloak, Shoulders)

 Honor: High

 Goal: Reach 2,000 Resource Points Before Your Enemy By Capturing Locations

 Requirements: Eight People per Team Minimum

Arathi Basin is really in a class of its own; this Battleground is a race with a dynamic timelimit. Unlike the other Battlegrounds, both sides are in a rush to reach a goal that will occur sooner or later. You will never see a one-hour Arathi Basin, because somebody is going to hit 2000 point sooner or later; these matches last from 8 to 40 minutes, and are most often around 25 for a complete match.

There are five resource nodes (Farm, Gold Mine, Blacksmith, Lumber Mill, and Stables). Each generates resources for the team that controls them. If one team holds three and the other holds two, the leading team will gain 50% more points over time. With a 4-to-1 lead, the winning team gets points at quadruple the speed. And with a 5-0 occurring, points come in at an amazing rate, finishing the match at a very early point.

So, your team wants to get as many sites as they can comfortably hold. It's no good to rush for all five sites and lose your battles at four of them, so there is a great deal of strategy and tactical work in figuring out what to hit. Initially, the Alliance gets the Stables while the Horde gets the Farm. The bulk of the forces for both sides rush on to contest the three other sites while a minimal defense guards the "safe" areas while they convert.

After right-clicking on a flag, it takes one minute for the site to become yours. While contested, it only takes the other team a few seconds to right

click and defend the flag (or, in the case that nobody hold the site beforehand, the site becomes contested in their favor). If the other team previously possessed the site, they can score a Defense; this instantly puts the site back in their possession.

Once a site is under control, resources begin to flow from it. In addition, the Spirit Healer at that location becomes active for the controlling side. This makes it easier to defend the area. Contested sites have no active Spirit Healer for either side; this is why it is very important for attackers to hit the flag early. You don't want a stream of reinforcements to appear every 30 seconds!

Use shorthand to let people know about the sites (Farm for the Farm, Mine for the Gold Mine, LM for the Lumber Mill, Stab for the Stables, and BS for the Blacksmith). Keep everyone abreast of enemy movements; from good vantage points like the Lumber Mill, your people can see a huge portion of the map.

Because it takes several seconds to use the flags, it is quite possible to interrupt attackers. Use instant abilities to deal damage and knock them off of the flag. If they don't turn to fight you, continue to deal damage to thwart their efforts. If several people pile onto a flag, drop totems, use any AoEs you have, try group Fear abilities, and so forth.

Defenders should try to fight near the flags whenever possible. Even if drawn off, by a Hunter, you must keep your eyes on the flag at all times. When someone jumps onto it, be ready to hurry back and shoot them, hit them, or do whatever you can. As an attacker, it's wise to draw people off as often as you can. If there are too many defenders to defeat, send one person ahead of the group to annoy and flee from the defenders; if they are stupid enough to chase the lone attacker, move in with others and take the site. This works more often than you might think.

Try not to let your sites get divided. Holding the Stables, Blacksmith, and Farm puts you in the lead. But, it also presents a daunting fight, because your forces are strung out across the map. When you can, try to hold territory that supports other nodes. Keeping the LM and Farm in the south, and taking the BS means that you have a triangle of defense that is extremely hard to break. From the BS, your people can see attack forces coming to either side, so your defenders always know what is being hit and can quickly rush to intercept a large group.

Low DPS classes have much more value in Arathi Basin than they do in many other PvP situations. As a defender in the Basin, your job is **not** to kill enemies. It's true! Your job is to slow enemies down for long enough that reinforcements respawn or arrive from other points. Thus, you don't need to kill to be a great defender.

Paladins, Druids in Bear Form, Priests, Protection Warriors, and other survivors have a great place in the Basin. Use their abilities to heal, slow, disrupt, and antagonize enemies. Paladins are so good at this that they have quite a reputation for annoyance; take damage while defending the flag, bubble, heal, drop bubble and attack anyone who got on the flag. For Druids, stay away from the flag, use Moonfire at range to disrupt capturing attackers, then switch to Travel Form and flee if too many people come after you. Even if the enemies are much higher in level, repeating this is wonderfully successful.

The best attackers are classes that have long-duration crowd control or high burst damage. Rogues and Mages have an especially good time Sap/Polymorphing targets and capturing the flags when there are solo defenders. For groups of attackers, lay on the DPS while focusing on enemy healers first. Once your group outnumbers the defenders, have one person try to ninja the flag (by grabbing it during the fighting). If the defenders don't see this, you win. If you do, it disrupts their current battleplan because someone needs to break off and stop the capture.

Overseeing the Basin

There are two major schools of thought on the leadership of Arathi Basin forces. For dealing with groups of people who are not as experienced in the game, one technique is to assign groups very clearly and encourage people to stick with their group the entire battle. A group is assigned for full attack work, another two groups for defense, then you have a floater group that defends sites if a third or fourth site is gained or joins the attackers if the team is behind.

The upside of a rigid team structure is that it gives inexperienced players the ability to follow veterans more closely and learn from them. Most of the strategy is clean, and obvious, and that helps to avoid confusion.

The downside of this pattern is that it lacks the strength and flexibility displayed by a team of full floaters! Such a team follows the other school of thought, that each force of 15 can be used fluidly. Those attackers require immense communication because they choose the ideal number of defenders for each site, at a given moment. As more people are needed for attack or specific defense, individual players call out that they will shift into that task.

For example, a fluid team leaves a single person at the farm early in the match while a heavy force hits the mill, BS, and mine. All three are taken, but the enemies swing around and are about to hit the farm with a few troops. The lone farm defender calls for help "Inc Farm 3," and two characters respond that they are going to the farm to assist.

Though this model has immense potential, it requires wonderful players who are used to working together. Quite PvPers make it difficult to determine where the force is needed, and a lack of discipline undermines the benefits that flexibility provides.

ALTERAC VALLEY

- Standard Rewards: Improved Ammo, Hi-End Quiver/Ammo Pouch, Epic Equipment (Rings, 2H Mace, Shield, Dagger, Off-Hand Items, Mount)

- Honor: Low

- Goal: Defeat the Enemy's Commander

- Requirements: Fifteen People per Team Minimum

Alterac Valley isn't available until the higher levels are reached. From level 50 onward, this is the Battleground that tests and defies many players. Up to 40 characters can enter Alterac Valley at the same time (per team), meaning that leadership is extremely difficult here. It's unusual to have everyone know each other and accept commands perfectly.

The goal is to push to the other team's base. The Alliance holds the northern keep, and the Horde leader is in the south. Killing the commander for the other team instantly ends the battle, but there is a lot to do along the way. There are resources to gather (mines are taken from NPC enemies to harvest for ground troops, Wolves and Rams are used to create cavalry, and Wing Commanders are rescued to summon aerial forces). Beyond that, Armor Scraps are taken from bodies and given to the Blacksmiths at your team's base to upgrade NPC armor. Blood is taken from bodies as well, and this is given to the summoner NPC at your team's base for calling a massive, elite creature later in the battle.

Thus, everything has a use in Alterac Valley. The rank and file characters are going to fight over graveyards, which are taken to keep the focus of the battle in different areas. Defenders work to hamper enemy forces, and can accomplish a great deal with AoE death runs, especially in the base defense (where elite NPCs are there to assist).

Along the way north/south, your team tries to take out enemy sub-bosses and locations. This not only reduces the attack force of your enemy (by removing their buffs); it also increases Honor of your side and adds additional Elite NPCs to guard your own leader.

There are quests for Alterac Valley that are given by the NPCs at the formal entrance to the zone (in the Alterac Mountains), and there are additional quests given by NPC inside the Battleground. Try to complete these as you go, and don't worry about finishing each on your first run through the Battleground. Try to get one or two done each time; the first one that is really important is the quest to clear the caves by your main base. This is a quest for either side, and the result is that you get an item to port back to your main base (very useful in Alterac Valley).

Try to have just a few, assigned people loot the bodies. This helps to keep the teams from having everyone run back every 30-40 minutes. Beyond that, the rewards are shared evenly, so there is no reason to have everyone waste their time looting.

AoEs are the king of Alterac Valley, on offense and defense. Mages and Warlocks especially are able to blast through massive groups of people who are trying to hold an area. Use these death rushes initially to soften a force, then hit them with standard DPS to finish the task. When taking flags or holding flags, keep the AoEs pounding on everyone to prevent them from having the opportunity to stay out of combat, touch flags, and so forth. The side that has fewer AoE characters is forced to be extremely aggressive when taking areas (if they can't take something quickly, the superior AoE forces of their enemy are likely to settle in and defend for a **long** time).

Beating the Valley

Even with the reduction in NPCs on the field (done in previous patches), defenders are still able to hold areas quite brutally if one side abandons there attempt to take enemy territory. These turtles heavily favor the faction with a higher player population. The players that drop out of the long matches eventually aren't replaced for the side with fewer members, leading to an imbalance in sides.

Luckily, the revamp to the battleground system makes it so that populations are smoother than they once were. Server clusters are better balanced and have the potential for both sides to receive reinforcements even late in the evening. Because of this, turtling doesn't have quite the finality that it once did.

There are still extensive arguments over the need to take and hold as many sights as possible in Alterac Valley. If you lets your enemies take many of your sites, this increases the number of defenders at the enemy commander's location (not a good thing). However, devoting people to slow or stop your enemy's advance keeps your main force from going forward as quickly too.

There isn't a clear or simple answer to this. Each commander has to decide how to distribute their forces. A heavy assault early on leads to a strong push, but it allows your enemies to do the same. Ultimately, both groups end up facing a powerful wall at the end of the match where turtling is quite successful.

One alternative that is very potent (if you have the right team for it), is to have a capable defense that holds the enemy in a stalemate while one or two stealth groups hit the targets on the opponent's end of the map. Taking four Rogues and a Druid in each of these groups makes it possible to stay in full stealth, have healing, and be strong enough to free Wing Commanders, kill enemy targets, and seize lightly-defended Graveyards. Of course, you need ten stealthers with skill to be able to try this.

Alterac Valley Legend

1	Frostwolf Keep (Commander: Drek'Thar)	8	Field of Strife	14	Alliance Starting Point	20	Icewing Bunker
2	Wildpaw Cavern (Trinket Quest Target)	9	Snowfall Graveyard	15	Irondeep Mine (Alliance Mine)	21	Lumber Mill Area
3	Frostwolf Graveyard	10	Stonehearth Outpost (Alliance Captain: Balinda Stonehearth)	16	Dun Baldar (Commander: Vanndar Stormpike)	22	Ram Territory (Cavalry Targets)
4	Coldtooth Mine (Horde Mine)	11	Stonehearth Graveyard	17	Tower Point	23	Wolf Territory (Cavalry Targets)
5	Horde Starting Point	12	Icewing Cavern (Trinket Quest Target)	18	Iceblood Tower		
6	Iceblood Garrison (Horde Captain: Galvangar)	13	Stormpike Graveyard	19	Stonehearth Bunker		
7	Iceblood Graveyard						

CRAFTING & PROFESSIONS

CHOOSING A PATH

Azeroth is full of many exciting discoveries and, for some, it comes in the form of its robust crafting system. Players can create various items and equipment as long as they have the right materials, tools, and know-how.

Players are restricted to two primary professions per character. Those choices are: Alchemy, Blacksmithing, Enchanting, Engineering, Herbalism, Leatherworking, Mining, Skinning, and Tailoring. To complement these profession options, there are secondary skills available to all characters. Secondary professions are not limited in the amount you can learn so every character can learn all three: Cooking, First Aid, and Fishing.

Professions are a way to improve your character by offering more adventuring options beyond questing and grinding. The available products are wondrous: weapons and armor, potions and oils, bombs and shrinking devices. True, you can't do all of them at once, so one of your first decisions is which professions and secondary skills you'd like to explore.

Consider the Options

Each class may, at first glance, look to be geared toward a certain profession. Decide what's important to you. Do you wish to have a profession that can supplement your character class or one focused solely on extra cash flow? Are you interested in more effective combat (PvE and PvP) with gadgets and bombs or does having the ability to enchant your equipment sound more interesting? You're not restricted to a specific profession based on your class. Mages can be Blacksmiths if they wish and Paladins can work with cloth; it's up to you.

PRIMARY

There are two primary types of professions; gathering and manufacturing.

Gathering professions are used to harvest materials from the world and prepare them to be used by a manufacturing profession. Gathering professions aren't reliant on other professions, but in such cases the gains are purely monetary.

Manufacturing professions use materials obtained from several sources to create new products or services. These rely heavily on gathering professions (the two exceptions are Enchanting and Tailoring).

Profession Quick List

Profession	Typical Partner Skill	Profession Type	Description
Alchemist	Herbalism	Manufacturer	Makes potions and elixirs with various attributes. Transmutation of metals and elements is also available to those that reach higher levels of Alchemy.
Blacksmith	Mining	Manufacturer	Makes mail and plate armor, as well as metal weapons of all types. At higher levels of skill Blacksmiths can choose to specialize in either Weaponsmithing or Armorsmithing. Weaponsmiths are able to further specialize in Axesmithing, Hammersmithing, or Swordsmithing.
Enchanter	Any	Gatherer/ Manufacturer	Disenchants uncommon or rarer items to attain resources. Enchants weapons and armor with permanent spell effects.
Engineer	Mining	Manufacturer	Engineers create gadgets, guns, bombs, etc. Many of the gadgets are usable only by other Engineers. The also create mechanical pets and trinkets. At later levels, Engineers can choose to specialize in Goblin or Gnomish Engineering.
Herbalist	Alchemy	Gatherer	Trackingdown herbs to be used by other professions. Alchemists, Enchanters, and Leatherworkers are just a few of the professions that use herbs on occasion (with Alchemists being dependant on them).
Leatherworker	Skinning	Manufacturer	Creates leather armor at lower levels and branches into both leather and mail armor at higher levels. Leatherworkers can also produce armor kits that can increase the armor on certain equipment. Proficient Leatherworkers can specialize in either Tribal Leatherworking, Elemental Leatherworking, or Dragonscale Leatherworking.
Miner	Blacksmithing or Engineering	Gatherer	Discovering the mining deposits of ore is restricted to Miners. In addition to the raw ore, rare gems can be found within the earth. Miners also smelt the ore into bars that other professions can make use of.
Skinner	Leatherworking	Gatherer	Harvests the leather and hides from beasts slain in combat. Skinners supplement many of the professions to a small extent with Leatherworkers being fully reliant on them.
Tailor	Any	Manufacturer	Creates cloth armor and bolts from the cloth pieces found on the bodies of enemies. Tailors can also create bags to increase characters' inventory space (these are generally quite sought after). As the primary sources of cloth are dead enemies, Tailors are only slightly dependant on Miners, Skinners, and Herbalists for some of the more rare materials.

Secondary Skill Quick List

Trade Skill	Description
Cook	Gather meats and parts of slain beasts and turn it into useful foods that replenish health. At higher levels certain foods also give statistic bonuses for a limited time.
First Aid	Uses cloth from fallen enemies to create bandages. These can be used to quickly heal yourself or others between fights.
Fisher	Gathers fish and treasure from the bodies of water spread across Azeroth. Alchemists make use of some fish while Tailors, Leatherworkers, Blacksmiths and Enchanters use various pearls.

All items necessary to excel in your chosen line of work can be purchased from others in the game if necessary. It's very possible to be an Engineer if you have the gold to buy the ore and stone you need. Guilds and friends are often key (exploited) in providing materials for such pursuits. Teamwork can be a huge advantage. One person producing ore to barter for armor and weapons is the foundation of a budding economy.

Of course, there's no rule saying that you must "make" something. Some players focus on gather resources in exchange for gold or lower costing equipment. There's plenty of room for players who wish nothing else than to sell the bounty of the land. The truth is, those with an abundance of gold are often willing to pay a premium in lieu of gathering the materials themselves. Gathering raw resources is almost free (the only expense is the price of a pick or skinning knife, and training), so anything you make is profit.

The obvious goal is to become the best crafter possible, regardless of which profession you choose. Maximizing your gold to do so in the cheapest and most efficient way possible is key. Everything available to crafters has a color. For example, Tailoring patterns and ore deposits each have a specific color depending on your level in the appropriate profession.

Difficulty vs. Reward

Color	Difficulty	Reward
Gray	None	These tasks are effortless and cannot fail unless interrupted. No skill gains are possible.
Green	Trivial	Very easy tasks that rarely fail. Skill gains are rare, but possible.
Yellow	Average	With a modest chance of failure, the chance for skill gain is significant.
Orange	Challenge	Failures are common (you won't lose any materials…only time) and skill gains are guaranteed on success.
Red	Impossible	Your skill is too low currently to even attempt these tasks.

It doesn't matter if you're Mining, Tailoring, Smithing, etc. These colors are uniform across the crafts. If you're trying to level up, focus on tasks that give a solid return while using as little of your resource pool as necessary. A good example of a trade off is when a yellow recipe uses two items and an orange uses six. Sure, you get a point for the orange one, but by making the yellow you have the potential for gaining three points with the same materials. However, there's also a slim risk that you'll make no progress.

Always watch for the change in color as you level. If you're just creating the same item over and over, it could very well change to a green status and have little value beyond the item itself. It doesn't always happen on a set number so pay attention (but it does tend to happen at five and ten number breaks). For this one reason, it's not always smart to hit the "create all" button. Follow this rule: if you're interested in skilling up, pay attention. If you want the items, create as many as you like.

All professions have specific trainers that teach their craft. The six capital cities typically house them all, but there are trainers hidden in the wild, in smaller towns, and even in dungeons/instances that offer more specialized training. It's important to visit the main trainers once ever 5-10 ranks while starting out. After you begin attaining higher levels, pay attention to your rank and only visit when you must. As you learn new skills, they're automatically added to your menu. You need to advance in a profession to learn better skills.

Ranks

Rank	Maximum Skill Level
Apprentice	75
Journeyman	150
Expert	225
Artisan	300

Not all trainers can teach you something new. As you level up, it's inevitable that you begin to surpass the knowledge of some trainers. When you've learned all a trainer can teach you, they often point you in the direction of the next trainer for you to contact.

Plans, recipes, and schematics can be purchased at your trainer. However, there are some that are dropped, received as quest rewards, or purchased from merchants throughout Azeroth. Some drops are extremely rare. Getting your hands on a rare set of plans and being the first to make that item for the market can make you quite rich quite quickly. Dropped plans generally make more powerful items. Rare plans, recipes, etc. are often some of the items that create the most voracious bidding. If you find a recipe or schematic as a drop, make sure to consult with someone before tossing it on the Auction House for a few silver.

Equipment and Tools

Some professions require equipment, but not all of them. Blacksmiths need a hammer (Blacksmith's Hammer), but Herbalists need only their hands. There are three types of equipment geared toward the professions in the game.

STORE-BOUGHT

Items and components like Blacksmith's Hammers, Mining Picks, Skinning Knives, vials, thread, etc. are all purchasable from vendors. You can generally get most items at the general vendors and you only need to buy these once. In the case of equipment, they simply need to be in your packs (not your bank) and you use the item once you initiate the action, whether it's mining ore or skinning a boar. However, for vials, thread, flux, etc. you need the item on you.

PLAYER-MADE

Some skills, as you level, require the trader to use different, player-made items. This can be a potion for a Tailoring pattern or an Arclight Spanner for an Engineer. Keep the items in your packs when you wish to use them.

ENVIRONMENT

Some items require you to travel to them. An anvil isn't something that you can put in your backpack and carry around. When something like this is required, it is noted in the recipe/pattern. You don't need to click the item, just stand near it, to make use of it.

Gathering Professions

The skills of Mining, Skinning, and Herbalism are gathering skills. You won't be making anything, or need to make anything to gather. These vocations supply other professions with resources.

HERBALISM

Your first skill is Find Herbs. Drag this icon from your ability book (defaulted to "p") onto a hotbar. Push the corresponding number or click it to activate. Once you activate it you'll only need to refresh it on death or after logging in.

While out adventuring, yellow dots appear on your mini-map. These denote an herbs location. If you mouse over the dot, you can discover which type of herb is shown.

When you're next to the plant, mouse over it to check the skill level required to harvest it. If you are able to harvest it, right-click on the plant to gather the herbs. It takes a few seconds and, if you're successful, a loot window opens with the herbs you found. To speed this you can hold shift and right-click the plant. The time to harvest will be the same, but it puts the fruit of your labor directly into your pack instead of bringing up a loot window.

It's possible to get as many as three herbs from each harvest as well as a bonus herb (Swiftthistle can be found in Mageroyal, Bruiseweed, Briarthorn, etc.).

MINING

Mining ore is crucial to the economy and may be used by your other profession. Copper, tin, and others are available at the swing of a pick, but jewels await the lucky. Find Minerals is the first skill granted to miners. Buy a Mining Pick, and head out to find your copper. Drag this icon from your ability book (defaulted to "p") onto a hotbar. Push the corresponding number or click it to activate. It remains active until you log, die, or change tracking types. A yellow dot appears on your mini-map when ore is nearby.

Mouse over the yellow dot to discover what kind of mineral awaits. Once you reach the vein, mouse over it to check the required skill level.

Right-click the node to begin mining. After a few swings, your character kneels down to check what you've found and a loot window opens. If you fail, simply try again. To speed the process, you can hold shift and right-click the vein to immediately deposit the spoils in your back after a success.

Unlike herbs, mines have to be used several times before they are depleted. If you fail to mine anything on your first try, you still have the chance to skill up until you mine ore for the first time on that vein. Failing to mine does not count against getting a skill-up.

Once you gather a load of ore, return to a forge and smelt it into bars. Again, pull the Smelting icon from your ability book (defaulted to "p") and drag it onto you hotbar. Activate the skill to bring up the smelting menu. Click "create all" or "create" to smelt the ore into useable bars.

SKINNING

When beasts are killed in the wild, Skinners swoop in to take the hides and any leather from their corpses. You need a Skinning Knife in your pack to strip the hide from the corpse (only after the corpse is fully looted can be skinned). Right-click on the body and wait for the skinning to be finished. A loot window appears. You can bypass the loot window if you hold shift when you right-click.

The types of leather and hide depend on the level of the animal you're skinning and a bit of randomness. Animals bordering on the next tier may have several of the lower tier instead of one of the higher tier. As the enemy's level increases, the level of leather received increases as well.

What's This?

Not all enemies are skinned for leather alone. Dragonkin, scorpids, turtles, and many others can be skinned for scales, as well as leather.

One thing you notice while hunting is that groups without a Skinner tend to leave corpses strewn about. It's quite a find and Skinners often follow such parties and clean up after them for some time.

Manufacturing Professions

Making items can be very rewarding. The ability to take raw resources and use what knowledge you've gained to create useful armor, weapons, potions, or enchants is worth pursuing. It's not a bad way to increase the size of your purse either.

All the skills ramp up quickly at first but, as you gain higher levels, your progress slows to a more steady pace. As long as you continue to make items of appropriate levels you continue to skill up. Having a guild to supply you with gold or resources is a great way to whip through the early levels, but it can be done without any aid as well. Even on your own you'll be able to become an artisan in your chosen field with the proper application of time.

Along with the decrease in skill gain, notice the additional components many of the higher level items require. A high end item may require you to adventure for a week to accumulate enough rare materials to create it. It's common to see such a rare item sell for great money if it's used in a recipe or pattern. Pearls and gems are common examples of additional components.

It's fair to say that if you bought all the resources to create a high level item that someone, in return, is going to have to pay a pretty penny to have you create it for them. However, some items require you to pay more for the resources than buyers are willing to pay for the completed item. Be careful when choosing what to make and what to buy.

There are times when money is no object. If you can make a robe that doubles a caster's current bonuses, they will likely pay a good deal for it.

ALCHEMY

Taking herbs, mixing them in a vial, and creating a potion that makes you several feet taller sounds exciting, no? The low level potions are typically the least interesting, but that makes them no less useful. Low level adventurers would be glad to pay for Lesser, and even Minor, Healing and Mana Potions. However, it's the high end potions and elixirs that really get people to dig into their pockets.

Invisibility Potions, Strength Potions, Defense Potions, Agility Potions—all of these are within reach of the alchemist. The list is huge and everyone has their favorites. There are no tools required for this profession, but you have to purchase vials constantly.

To create a potion, open your ability menu (defaulted to "p") and drag the Alchemy icon onto a hotbar. Activating the icon opens the Alchemy menu and immediately displays what potions you know how to create.

Click on the name of the potion to discover which reagents you need. It shows how many of each item as well. Make sure you have all the appropriate ingredients (including the vials) in your bags before trying to create potions. The menu indicates which potions you can make and how many of each (depending on your resources) can be made also. Mouse over the icon to see what the effects of the potion are.

As soon as you create a potion, it appears in your packs. To use it, either right-click it or drag it onto your hotbar for quick access.

Alchemists can also transmute semi-rare ore and elements into rarer types. You can, given the appropriate skill and a Philosopher's Stone, transmute iron to gold, mithril to truesilver, and more. Transmutes have a cooldown of one to two days, but are well worth the wait.

It's not hard to level up this skill if you have Herbalism. The herbs you find are free and, as long as you remember to have your Find Herbs skill active, you don't have to go out of your way. Groupmates, guildmates, and strangers in the field appreciate useful potions, and you're likely to develop quite a fan-base. They also sell very well in the auction houses.

No Room

If you're trying to create potions when your bags are full, you won't be able to add the potion to your inventory. This may become a problem at the lower levels when inventory space is limited. Making use of the bank to store your herbs when you aren't making potions is a good idea and will save you a headache.

BLACKSMITHING

Smiths are some of the most popular crafters. Not only do you create mail and plate armor, but weapons too! True, only four of the nine classes ever require a Blacksmith for armoring needs, but each class could benefit from a new weapon now and then. Even Priests choose to learn how to use daggers when they need. However, the best creations require leather, cloth, jewels, and more.

A Blacksmith's Hammer must be in your pack. Though that may sound obvious, it's often forgotten in the bank or ditched in the field for more bag space. You'll also need an anvil upon which to bang that hammer. Pull the Blacksmithing icon from your ability book (defaulted to "p") onto a hotbar and activate it. Your Blacksmithing menu pops up and shows all plans currently available.

Click on the name of the plan to see what components it requires. It shows you how many of each component you have in your bags and how many items of that plan you can make. It also gives you the option to make one or many in a row. Mouse over the icon of the item to see its stats.

Once you've made an item, it drops into your packs automatically. By level 250, it's difficult to find a trainer in a main city that can teach you anything new. However, by finding dropped patterns and hidden trainers, you can continue to progress in your craft. Some quests offer rewards for you also. These require you to craft certain items and, in return, they teach you new patterns. One of the quest lines leads you to the Mithril Order. It's not an easy quest chain, but the reward is the ability to craft a full suit of mithril plate armor!

Once you've attained a high enough skill level, you must choose a new path. Decide whether you wish to focus on weapons and carry the title Weaponsmith or become an Armorsmith. Both paths require quests and both are mutually exclusive. If you choose one path, the other is forever closed to this character. If become a Weaponsmith interests you, you may be interested to discover that an even more specialized choices await. The mutually exclusive

Hammersmith, Swordsmith, and Axesmith titles are often required for the highest level weapon patterns.

Blacksmithing is not a very fast skill to increase. You're often sharing ore available to Engineers and they're not scarce. Other Blacksmiths also compete for available ore and gems in the auction houses. It's expensive to buy since the demand is so high. In the early stages, it doesn't seem that bad, but it gets worse.

It's not a get rich quick profession, but some of the high end items are truly impressive. Of course, it's because they are so difficult to make. Casual players can expect to either drop a good chunk of money on the resources or spend several weeks gather all the materials required. Take it slow and don't rush.

The good news is you can make some money. Every class needs something at a certain level. The market demands for Blacksmiths fill these gaps and this gives you that extra surge of cash you need. You won't sell most of what you make early on, but certain pieces sell like clean air in Gnomeregan.

ENCHANTING

This is probably the simplest profession and also the most expensive to master. Components are not gathered from the field or from the corpses of beasts; instead, you must disenchant items of worth. This, of course, implies that you must find or purchase the items to be disenchanted. Disenchanting destroys the original item and leaves you with components to be used plying your trade. Items of higher level or rarer quality disenchant into better materials.

Only the Good Stuff

Only items of Uncommon quality or higher (Rare, Epic, Legendary, etc.) can be disenchanted for resources. You're not going to be able to get anything from common items.

Nearly every magical item can be disenchanted. The difficult part about this method of resource gathering is that you really need to think twice about destroying some item. If an item was given to you from a quest and its soulbound, but you can't use it, the choice is still difficult. These items sell for a good bit. In the long run, enchanting can make up for the long and expensive trek to artisan.

If you are with a party while hunting that doesn't need a certain item, ask for it; you may find that your party is willing to let you have a great deal of items. It's a standard to see a guild Enchanter snagging anything that someone doesn't immediately need. The Enchanter needs to keep everyone's weapons glowing, but that's a fair trade for resources that are typically hard to come by.

To disenchant an item, open your ability book (defaulted to "p") and drag the Disenchant skill onto a hotbar. Activate the ability and then click on the item you wish to disenchant. Grab the items from the loot menu and continue.

Once you've obtained a reasonable supply of dust and shards, move the Enchanting icon onto your hotbar in a similar fashion. Activating the Enchanting skill brings up a window that shows all enchants you are currently proficient with.

Click any recipe to see the components required. To enchant an item, open your inventory (or have someone put an item in the "Will Not Be Traded" slot of the trade window). Activate the appropriate enchant and click on the item. Enchantments are permanent until replaced. If you wish to replace an enchantment, it erases the previous one in favor of the new one.

The quickest way to master this profession is to have friends willing to offer items that they don't need. Whether this is through a guild or just a group of players you've begun to hang out with, it's nice to be up front and explain to them that you've chosen the path of the Enchanter. Be generous with your services and you're certain to receive goodwill in kind.

Low-level Enchanters underbid one another to level up quickly. However, by the time they reach a level with solid enchantments that people crave, the prices skyrocket. The resources aren't cheap and the enchantments are permanent. Imagine two Warriors. Each has attained level 50 and they're wearing the same equipment, they've chosen the same talents and use their abilities in the same fashion. However, one has every possible item enchanted and the other is in unenchanted equipment. Who's going to win?

People are constantly trying to get the edge over the competition and enchantments are sure ways to do that. If you're planning on holding onto an item for a while, get it enchanted early on and really take advantage of it.

ENGINEERING

If you like toys, gadgets and things that go *boom*, become an Engineer. It's a great match if you've already chosen to be a Miner since you use a lot of stone and ore. Gems are also used in Engineering and miners have the greatest access to them. Engineers can create bombs, guns, pets that are cute, pets that attack, and pets that explode. It's definitely not a boring profession.

Snag the Engineering icon from your ability book (defaulted to "p") and place it on a hotbar. Activate it to bring up your Engineering window.

Click on the name of a schematic to see what components are needed, what tools are required, and how much you have in your inventory. You can also mouse over the item to see what it does before making it.

Click the "create" or "create all" button to make the item. It's put directly into your pack on creation.

Bombs and Dynamite: Right-click the icon if it's in your pack or use your hotbar for faster access. A green circle appears once you've activated it. Choose the area of effect and left-click to toss your creation into the world. **Pets:** Pets work from your pack or hotbar keys as well. Battle Chickens and Mithril Dragonlings fight alongside you for some time while Explosive Sheep run at the enemy and…explode.

Trinkets: Many items constructed at higher levels are trinkets. There are two trinket slots on your character screen (defaulted to "c"). Trinkets must be equipped to be used and can't be swapped during combat. Activate a trinket by clicking on it from your character screen or using a hotbar key. Trinkets have cooldowns varying from five minutes to an hour. If you have a lot of trinkets, it's best to switch them out as you use them. The time works whether it's equipped or in your bag. However, if you carry five of the same item, Battle Chickens for example, they have a shared cooldown. So, using one activates the timer on all of them. There's no need to have more that one of any trinket equipped at the same time.

At skill level 150, you must pick Goblin Engineering or Gnome Engineering. Goblins are more of the blow'em up type and gnomes love to make gadgets and trinkets. Either takes a quest to get and once you learn one, this character is forever locked out of the other.

Engineering is the anti-wealth skill. Just about everything you make can only be used by other Engineers and there's a good chance that they can make their own. Rare schematics are the only things that give you a bit of an edge over the competition. Hold onto those and try to get as much as you can from this career. This path is all about improving your character. You make bombs, pets, goggles, parachutes, lasers, and all kinds of things that blow up and burn. It's what the killers and PvPers like to use. You'll be broke, but you'll be a walking time bomb with a bag full of tricks to pull out for a multitude of reasons.

LEATHERWORKING

Leather armor is something that many classes need desperately, especially early. Leatherworkers can gain access to mail armor at higher levels. Skinning, obviously, is a fantastic partner profession to have. Controlling your own resources is a great way to gain an edge over those wishing to buy from other players.

Open you ability book (defaulted to "p") and drag the Leatherworking icon onto a hotbar. Activating the ability brings up your Leatherworking screen. At first, you don't know much but that changes quickly. Click the name of a pattern to see how many of what components are required. Mousing over the item reveals the stats of the item.

Once you begin to make even the simplest of armor pieces, you'll need to visit your trainer often to learn new recipes. As your skill increases, the breadth of what you can craft increases and your ability to skill up slows.

You can create items one at a time or several one after another. Created items are automatically dropped into your packs.

At rank 225, you have three specialties to choose from; Tribal, Elemental, and Dragonscale. Each one requires a quest to learn and they are mutually exclusive. Once your character chooses one, they can never choose another. Tribal Leatherworking uses the special leathers taken from unusually creatures in the land. As the items are all leather, it's suited for Druids and Rogues most. Elemental Leatherworking harnesses the powers of the elementals running around the world. Also leather armor, Elemental Leatherworkers often sell their wares to Druids and Rogues. Dragonscale Leatherworking creates mail armor from the scaled beasts of the land and is generally sold to Shamans and Hunters, who at higher levels wear mail instead of leather armor.

Leatherworking combined with Skinning is a very intuitive and lucrative trade. You supply your trade by killing things you're already killing. There is no need to go out of your way for stray herbs or ore. While Leatherworkers are confined to armor, they can also make armor kits. These can be applied to any type of armor for the head, hands, chest, or legs slot and increase the armor of the item.

There another bonus to being a less-flashy profession. Chances are that when you're in a group, you'll be the only person collecting skins. Wearing the armor you make keeps you up to date and generally ahead of the curve until the late game. End game gear is hard to make and requires components that are difficult to find in large quantities.

TAILORING

When people think of Tailors they immediately think of cloth armor. However, when a non-caster thinks of Tailors, they think of bags! Sure, Tailors make cloth armor and caster chase after them in droves trying to pick up some of the nicer equipment, but bags and cloaks are used by everyone.

Open your ability book (defaulted to "p") and drag the Tailoring icon onto a hotbar. Click or push the appropriate hotkey to activate the icon and open you Tailoring window.

Click on the name of a pattern to see what components are needed to create the item. It shows you how many of each component you have in your bags and how many items of the pattern you can create. It gives you the option to make one or many in a row. To see what the pattern makes, mouse over the icon and the item's statistics are shown. Once an item is made, it is automatically put into your packs.

There isn't a partner profession needed for Tailoring. The main supplies for this skill are cloth which is dropped by humanoid enemies. By killing humanoid mobs, which is inevitable, you build a supply of cloth. Tailors also buy a lot of thread and dye from the vendors however. These items cannot by found in the field, so be ready to put down some money whenever you want to make an item. Since Tailoring doesn't need a partner profession to gather materials, you can choose one of the other gathering professions and sell the harvest to make up the money you spend making items.

In addition to the obvious, Tailors learn several patterns that have little combat value and are strickly for role players. Tuxedos, dresses, shirts, and the like are all within the realm of learning for a Tailor.

Secondary Skills

Secondary skills have no restrictions on how many a player can learn. Anyone can learn them and they don't count against your maximum of two professions. So, if you wish to take all three, go nuts! These skills general reduce your downtime and/or help your cash flow.

COOKING

Raw meat is often found on the beasts of Azeroth. However, turning piles of flesh, legs, ribs, eggs, etc. into delicacies is the cook's advantage. The food that cooks create often heals at a better rate than store-bought food. In addition, it often gives a short statistic bonus if you eat enough. Animals drop all sorts of ingredients for the avid cook.

To use your Cooking skill, open you ability book (defaulted to "p") and drag the icon onto a hotbar. Open the Cooking menu by clicking on the icon or pushing the appropriate hotkey and see what recipes you've mastered.

Click on the name of a recipe to see what ingredients you need. It shows how many of each ingredient you currently possess in addition to how many of the item you can currently cook.

Finished food is placed in your packs automatically, but a fire is needed to make anything. Using fires you find in the world is convenient unless you happen to be in the middle of nowhere. Merchants sell Simple Wood and Flint and Tinder. You only need one Flint and Tinder, but you need one Simple Wood for each fire you create. This allows you to cook almost anywhere!

FIRST AID

First Aid offers non-healers the opportunity to heal themselves and others. No, it's not as amazing as the magical healing abilities of the Priest, Druid, Shaman, or Paladin, but it's something! It's great for those non-healers while they're soloing or for a quick fix when your main healer goes down. Bandages of all types can heal wounds and lessen downtime. Also, Anti-Venom can cure poison and halt the steady assault on your health.

When you apply a bandage, it activates instantly, healing over time, wither 6 or 8 seconds. A character must wait 60 seconds after a bandage is applied before another can be used. First Aid is a stop gap or emergency measure and isn't intended to be the focus of a characters combat time. If you're hit at any time during the bandaging, the healing is stopped and you are left with the debuff. Bandaging the main tank usually doesn't do much because of this, but it can be the difference in a close fight.

Pull the First Aid icon from your ability book (defaulted to "p") onto a hotbar and activate it to open your First Aid window. Click on the item to see how much cloth is required to create the bandage and how many you can create presently. Bandages are automatically placed in your packs upon creation.

You never have enough cloth. There are times when you sell excess cloth only to run out of bandages the next day. Many players keep large quantities in their bank and several stacks on them at all times. Bandages are best used after a fight and perfect for soloing. Applying one right after a fight can keep you going endlessly with little downtime. Remember, if you get hit while applying a bandage, you lose the healing and retain the 60 second cooldown timer. Once you learn the next level of bandage and are pulling in enough of the required cloth, sell the old bandages.

To apply a bandage simply select the target you wish to heal (using F1 for you and F2-F5 for other party members is fast and easy) and push the hotkey you have the bandages set to. If you don't want to lose your current target and it's an enemy, you can activate the bandage then select your target.

FISHING

Fishing has two nice perks to it. The general ability is to catch fish. Fish can be cooked into some useful foods. It's great for Hunters with pets that eat fish. Some skills, like Alchemy, use certain types of fish in their recipes.

The second ability is the possibility of hauling up clams, boxes, chests, and mollusks. These can have items of worth or gems within and are quite a find!

Open your ability book (defaulted to "p") and drag the Fishing icon onto a hotbar. Equip your fishing pole (these can be bought at many vendors and stronger poles can be found or given as quest rewards). Move to a body of water and use the Fishing ability.

You cast line and bobber into the water and wait. Keep your mouse hovering over the bobber and wait for a fish to bite (this is shown by the bobber…bobbing). Click on the bobber to reel in your catch. If you were successful, your bounty shows in a loot window.

Fishing Poles Don't Make Good Weapons

Be sure to equip your weapons before going into combat. This can happen if an enemy comes upon you while fishing or if you simply move onto other activities. Hitting someone with a Fishing Pole, while funny, isn't effective.

Fresh and ocean waters have different types of fish as do some of the rare ponds and lakes in Azeroth. The best way to skill up is to fish in areas where your character can defeat the enemies. This keeps you fishing in areas where you can succeed and allows you to defend yourself if a monster wanders too close. Purchasing and using lures can temporary increase you fishing skill to make transitioning into a new area easier.

To use a lure, open your inventory. Right click on the lure and then left click on your fishing pole. Lures only last a certain length of time, but your skill can be greatly increased by these.

BATTLE CHEST

ISBN: 0-7440-0861-1

Printing Code: The rightmost double-digit number is the year of the book's printing; the rightmost single-digit number is the number of the book's printing. For example, 05-1 shows that the first printing of the book occurred in 2005.

14 13 12 11 10   16 15 14

Manufactured in the United States of America.

BRADYGAMES STAFF

Publisher
David Waybright

Editor-In-Chief
H. Leigh Davis

Creative Director
Robin Lasek

Licensing Manager
Mike Degler

CREDITS

Development Editor
Brian Shotton

Screenshot Editor
Michael Owen

Lead Designer
Brent Gann

Layout Designers
Areva

BLIZZARD ENTERTAINMENT

Creative Development Manager
Shawn Carnes

Director of Global Licensing
Cory Jones

Producer
Gloria Soto

Art Approvals
Joanna Cleland-Jolly

QA Approvals
Daniel Polcari
Andrew Rowe
John Lynch

Additional Support
Jason Weng
Joseph Magdalena

QA Feedback
Joseph Ryan
Timothy Ismay
Asher Litwin
Morgan Day
Dan Kramer
Sean Reyes
Foster Elmendorf
Art Peshkov
Jason Weng
Joseph Magdalena
Robert Boxeth

Licensing Specialist
Brian Hsieh

Blizzard Special Thanks
Chris Metzen
Ben Brode
Michael Gilmartin
Shane Cargilo